The Postmodern History Reader

'This is an authoritative selection of texts representing fairly all the principal positions in the current debate about the status of historical knowledge "after modernism". Keith Jenkins' superb introduction adroitly sorts out the issues and points the way to further profitable discussion for the near future. The collection amply illustrates that the "discourse of history" has entered a new era.'
Hayden White, *University of California, Santa Cruz*

'With clarity of purpose and a discerning eye for the apt text, Keith Jenkins has pulled together major postmodernism themes for adventurous historians,'
Joyce Appleby, *University of California, Los Angeles*

The Postmodern History Reader is the most comprehensive collection of influential texts on historiography and postmodernism yet compiled. Keith Jenkins expertly selects from the books and journal articles across the whole historiographical range that have been key to the transforming debates.

This unique reader is a clear introduction to the impact of postmodernism on historical debate, allowing easy access to one of the more stimulating and exciting areas of current history.

It provides:

* extracts from influential historians, such as Barthes, Joyce, White, Foucault and Baudrillard
* individual introductions to each carefully defined debate
* advice of further reading
* many thoroughly up-to-date as well as 'classic' pieces
* texts from a range of subdisciplines in history and theory
* arguments both for and against postmodernism
* access to key writings which are not normally readily available

Presented in a format that is both easy to use and challenging, *The Postmodern History Reader* will serve as an invaluable course text and reference tool for students and postgraduates.

The Postmodern History Reader

Edited by
KEITH JENKINS

London and New York

First published 1997
by Routledge
11 New Fetter Lane, London EC4P 4EE

Simultaneously published in the USA and Canada
by Routledge
29 West 35th Street, New York, NY 10001

Reprinted 1998, 2001

Routledge is an imprint of the Taylor & Francis Group

© 1997 Introduced and edited by Keith Jenkins

Typeset in Palatino and Helvetica by Intype London Limited

Printed and bound in Great Britain by
TJ International Ltd, Padstow, Cornwall

British Library Cataloguing in Publication Data
A catalogue record for this book is available from the British Library

Library of Congress Cataloguing in Publication Data
A catalogue record for this book has been requested

ISBN 0–415–13903–1
    0–415–13904–x (pbk)

For Maureen, Philip and Patrick

Contents

PART IV *DEBATES FROM THE JOURNALS*

CONTENTS

Acknowledgements

The author and publishers would like to thank the following who have kindly given permission for the use of copyright material; every effort has been made to contact copyright holders; any queries should be addressed to Routledge, London.

J. F. Lyotard, *The Postmodern Condition* (1984); reprinted by permission of Manchester University Press. J. Baudrillard, *The Illusion of the End* (1992); reprinted by permission of Blackwell Publishers and Stanford University Press. E. D. Ermarth, *Sequel to History* (1992); reprinted by permission of the author and Princeton University Press. D. Elam, *Romancing the Postmodern* (1992) and *Feminism and Deconstruction* (1994); reprinted by permission of Routledge. R. Young, *White Mythologies* (1990); reprinted by permission of Routledge. I. Chambers, *Migrancy, Culture, Identity* (1994); reprinted by permission of Routledge/Comedia. E. Fox-Genovese, "Literary Criticism and the Politics of the New Historicism", in H. A. Veeser (ed.) *The New Historicism* (1989); reprinted by permission of Routledge. C. Norris, "Postmodernising History: Right Wing Revisionism and the Uses of Theory" (1988); reprinted by permission of the author and *Southern Review*. B. Palmer, "Critical Theory, Historical Materialism, and the Ostensible End of Marxism", in the *International Review of Social History* (1993) 38; reprinted by permission of the author, the *International Instituut voor Sociale Geschiedenis*, and Cambridge University Press. R. Barthes, *The Discourse of History* (1967); reprinted by permission of Cambridge University Press. M. Foucault, "Nietzsche, Genealogy, History" in, *Language, Counter-Memory, Practice; Selected Essays and Interviews* with an Introduction by Donald F. Bouchard, Copyright © 1977 Cornell University Press; reprinted by permission of Cornell University Press. H. Kellner, *Language and Historical Representation* (1989); reprinted by permission of the University of Wisconsin Press. R. Berkhofer, "The Challenge of Poetics to (Normal) Historical Practice", reprinted by permission of *Poetics Today*, © 1988, Porter Institute for Poetics and Semiotics, Tel Aviv University. G. Himmelfarb, "Telling It As You Like It" (Oct 16, 1992); reprinted by permission of the author and *The Times Literary Supplement*. G. Elton, *Return to Essentials* (1991); reprinted by permission of The Royal Historical Society and Cambridge University Press. G. Spiegel, "History, Historicism, and the Social Logic of the Text in the Middle Ages" (1990); reprinted by permission of the author and *Speculum*. J. Appleby, L. Hunt and M. Jacob, *Telling the Truth About History* (1995); reprinted by permission of W. W. Norton, Inc. T. Bennett, *Outside Literature* (1990); reprinted by permission of the author and Routledge. T. Bennett, "Texts in History", in D. Attridge *et al.* (eds) *Poststructuralism and the Question of History* (1987); reprinted by permission of the author and Cambridge University Press. S. S. Friedman, "Making History: Feminism, Narrative and Desire", in D. Elam and R. Wiegman (eds) *Feminism Beside Itself* (1995); reprinted by permission of Routledge.

The contributions by L. Stone, P. Joyce, C. Kelly and G. Spiegel from the journal *Past and Present: A Journal of Historical Studies* (131, 1991 and 135, 1992 (Stone); 133, 1991 (Joyce and Kelly) 135, 1992 Spiegel); reprinted by permission of the authors and *Past and Present*, © The Past and Present Society. The contributions by F. R. Ankersmit and P. Zagorin from *History and Theory*; reprinted by permission of the authors, *History and Theory* and Wesleyan University © Wesleyan University.

The contributions by N. Kirk, P. Joyce, G. Eley and K. Nield from *Social History* (19, 2, 1994; 20, 1, 1995; 20, 3, 1995 and 21, 1, 1996 respectively); are reprinted by permission of Routledge. S. Friedlander, *Probing the Limits of Representation* (1992); reprinted by permission of Harvard University Press, Cambridge, Mass., Copyright © by the President and Fellows of Harvard College. H. White, "Historical Emplotment and the Problem of Truth", in S. Friedlander (ed.) *Probing the Limits of Representation* (1992); reprinted by permission of Harvard University Press © by the President and Fellows of Harvard College.

The contributions by H. Kellner, W. Kansteiner, R. Braun and B. Lang (*History and Theory* 33, 2, 1994 and 34, 1, 1995 (B. Lang)); reprinted by permission of the authors, *History and Theory* and Wesleyan University © Wesleyan University.

I would like to thank friends and colleagues for their advice and comments on this Reader; in particular, Peter Brickley has been, as usual, constructively critical. I would also like to thank Katherine Shakespeare and Marjory Heron of the Chichester Institute for their help in tracking down pieces which appear in this volume – and many more besides.

Keith Jenkins
October 1996

1 Keith Jenkins

Introduction: on being open about our closures

Today we are surrounded by *Readers* either on postmodernism itself or on aspects of postmodernism and something else; thus, postmodernism and feminism, postmodernism and literature, postmodernism and architecture, and so on. But, at the time of writing (October 1996) I am unaware of the existence of a volume on postmodernism and history: *A Postmodern History Reader*. I suppose it's not too difficult to see why this should be the case. Protected by a continued adherence to common-sense empiricism and realist notions of representation and truth, most historians – and certainly most of those who might be termed "academic" or professional "proper" historians – have been resistant to that postmodernism which has affected so many of their colleagues in adjacent discourses. Their residual disinterest in and/or hostility to philosophy has enabled them to cling to an ostensible "a" or anti-theoretical position. Yet even historians like these are beginning to realize that what is going on in the wider intellectual world has some importance for historical work(s) (historiography), whilst a minority have actually gone over to theory, this haemorrhaging causing various "traditionalists" (drawn from across the left-right ideological spectrum) to take to the barricades lest "history as we have known it" should be subverted. Consequently, what this increasingly engaged debate means, is that both under- and post-graduates are likely to hear on their courses at least faint echoes of this meeting of minds and interests, whilst, on a small number, the impact of theory in general and postmodernism in particular may have already become an important element in the understanding of historical discourse. Indeed, postmodernism may even have become constitutive of historical consciousness.

This *Reader* is based on the belief that history is theoretical "all the way down," and that all history students should not only consider the question of the nature of history/historiography in its various ontological, epistemological, methodological and ideological/discursive manifestations, but that they should be especially aware of that theorizing which currently lives under the rubric of postmodernism. As a *Reader* this book is therefore compiled primarily – though obviously not exclusively – for an introductory audience. This is not really a book for the initiated, the insider. It is for newcomers. It is a *Reader* compiled particularly for teachers of, say, undergraduate/postgraduate students and very obviously for the students themselves; teachers who are aware of the impact postmodernism is having or could be having on historiography and who will know some of the debates in some of the journals and books wherein they are contained, and who would like (at least) to introduce this writing to their classes. Indeed, such teachers might be considering establishing or modifying a course on "the nature of history" and would therefore like to have a convenient collection of readings to provide the basis for such an offering: *a course book*. In that sense this is a very teacherly text. It pulls together a cross section of influential and/or representative works both advocating and criticizing postmodern approaches to historiography. This is not to say the readings collected here are nicely balanced, however. For although this *Reader* presents extracts from works as engaged in a series of oppositional debates (and thus, I suppose, gives a further lease of life to "binary oppositions") I hope the weight of the readings come down in favour of postmodernism.[1] In this *Reader* I am supporting postmodern approaches in general because I think that through them historiography can be studied in ways that are both challenged and challenging; in ways which may help students lose their "theoretical innocence." It is hoped, for example, that they question the *doxa* which states that the "proper" study of the past is a study "for its own sake"; that the only legitimate study of the past is one which disinterestedly and objectively understands it "on its own terms," and that "proper" historians should always attempt to get to "the truth of the past." This *Reader* is thus dedicated to the idea that postmodern approaches are currently amongst the most stimulating and exciting available. Such approaches enable historians to be increasingly reflexive as to what they think history is, and to explicitly position themselves within and/or against traditional discourse. In its mainstream realist, empiricist, objectivist, documentarist, lower case, liberal/plural expressions, orthodox discourse still advocates working practices now seen, in the light of the postmodern, as both extremely problematical and demonstrably ideological.

So much for some indication of the purpose of this *Reader*. What I want to do in the rest of this Introduction is to explain some of the assumptions and thus the position I bring to postmodernism and history – how I read postmodernism and history – and how these are "reflected" in the organization of the *Reader* and the selected extracts. I have divided the rest of this Introduction into three sections to achieve this. In Section 1 (On Postmodernity, Postmodernism and History) I sketch in what I think is meant by the term *postmodernity* (the term which is arguably the best concept under which to signify our socio-economic, political and cultural condition) and the term *postmodernism* (as signifying the best way of making sense of various expressions at the level of theory). I then examine the general implication of these concepts for what passes under the signs of History/history. Thus, in Section 2 (On the Collapse of the Upper Case and Collateral Damage) I look at what I shall by then have explained and termed "the collapse of the upper case," arguing that the impact of this collapse is felt not only on upper case history, but indirectly on lower case "proper" history too. In Section 3 (The Organization of the Readings) I then draw up – in the light of the discussions in Section 1 and 2 – what I think "metaphorically" underlies postmodern attitudes toward history/historiography, and the way in which historians' reactions to these can be put into five different categories, which explain the way in which the readings in this volume have been organized. I conclude with brief remarks on some of the limits of this *Reader*.

SECTION 1: ON POSTMODERNITY, POSTMODERNISM, AND HISTORY

As I have argued on another occasion, I think that we live today within the general socio-economic and political condition of postmodernity.[2] I don't think we have a choice about this. For postmodernity is not an ideology or position we can choose to subscribe to or not, postmodernity is precisely our condition: it is our historical fate to be living now. As to how we should read the details of this moment – as, say, a period of post-Fordist flexible accumulation as opposed to modernist Fordism; as a period of capitalist de-differentiation; as a period of late capital; as part of a general time-space compression involving spatial reorganizations or as a combination of all of these and other factors – is subject to much debate.[3] But I would like to leave such details for now, important as they are, and argue more generally that the condition of postmodernity and the postmodern theoretical expressions concomitant with it are due to the overall failure of that experiment in social living we can term "modernity." That is, the general failure, as measured in its own terms, of the attempt, from the eighteenth century in Europe, to bring about through the application of reason, science and technology, a level of social and political well-being within social formations which, legislating for increasingly generous emancipation of their subjects/citizens, we might characterize by saying that they were trying, at best, to become "human rights communities."

Obviously this general failure has not been unrelieved; over the last two hundred odd years there have been many substantial successes. But, notwithstanding these, I think that we can now see that the two (contradictory) Eurocentric ideological/social system variants set to provide the vehicles for the universal emancipations of modernity – a bourgeois version and a proletarian version most cogently articulated (as it has turned out) by various total(itarian) Marxisms – have now either faded enough for us to rethink our earlier assumptions, or have disintegrated enough for us to revise our earlier hopes.[4] Accordingly, it is our existence at this disappointing stage that, particularly in the West, has given rise to either a series of jaded or nostalgic reassessments of modernity or to a range of radical critiques which still stubbornly hold out for an emancipatory future beyond modernity. And it is arguably here, in the variously articulated interconnections of such reappraisals as to what has gone wrong and why, that theorists have undertaken detailed critiques of the foundations not only of modernity but of that longer Western Tradition of which modernity can be seen as just one particular episode. These critiques which are historically unique in their sophistication, intensity and scale, conclude that there are not (and nor have there ever been) any "real foundations" of the kind normally considered to have underwritten the experiment of the modern. We must accept that we live and have always lived amidst social formations having no legitimating ontological, epistemological, methodological or ethical grounds for beliefs and actions beyond the status of an ultimately self-referencing (rhetorical) conversation. And it is the recognition of this, expressed in "postist" formulations (poststructuralism, post-feminism, post-colonialism, post-Marxism, neo-pragmatism . . .) at the level of theory from the actuality of living within postmodernity, which I want to refer to here under the general rubric of *postmodernism*.[5] And at this point there is a sort of choice available. For although I don't think we can choose to live in postmodernity or not, we can (and many of us still do) exercise a bit of picking and choosing between the residues of old "certaintist" modernisms (objectivity, disinterestedness, the facts, unbiasedness, Truth . . .) and rhetorical, postist formulations (readings, positionings, reality effects, truth effects . . .) rather than going for one or the other. Consequently, I think it is here, between old "certaintist" and new rhetorical discourses, that the current "battles" over "what is history" and how historical knowledge is methodologically "made up" and to what end, live.

Now, the detailed reasons for saying this are complicated. But generalizing for now, the argument for saying that this is where history is located today rests not least on the ideological importance given to history in modernist projects. For both bourgeois and proletarian versions of the modernist project – their obvious class differences notwithstanding – articulated as key elements in their respective ideologies a shared view of the past/history as a movement with an immanent direction, a past/history which was held to be going somewhere, differing only in the selection of "its" ultimate destination. For the bourgeoisie this was a harmonious capitalism; for the proletariat global communism. Both bourgeois and proletarian ideologies therefore expressed their historical trajectories in versions of the past/history articulated in the upper case (as History with a capital H) that is, a way of looking at the past in terms which assigned to contingent events and situations an objective significance by identifying their place and function within a general schema of historical development usually construed as appropriately progressive. And today, with the collapse of the optimism of the modernist project in ways which, metaphorically speaking, sink right down to its once ostensible roots, so we have witnessed the attendant collapse of histories in the upper case; nobody believes in those particular fantasies any more.

But it is not only that postmodernism has made the upper case look absurd, as we now have towards it what Lyotard has called an attitude of "incredulity towards metanarratives," but history in the lower case too. It is not only that we now appreciate that an upper case history is a formal and thus empty mechanism to be filled according to taste. For whilst these metaphorical/allegorical versions of the past were one crucial part of modernist ideologies, another way of reading the past was also being developed within the bourgeois version. This version is just as ideological as any upper case version ever was but, expressive of the more conservative elements of the bourgeoisie, this peculiar variant has become increasingly cultivated until, as more and more of the bourgeoisie "made it," it has achieved dominance. This version is, of course, history in the *lower* case. That is, history construed in "academic" and "particularistic" forms which, whilst insisting with as much force as any upper case history ever did that it was "proper" history, modestly eschewed metanarrative claims that it was discovering in the past meaningful trajectories, purposes and teleologies. Consequently, within increasingly bourgeois social formations that were able to jettison and/or marginalize upper case "History," this mere *species* of historiography has become so commonly accepted as being identical to its *genus* that it no longer looks like a mere species at all. This is the version of history that most of us will have been brought up with. Still ensconced within the universities and other academic institutions, this way of regarding the past (as the study of the past "for its own sake" as distinct from the study of the past explicitly for the sake of the bourgeoisie or the proletariat) has thus become almost natural.

But in a culture nothing is natural. And in our culture, thanks not least to postmodernism, this particular "naturalist fallacy" is now increasingly transparent. For the attempt to pass off the study of history in the form of the ostensibly disinterested scholarship of academics studying the past objectively and "for its own sake" as "proper" history, is now unsustainable. History in the upper case has been undercut by theorists for reasons to do with their own rethinking of the modernist project, and the argumentative means to do this fundamental re-evaluation of the foundations of these relative failures has impacted upon the foundational verities of lower case history too. The result is the problematicization of both *History* and *history*. Consequently, today we recognize that there never has been, and there never will be, any such thing as a past which is expressive of some kind of essence. At the same time, the ridiculous idea that the only proper study of the past is "own-sakism" is recognized as just the mystifying way in which a bourgeoisie articulates its own interests as if they belonged to the past itself. As a result, because of the way the upper case has been undercut, not only do upper case claims to be producing "true" knowledge of the past look utterly problematic, but so do lower case claims too. Accordingly, the whole modernist History/history ensemble now appears as a self-referential, problematical expression of interests, an ideological – interpretative discourse without any non-historicized access to the past as such. In fact history now appears to be just one more foundationless, positioned expression in a world of foundationless, positioned expressions.

SECTION 2: ON THE COLLAPSE OF THE UPPER CASE AND COLLATERAL DAMAGE

In the account I have just given, both upper and lower case histories are affected by postmodern critiques, but (as noted), because of the continuing discursive power of the bourgeoisie in the present historical culture of "our" social formation, it is the collapse of the upper case that is seen as being the major – and in many analyses – the only casualty. *The vast bulk of the literature about postmodernism and history talks of the way it undercuts the upper case.* In our social formation, where lower case history represents the "normal" way of finding out about and knowing the past, lower case mainstream academic historians consider that the collapse of the upper case (of ideological histories) does not affect their practices, not registering the fact that their histories are every bit as ideological as those of the upper case. I mean such proper historians don't need to be told by postmodern gurus like J. F. Lyotard (in *The Postmodern Condition*)[6] that his definition of postmodernism as "incredulity towards metanarratives" means that grand narratives (overarching philosophies of history like the Enlightenment story of the steady progress of reason and freedom, or Marx's drama of the forward march of human productive capacities via class conflict culminating in proletarian revolution) are a priori impositions on the past rather than being based on the "objective facts." Nor do they need to be told by Lyotard (in *The Differend*)[7] that you cannot extrapolate from one category of "phrase regime" to another (say, from the category of cognitive reason which may help one find the facts, to speculative reason whereby, from the findings of cognitive reason one can legitimately infer that such facts are leading to the inevitable victory of the proletariat, or progress, or whatever) as though the latter were absolutely entailed by the former. For "proper" historians know all about the absurdity of metanarratives and the problems involved in both inductivism and deductivism. Have drunk in with their milk the fact-value problematic. Have read – for goodness sake! – their Popper, their Oakeshott, their Hexter and their Elton. Indeed, it is precisely because they have done this reading, that it is perfectly clear why, for most "proper" historians, debates about postmodernism look both stale (I mean, what's new?) and irrelevant (I mean, so what?). Not being upper case historians themselves, the fact that such constructions are now recognized as absurd doesn't seem to affect their own practices in any way nor their own lower case "craft." Why should it? Thus they can carry on doing what they have always been doing and ignore postmodern theorizing with impunity. In that sense postmodernism in particular (and one might add "theory" in general) doesn't seem to have much to do with them.

But on my reading it does. And as I read it at least some lower case historians recognize that it does; recognize that the collapse of the upper case causes collateral damage to the lower. For if this is not the case – if postmodern type critiques were actually restricted to the upper case – if postmodernism really was irrelevant to lower case histories, then we have some difficulty in explaining why defenders of "proper," professional lower case history (from Lawrence Stone to Gertrude Himmelfarb, from Carlo Ginzburg to Geoffrey Elton *et al.*) seem to be so hostile to it. Of why they critique it and often construct *ad hominem* arguments against its advocates. Of why, generally sceptics themselves, they fear post-modern-type scepticism which, in their eyes, seems nothing less than an irresponsible invitation to a "read the past any way you like relativism" and/or, even worse, nihilism. Of why they see postmodernism as destroying at least "history as we [sic] have known it" or, more extrava-gantly, the whole historical enterprise. And I think the answer to these queries is because such historians reluctantly sense (I put it no stronger than that) that postmodernism really does have something to do with them. Far from it being the case that postmodern critiques only effect the ideological upper case, proper historians are now increasingly real-izing that it undercuts the working assumptions of the (ideological) lower case too: that nothing is sacred.

In a nutshell, then, my argument about the impact of postmodernism on the collapse of upper case history is that the collateral fall-out experi-enced by lower case history undercuts it too. To put it another way, that we can now see how both upper and lower case histories, being "metahistorical" constructions, are, like all constructions, ultimately arbi-trary ways of carving up what comes to constitute their field. Both upper and lower case histories are actually just theories about the past and how it should be appropriated. In particular, they are theories which, being sired, developed and made pragmatically useful to the "experiment of the modern" are now, with the end of that experiment, at their end too. My argument is thus a sort of "end of history" argument. Not (necessarily) the end of history as such, but arguably the end of those upper and lower case variants expressive of that part of our recent Western past. In short, *the end of the peculiar ways in which modernity conceptualized the past; the way it made sense of it in upper and lower case forms.*[8] And if this is so, then alert lower case defenders are quite correct to see postmodernism as signalling the end of history as they (lower case modernists) have known it. They too live within the post-modern condition.

It is because of the way postmodernism theorizes and problematic-izes the entire modernist History/history ensemble that students ought to be thus aware of the impact of postmodernism on history as such so that they can come to their own position on the question of "the nature of history" nowadays. And to help this awareness a little further, I now want to very briefly sketch out the sort of lower case history that most students will meet on their courses. This history will not refer to itself as lower case history of course but – in that universalizing trait of all ideology – forget the qualifying adjective and pass off its "species" of history as if it was history as such. That having been done, I then want to look at some of the ways in which that history is now being undercut by post-modern-type critiques. I take space to do this here because whilst in the literature it is (again as I have noted) overwhelmingly the upper case that seems to be affected by postmodernism, it is my argument that nothing escapes its impact. The next few paragraphs thus attempt to redress, *vis-à-vis* mainstream history culture, an obvious imbalance by stressing the way postmodern type critiques subvert lower case history. For though not so powerful as it once was, most professional academic historians – and the students taught by them – still subscribe to a discourse which continues to constitute historiography through employing lower case, realist, empiricist, objectivist, documentarist and liberal-pluralist ways of thinking about their discipline. What do each of these terms mean, then, and how do they add up to form a fairly coherent whole, the *doxa* against which postmodern approaches are arguably counterposed? Let me look briefly at each of them in turn so that my argument as to the necessity of thinking about/with postmodernism can be further clarified.

In a perceptive essay, Gregor McLennan has argued that most proper historians still run together realism and empiricism as the basis of their "discipline."[9] Such historians, says McLennan, claim to have enough experience to just know that the past was once real. Their labours are primarily directed towards describing that hitherto existing reality rather than constructing it, and the reality so disclosed in their accounts typically takes the form of discrete/unique events distilled (by processes of source generation, source interrogation, etc.) into historical facts. In effect, there is thus a characteristic conflation or slippage in commonsense realism "from a belief in the reality of the past to an empiricist conception of the historian's practice."[10] And McLennan has three points to make about this.

First, empiricism is not entailed by realism. It only appears as if empiricism is a property of realism rather than just being contingently connected on occasion. Therefore from the acceptance of the ontological actuality of the past no epistemology or method of any kind whatsoever necessarily follows (in postmodern terms, nothing connects). Second, McLennan argues that the still dominant entailment of empiricism from realism is of two main types. One the idea that the historian approaches the past directly, or two, uncovers bits of it descriptively. These constitute, says McLennan, the two planks of empiricism, planks which, when slid together, allow us to speak of ontological empiricism or, when only the second plank is in place, of methodological empiricism. And McLennan is of the view that the latter position is now the predominant one. Few historians subscribe to the idea (though they occasionally lapse into it rhetorically) that the past as such is directly appropriated as opposed to the idea that as historians they work with traces/sources which, by the use of evidential investigation, are mobilized into narrative accounts rather than just falling into shape under the weight of the sheer accumulation of "the facts." And, third, McLennan argues that neither type of empiricism is "acceptable as an account of what historians do," in that any defence of realism requires the recognition that "the indirectness of access to the past is due in part to the incompleteness and range of the evidence and in part to the structuring role of theory in any account of the 'real world'." Consequently, though, most empiricist historians see theory as "an unwelcome aberration which might rapidly spread into an intellectual disease," empiricism is not only (a) a theory itself, but also (b) an inadequate one.[12] Empiricism's quietude around theory can be seen not so much as a rejection of theoretical underpinning but rather as a consensus around a set of practical norms which discourage theory in the promotion of "a commonsense embargo on 'useless' speculation as a diversion from everyday practical consciousness – including that of the practical historian." For empiricism as a method, just cannot account for the significance it gives to the selection, distribution and weighting of "the facts" in finished narratives. The facts cannot themselves indicate their significance as though it were inherent in them. To give significance to the facts an external theory of significance is always needed. And whilst McLennan points out that it is difficult to know how widespread and/or how consciously or naively held professional historian's conflation of realism and empiricism is, nevertheless, I think the assumption is still made by historians that if you combine realism and empiricism the representation of the past as it actually, objectively was, can be achieved. At any rate, this type of objectivity remains high on the agenda of the "proper" historian.

As its title indicates, Peter Novick's *That Noble Dream: The "Objectivity Question" and the American Historical Profession*, examines the history of the desire by the bulk of American historians for objectivity. But Novick's argument has a wider resonance, particularly his comment, at the start of the book, that at the "very centre of the professional historical venture is the idea and ideal of 'objectivity'."[13] To be sure, says Novick, there is less confidence today than there was in the ability to actually be objective – there is less talk of "letting the facts speak for themselves." But that having been said, Novick is surely correct to argue that despite recent relativistic incursions into mainstream historiography, older usages endure. The principal elements of objectivity are outlined by Novick thus:

> The assumptions on which it [objectivism] rests include a commitment to the reality of the past, and to truth as correspondence to that reality; a sharp separation between . . . fact and value and, above all, between history and fiction. Historical facts are seen as prior to and independent [not constituted by] interpretation . . . Truth is one, not perspectival. Whatever patterns exist in history are "found", not "made" . . . The objective historian's role is that of a neutral, or disinterested, judge; it must never degenerate into that of advocate or, even worse, propagandist. The historian's conclusions are expected to display the standard judicial qualities of balance and even-handedness . . . qualities . . . guarded by the insulation of the historical profession from social pressure or political influence, and by the individual historian avoiding partisanship or bias . . . the historian's primary allegiance is to "the objective historical truth", and to professional colleagues who share a commitment . . . to advance toward that goal.[14]

Novick expresses here some familiar injunctions then. Few undergraduates and postgraduates will be unaware of the strictures to be "balanced," "unbiased," "even-handed," and "impartial." And in the land of proper history the way to achieve this state of grace – moral and professional integrity taken as read – is through the demand that, above all, historians should go back to the sovereignty of the sources, to the primary evidence. Historians should not remain at the level of secondary (and thus second-hand and soiled texts) which may still be – despite the above demand for historians to purge themselves of "interests" – dangerously positioned. Back to the original sources – *Ad Fontes* – is thus the further dominant injunction urged on the "proper" historian.

That injunction echoes throughout the practices of those umpteen American professionals examined by Novick, and is re-echoed by the majority of historians in the United Kingdom. It still occupies pride of place in those student orientated manuals and general introductions to the proper way to pursue history (Elton, Tosh, Stanford *et al.*)[15] The advice of the injunction centres not just on the sources but picks out one type of source as having particular value – the document. Consequently, there seems little doubt that Dominick LaCapra's labelling of the proper historian's *metier* as being *documentarist* is a pertinent one.[16] According to LaCapra, in the documentary mode the basis of historical research is, once again, hard facts. These hard facts are derived from a critical sifting of the traces/sources of the past, the purpose of such work being to furnish either narrative accounts or thick descriptions of documented facts, or to submit the "historical record to analytic procedures of hypo-thesis-formation, testing and explanation."[17] In this process, LaCapra thinks that the historical imagination is limited to the modest task of filling in the inevitable gaps in the record and/or throwing new light on a phenomenon by finding new information. Additionally, adds LaCapra, to demolish the possibility of speculative theorizing, all sources tend to be treated in "documentary" terms as if there was a real hierarchy of sources whereby those which seemed to be direct informational docu-ments – bureaucratic reports, state papers, wills, eye-witness accounts – are valorized. Other texts, if treated at all, are "reduced to elements that are either redundant or merely supplementary (and, if not checked against 'hard data,' purely suggestive) with respect to privileged 'infor-mational' documents."[18] In this construction the really significant questions are those answerable by empirical and archival research. Whilst this approach does not exactly prohibit interpretation (and whilst not unaware of the limited and ambiguous nature of documents as such), it fails to see such interpretive necessity or ambiguities as – as in postmodernism – radical opportunities and exciting gaps to be worked. Rather they are seen as problems to be eradicated and overcome, as biases to be detected, distortions to be rectified, and readings to be "balanced-out." Here, as LaCapra comments, a wedge is driven between the presuppositions and methods of the proper historian and "critical theory." For while the latter may suggest new ways of seeing or enable the historian – generally in the conclusion of his or her work – to "change voices" and "pronounce a few sententious *obiter dicta*," any sustained relationship between proper history and an "opportunistic theory" is condemned as unhistorical: such theory gets in the way of the factual objectivity that the discipline demands. Thus LaCapra links documentarism back into Novick-type objectivity:

> Reconstruction of the past, putatively "in its own terms," remains the overriding consideration, and the objective is to be as objective as possible by controlling for "bias" or "subjective preferences" . . . . The affirmation of an objectivist frame of reference may be fostered by anxiety over a "relapse" into "relativism," and the charge of "projection" may be directed at the historian whose interpretation – or entire interpretative orientation – one rejects.[19]

Now, as I have already indicated and as we shall see further, postmodern approaches not only ideologize any talk of "reconstructing the past on its own terms" but also, by embracing relativist-type variants, undercut both the correspondence theory of truth and problematicize the generally associated notion of internal coherence and consistency found within the objectivist position. But, in passing, we might note that LaCapra also offers another objection to documentarism; namely, that the documentarist approach commits the "technicist fallacy." That is to say, it commits the fallacy of taking just one part of the technical instrumentation of history (source investigation, etc.) as if it constituted its "essence." It is as if the complicated epistemological, methodological, ideological, problematical positionings of historical representation could be solved "technically." For as LaCapra puts it, this fallacy "takes what is in certain respects a necessary condition . . . of historiography and converts it into a virtually exhaustive definition."[20] And he adds that this not only diverts attention from the way documents and sources are themselves texts, but also plays down the fact that as such they require a critical reading that goes beyond traditional *Quellenkritik*: "to the extent that components of a documentary model constitute a necessary condition of professional historiography, the historian will face the recurrent temptation of making a fetish of archival research."[21] What is thus privileged, then, in the areas I have lightly sketched in so far – realism, empiricism, objectivism and documentarism – are positions which add up to the view that proper history really is history in the lower case (to recall, a mere *species* of history after all, which, in this rendition, identifies it with its putative *genus* as if this species type is identical to history as such).

Thus it can be seen why lower case historiography should consider itself to be outside of and/or antithetical to theory. In the above construal, proper, professional, scholarly, "for its own sake" historiography is not seen as a theoretical expression at all but rather as, say, a concrete practice (Elton) or as a craft (Hexter), uncontaminated by "anti-historical" (ideological) assumptions. So we witness attempts in lower case ortho- doxy at "theoretical cleansing." By holding that it is based on anti- theoretical and non-present-centred concerns, lower case history pres- ents itself as (relatively) free of contemporary interests and future- orientated desires. Again, all this is stated clearly in the mainstream manuals and introductory texts. To study the past academically so as to be able to deliver the past as it ostensibly was and not the past we would variously like it to be, is of paramount importance. Moreover, that past is one which must be presented as clearly as possible in unam- biguous, plain, commonsense language. Lower case historians therefore overwhelmingly use a "communication" type of language, avoiding or in many cases not even being aware of the existence of the quite devas- tating critiques of this language form by, amongst others, Hayden White.[22]

For these sorts of reasons, then, lower case history defines its identity in terms of what it is not – against its "other" – against its alleged antithesis; namely ideological history as construed in the upper case. For as we have seen, this kind of history – when pejoratively construed in the lights of the lower case – is not considered history at all, but improper, positioned ideology. It is a fake historiography which finds in the past – because it puts them there – meanings, purposes, teleologies, etc., to be used for present-centred and/or future programmes, pro- grammes which form, from this lower case position, generally radical political agendas of both the left and right (but generally of the left) as informed by, say, Marxism, feminism, ethnic interests, and so on. From the perspective of the lower case, then, upper case history is seen as the stuff of political correctness: as such it cannot be seriously considered or tolerated.

But what is most interesting here, of course, is how this banishment of upper case historiography beyond the boundaries of proper history casts an interesting shadow not over the ideology of the upper case (which is quite correctly seen as being positioned; why shouldn't it be?) but on the putatively non-ideological lower case. For on my reading lower case history is, as I have already suggested, bourgeois ideology.

Let me look briefly at this last statement because it is important. I have noted already that whilst in the lower case version interpretations should be capable through synthesis of creating a "true" account of the past, unsynthesizable interpretations are a fact of lower case life. Out of necessity, then, such interpretive flux has to be recuperated back into and normalized as a welcome feature of the lower case, its "flexibility" then being announced as indicative of its "openness," its willingness to "revise," its tolerance towards the "unconventional." Here lower case historiography gains credit for its liberal pluralism, for its guarantee of academic freedom as opposed to the closures of upper case ideology.

But in fact this only partly works. In practice liberal pluralism restricts its tolerances to those histories and historians who variably subscribe to the values of "the academic" lower case. For if liberal pluralism accepts that any sort of representation of the past is permissible – if it looks as if due to its liberal tolerance "anything goes" – then clearly other types of historiography such as upper case versions driven by Marxist or feminist or ethnic concerns (or even Whig ones) are not "not history" but just "different." Consequently, at this point lower case history has to lose its innocence and become as positioned and as interested as any other history. In preventing just anything counting as history, a tolerant liberal pluralism in the lower case becomes an intolerant Liberal Ideology in the upper. Accordingly, what we have here is the ideologization/politicization of all histories, such that we can now begin to legitimately address to the lower case all those questions it itself addresses to the previously construed ideological upper case. These questions in the end boil down to one: in whose interests is the particularistic history of the lower case masquerading as a universal? We can now see how lower case history's ostensible non-present-centredness is precisely what makes it ideological. In fact, we can see how lower case history fulfils the very criteria it itself erects as a definition of "ideological."

For to argue, as lower case practitioners do, that the study of the past should not have anything to do with being present/future orientated is, of course, exactly as present and future orientated as the argument that it should. Upper case historiography is generally quite explicit that it is using the past for, say, a trajectory into a different future. The fact that the bourgeoisie doesn't want a different future (the fact, that as we saw above, it has now arrived at its preferred historical destination – liberal, bourgeois, market capitalism) means that it doesn't any longer need a past-based future-orientated fabrication. Thus at this point, the point where the links between the past, present and future are broken because the present is everything, the past can be neutralized and studied not for our various sakes but for "its own." For this is exactly what is currently required, a history which is finished now that it has led right up to us. Thus to "pretend" not to be present-orientated is precisely what constitutes the present-centredness of the lower case. Accordingly, both upper and lower case histories serve – by the way they variously situate themselves in the present – their own past-sustained, suasive, present-centred needs and desires.

Let me now draw together the main points I have been making about history in the lower case. I think that the above thumb-nail *sketch* is very probably the thumb-nail *impression* which most students coming to (and indeed coming from) the study of the "discipline" of history in, say, higher education, will (with the exception of the last point – that proper academic history is actually liberal ideology) hold. The above construct – broad-brush and identifying only some of its components – is the still hegemonic discourse vis-à-vis the nature of history in our social formation. Accordingly, for convenience (for "summing up" purposes) this rendition of proper history might now be put into a tabular form so that I can go on to juxtapose against it postmodern-type critiques to which it is arguably vulnerable. So let us say that "proper" history can today be read as being:

(1)   realist, empiricist, objectivist and documentarist;
(2)   that it follows a non-rhetorical, commonsense, communication model of historical writing;
(3)   that it construes itself in the lower case wherein it transforms the "vice" of endless interpretive "differences" into the "virtues" of liberal pluralism;
(4)   that in its own rendition of liberal pluralism it portrays itself as anti-theoretical, anti-a priori and as non present-centred; that it studies the past ostensibly for the pasts "own sake" (own-sakism) as distinct from the study of the past for the ideological sakes of the proletariat, women, blacks . . . so that,
(5)   "other" histories are not really histories at all but fakes. However,
(6)   what this construction conceals is the fact that it is not in any way (as a mere species of history) identical to any putative genus; it is just one way of "doing history," so that both
(7)   lower and upper case histories are ideologically positioned and modernist, and so are
(8)   both susceptible to problematicization through what I want to call postmodern-type critiques.

So, how is this construct problematicized by postmodern critiques? Well, in a way this is a difficult area to summarize, for as soon as you begin to actually look for them, critiques of empiricism, realism, documentarism, "own-sakism," etc., are everywhere. But for introductory purposes and concentrating on only one angle, most critiques of lower case history seem to concern themselves with the implications of how the historian's referent – the thing to which historians refer as if it stands outside of representation, there to act as an independent resistance to wayward interpretations – is in fact constituted through the processes of representation. Consequently, it is this dissolution of the referent into representation which, for many lower case historians, signals the dissolution of their history by postmodern means.

How does this dissolution of the referent through the processes of representation work? Again, the detailed critiques of facticity (and of the empiricist methodology most closely associated with it) are a legion. These include not only critiques of a hermeneutic, phenomenological, constructivist or deconstructionist type, but individual exponents from, say, Dilthey to Collingwood, Danto to Mandelbaum, Oakeshott to P. Q. Hirst, Richard Rorty to Hayden White, and so on (whilst other theorists are represented in some of the readings in this volume). But in order to establish at this point the kinds of arguments which lower case exponents have to engage with, I give three short examples which suggest that (a) facts are always facts within the way the "referred-to past" has been "put under a description" (here I draw on Arthur Danto and Chris Lorenz); (b) allegedly referential independent facts are always theory dependent (here I draw on Alex Callinicos) and (c) the dissolution of the referent into representation can be seen, *pace* the way proper historians see it, in positive ways (here I draw on Robert Berkhofer).

The factualist/empiricist idea so rooted in traditional historical thinking, that if we can find "the facts" then this will stop interpretive flux, fails because only theory can constitute what counts as a fact in the first place. When we talk about facts we always do so under a description, so that to claim that "x" is a fact can only mean that the description it is under is adequate. Arthur Danto has made this point: when we talk about facts and reality we always refer to them within a specific framework of description. Phenomena as such are therefore never the things explained, it is only phenomena *as covered by descriptions*, so that when we speak of explaining them it must always be with reference to that description: "So an explanation . . . must . . . be relativized to a description of that phenomenon."[23] Danto's point has been illustrated "historically" by Chris Lorenz who asks:

How is it possible that with regard to an individual subject – National Socialism for instance – different historians *keep* referring to different states of affairs as facts and *keep* referring to different statements as true, and thus how is it possible that there is no guarantee of consensus in history. This fact is explained by the circumstance that factual statements and their truth vary with their frames of description . . . if one realizes what "reality" looks like always depends on a frame of description – and therefore a perspective – it comes as no surprise that "reality" cannot be used as an argument in favour of, or even for the "necessity" of, a particular perspective. [For] This presupposes a direct fit between reality and a specific linguistic framework – a presupposition linked up with naive realism and discarded with empiricism in epistemology. It is rather the other way round: it is the historian who tries to determine what the past "really" looks like . . . it is the historian, not the past, which does the dictating in history.[24]

The idea that facts/reality can thus exist independently of the historian so as to stop what Hayden White has termed the "de-realization of the event" is thus an implausible idea. For as Callinicos has put it (not at all approvingly – for later on in his text he will try to reconnect fact and value) statements about the observable/authenticated facts always have an "irreducibly conjectural" and thus "theoretical" character. Consequently,

it follows that, should some observation [fact] appear to refute a well-established theory, it is logically permissible to save the theory by rejecting the basic statement reporting this inconvenient observation [fact] perhaps by adjusting the . . . theory by means of which . . . results are interpreted. So instead of theory confronting – and being put to the test of – independently established facts, we have a clash between two theories – the one which is apparently refuted by the observation, the other the observation theory. If we explain away the observation [fact] we are preferring the first theory to the second (which we alter in order to get rid of the observation [fact]); if we uphold the observation [fact] we have chosen the second over the first. There seems to be no objective criteria governing these decisions. It may come down, as W. V. Quine argues, to how well entrenched the theories are within the overall system of our belief, or, if Richard Rorty is right, it is a matter of aesthetic preference, no more a matter of rational adjudication than my liking one painting better than another.[25]

Finally, these points are fleshed out and possible conclusions drawn by Robert Berkhofer. I give here the gist of Berkhofer's argument against "referential factuality" (his paper, "The Challenge of Poetics to (Normal) Historical Practice") is reproduced as Chapter 14.[26]

Berkhofer's argument is that literary theory – poetics – undercuts the foundations of normal professional historical practice by "denying the factuality that grounds the authority of history itself" and thus releases it into new areas of possibility.[27] How does this work? Well, in normal historical practice it is the referential facts which allegedly act as an independent check against the representations of the past by historians. It is on the basis of factuality that such values as accuracy, objectivity, and loyalty to the past as it really was, stand. But where, asks Berkhofer, do such facts come from? Nobody is denying, of course, that the actual past occurred. However, the facts that constitute that now absent past and which get into representations have clearly been extracted from the now extant "traces of the past" and combined through inference by historians into synthetic accounts that mere reference back to the facts as such could never entail. Therefore, because such factuality only becomes available for historical appraisal and debate as historiographical constructs, the alleged checks on such historiography by the facts are never checks on or by *independent facts* but always checks on *"already" historicized* ones. In other words, the effect normal historians try to achieve in their representations is the fusion of the structures of interpretation and factuality to try and prove that the structure of interpretation is the structure of factuality, instead of showing how the representation is structured "to *look like* total factuality." Although normal historians try to reconcile disparate interpretations of the same phenomenon by reference to the facts (through the presumption that factuality possesses some sort of independent, coercive "reality"), in actuality most if not all of what is presented as (f)actuality "is a special coding of the historian's synthetic expository texts, designed to conceal their highly constructed basis." In Berkhofer's words:

> That normal historical practice attempts to make its representations appear to present information as if it were a matter of simple referentiality indicate that the premises of realism are basic to the paradigm. Realism enters historical practice to the extent that historians try to make their structure of factuality seem to be its own organizing struc-

ture and therefore conceal that it is structured by interpretation represented as (f)actuality. This is as true of analytic as narrative expositions.[28]

For Berkhofer, then, the challenge coming from a postist poetics means that normal historical practice is seen as a mode of coding words and texts according to "conventional presuppositions about representing the past as if it was effectively always already history." That such coding is conventional, adds Berkhofer, also means that it is ultimately arbitrary, in that realism is a chosen cultural and not a natural category of representation. The upshot is that such beliefs about realism and the arbitrary coding of the past in the present as history arguably collapses the distinctions between representation and referentiality. The signified (the past) is thus nought but the signifier (history). No referent (fact/the past) exists outside the history texts themselves. Consequently, this capsizal of the referential side into the representational side (what John Zammito calls "pan-textualism")[29] destroys the effect of overall factual authority as claimed for normal historical work: "demystification of a historical enterprise, therefore, also delegitimizes it." Such demystification can thus "free up" historians to tell many equally legitimate stories from various view points, with umpteen voices, emplotments and types of synthesis. It is in that sense that we can interpret the past "anyway we like." And it is this conclusion which signals to many (normal) historians the end of their kind of history. By opening up historical work to many possibilities of narrative structuring and interpretive coding than normal history in its empirical/factual, realist, documentarist, "for its own sake" paradigm allows, it thus appears that one has indeed eliminated what, for Berkhofer, poetics has promised to eliminate; namely, "the legitimating authority of factuality for history itself according to traditional premises."[30]

But Berkhofer doesn't stop there. He goes on to ask: but why is this a problem? Why are historians (in this context "normal historians") worried by this opening up? And his answer, a quite correct one I think, is because "normal history orders the past for the sake of authority and therefore power."[31] As with metanarrative historians, normal historians must also "prove" their case by a single interpretive coding of the past, otherwise the arbitrary nature of the produced history becomes so evident that it loses its intended natural effect and thus its privileged position as having represented the past as it actually was.

To conclude Berkhofer's argument. The only referent that he thinks can be found for historical accounts is in the intertextuality which results from the reading of sets of sources combined with the readings of other historians of these same sources as synthesized in their expositions. Thus Berkhofer fails to see much, if anything, in the distinction drawn by normal historians between fact and fiction, "for factual reconstruction is really nothing but construction according to the working 'fictions' [the discipline] of normal historical practice which, in turn, are the premises of [an untenable] . . . historical realism and realistic mimesis."[32]

It is these kinds of arguments, then, which have thus caused "postist" interpretations (often just referred to demonically as "theory") to be quite correctly seen by many traditional lower case historians as life-threatening to their practices. Accordingly, the argument I have been putting throughout this Introduction – that history students ought to be aware of this situation and ought to take seriously postmodern-type critiques of both upper and lower case histories – is an essential one if they are to become reflexive practitioners in control of their own way of stabilising their texts; if they are to have their "own semantic authority" and thus be "in control of their own discourse." And to achieve this I hope that the readings in this volume will make some contribution. All that is left for me to do now, therefore, is to say something about how I have organized this *Reader* and selected the extracts which make it up relative to the way I have – in my above comments – put History/history "under a description."

SECTION 3: THE ORGANIZATION OF THE READER

The situation just sketched in – a situation where postmodern-type critiques arguably undercut both upper and lower case histories – now allows me to suggest how historians have recently been taking up positions *vis-à-vis* this phenomenon. For what historians make of the present condition (whether they radically welcome the new opportunities to work in the cracks opened up in upper and lower case orthodoxies or fearfully see in this capsizal the collapse of, if not the best of all possible worlds, at least the end of theirs) determines pretty much where they stand with regard to postmodern critiques of the History/history ensemble.

Accordingly, I think it is possible to distinguish between at least five different categories of historian with regard to the general attitude they adopt towards postmodern histories; two groups which I term *radical*, two which I would term *traditionalist*, and a fifth group (*undecided* or *nuanced others*) who can see both the benefits and the drawbacks of postmodernism, combining positive and negative readings to "suit themselves." Of course – and I add this caveat immediately – in any enabling categorization such as this, the boundaries between the categories must be acknowledged as both blurred and subject to continuing seepage. Nevertheless, I think there are good reasons for adopting the chosen categorizations – and I turn to them now.

First, then, I think we can distinguish a group of *radical* theorists who, heterogeneous though they may be as they bring to current debates different historical baggages and agendas, are nevertheless all positive about the impact of postmodernism on history as such but especially about the collapse of the upper case. That collapse is seen as allowing people(s) who, hitherto negatively represented and/or ignored by Western logocentric/phallocentric metanarratives, have not yet had the opportunity to construct histories of their own; histories of emancipation and empowerment. This is a large group of historians/theorists which includes some of the biggest names (Derrida, Lacan, Lyotard, Baudrillard, Spivak, Iragary, Fish and Rorty) as well as a host of others (Bauman, Laclau, Giroux, Young, Chambers *et al.*) theorists who can live with the kind of deprivileging postmodernism causes; who can live with upper and lower case histories that are demystified, which overtly call attention to their own processes of production, flag their working assumptions, and indicate explicitly and repeatedly the constituted rather than the found nature of their referent – the historicized past.

Second, there is a series of *radical* critiques of history in the lower case made by historians/theorists who accept the collapse of both the upper and lower cases but who, taking the collapse of the upper case as read, have tended to concentrate on the lower. This is a group which includes Barthes, Foucault, F. R. Ankersmit, Hayden White, Robert Berkhofer, Joan Scott, Diane Elam, David Harlan, Dominick LaCapra *et al.*, some of whom are represented in this volume.

Third, there is a group which I would like to call *traditionalists* – people drawn in this volume overwhelmingly from the left. This group, whilst happy to see the undercutting of lower case history by White and Ankersmit *et al.*, and who can generally admit (albeit somewhat reluctantly) that radical critiques of metanarrative histories have reduced them to the status of extended metaphors/allegories, still see the need to retain a hold on "right reason," factuality, truth, justice, etc., as bases for emancipation and empowerment along old fashioned lines. This group sees in postmodernism a potentially hapless relativism or even a thorough-going nihilism. They see in its endless deferments, in its celebration of difference and alterity, in its anti-ontological, anti-epistemological, anti-methodological stance, a mode of thinking which "conveniently" under-cuts their radical gestures such that postmodernism is seen as arising from, and working in the interests of, contemporary, commodifying con-sumer capitalism. This is a group which includes Christopher Norris, Terry Eagleton, Fredric Jameson, Perry Anderson, David Harvey, Alex Callinicos, Elizabeth Fox-Genovese, Norman Geras et al.. These are theorists who can go along with, say, recent postmodern developments in literary criticism and the turn against naive representationalist ideas of language. This is a group which can accept that anti-foundational philosophy has brought a new awareness as to the ways narrative structuring, emplotment and metaphor enter into our readings of the world. They also accept, so far as history is concerned, that we now have a much greater awareness as to the means of its construction. But, having gone this far, such theorists consider there is no need to go along with utterly relativistic postmodern views, in that there are still methods of comparing more or less plausible (historical) accounts in ways which do not give in to a feckless relativism. They believe that there are still ways of retaining the "facts" in order to resist the endless play of simulation and deferment. Norman Geras has typically put the problem as he/they see it:

> If there is no truth, there is no injustice . . . if truth is wholly relativized or internalized to particular discourses or language games . . . final vocabulary, framework of instrumental success, culturally specific set of beliefs or practices of justification, there is no injustice . . . The victims and protestors of any putative injustice are deprived of their last and often best weapon, that of telling what really happened. They can only tell their story, which is something else. Morally and politi-cally, therefore, anything goes.[33]

The argument from left traditionalists is that postmodernism's undercut-ting of any principled grounds for truth disables their attempts to resist capitalist practices and alternative scenarios. But for another group – group four, postmodernism comes from, is in the interests of, and even belongs to, not the right at all but the left. This is a group not of upper but of lower case traditionalists, a group which includes, say, Lawrence Stone, Perez Zagorin, Gertrude Himmelfarb, Geoffrey Elton, Carlo Ginz-burg et al., all of whom speak in the name of "proper" history. For this group, postmodern history in the hands of lower case radicals such as Ankersmit and White unprivileges its legitimate status. Having no objection whatsoever to the radical critiques of the upper case by Lyotard *et al.* historians like Stone see with unease the proper lower case baby being thrown away with the crazy upper case bath water. Their conclusion is that with no viable upper or lower case history left, history as such disappears in the postmodernist air. Accordingly, pretty much on the basis that something which doesn't benefit them and their view of history must benefit somebody else, they are led towards the conclusion that postmodernism is a left phenomenon. In this way we can see that traditionalists of both left and centre/centre-right consider – precisely because postmodernism seems to undercut their own practices – that such a postmodernism is in the service of those they are unsympathetic to. Either way, we can see that traditionalists of both the upper and lower case would like some sort of "certaintist" fix against the postmodern.

I come now to the *fifth* group. This is a group of historians who might best be described as "undecided or nuanced others." Its members can appreciate the advantages of postmodern demystification but they remain nostalgic for, say, a definitive method which would again prevent a situation of "anything goes"; which would privilege/legitimate their particular readings. I am thinking here of such people as Joyce Appleby, Lynn Hunt, Margaret Jacob, Tony Bennett, Raphael Samuel, *et al.*, people who still hope that their positions are not just capricious choices but are capable of being "underwritten."

We now have a situation where the historians in this volume can be classified as follows:

(1) Historians who like the collapse of the upper case (Lyotard *et al.*).
(2) Historians who especially dislike the collapse of the upper case (Christopher Norris *et al.*).
(3) Historians who like the collapse of the lower case (Robert Berkhofer *et al.*).
(4) Historians who like the collapse of the upper case but not the collateral fall-out on the lower (Gertrude Himmelfarb *et al.*).
(5) Historians (nuanced/ambiguous others) who can see the pluses and minuses of postmodernism and who mix postmodern positions with older radical commitments and practices (Tony Bennett *et al.*).

This constitutes the rationale for the inclusion of the above types of historian/theorist in this volume. I now want to explain how I have placed these five types into the *four* Parts which make up this Reader.

I have organized the extracts from the historians who fall into the above five categories in *two* ways, one where, within their Parts, individual historians "stand alone," the other where they are embedded in a series of debates generally taken from journals. That is, to spell this out, the first "half" of the volume is made up of three Parts:

Part I: On History in the Upper case: For and Against Postmodern Histories (i.e., Lyotard *et al.* v. Norris *et al.*)
Part II: On History in the Lower case: For and Against the Collapse of the Lower case (i.e., Berkhofer *et al.* v. Himmelfarb *et al.*)
Part III: Nuanced or Ambiguous Others (i.e., Bennett *et al.*).

In these three Parts the readings (overwhelmingly drawn from books) will be relatively short. This is where historians "stand alone." The extracts reproduced in them are, if you like, a series of "positioned tasters"; a series of extracts which allow the divisions, the issues, and the differences between historians' attitudes to the postmodern to be cast in sharp relief. Part IV (in effect constituting the second "half" of the volume) will then be made up of a series of debates taken overwhelmingly from the journals wherein the positions outlined in Parts I to III are articulated within particular arenas: within, say, Social History or the History of Ideas. These readings are generally longer than those in Parts I to III. Indeed, wherever possible I have tried to reproduce full articles, often complete with footnotes, so that readers may have before them fairly self-contained debates. I think that in the case of the extracts in Parts I to III, readers will have to go to the books anyway simply because from a book of, say, some 200 pages, a taster is all that can be given. But in the case of articles, if these can be given pretty much in their entirety, then this avoids readers having to search out often elusive back numbers of journals. Having more or less complete articles which are often part of an ongoing debate also means that the juxtaposition of opposing views sharpens the issues, and so may aid discussion by students in, say, seminar groups. Part IV is thus made up of readings taken from the journals: *Past and Present*, *Social History*, and *History and Theory*; and one book: S. Friedlander (ed.) *Probing the Limits of Representation: The Holocaust Debate*, Cambridge, Mass., Harvard University Press, 1992.

At this point it may be useful to readers to have the contents of the book sketched out in full and "in context":

PART I: ON HISTORY IN THE UPPER CASE: FOR AND AGAINST POSTMODERN HISTORIES

For Postmodern Histories:

(1) J. F. Lyotard, *The Postmodern Condition*
(2) J. Baudrillard, *The Illusion of the End*
(3) E. Ermarth, *Sequel to History*
(4) D. Elam, *Romancing the Postmodern; Feminism and Deconstruction*
(5) R. Young, *White Mythologies*
(6) I. Chambers, *Migrancy, Culture, Identity*

Against Postmodern Histories:

(1) E. Fox-Genovese, *Literary Criticism and the Politics of the New Historicism*
(2) C. Norris, *Postmodernizing History: Right-wing Revisionism and the Uses of Theory*
(3) B. Palmer, *Critical Theory, Historical Materialism, and the Ostensible End of Marxism: The Poverty of Theory Revisited*

PART II: ON HISTORY IN THE LOWER CASE: FOR AND AGAINST THE COLLAPSE OF THE LOWER CASE

For the Collapse of the Lower Case:

(1) R. Barthes, *The Discourse of History*
(2) M. Foucault, *Nietzsche, Genealogy, History*
(3) H. Kellner, *Language and Historical Representation*
(4) R. Berkhofer, *The Challenge of Poetics to (Normal) Historical Practice*

Against the Collapse of the Lower Case:

(1) G. Himmelfarb, *Telling It As You Like It: Postmodernist History and the Flight from Fact*
(2) G. Elton, *Return to Essentials*
(3) G. Spiegel, *History, Historicism, and the Social Logic of the Text in the Middle Ages*

PART III: NUANCED OR AMBIGUOUS OTHERS

(1) J. Appleby, L. Hunt, M. Jacob, *Telling the Truth About History*
(2) T. Bennett, *Outside Literature; Texts in History*
(3) S. Stanford Friedman, *Making History: On Feminism, Narrative and Desire*

PART IV: DEBATES FROM THE JOURNALS

Past and Present

(1) L. Stone, "History and Postmodernism"
(2) P. Joyce, "History and Postmodernism"
(3) C. Kelly, "History and Postmodernism"
(4) L. Stone, "History and Postmodernism"
(5) G. Spiegel, "History and Postmodernism"

History and Theory

(1) F. R. Ankersmit, "Historiography and Postmodernism"
(2) P. Zagorin, "Historiography and Postmodernism Reconsiderations"

Social History

(1) N. Kirk, "History, Language, Ideas and Postmodernism: A Materialist View"
(2) P. Joyce, "The End of Social History?"
(3) G. Eley, and K. Nield, "Starting Over: The Present, The Postmodern and the Moment of Social History"
(4) P. Joyce, "The End of Social History? A Brief Reply to Eley and Nield"

History and Theory and S. Friedlander (ed.) *Probing the Limits of Representation: The Holocaust Debate*

(1) S. Friedlander, "Probing the Limits of Representation"
(2) H. White, "Historical Emplotment and the Problem of Truth"
(3) H. Kellner, "'Never Again' Is Now"
(4) W. Kansteiner, "From Exception to Exemplum"
(5) R. Braun, "The Holocaust and Problems of Representation"
(6) B. Lang, "Is It Possible to Misrepresent the Holocaust?"
   I now have just two final comments to make, both of which are to do

with what this volume has "left out." First, it will be obvious by now that this *Reader* is primarily on postmodern-type theories and historiography: on "the nature of historiography" under the impact of the "posts." But questions which often arise in this context are what, after all this theorizing, do (or would) postmodern histories actually look like; how are they (or how would they be) different from modernist historiography? These are not easy questions to answer. One thing we can be fairly sure about is that (if they exist) they will not be like "histories in the upper case." Less certainly, we might say that they will not be much like lower case histories either in their old realist, "for its own sake" formulations. But this is still to beg the question, to say what they won't be rather than what they will. No, what are required, it is still said, are concrete examples of the new.

I have already suggested why this rather reasonable request is difficult to fulfil. For if postmodern histories are "histories of the future," are histories "which have not yet been," then they are clearly not yet in existence. There are, however, in the already existing works of, say, Hayden White, Jean Baudrillard, Natalie Zeman-Davis, Simon Schama, Stephen Bann *et al.*, intimations of postmodern-type histories at least according to some "trend spotters," (for example, Hans Kellner, F. R. Ankersmit, Raphael Samuel, Linda Hutcheon and Robert Berkhofer). But, as I say, it is difficult to find thorough-going examples of this new genre (Berkhofer, for example, cites Greg Dening's *Mister Bligh's Bad Language: Passion, Power and Theatre on the Bounty*; Richard Price's *Alibi's World*; Robert Rosenstone's *Mirror in the Shrine: American Encounters with Meiji Japan*),[34] and, perhaps more importantly here, short extracts from such works which would be illustrative. Consequently, I think that here I can only recommend that readers go to Kellner *et al.* for further reading and particularly to Berkhofer's recently published volume, *Beyond the Great Story: History as Text and Discourse*. This is one of the most comprehensive volumes so far produced on the impact of postmodernism on history (and especially on history in the lower case) and it pulls together much of the literature (Berkhofer's footnotes, running to eighty-one pages, are a veritable gold mine).[35]

So to my second and final point. This *Reader*, like every other, has been compiled under many constraints: of word limits, of time pressure, of the potential readership, of my own familiarity with the areas under scrutiny, of the decision to organize the *Reader* in four parts, and so on. Obviously many things have been left out. Whole areas which could have been included have been omitted entirely. From a different perspective, or with hindsight, a different set of readings could have been selected, and a different organization of the text could have centred or marginalized them. Nevertheless, I hope in what follows I have given a helpful and workable cross-section of readings which "are as they are" for the sorts of reasons I have tried to explain in this Introduction. Indeed, it is for this reason that I have tried to sketch out the position I hold towards postmodernism and historiography. For my own position on postmodernism explains why this volume has the shape it has. What I have tried to do here is therefore what I think we all ought to try and do as we edit and abridge and present to others what makes sense to us; that is, to be as "open about our closures" as we possibly can. For at least this enables the reader to review his or her own position "and so make the adjustments necessary for dialogue."[36]

NOTES

1. The reason why this *Reader* is not necessarily balanced and dis-interested is not least because, as this is a *Postmodern History Reader*, so people coming to it might reasonably expect postmodern readings to be what the book substantially contains. Looking through other Readers I find very few examples of oppositional arguments having much space in them (for example, in post-colonial Readers you don't see lots of apologies for colonialism). In point of fact, however, because much of this *Reader* is arranged in terms of debates which do give both pro and anti positions, then there is actually a considerable "balance" within it, and hopefully both pro and anti positions will give "food for thought."
2. The next few paragraphs follow the argument which I put forward in my *On "What Is History?": From Carr and Elton to Rorty and White*, London: Routledge, 1995.
3. The various debates as to the types of postmodernism and the nature of postmodernity can be conveniently followed in, for example, David Harvey's *The Condition of Postmodernity*, Oxford: Blackwell, 1989; T. Docherty, *Postmodernism: A Reader*, Hemel Hempstead: Harvester Wheatsheaf, 1993.
4. A similar argument to mine can be found in John Gray's *Enlightenment's Wake*, London: Routledge, 1995 – though my position is somewhat different to his.
5. This has been put somewhat differently by J. C. Alexander in his *Fin-de-Siècle Social Theory: Relativism, Reduction and the Problem of Reason*, London: Verso, 1995. See also H. Berten's *The Ideal of the Postmodern: A History*, London: Routledge, 1995.
6. J. F. Lyotard, *The Postmodern Condition*, Manchester: Manchester University Press, 1984.
7. J. F. Lyotard, *The Differend: Phrases in Dispute*, Minneapolis: University of Minnesota Press, 1988. For a hostile treatment of *The Differend* see Christopher Norris' *What's Wrong with Postmodernism?* Hemel Hempstead: Harvester-Wheatsheaf, 1990, especially the Introduction.
8. See Robert Young, *White Mythologies: Writing History and the West*, London: Routledge, 1990; Iain Chambers, *Migrancy, Culture, Identity*, London: Routledge, 1994.
9. G. McLennan, "History and Theory," in, *Literature and History*, 10, 2, 1984, pp. 139–64; see also his *Marxism and the Methodologies of History*, London: Verso, 1981, *passim*.

10. McLennan, "History and Theory," p. 141.
11. Ibid. p. 142.
12. McLennan, *Marxism and the Methodologies of History*, op. cit. p. 97.
13. P. Novick, *That Noble Dream: The "Objectivity Question" and the American Historical Profession*, Cambridge: Cambridge University Press, 1988.
14. Ibid. pp. 1–2.
15. G. Elton, *The Practice of History*, London: Fontana, 1969; J. Tosh, *The Pursuit of History*, London: Longman, second edition, 1991; M. Stanford, *A Companion to the Study of History*, Oxford: Blackwell, 1994.
16. D. LaCapra, *History and Criticism*, New York: Cornell University Press, 1985, p. 17.
17. Ibid. p. 18.
18. Ibid. p. 18.
19. Ibid. p. 19.
20. Ibid. p. 19.
21. Ibid. pp. 20–1.
22. See, for example, H. White, *The Content of the Form, Baltimore*: Johns Hopkins University Press, 1987.
23. A. Danto, *Analytic Philosophy of History*, Cambridge: Cambridge University Press, 1965, p. 218.
24. C. Lorenz, "Historical Knowledge and Historical Reality: A Plea for Internal Realism," *History and Theory*, 33, 3, 1994, pp. 297–344; pp. 313–14.
25. A. Callinicos, *Theories and Narratives: Reflections on the Philosophy of History*, Cambridge: Polity Press, 1995, p. 78.
26. R. Berkhofer, "The Challenge of Poetics to (Normal) Historical Practice," *Poetics Today*, 9, 2, 1988, pp. 435–52.
27. Ibid. p. 435.
28. Ibid. pp. 446–7.
29. J. Zammito, "Are We Being Theoretical Yet? . . .," *The Journal of Modern History*, 65, 1, 1993, pp. 783–814, p. 807.
30. R. Berkhofer, op. cit p. 449.
31. Ibid. p. 449.
32. Ibid. p. 445.
33. N. Geras, "Language, Truth and Justice," *New Left Review*, 209, 1995, pp. 110–35, p. 110, p. 125.
34. F. R. Ankersmit and H. Kellner, *A New Philosophy of History*, London: Reaktion, 1995; R. Samuel, "Reading the Signs" (Parts I and II) *History Workshop Journal*, 32–3, Autumn 1991/Spring 1992; L. Hutcheon, *The Politics of Postmodernism*, London: Routledge, 1989; R. Berkhofer, *Beyond the Great Story: History as Text and Discourse*, Cambridge, Mass.: Harvard University Press, 1995.
35. Attention ought also to be brought here to Alun Munslow's analysis survey of the contemporary historiographical scene, *Deconstructing History*, London: Routledge (forthcoming). Munslow is also co-editor (with Robert Rosenstone) of a new journal of historiographical theory and practice, *Rethinking History*, published by Routledge three times a year, from July 1997.
36. D. MacCannell, *Empty Meeting Grounds*, London: Routledge, 1992, p. 10.

Part I On history in the upper case

For and against postmodern histories

EDITOR'S INTRODUCTION: FOR POSTMODERN HISTORIES

In this and the following two Parts, I have taken extracts, generally from books rather than journal articles, to illustrate debates over history in the upper and lower case. In this first Part I have chosen extracts which I hope introduce readers to some of the possibilities opened up by abandoning the upper case and some of the fears, particularly from traditionalists on the ideological left, occasioned by the loss of what are, in effect, metanarratives.

The first short extract is taken from J. F. Lyotard's *The Postmodern Condition*, first published in French in 1979 and in English in 1984. In it Lyotard has two attempts at defining postmodernism. In the first (the one reprinted here – Lyotard's further definition of postmodernism as invoking notions of the sublime is found in his Appendix) he famously defines postmodernism as "incredulity towards metanarratives." That is, postmodernism takes as incredible the notion that an idea (especially an idea of a scientific kind, including scientific histories in the upper case) can be legitimated by reference to a metadiscourse of the kind making an explicit appeal to some grand narrative. A grand narrative may be the "hermeneutics of meaning, the emancipation of the rational . . . or the creation of wealth." Such legitimations are, as Lyotard puts it, currently being dispersed "in clouds of narrative language elements." This radical, nominalistic pragmatism, illustrates the notion that various alleged unities (totalities, holisms, teleologies) are at best convenient fictions and, at worst, totalizing mystifications in which can be found intimations of totalitarianism. For Lyotard, radical indeterminacy, the perpetual openness of possibilities and a sceptical attitude towards all positions bearing down on us wearing the label of Truth, is one of the guarantees of human freedom. For Lyotard it is not so much radical scepticism that should be feared, but all those positions which claim "to know" – and know for sure.

Jean Baudrillard pushes this type of postmodernism towards its "logical conclusions"; towards nihilism. Unlike other postmodernists who in order to have an (albeit arbitrary) position from which to work, yoke "postist" scepticism to some reworked aspect of modernity (so that, for example, post-Marxists still yoke "postist" attitudes to some sort of Marxist political desire, or post-feminists still yoke their position to something recognizably "feminine") Baudrillard has no adjective with which to precede postmodernism: he is all postmodern.

The extract from Baudrillard given here is the beginning of his meditations on history from *The Illusion of the End* (1992). It is difficult to summarize the many arguments running through this suggestive text but, in a nutshell,

Baudrillard's argument is that there is neither rhyme nor reason in existence, and no reason to think that history is purposive: that it has in it a discoverable end. Baudrillard's book signals "the end of endism." In fact, to think of history as going somewhere, to suffer from the illusion of endism, is something which today we have overcome. We now live in a period in which hyper-reality allows us to understand that "reality" has always been based upon a foundationless "simulacrum." In the extract given here Baudrillard considers the conditions necessary for the creation of modernist-type histories and argues that these have disappeared. Accordingly, there will be a new sort of history in the future of a type which we have not yet seen, histories "without end."

Diane Elam, in extracts taken from her *Romancing the Postmodern* (1992) and *Feminism and Deconstruction* (1994) arguably continues in the spirit of Baudrillard (and Derrida). Again, Elam's general position is not easy to summarize but, at the risk of some simplification, she is concerned to show that, precisely because "woman" is something that has previously been defined through gendered (male dominated) discourse, then we have never yet known what "woman" is. Yet, to define "woman" as being something in particular, that something, if being realized ("realizing woman") closes down the endless possibilities of women of the future. Having something to realize reinvokes the ideas of essentialism and historical teleology. Consequently, Elam wants a future where women endlessly re-invent their (metaphorical) selves in ways which modernist-type definitions stabilize and so oppose the notion of "endless" becoming.

In the first of the two extracts given here (from *Romancing the Postmodern*) Elam invokes the notion of the future-anterior verb; the idea that what passes for our present is not a fullness or a total presence since it is always marked as a potential past of our own future; a present which "will not have been good enough." This is a refusal, then, to abstract the present from history as the single point from which a perspective on history can be adopted. "In place of the living present comes the recognition of presence as a lost object, grasped only in its passing . . . 'Tomorrow was another day.'" In the second extract (from *Feminism and Deconstruction*) Elam begins from the question of what – from the position of the radical, metaphorical alterity of women – would it mean to write a history of women, extending the work of Joan Scott and concluding that such a history (written in the future anterior) would be an endless repositioning and rewriting: "history written in the future anterior is a message that is handed to an unknown addressee and accepts that its meaning in part will have to depend upon that addressee. History rewritten for a public that will have to rewrite it ceaselessly." Here, "endism" is permanently banished.

Elizabeth Deeds Ermarth's *Sequel to History* (1992) examines the way in which modernist notions of linear time are subverted by postmodern notions of rhythmic time, an idea of time that "radically modifies or abandons altogether the dialectics, the teleology, the transcendence, and the putative neutrality of historical time . . . it replaces the Cartesian *cogito* with a different subjectivity whose manifesto might be Cortázar's 'I swing, therefore I am'." Whether or not postmodern rhythmic time invokes a new type of history remains, for Ermarth, an open question: "I attend mainly to how postmodern time works, what it offers, and what its implicit requirements, gains, and losses may be. The work that undermines history also opens new questions and provides new opportunities in practice." In the extracts offered here, I reproduce Ermarth's Prologue and her conclusion "Coda: On Contingency," in the hope that readers will themselves be driven to the quite brilliantly suggestive "book" in between.

The final two extracts – from Robert Young's *White Mythologies: History Writing and the West* (1990) and Iain Chambers' *Migrancy, Culture, Identity* (1994) – shift the perspectives on postmodern possibilities in ethnic directions. For both writers what might be termed modernist histories are examples of white, male, Euro-centred, metropolitan scripts – a local script which, nevertheless, wrote from its temporal and spatial particularity "the history of the world." And for both, postmodernism is the 'return of the repressed'; as Young concludes, today, "as 'History' gives way to the 'Postmodern', we are witnessing the disillusion of 'the West'." In *Migrancy, Culture, Identity* Chambers, in a series of evocative chapters, raises the question of what, in times of "ethnic mix," is history for: of why history?: "Put another way, what does the historian want?;" what does the "very desire" for history involve? Chambers' answer, only hinted at in the short section given here, is that today a history must give generous plural identities which respect alterity and which refuse the closure articulated in modernist, homogenized, totalizing scripts. Chambers thinks of the possibility of history in ways akin to Nietzsche's unbounded sea; open vistas of historical alterities "loyal to life."

2 Jean-François Lyotard

The postmodern condition

The object of this study is the condition of knowledge in the most highly developed societies. I have decided to use the word *postmodern* to describe that condition. The word is in current use on the American continent among sociologists and critics; it designates the state of our culture following the transformations which, since the end of the nineteenth century, have altered the game rules for science, literature, and the arts. The present study will place these transformations in the context of the crisis of narratives.

Science has always been in conflict with narratives. Judged by the yardstick of science, the majority of them prove to be fables. But to the extent that science does not restrict itself to stating useful regularities and seeks the truth, it is obliged to legitimate the rules of its own game. It then produces a discourse of legitimation with respect to its own status, a discourse called philosophy. I will use the term *modern* to designate any science that legitimates itself with reference to a metadiscourse of this kind making an explicit appeal to some grand narrative, such as the dialectics of Spirit, the hermeneutics of meaning, the emancipation of the rational or working subject, or the creation of wealth. For example, the rule of consensus between the sender and addressee of a statement with truth-value is deemed acceptable if it is cast in terms of a possible unanimity between rational minds: this is the Enlightenment narrative, in which the hero of knowledge works toward a good ethico-political end – universal peace. As can be seen from this example, if a metanarrative implying a philosophy of history is used to legitimate knowledge, questions are raised concerning the validity of the institutions governing the social bond: these must be legitimated as well. Thus justice is consigned to the grand narrative in the same way as truth.

Simplifying to the extreme, I define *postmodern* as incredulity toward metanarratives. This incredulity is undoubtedly a product of progress

in the sciences: but that progress in turn presupposes it. To the obsol-
escence of the metanarrative apparatus of legitimation corresponds,
most notably, the crisis of metaphysical philosophy and of the university
institution which in the past relied on it. The narrative function is losing
its functors, its great hero, its great dangers, its great voyages, its great
goal. It is being dispersed in clouds of narrative language elements –
narrative, but also denotative, prescriptive, descriptive, and so on. Conveyed within each cloud are pragmatic valencies specific to its kind.
Each of us lives at the intersection of many of these. However, we do not
necessarily establish stable language combinations, and the properties of
the ones we do establish are not necessarily communicable.

Thus the society of the future falls less within the province of a
Newtonian anthropology (such as structuralism or systems theory) than
a pragmatics of language particles. There are many different language
games – a heterogeneity of elements. They only give rise to institutions
in patches – local determinism.

The decision makers, however, attempt to manage these clouds of
sociality according to input/output matrices, following a logic which
implies that their elements are commensurable and that the whole is
determinable. They allocate our lives for the growth of power. In matters
of social justice and of scientific truth alike, the legitimation of that
power is based on its optimizing the system's performance – efficiency.
The application of this criterion to all of our games necessarily entails
a certain level of terror, whether soft or hard: be operational (that is,
commensurable) or disappear.

The logic of maximum performance is no doubt inconsistent in many
ways, particularly with respect to contradiction in the socio-economic
field: it demands both less work (to lower production costs) and more
(to lessen the social burden of the idle population). But our incredulity
is now such that we no longer expect salvation to rise from these
inconsistencies, as did Marx.

Still, the postmodern condition is as much a stranger to disenchantment as it is to the blind positivity of delegitimation. Where, after
the metanarratives, can legitimacy reside? The operativity criterion is
technological; it has no relevance for judging what is true or just. Is
legitimacy to be found in consensus obtained through discussion, as
Jürgen Habermas thinks? Such consensus does violence to the heterogeneity of language games. And invention is always born of dissension.
Postmodern knowledge is not simply a tool of the authorities; it refines
our sensitivity to differences and reinforces our ability to tolerate the

incommensurable. Its principle is not the expert's homology, but the inventor's paralogy.

Here is the question: is a legitimation of the social bond, a just society, feasible in terms of a paradox analogous to that of scientific activity? What would such a paradox be?

The text that follows is an occasional one. It is a report on knowledge in the most highly developed societies and was presented to the Conseil des Universités of the government of Quebec at the request of its president. I would like to thank him for his kindness in allowing its publication.

It remains to be said that the author of the report is a philosopher, not an expert. The latter knows what he knows and what he does not know: the former does not. One concludes, the other questions – two very different language games. I combine them here with the result that neither quite succeeds.

The philosopher at least can console himself with the thought that the formal and pragmatic analysis of certain philosophical and ethico-political discourses of legitimation, which underlies the report, will subsequently see the light of day. The report will have served to introduce that analysis from a somewhat sociologizing slant, one that truncates but at the same time situates it.

Such as it is, I dedicate this report to the Institut Polytechnique de Philosophie of the Université de Paris VIII (Vincennes) – at this very postmodern moment that finds the University nearing what may be its end, while the Institute may just be beginning.

3 Jean Baudrillard

The illusion of the end

PATAPHYSICS OF THE YEAR 2000

A tormenting thought: as of a certain point, history was no longer *real*. Without noticing it, all mankind suddenly left reality; everything happening since then was supposedly not true; but we supposedly didn't notice. Our task would now be to find that point, and as long as we didn't have it, we would be forced to abide in our present destruction.

Elias Canetti

Various plausible hypotheses may be advanced to explain this vanishing of history. Canetti's expression "all mankind suddenly left reality" irresistibly evokes the idea of that escape velocity a body requires to free itself from the gravitational field of a star or planet. Staying with this image, one might suppose that the acceleration of modernity, of technology, events and media, of all exchanges – economic, political and sexual – has propelled us to "escape velocity," with the result that we have flown free of the referential sphere of the real and of history. We are "liberated" in every sense of the term, so liberated that we have taken leave of a certain space-time, passed beyond a certain horizon in which the real is possible because gravitation is still strong enough for things to be reflected and thus in some way to endure and have some consequence.

A degree of slowness (that is, a certain speed, but not too much), a degree of distance, but not too much, and a degree of liberation (an energy for rupture and change), but not too much, are needed to bring about the kind of condensation or significant crystallization of events we call history, the kind of coherent unfolding of causes and effects we call reality [*le réel*].

Once beyond this gravitational effect, which keeps bodies in orbit, all the atoms of meaning get lost in space. Each atom pursues its own trajectory to infinity and is lost in space. This is precisely what we are seeing in our present-day societies, intent as they are on accelerating all bodies, messages and processes in all directions and which, with modern media, have created for every event, story and image a simulation of an infinite trajectory. Every political, historical and cultural fact possesses a kinetic energy which wrenches it from its own space and propels it into a hyperspace where, since it will never return, it loses all meaning. No need for science fiction here: already, here and now – in the shape of our computers, circuits and networks – we have the particle accelerator which has smashed the referential orbit of things once and for all.

So far as history is concerned, its telling has become impossible because that telling (re-citatum) is, by definition, the possible recurrence of a sequence of meanings. Now, through the impulse for total dissemination and circulation, every event is granted its own liberation; every fact becomes atomic, nuclear, and pursues its trajectory into the void. In order to be disseminated to infinity, it has to be fragmented like a particle. This is how it is able to achieve a velocity of no-return which carries it out of history once and for all. Every set of phenomena, whether cultural totality or sequence of events, has to be fragmented, disjointed, so that it can be sent down the circuits; every kind of language has to be resolved into a binary formulation so that it can circulate not, any longer, in our memories, but in the luminous, electronic memory of the computers. No human language can withstand the speed of light. No event can withstand being beamed across the whole planet. No meaning can withstand acceleration. No history can withstand the centrifugation of facts or their being short-circuited in real time (to pursue the same train of thought: no sexuality can withstand being liberated, no culture can withstand being hyped, no truth can withstand being verified, etc.).

Nor is theory in a position to "reflect (on)" anything. It can only tear concepts from their critical zone of reference and force them beyond a point of no-return (it too is moving into the hyperspace of simulation), a process whereby it loses all "objective" validity but gains substantially in real affinity with the present system.

The second hypothesis regarding the vanishing of history is the opposite of the first. It has to do not with processes speeding up but slowing down. It too comes directly from physics.

Matter slows the passing of time. To put it more precisely, time at the surface of a very dense body seems to be going in slow motion. The phenomenon intensifies as the density increases. The effect of this slowing down will be to increase the length of the light-wave emitted by this body as received by the observer. Beyond a certain limit, time stops and the wavelength becomes infinite. The wave no longer exists. The light goes out.

There is a clear analogy here with the slowing down of history when it rubs up against the astral body of the "silent majorities." Our societies are dominated by this mass process, not just in the demographic and sociological sense, but in the sense of a "critical mass," of passing beyond a point of no-return. This is the most significant event within these societies: the emergence, in the very course of their mobilization and revolutionary process (they are all revolutionary by the standards of past centuries), of an equivalent force of inertia, of an immense indifference and the silent potency of that indifference. This inert matter of the social is not produced by a lack of exchanges, information or communication, but by the multiplication and saturation of exchanges. It is the product of the hyperdensity of cities, commodities, messages and circuits. It is the cold star of the social and, around that mass, history is also cooling. Events follow one upon another, cancelling each other out in a state of indifference. The masses, neutralized, mithridatized by information, in turn neutralize history and act as an *écran d'absorption*.[1] They themselves have no history, meaning, consciousness or desire. They are the potential residue of all history, meaning and desire. As they have unfurled in our modernity, all these fine things have stirred up a mysterious counter-phenomenon, and all today's political and social strategies are thrown out of gear by the failure to understand it.

This time we have the opposite situation: history, meaning and progress are no longer able to reach their escape velocity. They are no longer able to pull away from this overdense body which slows their trajectory, which slows time to the point where, right now, the perception and imagination of the future are beyond us. All social, historical and temporal transcendence is absorbed by that mass in its silent immanence. Political events already lack sufficient energy of their own to move us: so they run on like a silent film for which we bear collective irresponsibility. History comes to an end here, not for want of actors, nor for want of violence (there will always be more violence), nor for want of events (there will always be more events, thanks be to the media and the news networks!), but by deceleration, indifference and stupefaction. It is no longer able to transcend itself, to envisage its own finality, to dream of its own end; it is being buried beneath its own immediate effect, worn out in special effects, imploding into current events.

Deep down, one cannot even speak of the end of history here, since history will not have time to catch up with its own end. Its effects are accelerating, but its meaning is slowing inexorably. It will eventually come to a stop and be extinguished like light and time in the vicinity of an infinitely dense mass ...

Humanity too had its big bang: a certain critical density, a certain concentration of people and exchanges presides over this explosion we call history, which is merely the dispersal of the dense and hieratic nuclei of previous civilizations. Today we have the reversive effect: crossing the threshold of the critical mass where populations, events and information are concerned triggers the opposite process of historical and political inertia. In the cosmic order, we do not know whether we have reached the escape velocity which would mean we are now in a definitive state of expansion (this will doubtless remain eternally uncertain). In the human order, where the perspectives are more limited, it may be that the very escape velocity of the species (the acceleration of births, technologies and exchanges over the centuries) creates an excess of mass and resistance which defeats the initial energy and takes us down an inexorable path of contraction and inertia.

Whether the universe is expanding to infinity or retracting towards an infinitely dense, infinitely small nucleus depends on its critical mass (and speculation on this is itself infinite by virtue of the possible invention of new particles). By analogy, whether our human history is evolutive or involutive perhaps depends on humanity's critical mass. Has the history, the movement, of the species reached the escape velocity required to triumph over the inertia of the mass? Are we set, like the galaxies, on a definitive course distancing us from one another at prodigious speed, or is this dispersal to infinity destined to come to an end and the human molecules to come back together by an opposite process of gravitation? Can the human mass, which increases every day, exert control over a pulsation of this kind?

There is a third hypothesis, a third analogy. We are still speaking of a point of disappearance, a vanishing point, but this time in music. I shall call this the stereophonic effect. We are all obsessed with high fidelity, with the quality of musical "reproduction." At the consoles of our stereos, armed with our tuners, amplifiers and speakers, we mix, adjust settings, multiply tracks in pursuit of a flawless sound. Is this still music? Where is the high fidelity threshold beyond which music disappears as such? It does not disappear for lack of music, but because it has passed this limit point; it disappears into the perfection of its materiality, into its own special effect. Beyond this point, there is neither judgement nor aesthetic pleasure. It is the ecstasy of musicality, and its end.

The disappearance of history is of the same order: here again, we have passed that limit where, by dint of the sophistication of events and information, history ceases to exist as such. Immediate high-powered broadcasting, special effects, secondary effects, fading and that famous feedback effect which is produced in acoustics by a source and a receiver being too close together and in history by an event and its dissemination being too close together and thus interfering disastrously – a short-circuit between cause and effect like that between the object and the experimenting subject in microphysics (and in the human sciences!). These are all things which cast a radical doubt on the event, just as excessive high fidelity casts radical doubt on music. Elias Canetti puts it well: beyond this point, nothing is true. It is for this reason that the *petite musique* of history also eludes our grasp today, that it vanishes into the microscopics or the stereophonics of news.

Right at the very heart of news, history threatens to disappear. At the heart of hi-fi, music threatens to disappear. At the heart of experimentation, the object of science threatens to disappear. At the heart of pornography, sexuality threatens to disappear. Everywhere we find the same stereophonic effect, the same effect of absolute proximity to the real, the same effect of simulation.

By definition, this vanishing point, this point short of which history *existed* and music *existed*, cannot be pinned down. Where must stereo perfection end? The boundaries are constantly being pushed back because it is technical obsession which redraws them. Where must news reporting end? One can only counter this fascination with "real time" – the equivalent of high fidelity – with a moral objection, and there is not much point in that.

The passing of this point is thus an irreversible act, contrary to what Canetti seems to hope. We shall never get back to pre-stereo music (except by an additional technical simulation effect); we shall never get back to pre-news and pre-media history. The original essence of music, the original concept of history have disappeared because we shall never again be able to isolate them from their model of perfection which is at the same time their model of simulation, the model of their enforced assumption into a hyper-reality which cancels them out. We shall never again know what the social or music were before being exacerbated into their present useless perfection. We shall never again know what history was before its exacerbation into the technical perfection of news: we shall never again know what anything was before disappearing into the fulfilment of its model.

So, with this, the situation becomes novel once again. The fact that we are leaving history to move into the realm of simulation is merely a consequence of the fact that history itself has always, deep down, been an immense simulation model. Not in the sense that it could be said only to have existed in the narrative made of it or the interpretation given, but with regard to the time in which it unfolds – that linear time which is at once the time of an ending and of the unlimited suspending of the end. The only kind of time in which a history can take place, if, by history, we understand a succession of non-meaningless facts, each engendering the other by cause and effect, but doing so without any absolute necessity and all standing open to the future, unevenly poised. So different from time in ritual societies where the end of everything is in its beginning and ceremony retraces the perfection of that original event. In contrast to this *fulfilled* order of time, the liberation of the "real" time of history, the production of a linear, deferred time may seem a purely artificial process. Where does this suspense come from? Where do we get the idea that what must be accomplished (Last Judgement, salvation or catastrophe) must come at the end of time and match up with some incalculable appointed term or other? This model of linearity must have seemed entirely fictitious, wholly absurd and abstract to cultures which had no sense of a deferred day of reckoning, a successive concatenation of events and a final goal. And it was, indeed, a scenario which had some difficulty establishing itself. There was fierce resistance in the early years of Christianity to the postponement of the coming of God's Kingdom. The acceptance of this "historical" perspective of salvation, that is, of its remaining unaccomplished in the immediate present, was not achieved without violence, and all the heresies would later take up this leitmotif of the immediate fulfilment of the promise in what was akin to a defiance of time. Entire communities even resorted to suicide to hasten the coming of the Kingdom. Since this latter was promised at the end of time, it seemed to them that they had only to put an end to time right away.

The whole of history has had a millennial (millenarian) challenge to its temporality running through it. In opposition to the historical perspective, which continually shifts the stakes on to a hypothetical end, there has always been a fatal exigency, a fatal strategy of time which wants to shoot straight ahead to a point beyond the end. It cannot be said that either of these tendencies has really won out, and the question "to wait or not to wait?" has remained, throughout history, a burning issue. Since the messianic convulsion of the earliest Christians, reaching back beyond the heresies and revolts, there has always been this desire to anticipate the end, possibly by death, by a kind of seductive suicide aiming to turn God from history and make him face up to his responsibilities, those which lie beyond the end, those of the final fulfilment. And what, indeed, is terrorism, if not this effort to conjure up, in its own way, the end of history? It attempts to entrap the powers that be by an immediate, total act. Without awaiting the final term of the process, it sets itself at the ecstatic end-point, hoping to bring about the conditions for the Last Judgement. An illusory challenge, of course, but one which always fascinates, since, deep down, neither time nor history has ever been accepted. Everyone remains aware of the arbitrariness, the artificial character of time and history. And we are never fooled by those who call on us to hope.

And, terrorism apart, is there not also a hint of this parousic exigency in the global fantasy of catastrophe that hovers over today's world? A demand for a violent resolution of reality, when this latter eludes our grasp in an endless hyper-reality? For hyper-reality rules out the very occurrence of the Last Judgement or the Apocalypse or the Revolution. All the ends we have envisaged elude our grasp and history has no chance of bringing them about, since it will, in the interim, have come to an end (it's always the story of Kafka's Messiah: he arrives too late, a day too late, and the time-lag is unbearable). So one might as well short-circuit the Messiah, bring forward the end. This has always been the demonic temptation: to falsify ends and the calculation of ends, to falsify time and the occurrence of things, to hurry them along, impatient to see them accomplished, or secretly sensing that the promise of accomplishment is itself also false and diabolical.

Even our obsession with "real time," with the instantaneity of news, has a secret millenarianism about it: cancelling the flow of time, cancelling delay, suppressing the sense that the event is happening elsewhere, anticipating its end by freeing ourselves from linear time, laying hold of things almost before they have taken place. In this sense, "real time" is something even more artificial than a recording, and is, at the same time, its denial – if we want immediate enjoyment of the event, if we want to experience it at the instant of its occurrence, as if we were there, this is because we no longer have any confidence in the meaning or purpose of the event. The same denial is found in apparently opposite behaviour – recording, filing and memorizing everything of our own past and the past of all cultures. Is this not a symptom of a collective presentiment of the end, a sign that events and the living time of history have had their day and that we have to arm ourselves with the whole battery of artificial memory, all the signs of the past, to face up to the absence of a future and the glacial times which await us? Are not mental and intellectual structures currently going underground, burying themselves in memories, in archives, in search of an improbable resurrection? All thoughts are going underground in cautious anticipation of the year 2000. They can already scent the terror of the year 2000. They are instinctively adopting the solution of those cryogenized individuals plunged into liquid nitrogen until the means can be found to enable them to survive.

These societies, these generations which no longer expect anything from some future "coming," and have less and less confidence in history, which dig in behind their futuristic technologies, behind their stores of information and inside the beehive networks of communication where time is at last wiped out by pure circulation, will perhaps never reawaken. But they do not know that. The year 2000 will not perhaps take place. But they do not know that.

NOTE

1. The French is retained here, since to translate this by the English term "dark trace screen" would be to forfeit the connection Baudrillard wishes to maintain with the idea of absorption.

4 Elizabeth Ermarth

Sequel to history

PROLOGUE: WHY TEXT?

This book is about postmodern temporality, and about the multivalent crises of historical thinking that appear across a very broad spectrum of cultural practice. I sketch these broad arguments in three main parts, often using literary analogies to specify a point, and then I punctuate the argument with a final "Rhythm Section" on one narrative text. This is, then, not precisely literary criticism, nor is it precisely social, philosophical, political, or cultural analysis. It is all of these and none. A conventionally disciplined reader might question this mixing of species, regarding it as an unnatural act. A more theoretically up-to-date reader would take a different line but one that also arrives at a difficulty: since I accept the expanded use of the term "text" which includes artifacts ranging from architecture to events, why not use historical events as examples instead of literary narratives? In other words, and from both sides of the interpretive situation, "Why Text?"

First, and for the empiricist who believes that rocks and stones and trees are more "real" than play and poetry, and that, like minerals, political systems belong to nature not art, my implicit argument is this now familiar one: that the distinction between what is invented and what is real is one that for many reasons we can no longer afford. As Claude Simon, the 1985 Nobel-Prize winner has said, art and literature meet human needs as basic as hunger and thirst. Second, and for the collegial discourse-analyst who finds textuality in historical events, my explicit argument is this: that the term "event," like "text" or "self" or "historical," retains the essentialism that postmodernism challenges. In a postmodern process every event may be a text, but no text is single. It is the nature of the process, the series, the sequence that most interests me in this book and that can scarcely be called an "event" in any traditional sense. The revision of sequence at the level of language is where the practical, embedded resolutions of postmodernism become available.

The complex answer to the question "Why text?" turns on the new priority postmodernism gives to language in defining any system. Postmodernism conceives language as a system of signs, that is, as something internally coherent and not merely a neutral collection of traveling pointers with which we indicate "real things." While this may be widely understood, its implications, I think, are not. The materiality of language is always in view in a postmodern text, and any putative "neutrality" that language might once have appeared to possess remains conspicuously absent. Language is not neutral and not single. In postmodernism, language means residence in a particular discourse, and alternate semantic systems or discourses are not just alternate views or versions of "a reality" that remains beyond them. This is just as true of the "languages" of socialism, capitalism, feminism, sexism, or fashion as it is of French or Spanish or English. Language, in other words, is the constant by which we compare forms of "writing" in the expanded sense that postmodernism gives to that word: writing, that is, conceived as a unique, finite, and local specification of a particular sign system. Considered as discursive "writing," activities are not instruments of production but the activation of different opportunities of residence and of engagement. A "text," furthermore, is no longer a singular "thing" because it is constituted by the process of enactment that engages this or that particular personnel or material.

The term "postmodern" has acquired considerable currency in recent decades, spreading from architectural theory and linguistic esoterica to sweater advertisements in the *New York Times*. This multivalence, this "play" in the term, certainly contributes to its vitality, but it means quite different things in different contexts, and these differences need to be acknowledged. In architecture, for example, postmodernism succeeds and copes with the results of early twentieth-century modernism, particularly the razing effects of Bauhaus and the reduction of detail in favor of Euclidean forms. In philosophy and discourse analysis, on the other hand and partly as a result of Nietzsche's influence, postmodernism succeeds a modernism formulated in a much broader sense, going even so far as to consider postmodernism the successor to a "classicism" traceable to the Greeks.[1] It is important to achieving some political focus on postmodernism to remember that two related but quite distinct things are at stake: first, the modernity that began with

the Renaissance and Reformation, and second, the representational discourse traceable to classical philosophy and science.

In my usage "modern" indicates a period and a discourse that had
preeminence between the Renaissance and the turn of the twentieth
century; that is, I conceive "modern" culture to be the discourse that,
however unevenly and gradually, supplanted medieval culture and
enjoyed hegemony until fairly recently. The case for this I make at
length in *Realism and Consensus in the English Novel*, my book on the
construction of historical consciousness from its roots in Renaissance
perspective through the complex historical forms of the nineteenth
century. What succeeds *that* "modern" culture is "postmodern." What
postmodernism supplants, then, is the discourse of representation
characteristic of the long and productive era that produced historical
thinking, or what Meyer Schapiro calls "the immense, historically
developed capacity to keep the world in mind."[2] This usage assumes a
broader definition of "modern" than the one synonymous with early
twentieth-century "modernism," and a narrower definition than the one
synonymous with "classical" discourse. The related crises of the subject
and of history involve discursive conventions much newer than those
of the Greeks who had no conception of history in the modern sense
and no conception of the subject.[3] By taking up this "classical" discourse
at the familiar fictional threshold of the Renaissance I can focus on the
formation that has favored institutions that we still take very much
for granted, including, to mention a few, representational government,
Newtonian and Darwinian science, realistic art, and capitalism. This
middle-range conception of the "modern," which is by no means unique
to my argument,[4] informs my estimate of the difference postmodernism
makes. In terms of temporality, postmodern writing moves beyond the
identity-and-similitude negotiations that characterize the construction of
historical time and its rationalized consciousness. The tellable time
of realism and its consensus become the untellable time of postmodern
writing.

That the terminological situation with regard to these new currents
is unstable and sometimes parochial seems quite understandable considering the vast implications of postmodernism. Even the term
"postmodern" has emerged relatively late in the historical situation I
describe, and some of the people I quote use the terms "modern" or
"contemporary" to indicate the same thing I describe as "postmodern."
I prefer "postmodern" over "contemporary" for discussing narrative to
avoid any implication that the new writing I describe might include

any of that large number of authors still writing traditional plot-and-character novels; and I prefer "postmodern" over "modern" not only for the general reasons already advanced but also because the writing I discuss differs markedly from the achievements of high modernism. The term "postmodern" is after all a mere chronological indicator, a concession to the difficulty of talking sense about one's own immediate cultural definition, and a mark of general awareness that something, indeed, is happening to discourse in the post-Renaissance, post-Reformation, and post-Enlightenment West. Across a broad range of cultural manifestations a massive reexamination of Western discourse is underway: its obsession with power and knowledge, its constraint of language to primarily symbolic function, its ethic of winning, its categorical and dualistic modes of definition, its belief in the quantitative and objective, its linear time and individual subject, and above all its common media of exchange (time, space, money) which guarantee certain political and social systems (see *Realism and Consensus* on the culture of humanism).

Because postmodernism subverts very basic habits, it is not surprising that its assertions alarm those with vested interests in the modernist order of things: an order where imaginative constructs ("art") are exported (along with "the subject" and even creativity in general) to the margins of discourse where they act as the repressed foundation for rationalist order. Feminist theory has had much of a revisionist nature to say about the repressed of Western culture, and it provides essential terms for the present argument about the postmodern collapse of the dualisms that have served modernist hegemony and its forms of transcendence. An example is the dualism between invention and reality. By refiguring fiction-making as the primary mode of consciousness (it replaces mirrors, lamps, and other such metaphors), postmodern narrative emphasizes the power of invention and fabrication to the point, as Robbe-Grillet says, of making it the foundation of discourse, the subject of the book.

The postmodern reformation that most interests me in *Sequel to History* is the subversion of historical time. The humanist construction of time is historical, and postmodern writing subverts this temporality and its projects. Given the scale and profundity of Western, especially Anglo-American and Northern European investment in this construction of temporality, its subversion merits much more attention than it has had in theoretical writing, which often seems riveted to static models. Time is often the missing link in discussions of postmodernism, which cycle through endlessly reflexive spatial and static models without ever revealing the disappearance of history and the practical reformation this implies. Usage almost invariably betrays a view of "time" that is fundamentally historical and without alternative. Habermas, for example, notes the importance of "time" but does not distinguish one construction of temporality from another. When he speaks of "a changed consciousness of time" in dada and surrealism (he calls these "aesthetic modernity"), what changes seems to be consciousness, but "time" remains the same. Habermas even seems to agree with Lyotard that "the relation between 'modern' and 'classical' has definitely lost a fixed historical reference," meaning that the sense of Big Change reappears variously "in" time which itself remains the same.[5]

The challenge in postmodern writing to this hegemony of History understandably appears threatening. At the same time, the effect of such writing is often the opposite of threatening, and it opens a sense of alternative possibility foreclosed by History. It takes only a slight disciplinary shift to bring into view some profound preparation for this reformation of time. Twentieth-century phenomenology has massively revised the modern formulations of time and consciousness inherited largely from the seventeenth century, which formulated time as a categorical imperative "natural" to human thought and inseparable from the conception of the individual subject, the founding *cogito*, that has developed its powers since then. By focusing on a phenomenal "event" in which subjectivity and objectivity cannot be distinguished, phenomenology anticipates the always-embedded and in-process postmodern subjectivity. Like surrealism, phenomenology seeks to "bracket" preconceptions in order to make palpable a world of experience that precedes rational knowledge, including the very act of perception itself. For example, this bracketing of preconceptions is an implicit motive in the art of collage: a characteristic form of the early twentieth century that promotes the imaginary and neutralizes the principle of non-contradiction by disconnecting material objects from their "normal" (read, habitual) connections and conditions.[6] Postmodern narrative can be instructively thought of as a temporal instance of collage, or rather collage in motion.

The best-known twentieth-century revision of the modern view of time is Einstein's General Theory of Relativity, where time is no longer a constant but instead a function of relative motion, a dimension of events. Just as the classical object has been redefined in physics, so the phenomenological subject is no longer discrete, apart from the event, but, like time and space themselves, functions of specific events and bound by their limitations. And beside physics and philosophy appear other efforts that subvert historical thinking and its supporting discourse of realism and empiricism. The period of Einstein's papers on relativity and Edmund Husserl's logic, for example, also saw the publication of Franz Kafka's stories, the poetry of Guillaume Apollinaire, Sigmund Freud's papers on the unconscious, the cubism of Georges Braque and Pablo Picasso.[7]

For strategic as well as substantive reasons it is important to remember that the work of postmodernism is *not new* (it is fully evident in surrealism and, as André Breton saw, already present in romanticism), and it is *not over*. Many so-called modern and postmodern achievements are already in evidence in the nineteenth and even the eighteenth centuries, although the cultural critique they implied did not yet have critical mass. Non-Euclidean mathematics belongs to the nineteenth century, as does phenomenology, which even extends back to the eighteenth. The relativization of religious systems that began in the Renaissance got a major redirection in the nineteenth century in the German religious revolution known as the Higher Criticism, which historicized Christianity and in some forms came very near to using linguistic models. The denunciation of "this ridiculous illusion of happiness and *understanding*" belongs, as Breton says, to romanticism as well as to surrealists a century later and their postmodern heirs.[8] In other words, the work of postmodernism is quite broadly prepared for, not rootless or unmotivated.

It is also important to keep in view the politically quite stunning fact that, while there is considerable Anglo-American interest in postmodernism and its predecessors, the cutting edge of theory and practice has remained primarily based in Romance-language countries in Europe and Latin America. England and the United States may have too much invested in the empiricist models responsible for their material and political hegemony to absorb the critique of empiricism so persuasively underway elsewhere in Western culture.

The changes evident in postmodern writing cannot be ignored, but should they be resisted? While I think not, the question is important because the stakes are very high: it is not often noted how high. The critique of historical time involves a critique of everything "in" it: not just anthropomorphism, not just the metaphysics of presence, transcendence, and depth, not just the structure of the human sciences, not just the definition of subjectivity as "individuality." The postmodern subversion of historical time threatens other things still broadly taken for granted in universities and constitutional governments: the idea of "natural" or "human" or "inalienable" rights, the definition of disciplines and fields of research and perhaps the very notion of research itself, the possibility of "representation" in political as well as aesthetic terms, the nonceremonial (i.e., informational) functions of language. There are some who fear that postmodernism, by depreciating traditional causalities, portends an end to morality itself, and the fear is not unfounded so far as traditional morality is concerned. After all, how *do* we deal with each other domestically or globally when we can't be certain who or where each other is? And who, for that matter, is "we"? So how broad and practical might be the changes that postmodernism implies? Is it cause for unease, for instance, that business seems still to be conducted in empiricist not to say Aristotelian terms (profit-loss, cause-effect, ends-means, provider-recipient, product-market)? The systemic consequences of this inertial rest are becoming hard to ignore. On a more intimate and potentially more powerful level, the affairs of questionable subjects-in-process, is it just the least bit unnerving to consider that, in Irigaray's words, "if we continue to speak the same language to each other, we will reproduce the same story"?[9]

It is, as an academic must be only too well aware, quite possible to live an unregenerately representational existence in this era of postmodernism. At the same time it seems likely that the postmodern reformation belongs to an inalienable shift of cultural disposition. The description of the physical world has changed, and with it the relative importance of habits formulated prior to that mutation. We are surrounded by a world that operates on the principles of quantum theory; we are living in mental worlds that operate on the principles of Newton. The object is not simply to modernize – or postmodernize – for its own sake; Newton's mechanics still operates at the everyday level of practical affairs, like dropping the apple and lifting the bag of groceries. But in the subvisible and stellar worlds that surround us, things have changed, and those changes limit the scope and importance both of Newtonian mechanics and of historical thinking. This change may seem evident as a constraint on discourse, but methodologically few observe it, and that is because it is very difficult to do so. My intention here is not to lobby for postmodernism at the expense of history, any more than it was my intention in writing about the historical conventions of realism to lobby for history at the expense of alternative conventions; my intention is to locate a major discursive shift in our understanding of temporality and to explore some of its implications. Many irreversible events have rendered historical thinking problematic; at the same time, postmodernism is not as new as recent terminology for it might suggest. For those interested in exploring postmodern alternatives, this book shows the importance of temporality to the postmodern reformation and explores some links between postmodernism and other, older achievements; for those interested in defending historical thinking from postmodern assault, this book renders problematic the historical convention on the assumption that what remains self-evident cannot be defended or maintained.

Postmodern narrative, then, by a complex and broadly prepared act of redefinition, explores in terms of consciousness and time some reformations being explored elsewhere in the physics, philosophy, and visual art of our time. Postmodern narrative is not a translation or a marginal instance of that physics or philosophy or art; it is an enactment that redefines time as a function of position, as a dimension of particular events. Furthermore, both position and event are described in terms of language. While all narrative is temporal by definition because its medium is temporal, postmodern sequences make accessible new temporal capacities that subvert the privilege of historical time and bind temporality in language.

The emphasis on the reflexivity of language, on its function as a system, has proven a valuable model for the treatment of various other systems (e.g., political, social, institutional) which thus can be broadly considered as "languages" in terms of their systemic or "differential" function: that is, a system in which difference, far from being expendable, is precisely what constitutes the system. There has been considerable theoretical exploration of this and related problems since Saussure, from his own analyses of the reflexivity of signs to the deconstruction and new historicism based on Derrida and Foucault and the new theoretics of language and writing developed by Kristeva, Irigaray, and Cixous. Common to all these theoretical efforts, though voiced in different ways, is a critique of the language of rationalism on the grounds that it reinforces one discursive function at unnecessary expense to another.

For example, this postmodern critique applies broadly to the discourse of the so-called "human sciences" and their opportunistic imports of methods and categories from the restricted and disciplined realm of modern physical science into a broad range of social, political, military, and other nonscientific areas of life. Such "sciences" produce a kind of interpretation that "always 'fits' because," as Heidegger says, "at bottom it says nothing" about phenomenal and mortal being-in-the-world.[10] This broad postmodern discursive critique subverts the metaphysic that posits essences like stable, self-identical, nondiscursive identities and the transcendental "laws" that operate "in" them. Such a metaphysic simply becomes inadequate in the discourse where essence or identity is multiplied because it is always *situated*, and where the situation is always discursive, which is to say always constructed by systems of signs whose function is differential.

With "text" and "writing" conceived in this way as modes of discursive engagement, the importance of so-called literary texts and writing becomes obvious: they are among the most highly achieved, most economical exercises of discursive engagement; they take up and improve the forms of discourse we inhabit every day in sloppier, less visible versions; they make the premises of discourse evident. And there is another, less obvious reason to use so-called literary texts. Postmodern narrative language engages pulse and intellect simultaneously and consequently permits no easy escape from practical problems. It focuses on *practices* and refuses in so many ways to accept the distinction between practice and thought, between material and transcendental "reality." Such narrative literally recalls readers to their senses by focusing acts of attention on the actual practices of consciousness and sensibility as they operate in process, and not as they might operate if the world were the rational, natural, logocentric place that so many of our models still describe. In short, postmodern narrative does much to show what the contemporary critique of Western metaphysics amounts to in practice and for a subjectivity in process. It is arguable that, at least in terms of temporality and language, novels articulate the postmodern critique more fully and certainly more accessibly than do most theoretical texts.

The most direct answer to the question "Why text?" however, is "Why not?" The separation between a world of texts and a world of affairs, between history and text, is a separation that served modern discourse; it is the same distinction as the one between politics and aesthetics. Such distinctions disappear in postmodernism along with the agendas they serve, even though the *language* that maintains these distinctions is very hard to change, even for those interested in doing so. Andreas Huyssen, for example, in one breath argues eloquently for the end to this very dualism and in another says that the postmodern emphasis on textuality is aestheticism and thus "too high a price to pay" in terms of self-limitation, thereby retaining the modernist sense of "aesthetic."[11] The language is radioactive; we will get beyond its enforcements when we stop depreciating the "aesthetic" by distinguishing it from "politics" and start writing an Aesthetics of Capitalism, an Aesthetics of Feminism, an Aesthetics of Racism, an Aesthetics of the Corporation, an Aesthetics (with national differentia) of the Cartel, an Aesthetics of the Café/Bar: in other words, when we apply to material practices the precise and sophisticated knowledge of systems that since the Enlightenment we have called "aesthetic."

A word about my use of the term "representation": it is based in part on an argument I have made at length elsewhere,[12] but even so it needs some explanation. While I distinguish between "realism" and "representation," it seems to me important to keep them on the same leash if we ever are going to grasp the extent to which we have confused a specific, powerful, and possibly unique discursive convention – that of representation or realism as it has been defined in the culture of empiricism typical of Western culture since the Renaissance – with a universal norm for art, for narrative, for language, not to mention for other forms of organization.[13] I have argued that history itself is the most powerful construct of realistic conventions as we have known them since about 1400. This argument implies a large discursive frame of discussion, yet the term "realism" has been confined to disciplinary usages inconsistent with discourse analysis. One could argue, for example, that an image by Matisse, which is only incidentally realistic in the sense that it uses still recognizable shapes like a woman or a goldfish, also is only incidentally representational because its governing conventions have nothing to do with the agreements that produce "objects" and that Matisse's figures therefore have little to do with empirical objects and everything to do with design, *figura*, the condition of music – in short, with a nonreferential frame. To what extent a vestigial reference can act as a commanding convention is a question to be asked about much postmodern parody.

Postmodern writing has a kind of gravitational pull that is bound to influence any writing "about" it. The reflexive qualities of my writing (e.g., the rhythm sections punctuating the macro-sequence, the paralogical pulse of particular sentences, the repetition of key quotations, phrases, and points) may cause problems for diehard representationalists, dualists, and dialecticians who will want to factor them out as "noise." This, I assume, goes with the territory. A similar problem, for those who believe in the myth of comprehensive evidence, may be the fact that although I do mention a variety of writers, I concentrate on three texts, none of them especially recent (*Jealousy*, 1957; *Hopscotch*, 1963; *Ada*, 1969). These features of the book are clues to its purpose. What interests me here is the nature of the series, which can only be considered in detailed, material, embedded practices: practices that are textual in the large sense I have described. I mean to bring into view a new set of assumptions and practices that redefine time, a considerable task given the degree to which most of us take historical time for granted. I am counting on my readers to supply other examples. So, for instance, when I discuss the postmodern emphasis on plural semantic contexts, I hope that other examples from literature or science or economics will come to mind. I want to open the door, not ransack the room. The same spirit governs my use of sources, which I confine mainly to footnotes in order to concentrate in my own writing on the quality of the linguistic series.

On the other hand, this text "about" postmodernism is written in the language of representation; it produces meaning, assumes a consensus community, engages in historical generalization and footnotes. In short, in my own writing I do not entirely live up to the postmodern call, a methodological problem I recognize and settle in my own conscience with several assumptions. First, I assume that one need not give up history to challenge its hegemony, although I admit the perilousness of the undertaking and the ironies of the situation in which history must recognize its own historicity. Second, I assume that the play, the alliterating thematic echoes of a text, as of a life, may be heterogeneous to "meaning" and yet remain always in sight of it. Third, the essay form, as Cortárzar says (*Hopscotch*, ch. 79), permits among specialists a kind of "literature" or bridge of language that is endlessly allusive and intertextual *because* there exists a community of discourse, however problematic, in which certain questions and terms are in play; I count on that allusiveness when I write this or that phrase. Fourth, I assume a discourse community, but I write at risk. Who is my audience? Will the specialists whose work I read, read mine? Will the specialists whose work I do not read, read mine? Is judicial resolution between one discussion and another important when the fact of cultural reformation calls for sustained writerly experiment and not the same old arguments? At a time when the discourse community for such work as this is sustaining the very reformation under consideration here, to what audience can I say, "This, our text"? And yet this text makes room for an audience, takes place at the hands of and in sight of an audience: one that experience has taught me to find broadly dispersed across disciplinary, ideological, and national interests.

My thesis in brief is this: postmodern narrative language undermines historical time and substitutes for it a new construction of temporality that I call rhythmic time. This rhythmic time either radically modifies or abandons altogether the dialectics, the teleology, the transcendence, and the putative neutrality of historical time; and it replaces the Cartesian *cogito* with a different subjectivity whose manifesto might be Cortázar's "I swing, therefore I am."[14] Whether or not it is meaningful to speak of a "new" history remains an open question, although the term "history" has become so saturated with dialectical value that it may no longer be very buoyant. My emphasis on the disappearance of historical thinking does not mean that I advocate either overthrowing "history" or rallying to its defense; the state of affairs is far more complex and interesting than such formulations imply, and more important. We face interesting questions in the history of consciousness now that the discourse which has supported historical thinking turns out itself to be discourse-bound like every other habit and belief. I attend mainly to how postmodern narrative time works, what it offers, and what its implicit requirements, gains, and losses may be. The work that undermines history also opens new questions and provides new opportunities in practice. In the postmodern frame, choice is not a question of either/or but a question of emphasis.

CODA: ON CONTINGENCY

In his book on the paleontological wonders of the Burgess Shale, Stephen Jay Gould explores some of its revisionary implications for our assumptions about history. Key to this revision is the role of contingency in the survival of species. With *Homo sapiens*, for example, many chance events during billions of years gave our species its opportunity: events that might have happened otherwise, like a comet shower or a change of climate in Africa. But for such events, life on earth could have developed without ever favoring the development of consciousness and, like most species, *Homo sapiens* would have perished: "one little twig on the mammalian branch, a lineage with interesting possibilities that were never realized, joins the vast majority of species in extinction. So what?

Most possibilities are never realized, and who will ever know the difference?"[15] And even though *Homo sapiens* has flourished, there is no particular biological or geological reason to expect the species to survive forever. Even our sun, which has shone on the development of conscious life for only a split second of geological time, has itself run more than half its life's course and, like other, similar stars, probably will explode (in about five billion years), taking with it whatever is left, if anything, of *Homo sapiens*; as Gould observes, "geological time may be long, but it is not infinite" (p. 233). At so many junctures "the unpredictability of evolutionary pathways asserts itself against our hope for the inevitability of consciousness" (p. 316). The denial of this hope, however, far from discouraging aspiration, may be precisely the circumstance to increase it. Gould puts it this way: "*Homo sapiens*, I fear, is a 'thing so small' in a vast universe, a wildly improbable evolutionary event well within the realm of contingency. Make of such a conclusion what you will. Some find the prospect depressing; I have always regarded it as exhilarating, and a source of both freedom and consequent moral responsibility" (*Wonderful Life*, p. 291).

Something like this assertion, and something like its attendant acceptance of contingency, can be felt in the ebullient pathways of postmodern writing. Whereas historical sequences, with their insistent rationalizations, convert chance into causality, the multivalent frequencies of rhythmic improvisations with their obscure enterprise of form find their opportunity in what is accidental, surprising, contingent. Where historical conventions formulate most questions in terms of quantity and extension in a neutral horizon overseen by a detached (potentially neutral) consciousness that is "in" history but not of it, rhythmic time, which focuses questions in terms of qualitative difference and precise, systemic differentiation, treats such detachment as an artifact and inscription of particular values. Where historical conventions use (more or less discrete and simply located) events, texts, and persons as bases for key rationalizations, rhythmic conventions of temporality – parataxis on the move – depend on local arrangements whose amplifications are unpredictable. The rhythmic sequence forks and reforks, exfoliating, proliferating details and thematic threads and then coming to an end that is by any rational standard arbitrary. Rhythmic time incorporates the convention of history – internalizes it as one game, one set of rules among many. Confined to a rhythmic sequence, history is a thematic formulation, like any other, and no longer a commanding (determining) premise.

Postmodern writing thus erases the privilege of certain ideas and habits of mind that have long seemed natural: those associated with the great rationalization of faculties accomplished in the Renaissance and Reformation and codified since in a thousand practices across cultures congenial to empiricism and capitalism. Postmodern narrative language raises unsettling and unsettled questions that reach the root of our assumptions about language and time. Narratives that circumvent "meaning" and confine attention to the detail and the moment undermine the traditional humanistic bases of subjectivity, temporality, and familiar forms of social order. This comes to the crux of the postmodern difficulty for readers. We are asked to give up logocentric, dialectical, dualistic, and other transcendental habits; we are asked to give up plot and character, history and individuality, perhaps even "meaning" as we have long conceived it. In their place we are offered "interminable pattern without meaning": an atomized system of details patterned paratactically, which is to say, asyntactically, which is to say, meaninglessly. While such narrative sequences seem to offer few footholds for habitual humanist readers, it is essential equipment for the postmodern person who, coerced perhaps by an emergent *episteme*, begins anew and at the root of the obscure discursive enterprise of form.

In demonstrating the powers of rhythmic temporality, then, I certainly do not mean to say that "history" no longer exists, although a nontrivial case can be made for this view. In attempting to convey a detailed impression of a new experience of temporality, one relatively independent of the usual historical conventions that we so easily assume in so many practical ways, my intention has nothing to do with trashing history and its cultural dispensation or with substituting play as the commanding mode of a new world. The multilevel play described in this book belongs to an effort to renew social codes by restoring powers that have been suppressed; it is not an effort to enforce another repression.

But this effort *does* involve a major revision of hegemonic arrangements. Systems that valorize production, progress, mobility, capitalization, and related ideas of identity have tended to depreciate and marginalize multi-level thinking, conceptions of personhood rooted in local systems and processes, and the capacity for play. The reinstatement of the repressed in this case is momentous because it involves a reformation of assumptions that have the most rooted practical exercise: for example, and to suggest only a few, the assumption that history is a single public medium, to which private histories are tributaries or "in" which they operate; the assumption that public can be more or less easily distinguished from private or the individual from the social; the assumption that losses can be sustained by regarding them as preparation for an as yet unfinished future gain; the assumption that, acknowledged complexities notwithstanding, psychic identity is as simply located and invariant as somatic identity; the assumption that there are regularities in experience, whether individual or collective, that enable us to learn from the past and control the future; the assumption that we can learn from the past in the first place because it is like the present and past persons are like us. In postmodern writing these things can no longer be taken for granted.

The rhythmic conventions of time offer new starting points for discursive reformation. To expand the richness of the moment, as multilevel thinking does, is not stupidly to stop all forward motion or to suppose that there is no "after" and "before"; instead, that expansion makes available more starting points and more alternative routes. Such a reformation is not without precedent. An historical sense quite different from the one implied by the term "history" is evident in the philological comparisons of Renaissance scholarship, which as yet had little or nothing to do with the teleological motives that later inspired the seventeenth-century vision of "time" as a universal constant both in the physical and the social universes. The fate of this time as "history" is linked with the fate of "humanism": and both are terms in need of significant reevaluation and redefinition. Rather than embalming the past in a commanding structure of significance, rhythmic time keeps its precise, concrete details in play and in process of constant renewal. In a complex and specific rhythm each sequence works out its exploratory repetition, its obscure enterprise of form, uniquely specifying the discursive potentials that belong to a collectivity, a text, a life. The result is an ineffably social achievement. It could never be achieved in solitude or by calculation alone or by a mob. It is, like a sentence, a unique specification of discursive possibility.

The challenge to the hegemony of historical thinking may seem to some like a challenge to be resisted. It seems to me like an invitation to take responsibility for conventions that we have naturalized, which is to say, assigned to a realm of undisputed truth where they need not be consciously maintained, modified, or managed. The challenge points up their fragility, their contingency, to be sure, but we do not alter that contingency by ignoring it. In any case, the contingency of all arrangements in rhythmic time seems appropriate to our circumstances.

The postmodern restoration of language attempts to bring back from repression an enduring creative power. If true exploration and experiment – that openness sometimes attributed to "thought" – really are a phenomenon of language in the widest sense of that term, then the creative originals of discourse are those who enable it to renew and not merely perpetuate itself, those who manage some play with the sign systems in which we operate day to day, and who manage some correction of habitual usages. The play of postmodern writing seeks to guarantee vitality, to affirm what remains open to surprise and capable of new formation.

NOTES

1. Charles Jencks, for example, wants for reasons of his own to limit the historical frame and to distinguish Post-Modern from Late-Modern in the twentieth century, although he does say that postmodernism is post-Christian (*What Is Postmodernism?* New York: St. Martin's Press, and London: Academy Editions, 1981, pp. 7–8, 38, 32–3). Fredric Jameson, who refers to architecture, also seems to find postmodernism a relatively local deformation appearing since the 1940s; this might follow if one takes history to be a permanent condition and not, as I do, an inflection of culture since around 1400 (Jameson, "Postmodernism and Consumer Society," in Hal Foster (ed.), *The Anti-Aesthetic: Essays on Postmodern Culture* Port Townsend, Wash.: Bay Press, 1983, p. 113). In localizing the definition of postmodernism, Jencks may be responding in part to Jean-François Lyotard's completely ahistorical definition of postmodernism as a constant cultural state and not historically specific (i.e., that modernity "in whatever age" is the shattering of belief and the "discovery of the 'lack of reality' of reality, together with the invention of other realities" (*The Postmodern Condition: A Report on Knowledge,* trans. Geoff Bennington and Brian Massumi, Minneapolis: University of Minnesota Press, 1984, pp. 77, 79, 81). "This crazy idea," says Jencks, "at least has the virtue of being original and it has led to Lyotard's belief in continual experiment, the agonism of the perpetual avant-garde and continual revolution, a confusion in Jenck's terms with Late Modernist avantgardism" (*What Is Postmodernism?*, p. 42). Jürgen Habermas, while he laments the habit of universalizing "modernity" by finding its roots in the dissolution of archaic life (à la Nietzsche), seems to agree with Lyotard at least on this, that "the relation between 'modern' and 'classical' has definitely lost a fixed historical reference." But the "determinate negation" he finds recommended by the practice of Max Horkheimer and Theodore Adorno does not offer anything very "ad hoc" when it is grounded in "dialectic" (Jürgen Habermas, *The Philosophical Discourse of Modernity: Twelve Lectures* [*Der philosophische Diskurs der Moderne: Zwölf Vorlesungen,* 1985], trans. Frederick Lawrence, Cambridge, Mass: MIT Press, 1987, pp. 87, 4, 128; on dialectic see Part I, sect. 1).
2. Meyer Schapiro, "Nature of Abstract Art," *Marxist Quarterly,* no. 1, January–March 1937, p. 85.
3. Michel Foucault, "Final Interview," in *Raritan Review* 5, no. 1, 1985, p. 12.
4. Stephen A. Tyler (*The Unspeakable: Discourse, Dialogue, and Rhetoric in the Postmodern World,* Madison: University of Wisconsin Press, 1987 and William Spanos (*Repetitions:*

The Postmodern Occasion in Literature and Culture, Baton Rouge: Louisiana State University Press, 1987) both take modernism to be a post-Renaissance phenomenon and, although they differ in their estimates of the value of modernism, are intent on the political dimension of the problem postmodernism poses. For Tyler, "postmodernism is the culmination of modernism's assault on the idea of representation, but unlike modernism, it also undermines the idea of form"; and "postmodernism is the writing of the history of the repression of the paradigmatic axis of reading and representation, and it is the breaking of the mirror, and the 'opening of the field' of the signifier," the ultimate goal of which is, perhaps, to return us to the world of "speech" and "quotidian talk" (pp. xi, 4, xii). Tyler attends to the important political role of language, and on postmodernism's attempt to erase the "plain style" that was inspired by science and that "above all else, seeks to erode the presence of the speaker by eliminating all marks of individuality that speak of the speaker's difference from the text" (pp. 6–7). I part company with Tyler when he opts for "dialogic" as a postmodern solution.

Spanos is interested in the political consciousness of modernism as a "Western" tradition: "the structure of consciousness into which post-Renaissance man has wilfully coerced his classical inheritance" (p. 18). He, too, is interested in language ("the authorizing logocentric forms and rhetorics of the entire literary tradition," p. 195), although his argument does not allow for what I take to be crucial to postmodern writing: that its interrogations of those forms takes place, to the extent it does take place, entirely as a phenomenon of language. It is not possible, really, to conduct this interrogation in any other way, or at least not in the conventional philosophical or "historical" terms that are themselves authorizing and logocentric. If we can speak of postmodern hermeneutics at all, it "is open ended, ongoing, (im)provisational," but it is not at all "interminably historical" (p. 218).

5. Jürgen Habermas, "Modernity – An Incomplete Project," in Hal Foster (ed.) *The Anti-Aesthetic*, pp. 4–5.
6. On collage see Robert Delevoy, *Dimensions of the Twentieth Century, 1900–1945*, trans. from French by Stuart Gilbert, Geneva: SKIRA, 1965, especially Part III: The Principle of Indeterminacy; and Marjorie Perloff, "The Invention of Collage," in *The Futurist Moment: Avant-Garde, Avant Guerre, and the Language of Rupture*, Chicago: University of Chicago Press, 1986, pp. 42–79.
7. For an illuminating discussion of relativity theory see Delo E. Mook and Thomas Vargish, *Inside Relativity*, Princeton: Princeton University Press, 1987. I am grateful to the same authors for sharing their work in progress on relativity theory and its cultural contexts.
8. *Manifestoes of Surrealism*, trans. Richard Seaver and Helen Lane, Ann Arbor: University of Michigan Press, 1972, p. 153.
9. Luce Irigaray, "When Our Lips Speak Together" ("Quand nos lèvers se parlent," *Cahiers du Grief* no. 12), in *This Sex Which Is Not One (Ce sexe qui n'est pas un*, 1977), trans. Carolyn Burke, Ithaca: Cornell University Press, 1985, pp. 205–6. Also in *Signs* 6, no. 1, Autumn 1980, pp. 69–70.
10. *Being and Time (Sein und Zeit*, 1926), trans. John Macquarrie and Edward Robinson, New York: Harper & Row, 1962, p. 108; I.3.17. Heidegger asserts the *"equiprimordiality"* of whatever constitutes Being against the methodologically unrestrained tendency to derive everything and anything from some simple 'primal ground'" (p. 170; I.5.28; p. 71; 1.1.10). The principle of noncontradiction (along with primal ground, origin, and end) is a conception widely violated in postmodern narrative where essence can't really be said to exist at all because "it" is always multiple.
11. Andreas Huyssen, "Mapping the Postmodern," in Linda Nicholson (ed.) *Feminism and Postmodernism*, New York: Routledge, 1990, pp. 271, 257, and 261. Laura Kipnis links

the antipopular inclination of what she calls "modernism" with a slide to what she calls "aesthetic," thus also using "aesthetic" in its post-Enlightenment and empiricist sense ("Feminism: The Political Conscience of Postmodernism?" in Andrew Ross, *Universal Abandon?: The Politics of Postmodernism*, Minneapolis: University of Minnesota Press, 1988, p. 154.

12. *Realism and Consensus in the English Novel*, Princeton: Princeton University Press, 1983, a discussion of the construction of history and of historical consciousness from Alberti to Henry James.

13. Jacques Attali also uses "representation" for a certain phase of (primarily Western) culture in *Noise: The Political Economy of Music (Bruits: essai sur l'économie politique de la musique*, 1977), trans. Brian Massumi, Minneapolis: University of Minnesota Press, 1985.

14. Julio Cortázar, *Hopscotch (Rayucla*, 1963), trans. Gregory Rabassa, New York: Random House, 1966, ch. 16.

15. Stephen Jay Gould, *Wonderful Life: The Burgess Shale and the Nature of History*, London, Sydney, Auckland, Johannesburg: Hutchinson Radius, 1989, pp. 318–20.

5 Diane Elam

Romancing the postmodern
Feminism and deconstruction

ROMANCING THE POSTMODERN

Nietzsche articulates an important problem that occurs when we first acquire a sense of the historical:

> Then [the child], learns to understand the words "once upon a time," the "open sesame" that lets in battle, suffering, and weariness on mankind and reminds them what their existence really is – an imperfect tense that never becomes a present.

Language makes possible the child's awareness of the burden of the past, yet the language that performs his work is the rhetoric of romance – "once upon a time" and "open sesame." So history, which is the burden that we must forget in order to enter the romance of unhistorical action, to come into our destiny, is always already part of romance, just as romance is always already part of history. Romance exists impossibly on both sides, past burden and future freedom: condemning the present to the imperfect tense. In a radical sense, the historical event, like existence, is unhistorical in that it must be understood through the rhetoric of romance. But then the unhistorical as romance is also strangely historical, because it gives voice to the events of the past. To put this another way, history is always "the yesterday of romance," a phrase borrowed from Conrad's *Romance*. In effect, Nietzsche notices the same problem that Scott sees – the origin of history is confused with that of romance. And the unhistorical – the art of forgetting the historical – proves difficult to perform.

It will come as no surprise that I want to rename Nietzsche's "imperfect tense" the "future anterior" of postmodernism. To return after so many pages to Lyotard: "*Postmodern* would have to be understood according to the paradox of the future (*post*) anterior (*modo*)." This is the temporarily announced in the belatedly apocalyptic opening of Derrida's *Dissemination*: "This (therefore) will not have been a book." The future anterior insists upon the fact that what passes for our "present" is not a fullness or a presence, since it is always marked as the potential past of our own future: postmarked, as it will have been. Insofar as the "now" is thinkable, it is as the possibility of its passing, its becoming a moment among others in a future history: that time in the future where even our own future will be the past. For the modernist, artistic production is organized according to rules delineated before the fact: the present fills the future and guarantees its truth as present. Postmodernity, by contrast, involves a recognition of the artistic event as unforeseeable, unpredictable. As Lyotard puts it, "The artist and the writer, then, are working without rules in order to formulate the rules of what *will have been done*." To say this is not willful self-blinding: it is a refusal to abstract the present from history as the single point from which a perspective on history can be adopted, an insistence upon the way in which any act of writing is written across by a temporality that it cannot itself inhabit, suspended in quotation marks as it were. In place of the living present comes the recognition of presence as a lost object, grasped only in its passing. The present is always a reconstruction from an imaginary absence, just as *Nostromo* can only be understood as history by virtue of a critical rereading. In this sense, its contemporary epigraph comes from another South American allusion, the title song of Terry Gilliam's film *Brazil*, which reminds us that: "Tomorrow was another day." History cannot be written, as such; but this does not make us nihilists. Rather we should recognize that history will have been written, whether we like it or not. Engaging in arguments about what history will have been, we take responsibility for our actions, yet we do not ground them in a truth of what history *is*.

FEMINISM AND DECONSTRUCTION

HER-STORY OR HIS-STORY

After centuries of Western history that has been in the strict sense his story (the narratives of "great" men), historians have gradually turned their attention to the problem of historically representing women. What would it mean to write the history of women? What would her story look like? These are by now familiar questions, as are the hoary chestnuts of his-story versus her-story. Nonetheless, I want to begin on this familiar territory in order to trace the ways in which women have become a problem for historical representation as much as they have become its ostensible subject.

First of all, history has become the ground on which feminism can challenge the exclusive universality of the (Anglo-Saxon) male subject. Within the discipline of history, as Joan Scott argues in *Gender and the Politics of History*, new knowledge about women has surfaced, which questions the central role that male subjects have traditionally played in historical narratives. In a sense, this new knowledge may more precisely be understood not as "new" *per se* but rather as old, hidden knowledge which has been discovered as a result of a full-scale re-evaluation of what counts as historical knowledge. That is to say, the type of information considered worth knowing, in order to uphold our obligation to representing the past, has changed along with the re-evaluation of women's place in history. History is not what it used be.

But history is more than a matter of obtaining information, as any historian knows, and historical knowledge is as much a result of methodology as anything else. In the absence of a well-established historiographic tradition, to continue with Scott's analysis, "the subject of women has been either grafted on to other traditions or studied in isolation from them." This absence of a tradition of specifically feminist methodologies has given rise to several different versions of her-story, which Scott does a good job delineating. According to Scott, we can find three distinct her-story methodologies that "developed in tandem with social history": 1. those which claim women's "essential likeness as historical subjects to men"; 2. those which "challenge received interpretations of progress and regress"; and 3. those which offer "a new narrative, different periodization, and different causes," so as to "discover the nature of the feminist or female consciousness that motivated" the behavior of both ordinary and notable women's lives.

Scott does not, however, recite these approaches without reservations. She warns us that if social history assumes that "gender is not an issue requiring study in itself," her-story methodologies, while they study gender, nonetheless do not adequately "theorize about how gender operates historically." Thus in the end, Scott faults social history for being too integrationist, and her-story approaches for being too separatist.

Singling out feminist literary history, Christina Crosby offers an even harsher critique of her-story feminism. Crosby argues that for feminists like Elaine Showalter, Sandra Gilbert, and Susan Gubar:

> To historicize is first to discover women where there had only been men, to see women in history, and recognize a fundamental experience which unites all women, the experience of being "the other." . . . Such a reading obviously is no longer wholly within the discourse which produces history as man's truth, no longer accepts that history has only to do with men. Yet in a fundamental way this feminist reading is still within the "space of formation" of that discourse, for where once history revealed the truth of man's identity as a finite being, revealed man's fate, now history reveals the truth of women's lives, the fate of being a woman, of being "the Other." The closed circle of recognition is still inscribed, for all women are women in the same way, and this discovery of identity is predicated on a whole series of exclusions. . . . A feminism that conceptualizes "women" as a unitary category which can be recognized in history works within the circle of ideological reflection, guaranteeing that women will be found everywhere and will be everywhere similar.

Crosby draws much of her own argument from Audre Lorde's similar criticism of white feminists who likewise fail to address the differences between women. As Lorde points out, by all accounts, her-story threatens to be a colorless narrative, where, as Crosby underlines, "unity is achieved at the expense of the differences of race, and class, not to mention ethnicity, sexual preference, age, and all the other differences which divide women."

Lorde and Crosby offer well-deserved criticism of her-story narratives, and I have no desire to become an apologist for discriminatory and exclusionary histories. However, I am reluctant simply to dismiss her-stories altogether. What if, for instance, Bell Hooks's *Ain't I a Woman*, Susan Cavin's *Lesbian Origins*, Esther Newton's *Mother Camp: Female Impersonators in America*, and Barbara Christian's *Black Women Novelists: The Development of a Tradition* were to be included in the list? The methodologies which these texts employ and their interest in developing a history of women are still common themes in each of these cases. The danger in this kind of thinking is, of course, the false belief that writing the true history of women is simply a matter of inclusion – of completing the list of texts which I have begun above.

What it is important to recognize, I would argue, is that *her-story is not one story*. An injustice is committed when any *one* history purports to speak for all women everywhere, when it does not underline the incompleteness of its own narrative. I would want to make clear, in a way that Crosby does not, that her-stories are valuable, but feminists must continue to examine how these narratives determine women, carefully looking at both what materials are included *and* excluded.

One way of going about this would be to argue that women's history or the history of women should be written and studied along with both discussions of the political implications of these histories and considerations of the alternatives. This seems to be Scott's solution, since she is careful to stress that it is not clear what the feminist rewriting of history might entail. Given this hesitation, she ventures that feminist history will become:

> not the recounting of great deeds performed by women but the exposure of the often silent and hidden operations of gender that are nonetheless present and defining forces in the organization of most societies. With this approach women's history critically confronts the politics of existing histories and inevitably begins the rewriting of history.

Along these lines, in *"Am I That Name?"* Denise Riley tries to get around the problem by emphasizing that "women" is an unstable category in history. According to Riley, "the history of feminism has also been a struggle against over-zealous identifications" of women. And rather than become the additional force which resolves the controversy, Riley's work encourages feminism to continue with the struggle. As Riley puts it, the indeterminacy of women is "no cause for lament"; "it is what *makes* feminism."

In this sense, Riley provides a useful perspective from which to view some of the ways in which indeterminacy has played (and continues to play) a role in feminism. She recognizes that the purpose of a history of women might be something besides discovering the answer to the question: "What is woman?" But this vantage point is not without its own blind spots. No fan of deconstruction herself, Riley would undoubtedly not wish to align her work with Derrida's, and it seems appropriate that she is willing to take the role of indeterminacy only so far. While her overall line of argument is compelling enough, there is little that is indeterminate about the historical chapters themselves. Riley's book consists of a fairly straightforward traditional history of the category of women at selected moments in Western cultures. It would not be unfair to describe her project as a history of women which purports to tell the truth about the historical progress of the changing determinations of "women."

Here it is possible to see that her story and history share a tendency to equate women with truth. In each of these instances, "woman" has a history insofar as she is associated with truth: woman is either the truth upon which history (or her-story) focuses, or she is the untruth which it is history's job to expose. One way or another, the narrative tries to relay the truth that woman has been, is, or will be.

The consequences of this historical association of women with truth has been a much debated topic, partially provoked by deconstruction. When Derrida reads Nietzsche and considers the figure of woman in *Spurs*, he rejects the association of woman with truth altogether. As far as he is concerned:

> There is no truth of woman, but it is because of that abyssal divergence of the truth, because that non-truth is "truth." Woman is one name for that non-truth of truth.

If Derrida is to be believed, woman is not truth, nor is there a truth of woman. The question of woman, according to Derrida, actually suspends the *decidable* opposition between the true and the non-true. The problem has been, however, that history, philosophy, and certain kinds of feminism have figured woman as truth in order to assuage hermeneutic anxieties by appealing to a true meaning of the text of gender. History, philosophy, or feminism could thus each claim to provide the true meaning of the text: the truth of woman. Derrida's analysis, however, has found its critics. Ruth Salvaggio accuses Derrida of sharing with Lacan a suspicious "quest for woman," which presumably is just another macho affectation. Rosi Braidotti is even harsher and claims that Derrida ignores "the reality of women" and that his argument in *Spurs* has caused vast numbers of otherwise critical feminist theorists to be seduced both by him and deconstruction. Turning Derrida's argument back on itself, Gayatri Spivak contends that Derrida actually does precisely what he finds fault with: identifies woman with truth by identifying her instead with the absence of truth. In light of such criticism, does the importance of *Spurs* lie in its function as cover-up for sloppy philosophy, machismo, and the seduction of innocent (though otherwise tough-minded) feminists?

Without sounding too much like an apologist for Derrida, I would like to say that his critics have missed a crucial point in his argument. The oversight is most evident in Spivak's case, where, as Drucilla

Cornell points out, the critique of Derrida rests on a confusion of "Derrida's reading of Nietzsche with an acceptance of [Nietzsche's] position." What Cornell understands too well, and what Derrida's critics too often fail to recognize, is that "woman cannot be contained by any definition, including Nietzsche's name for her as the non-truth of truth." Innocent feminists have nothing to fear and the philosophical standards bureau has no cause for alarm.

In rightfully calling attention to this aspect of Derrida's argument, Cornell nonetheless chooses to ignore the way in which Derrida's text moves between *woman* and *women* in making this argument. Derrida thus insists on the indeterminacy of woman in the singular, while at the same time proposing that women can be adequately determined by this single figure. Woman is indeterminate, according to Derrida, but all women fall under the singular rubric of woman. Derrida is cutting corners here, in a way which marks a limitation to his concern for feminism. My somewhat belabored emphasis here on the plural "women" is meant to underline what is at stake in writing her-stories or histories of women. Within these discourses a temporal predicament exists that threatens to return *women* to a single historical definition or figure of *woman* as truth. That is to say, history or her-story understood as continuous progress (which takes its strongest form as dialectical history) is oriented "towards a notion of woman's 'truth,'" to use Derrida's phrase, and risks determining what women can be and do.

The historical movement which appeals to the truth in order to determine women takes several temporal forms. This is best understood by looking at three tenses in which history can be written: the past, present, and future. To begin with, history written in the past tense defines what women *were*, attempts to discover what the truth of woman was in the past. The present is understood in terms of the past, and feminists are asked (in the name of the truth of woman) either to respect their elders or to be grateful that they no longer have to be part of the bad old days.

On the other hand, history written in the present tense tends to explain how women have always been what they are. Here the story may either trace the truth of an eternal femininity (the historical proof of the ahistorical truth of woman), or may, like a certain materialist feminism, only celebrate the past insofar as the truth contained in it responds to present concerns. In either case, the present determines the past insofar as we look to the past to show us what we are, and are not, now.

Finally, at the opposite extreme, the future tense might downplay the need to write history at all in favor of a concern for what women will be. This would be a feminism that believes it has nothing to learn from the past, because the past is always a compromised, imperfect version of what the future holds: the truth of woman.

Without implying that any dialectical progression is contained in these three ways of writing history, I want to ask what a history would look like that did *not* ground itself on the truth of woman or set out to determine what women will be and do. As I have already pointed out, women are determined, but not exhaustively. To write of women is thus always to incur an obligation: no feminist has not been a daughter, no woman is not indebted to past sisters. At the same time, there can be no just history of women that does not subject its methodology at every turn to the deconstructive effect of women's radical indeterminacy. This is part of what Derrida is getting at when he postulates:

> A history of paradoxical laws and non-dialectical discontinuities, a history of absolutely heterogeneous pockets, irreducible particularities, of unheard of and incalculable sexual differences; a history of women who have – centuries ago – "gone further" by stepping back with their lone dance, or who are today inventing sexual idioms at a distance from the main forum of feminist activity with a kind of reserve that does not necessarily prevent them from subscribing to the movement and even, occasionally, from becoming a militant for it.

While Derrida is right to insist upon the diffusion of feminine identify rather than upon its dialectical recovery, to stress the irreducible and the incalculable, he has not, to my mind, sufficiently considered how these could be understood given the temporal conditions of historical narratives. For that reason, I would propose that any history of women should not be written in the past tense, or even the present or simple future tenses – all of which necessarily ground themselves on the truth of woman – and should instead be written in the future anterior. The writing of history, that is, should expose itself to the *political* question of what women *will have been* and thus destabilize any claim to positive knowledge or restrictions on the non-category of "women."

Distinct from the three historical tenses of past, present, and future, history written in the future anterior doesn't claim to know in advance what it is women can do and be: the radical potentiality of women does not result from a break with the past, nor is it to be found in any form of assurance provided by the past or the present. Instead, the future anterior emphasizes radical uncertainty and looks to its own transformation. It would be a history that is a rewriting, yet is itself always all ready to be rewritten. Put another way, history written in the future anterior is a message that is handed over to an unknown addressee and accepts that its meaning in part will have to depend upon that addressee. History rewritten for a public that will have to rewrite it ceaselessly.

With this said, it is worth issuing a caution that what I have just outlined is not intended to be understood as itself a history – be it that of the progressive realization that the category of women is a representational construct, or be it the history of critics' increasing disregard for "real" women in favor of their own theorizing. Such would be the two sides in the debate between "constructionists" (who privilege theory) and "essentialists" (who privilege real women). Thus, it would be easy for me to argue that once constructionists and essentialists understand the truth of deconstruction (the magic third term), they will drop what they're doing to write proper histories of women.

However, there is no proper account of women to which deconstruction can appeal, although this is not the same thing as saying that there are no women. Deconstruction neither determines the representational space of women nor does it get rid of the category of women altogether, despite some protests to the contrary. I want to argue that feminist analysis must be a deconstruction of representation that keeps the category of women incessantly in question, as a permanently contested site of meaning. Therefore, no history of progress should be allowed to suggest a final goal, an end or solution, to the questions of women. For instance, sweeping away false constructions of "women" does not then reveal the real women behind them, nor does the perspective of "real women" correct the false constructions of men and their patriarchal discourses. We do not simply add Laura Mulvey to Sigmund Freud, Luce Irigaray to Jacques Lacan, Drucilla Cornell to Jacques Derrida, Julia Kristeva to Roland Barthes, or even Judith Butler to Kristeva.

This is not to dismiss the importance of the historical, only to caution against too much faith in histories of progress. Feminism is not made all at once or at the same time. Thus, feminisms have their histories; no feminism exists in a pure present, standing on foundations entirely of its own making. In different ways and at different moments, debts have been incurred by feminists, debts whose very inescapability marks the limitations of a merely progressive understanding of feminism. The history of feminism is not a history of simple progress, of leaving the past behind. Rather, if feminism has a history, it is one of debts and obligations. There will be no point in the history of feminism at which it will have become obsolete to read Simone de Beauvoir. One is not born a feminist.

[Editor's note: The footnotes of the original have been omitted.]

6 Robert Young

White mythologies: writing History and the West

Postmodernism can best be defined as European culture's awareness that it is no longer the unquestioned and dominant centre of the world. Significantly enough one of the very earliest uses of the term "post-modern," dating from the time of the Second World War, was that of Arnold Toynbee in his *A Study of History.* He used it to describe the new age of Western history which, according to Toynbee, began in the 1870s with the simultaneous globalization of Western culture and the re-empowerment of non-Western states. If this new period brought with it a phase of Spenglerian pessimism after the long years of Victorian optimism, Toynbee did not himself assume that the West was in decline as such, but rather that paradoxically the globalization of Western civiliz-ation was being accompanied by a self-consciousness of its own cultural relativization, a process to which Toynbee's own equally totalizing and relativizing history was designed to contribute. Reviewing the genesis of his whole project, he recounts that his history was written

> against a current Late Modern Western convention of identifying a parvenue and provincial Western Society's history with "History," writ large, *sans phrase.* In the writer's view this convention was the preposterous off-spring of a distorting egocentric illusion to which the children of a Western Civilisation had succumbed like the children of all other known civilisations and known primitive societies.

Postmodernism, therefore, becomes a certain self-consciousness about a culture's own historical relativity – which begins to explain why, as its critics complain, it also involves the loss of the sense of an absoluteness of any Western account of History. Today, if we pose the difficult ques-tion of the relation of poststructuralism to postmodernism, one distinction between them that might be drawn would be that whereas postmodernism seems to include the problematic of the place of Western culture in relation to non-Western cultures, poststructuralism as a category seems not to imply such a perspective. This, however, is hardly the case, for it rather involves if anything a more active critique of the Eurocentric premises of Western knowledge. The difference would be that it does not offer a *critique* by positioning itself outside "the West," but rather uses its own alterity and duplicity in order to effect its deconstruction. In this context, we may note, attempts to account for poststructuralism in terms of the aftermath of the events of May '68 seem positively myopic, lacking the very historical perspective to which they lay claim. Contrary, then, to some of its more overreaching definitions, postmodernism itself could be said to mark not just the cultural effects of a new stage of "late" capitalism, but the sense of the loss of European history and culture as History and Culture, the loss of their unquestioned place at the centre of the world. We could say that if, according to Foucault, the centrality of "Man" dissolved at the end of the eighteenth century as the "Classical Order" gave way to "History," today at the end of the twentieth century, as "History" gives way to the "Postmodern," we are witnessing the dissolution of "the West."

[Editor's note: The footnotes of the original have been omitted.]

7 Iain Chambers

Migrancy, culture, identity

The historian, despite the recognition that "consciousness is never fixed, never attained once and for all," still seeks the light, the illuminated path, evidently believing that truth lies there in a stable intellectual referent rather than in the intellectual (and worldly) turbulence that has been unleashed. This leaves historiography subject to internal critique and adjustment, but safe from the wider, more uncomfortable, questioning that might refuse or simply ignore its epistemological pretensions and their institutional authority.

So, if a redressing of the figure of history leads to a less universalistic, less positivist, more modest sense of practice and knowledge, it can still refuse to raise the question, "Why history?" Put another way, what does the historian want? Historians can refer to textuality and deconstruction but still shy away from the heart of the matter: history as an allegorical construction, as the constant return to the sense of our lives, of being. We are left, however sensitive to change and limits, working with the map of a lost world, where the discipline and directions of erudite knowledge take precedence over the complexities, confusion and contingencies of our being. This means to opt for the stability and self-assurance of the hermetic mode – subject of the institutional panopticon and the academic discourse – rather than the excesses of heteronomy and the de-situating responsibility for other places: the sites of the ambiguous, the unsaid, the silent, the repressed.

For the ethics of writing history surely emerges from our perpetual dialogue with the dead. To inter-pret the past is also, as Michel de Certeau points out, to inter it: to honour and exorcise it by inscribing it in the possibilities of language and discourse. To name and mark past time and recover it for the present is to produce a *tombeau*, a funeral commemoration that simultaneously celebrates life. For it "is to make a place for the dead, but also to redistribute the space of possibility, to determine negatively what must be done, and consequently to use the narrativity that buries the dead as a way of establishing a place for the living."

Historiography, Michel de Certeau suggests, emerges from the European encounter with the unknown other. As a product of the Renaissance it marks the emergence, the so-called "discovery," of non-European worlds – "whose only history was the one about to begin" – and their re-location within the physical, psychic and imaginary landscapes of the "West." The West, as the apparent maker and custodian of history in both geopolitical and scriptural terms, was the site of "truth." Under its institutional and technological aegis – universities, printing, museums, syllabuses, photography, sound recording, film – history transcribed all human practice; it recorded, reordered and rewrote the world.

Historiography did not merely study the past: it registered, transmitted and translated it. Its truth was the faith and mission of the West. So, the recent irruption of others into the heartland of European *savoir* poses disturbing questions about the status of *our* knowledge and the particular protocols of historiography. For this intrusion rewrites the conditions of the West: its sense of truth, its sense of time, its sense of being.

Much of what passes for history is trapped in a continual exchange between realism and representation that relies on a naïve metaphysics of truth (absolute, total, complete) as though it were the property of the West. Yet representation is not a natural or obvious thing. It is, in both its political and aesthetic dimensions, a process of continual construction, enunciation and interpretation. The multiple representations and voices of the once excluded, of women, of black peoples, of discriminated sexualities, in contemporary culture, history and society, for example, do not simply exist in creating a space for them, of widening academic disciplines, political institutions, and adopting a pluralist gaze. It lies, rather, in reworking the very sense of history, culture, society and language that had previously excluded or silenced such voices, such a presence.

This is not to propose a history that, now able to recognise what was previously hidden and ignored, is therefore more "complete," more convincing, more whole. It is rather to seek to propose a version that is more "authentic" to our conditions by discussing what the very desire for history might involve. This entails a recognition of responsibility for the "hunger of shadows," for the oblivion of being. Here in the West, "history," with its desire for mastery and its drive to fully explain, has provided the perennial testimony to the rewriting of the world as a European text. This observation carries us far beyond the obvious narratives of colony and Empire. For, concomitant with exploring, mapping and claiming the world, European identities were fashioning and defining themselves as the subjects of the modern *episteme*. While laying claim to the ownership of "universal" knowledge Europeans were simultaneously involved in the paradoxical exercise of inventing the myths and traditions of the emerging modern (European) state and the national identities that sustained such a claim. Knowledge and power were mirrored and sustained in an assumed global destiny. The European became the universal "we" – able to grant and withdraw history from others: the pervasive "I" that speaks in knowledge and science, never the object, the "they," of these discourses. Today, in a world in which the unity of knowledge and power meets with resistance and is being interrupted, challenged and decentred, such aspirations turn out to involve a limited account, and one, even in its critical and self-reflective moments, that remains deeply imbricated in the history of Eurocentrism. To recognise this aperture, and with it the falling away of a unique centre, is also to recognise the "pertinence of the critique of historicism to a world undergoing decolonization."

This particular sense of history – one that confidently appropriates the rest of the world to its point of view – depends upon the invariable and unquestioned sense of identity of the knowing subject. What cannot be reduced to his law and logic, and the gender is deliberate, is declared to be irrational. This universal "he" of mankind cannot accept or tolerate otherness: the idea that something or somebody might exist beyond its domain and empire. It proposes a sense of history from a unique perspective: the eye of God now secularised, brought down to earth to inhabit the measured voice of the expert, the scientist, the intellectual, and the infra-red surveillance eye of a Los Angeles Police Department helicopter. This appeal to the universal claims of modern rationalism, to the Cartesian certainties established in the singular abstraction of thought that avoids the differences of our historical bodies and their incorporation in diverse languages, encompasses everything within its possessive gaze and power. The observed is reduced to "a speechless, denuded, biological body." Alterity is swallowed up: the observed is removed from a precise historical and cultural economy and subsequently relocated in the scientific, literary and philosophical typologies employed to describe, fix and explain the "other." It is a mode of enquiry that refuses to let others be. Differences are reduced to a common measure, the complexity of life to the narrow path of Eurocentric knowledge, to its particular myths of reason, progress, authenticity, closure and truth. In this fashion, disinterested and "scientific" knowledge underwrites "colonial appropriation, even as it rejects the rhetoric, and probably the practice, of conquest and subjugation."

This is why the narrative of "history," which in some accounts stands for liberation – the rise of the nation state, of modern democracy and citizenship, of science and "progress," of the victories of the locally oppressed – can for others simply indicate the label of terror and repression. As other histories emerge from the archaeology of modernity to disturb the monologue of History, we are reminded of the multiple rhythms of life that have been written out and forgotten, as the ambiguous, the disruptive and the excessive were reduced to the European accounting of past, present and future.

If modern slavery, racism, imperialism, total warfare, the Holocaust, Hiroshima and ecological break-down represent the limits of Europe's attempt to devour the world, how can we learn to allow the other to remain as other? How can we live in difference, respecting alterity? Hence the very title of Emmanuel Lévinas' most famous work, *Totality and Infinity* (1969), in which he indicates the choice between reducing everything to the selfsame totality or letting beings be. Lévinas argues that instead of attempting to fully "explain" and assimilate the other, thereby reducing her or him to *our* world, we need to open ourselves up to a relationship that goes beyond ourselves, that exists beyond and apart from us. To acknowledge others, and in that recognition the impossibility of speaking for them, is to inscribe that impossibility, that limit, into my discourse and to recognize my being not for itself but for being with and for the other. Instead of reducing the encounter with the other to the rational transparency and finite closure of self-centred Cartesian subjectivity, Lévinas proposes the open web of language. In particular, it is the ethical event of dialogue that maintains a recognition of difference and distance: the surplus of the encounter that cannot be reduced to one or other of the speakers, that is irreducible to a common measure or totality, that remains vulnerable to the radical alterity of infinity.

Writing is re-presentation, a simulation of what has been lost to it. History comes to us not as raw, bleeding facts but in textual production, in narratives woven by desire (for truth) and a will (for power). Such knowledge amounts to the violence, the force, that activates thought.

For it deals with a memory that knows the impossibility of ever fully knowing either itself or the past. What are transcribed and translated are traces, residues, shadows and echoes. Here there is no obvious clarity to be narrated but rather a continual sorting through the debris of time. And as the accounting of the past constantly prefigures new questions, or else the most ancient of demands in new constellations, the chronicle is continually being re-written, re-viewed, re-presented. The resulting narrative can only be historical *and* fragmentary, structured *and* open, continuous *and* interrupted. For historiography involves both the re-membering and the re-covering of the past: its temporary coherence simultaneously invokes disclosure and disguise.

This terminates a discourse based on the assumption of an unequivocal distinction between truth and falsehood – as though the former were guaranteed by reason and the latter merely an appearance, a mask, to be stripped away. When every discourse is put together, articulated, fabulated, in the ambiguous territory between (or beyond) such poles, then the very idea of the "authentic" subject and its grammar of truth is displaced. We are left discussing the event of the gesture, the sign, the signature, simulation, language. This suggests an ethics whose only recourse lies in the recognition and acknowledgement of the transient mechanisms that sustain such a presence and representation: the contingency of the *mise en scène*. Here, in acknowledging the mechanisms of language, the instance of the genre (realist, surrealist . . .), and the mode of the narrative (historiographic, sociological, literary . . .), we also perceive that what is being represented is already in quotation marks, already a representation. It is not for that reason any less valid or true, given that language, representation and discourse are the unique modes that permit speech, a voice, and access to the truth.

[Editor's note: The footnotes of the original have been omitted.]

EDITOR'S INTRODUCTION: AGAINST POSTMODERN HISTORIES

The extracts chosen to illustrate the alleged problems which occur when upper case History is dropped, are drawn from the ideological/"traditionalist" left. For whilst there are obviously many on the left (and left of centre and, indeed, as in the case of, say, Jonathan Clark, of the radical right) for whom the capsizal of the upper case occasions little fear or trembling, traditional left-wing historians/theorists are suspicious of the sceptical postmodernism they tend to see as complicit with a commodifying capitalism. From this position, postmodernism is seen as emerging primarily from the exigencies of late-capital, a response to the fragmentation of the social into the commodity forms which underwrite it and which allows for unlimited "differences" to be recuperated back into it via both consumerism and a contrived political pluralism. Seen through this optic, tainted by capital, postmodernism cannot be embraced. For whilst this part of the left often uses postmodernism's ironic rhetoric to deconstruct lingering bourgeois certainties, it would still like to retain a few of its own: a basic rationality, some contact with the reality which is not hyper-reality (where one can actually engage with "your real referent") and, so far as history is concerned, some knowledge of the past which would be useful because to all intents and purposes it would be true. To this element of the left the attitude taken towards postmodernism is thus, at best, a variously ambivalent one (perhaps distinguishing in the manner of Norris postmodernism from deconstructionism) or, at worst, an outright rejection. The three extracts in this section seem to me to typify the approaches just briefly described. Thus, in the first, ("Literary Criticism and the Politics of the New Historicism") Elizabeth Fox-Genovese, whilst rejecting a vulgar Marxism in favour of what she calls "structural history", still insists that a postist textuality undercuts good (Marxist) history; namely, an inescapable structural history which is, however, neither reductionist, present-minded, or teleological. The second extract is by Christopher Norris, a Norris who has, by now, nailed his anti-postmodern colours to the mast, albeit finessing his general rejection by retaining a version of deconstructionism after Derrida, whom he champions. In a series of books (including *Deconstructionism; Derrida; The Truth About Postmodernism; What's Wrong with Postmodernism; Uncritical Theory;* and *Truth and the Ethics of Criticism*) Norris has radically critiqued especially the works of Lyotard, Baudrillard, Rorty and Stanley Fish, returning time and again to the point that without such notions as reality, reason, facticity, objectivity and realism, then "anything goes"; that the truth is nothing more than that which is "best by way of belief." In his books Norris addresses what he sees as the current problematic of historiography in many passages, but I reproduce here not a book extract but rather the bulk of an article which appeared in 1988 in an issue of the journal *Southern Review*; namely, "Postmodernising History: Right-Wing Revisionism and the Uses of Theory", which is broadly representative of his particular reading of postmodernism and history. It deserves a close reading.

Bryan Palmer has been addressing the question of the impact of post-modernism on Marxist historiography in general and social history in particular for many years, his *Descent into Discourse* (Philadelphia; Temple University Press, 1990) being his most extended piece of work in this area. Inhabiting much of the same territory as the journal *Social History*, many of Palmer's concerns will be "re-presented" in the extracts from that journal in Part IV (below pp. 315–83). The extract from Palmer's work reproduced here as Chapter 10 is taken from his incisive 1993 article "Critical Theory, Historical Materialism, and the Ostensible End of Marxism: The Poverty of Theory Revisited" which appeared in the *International Review of Social History*. Here, Palmer argues that counter to the prevailing postist "conventional wisdom," Marxist analysts have not been brought to their interpretive knees, and that historical materialism has lost neither its power to interpret the past "nor its relevance to the contemporary intellectual terrain.'

8 Elizabeth Fox-Genovese

Literary criticism and the politics of the new historicism

History consists in something more than "just one damn thing after another," in something more than random antiquarianism, even in something more than what happened in the past. Some of those who are turning to History to redress the excesses of contemporary literary theory are calling it a "discourse" – a label that at least has the virtue of acknowledging its claims to intellectual status, and more, of acknowledging its possible internal cohesion and rules, of beginning to recognize it as a distinct mode of understanding. But their strategy runs the risk of confusing history as accounts, narratives, or interpretations of the past, with history as the sum or interplay of human actions, notably politics. School children who first learn of history as what happened in the past may lack the intellectual sophistication to grasp that what we know of the past depends upon the records – implicit interpretations of who and what matters – and upon the ways in which subsequent human beings have written about and interpreted those records. Only later do they learn to recognize history as a genre, as one particular kind of text. We still use history to refer, however imprecisely, to what we like to think really happened in the past and to the ways in which specific authors have written about it. Contemporary critics tend to insist disproportionately on history as the ways in which authors have written about the past at the expense of what might actually have happened, insist that history consists primarily of a body of texts and a strategy of reading or interpreting them. Yet history also consists, in a very old-fashioned sense, in a body of knowledge – in the sum of reliable information about the past that historians have discovered and assembled. And beyond that knowledge, history must also be recognized as what did happen in the past – of the social relations and, yes, "events," of which our records offer only imperfect clues.

History cannot simply be reduced – or elevated – to a collection, theory, and practice of reading texts. The simple objection to the subsumption of history to textual criticism lies in the varieties of evidence upon which historians draw. It is possible to classify price series or coin deposits or hog weights or railroad lines as texts – possible, but ultimately useful only as an abstraction that flattens historically and theoretically significant distinctions. If, notwithstanding occasional fantasies, the nature of history differentiates historians from "hard" social scientists, it also differentiates them from "pure" literary critics. For historians, the text exists as a function, or articulation, of context. In this sense historians work at the juncture of the symbiosis between text and context, with context understood to mean the very conditions of textual production and dissemination.

In fairness, many literary critics or theorists seem also to be working at this juncture, and their best work is opening promising new avenues. I am hardly alone among historians in being heavily indebted to the work of Antonio Gramsci and Mikhail Bakhtin in particular, although admittedly both rank more as cultural philosophers than as literary critics. Thus, in important instances, the center of attention can be seen to be shifting from text to context, with a healthy emphasis on the concept of hegemony and the notion of struggle within and between discourses. But only in rare instances have new historicists embraced the full implications of this project. In most cases they have implicitly preferred to absorb history into the text or discourse without (re)considering the specific characteristics of history herself.

Such a blanket charge may appear churlish, especially since so much of the work in the new historicism has attempted to restore women, working people, and other marginal groups (although rarely, so far, black people) to the discussion of literary texts. Nor can a blanket charge pretend to do justice to the diversity of works that can be lumped under the general category of new historicism. Understandably, as with any fledgling enterprise, the new historicists, in all their diversity, have worked piecemeal, borrowing from the materials that lie to hand. And, in the vast majority of instances, they have drawn their materials from the new social history and have followed it in substituting experience for politics, consciousness for the dynamics and consequences of power. Feminist critics, to be sure, have attended to the consequences of power – from which they singlemindedly argue women to have suffered – but have tended to homogenize its dynamics under the mindlessly simplistic category of "patriarchy." The end result, despite the uncontestable value of discrete efforts, has been to take as given precisely the most pressing questions, namely the (changing) relations of power and their (multiple) consequences.

History, at least good history, in contrast to antiquarianism, is inescapably structural. Not reductionist, not present-minded, not teleological: structural. Here, I am using structural in a special – or, better, a general – sense, not in the sense developed by Saussure, Lévi-Strauss, or even Roland Barthes or Lucien Goldmann. By structural, I mean that history must disclose and reconstruct the conditions of consciousness and action, with conditions understood as systems of social relations, including relations between women and men, between rich and poor, between the powerful and the powerless; among those of different faiths, different races, and different classes. I further mean that, at any given moment, systems of relations operate in relation to a dominant tendency – for example, what Marxists call a mode of production – that endows them with a structure. Both in the past and in the interpretation of the past history follows a pattern or structure, according to which some systems of relations and some events possess greater significance than others. Structure, in this sense, governs the writing and reading of texts.

This use of structure requires a word of justification. Structure has lapsed in fashion in large measure because of our recognition of the multiple ties that link all forms of human activity, including thought and textual production. In other words, the preoccupation with structure has given way to the preoccupation with system. The very notion of textuality in the large sense embodies the insistence on system, interconnection, and seamlessness, and therefore leads inescapably to what Jameson calls totalization. That recognition is compelling, but it rests upon a denial of boundaries. The concept of structure, not unlike that of discourse, represents a commitment to drawing at least provisional boundaries. In this respect, structure, like discourse, attempts to take account of present and past politics. For politics consists in nothing if not the drawing of boundaries. If indeed, we live in and represent ourselves through a seamless web of textuality, ultimately the spoils of our living and representing accrue to those who draw the boundaries: boundaries of the law, of the literary canon, of superordination in all its manifestations. In this perspective, politics as the will to define and the ability to impose boundaries constitutes the irreducible core of experience, textuality, and history. Politics draws the lines that govern the production, survival, and reading of texts and textuality – of text and Text.

Here again, we have an irony of sorts. Contemporary criticism implicitly, when not explicitly, grants the text a status *sui generis*, as if it somehow defied the laws of time, mortality, history, and politics. But beneath that surface lies an implacable hostility to history as structure and to politics as the struggle to dominate others and thus to shape the structure of social relations. Thus the evocation of history reduces to history as accident (in the Aristotelian sense) of the text rather than its essence, and thus, implicitly, reduces politics to its textual embodiment.

At the core of the contemporary critical project lies the conviction that we think, exist, know, only through texts – that extratextual considerations defy proof and, accordingly, relevance. And how wonderful it is that these critics make precisely the same claims for their theory that the more reductionist, not to say vulgar, cliometricians and psychohistorians make for theirs. In this respect, contemporary criticism as a philosophical project returns through the thickets of modern philosophy to the eighteenth-century Berkeleyan dilemma: Does the falling tree make a sound if none is there to hear it? Or, to take the modern variant, does the thought exist if none is there to write it? The radical attempt to transcend this dilemma, which does command attention, proposes the text as society, culture, history, consciousness, on the grounds that it is all of them or all that we can know. And it further proposes that in addition to being all of them that we can know, it is the only form in which we can know them.

Life would be easier if we could dismiss this challenge to our commonsensical, intuitive apprehension of the solidity of things out of hand. We cannot. In the post-Einsteinian and post-Wittgensteinian universe of intellectual relativism in all spheres, in the post-capitalist world of modern technology and of a restively interdependent globe, our culture's received wisdom about order, about cause and effect, about subject and object no longer suffices. Most of us know all too well that complexity, uncertainty, and indeterminacy govern our world and have effectively shattered our abiding longing to grasp the scheme of things entire. And those who refuse to accept the evidence – notably religious fundamentalists of varying persuasions – engage in a massive effort of denial and self-deception. Bourgeois culture had bravely assumed that the scheme of things obeyed a logic that the individual mind could grasp – had rested on a commitment to what modern critics are now dismissing as "logocentrism." Bourgeois attitudes towards history, notably the whig interpretation, rested upon this commitment. We now know that what we called reality is but appearance, no more than the interplay of self-serving opinions. Historians told the stories that legitmated and served the perpetuation of the powerful's control of the weak. For some, the collapse of this illusion is taken to have opened the way to intellectual anarchism: to each his or her own history. For others, it may be opening the way to a new intellectual totalitarianism, or at least to an elitist thrust that divorces history from the perceptions of the general educated public.

The literary critics cannot absorb history piecemeal, as curiosity, landscape, or illustration. Nor can the historians restore history in all its innocence. The epistemological crisis of our times itself reflects the crisis of bourgeois society – a crisis of consciousness, certainty, hierarchy, and materially grounded social relations. I am not suggesting that we should return if indeed we could, to an untransformed Marxism any more than to sanctimonious whig interpretation. Not least, recent developments in history and literary studies have exposed the bankruptcy of the authoritative white male subject and pressed the claims of women, working people, and peoples of non-white races and non-Western cultures. I am suggesting that a structurally informed history offers our best alternative to the prevailing literary models. For serious attention to the claims of history forces the recognition of the text as a manifestation of previous human societies. The problems of "knowing" history persist. We remain hostage not merely to the imperfection but to the impossibility of precisely recapturing the past and, in this sense remain bound on one flank by the hermeneutic conundrum. But those constraints neither justify our abandoning the struggle nor our blindly adhering to the denial of history.

NOTE

The footnotes of the original have been omitted.

9 Christopher Norris

Postmodernizing history: right-wing revisionism and the uses of theory

I think we might start from some of Paul de Man's remarks on the "resistance to theory" in literary studies. This resistance doesn't only come from outside, so to speak, in the form of institutional prejudice or refusal to acknowledge new ways of reading and thinking. There is also a resistance internal to theory itself, a point at which texts have a habit of not turning out to mean what one expects them to mean according to this or that set of theoretical assumptions. This is why de Man admired the best of the "old" American New Critics. Certainly they were apt to raise local insights into a wholesale ontology of language and form, a rhetoric of "irony," "paradox" or whatever that supposedly defined the very nature of poetic meaning. But they were also (some of them) such fine close-readers that often their perceptions went clean against what they wanted to say and registered something quite different – maybe an odd turn of phrase or discrepant detail that called their whole approach into question. And de Man thought this the best possible way of teaching poetry, or for that matter any kind of text. That is to say, one needs theory to avoid reading stupidly, accepting language at face value, which is always the value placed on it by commonsense belief or ideology. In de Man this takes the form of a heightened attention to rhetoric and the way that rhetorical tropes can undermine the logic or the grammar of straightforward assertion. But theories of this sort are equally capable of turning into ironcast critical systems, as one already sees happening in certain quarters of the US deconstruction industry. So there also had to be this "internal" resistance to theory, one that held out against system and method, that continued to cultivate the virtues of analytical close-reading, but also found room for theoretical reflection when it came to diagnosing the sources of that resistance.

This might help to locate some problems with theory as currently taught at undergraduate and graduate levels. Too often it is a matter of running through the various systems on offer, presenting them as so many self-contained options, and leaving the students to apply one or another as best they can. This turns the whole business into a kind of intellectual supermarket where the main thing is to pick the most radical theory going, expound its claims from the nearest secondary source, and then show briefly that you know how to work it by pulling the appropriate levers. And the trouble is that all these theories (Marxist, feminist, poststructuralist or whatever) work perfectly well with just about any kind of text so long as they are applied at this level of abstract generality. Any resistance that the text might put up – any sign of its not responding ideally to the chosen method of approach – is rendered invisible by a whole new set of stubborn theoretical preconceptions. A brief glance at the current journals is enough to bear this out. It is not so much the canon that has changed as the variety of methods, theories and approaches that now have something like canonical status. So for every poem or novel in the Great Tradition there must be by now at least one reading that treats it from (say) a Freudian-Lacanian, or a New Historicist, or a Marxist poststructuralist, or a Derridean, or a feminist-psychoanalytic standpoint. Some of these readings are inventive, resourceful and convincing. Others are so remote from the text as scarcely to be "readings" at all. And very often, even with the best of them, there is an overriding need to prove the theory right at all costs, and a corresponding lack of that internal resistance – a resistance "specific to theory itself" – that de Man locates in the rhetorical aspect of language.

The most typical feature of so-called "literary" deconstruction is its tendency to fasten on to well-worn themes like the self-reflexive character of texts, the way that mimetic illusion is undone by the play of figural language, and the specular regress (or "mise-en-abyme") that results from a reading always on the look-out for signs of metaphorical slippage. Again, this is more or less guaranteed to work with just about any fictional text, since we know (after all) that novels aren't *really* windows on reality, that language can't provide an unmediated access to the world, that realism is in some sense a product of signifying codes and conventions . . . and so forth. Of course this gives room for displays of ingenuity in showing how the argument applies just as much to novels in the great realist tradition as to postmodern texts that positively flaunt their anti-mimetic character. Still there is something odd about the repeated demonstration, carried off each time with an air of triumphant discovery. On the other hand there seems little point in deconstructing postmodernists like Borges, Barthelme or Calvino, writers who effectively manage to preempt just about everything the critic might want to say. In the end such readings most often invite the Johnsonian riposte that nobody in their right mind ever actually confused fictive with real-life experience, or succeeded so far in suspending disbelief that all such distinctions dropped away. One problem with literary deconstruction is that it tends to come up with sophisticated reasons for believing what we always knew. Often this produces an uncomfortable sense that the theory is working all right, but that it couldn't really fail to work, given the basic absurdity of the beliefs it sets out to deconstruct. Again, it is the lack of any possible resistance from the text – any obstacle to theory on its otherwise triumphal progress – that renders such arguments decidedly suspect.

Perhaps this is simply to restate the familiar point that American deconstruction has been largely transformed from a philosophical activity into a branch of literary criticism. As a result, its procedures have been loosened up, foregoing the kind of consequential argument and analytic rigour that one finds in Derrida's essays on Plato, Kant, Hegel or Husserl, and becoming much more a species of elaborate verbal gymnastics. Of course it may be argued that such criticisms are beside the point, since Derrida has shown (hasn't he?) that there is really no difference between "philosophy" and "literature"; that all philosophical concepts come down to metaphors in the end; and that therefore we had much better drop such deluded categorical distinctions and read all texts with an eye to their covert structures of figural meaning. In fact this ignores the many passages (especially in *Margins of Philosophy*) where Derrida says just the opposite. If indeed it is true that the texts of philosophy are littered with dead or forgotten metaphors – if the very word "concept," along with others like "theory" or "idea," are ultimately tropes whose origin we have repressed, as Nietzsche argued, through the will-to-power that masquerades as philosophic truth – then equally it is the case that our very notions of metaphor, of literature, and of figural as opposed to literal language are notions that have always been produced and worked over by the discourse of philosophic reason. So Derrida is far from endorsing Richard Rorty's proposal that we should drop the idea of "philosophy" as a discipline with its own particular interests, modes of argument, conceptual prehis-tory and so on, and henceforth treat it as just one "kind of writing" among others, on a level with poetry, literary criticism and the human sciences at large. In fact his recent essays have laid increasing stress on this need to conserve what is specific to philosophy, namely its engage-ment with ethical, political and epistemological issues that cannot be reduced *tout court* to the level of an undifferentiated textual "freeplay."

This does have a bearing on the practical question of how best to teach "theory" at undergraduate and graduate levels. One thing that is happening in many universities is a gradual interpenetration of the disciplines, such that (for instance) people from departments of literature are offering courses to students of philosophy, history or the social sciences. The benefits of this arrangement are obvious enough. There is good reason to think that the old institutional boundaries no longer correspond to what is going on at the cutting edge of those disciplines. Thus students of philosophy might gain from some knowledge of current developments in literary theory (more specifically, from a reading of Derrida or de Man), and historians from a course in narrative poetics, perhaps starting out with Hayden White's *Tropics of Discourse* and then moving on to a detailed rhetorical analysis of texts in the manner that White proposes. Or again, there are many points of contact between literary theory and the interests of modern jurisprudence, including such basic issues as the interpretation of case-law precedent, the role (if any) of framers' intentions in fixing the scope and proper meaning of documents, and the whole vexed question of how far law can be treated – as the legal formalists believed – as a self-contained system of axiomatic rules and principles, ideally immune from the pressure of social and political interests. In each of these disciplines – philosophy, history and law – there are signs already of a challenge being mounted on terms that derive from literary theory, especially from the current poststructuralist critique of language, ideology and representation. So far it has happened mainly in American universities, where the credit system gives students more freedom to opt for courses outside their chosen major discipline. But the same broad trend is observable in Britain, and no doubt in other countries as it becomes steadily more difficult – more obviously an artificial exercise – to pretend that these disciplines truly exist as so many self-enclosed realms of special expertise.

Now of course I wouldn't want to deny the value and desirability of such inter-disciplinary contacts. In sheerly practical terms – as a matter of showing how "literary studies" can earn their keep at a time of economic cutbacks, cost-effectiveness as the universal yardstick and widespread scepticism as regards the humane or civilising role of the arts – it is obviously useful to strike up relations on as many fronts as possible. And if these seem merely opportunist arguments, there is also the mutual benefit to be had from the exchange of ideas across intellectual borderlines, and the testing of assumptions in a spirit of open dialogue. Besides, many teachers can attest to the feelings of professional bad conscience that result from continuing to profess a discipline – English Literature – whose ideological history has now been so thoroughly exposed to view, and whose reliance on a set of largely unargued and self-promoting values they can demonstrate easily enough in books and articles, but not when it comes to the business of day-to-day seminar teaching. Much better to give up that old, isolationist stance and replace it with a range of demystified alternatives: reception-theory, narrative poetics, discourse studies, "New Historicism" and the like. At least these are eminently teachable skills, of use across a range of contiguous disciplines and carrying none of the obscurantist overtones that dogged the inheritance of English Studies from Arnold to Leavis and beyond.

But there are, as I have suggested, certain dangers in the move to colonise other disciplines in the name of an all-embracing literary theory. One is the tendency to reduce those disciplines to the level of a generalized "intertextuality" that takes no account of their specific problems, their conceptual pre-history and characteristic modes of argument. The result – as seen most clearly in neopragmatist appropriations of Derrida's work – is to encourage a levelling consensus-view of language, truth and reason which deprives theory of its critical force by arguing that all such claims come down to a species of rhetorical imposition. This is no doubt why Derrida has insisted more emphatically in his recent writings that any deconstruction of philosophic truth-claims must at some point go by way of a meticulous and detailed close-reading of texts in the modern, post-Kantian enlightenment tradition. And the same applies to those current attempts to extend literary theory into the domain of history, jurisprudence or the social sciences in general. For the result may be not so much a salutary questioning of ideas, arguments and values standardly taken for granted, as a means of evading the forms of self-criticism that those disciplines have evolved in the process of examining their own distinctive truth-claims. Once again, I am not suggesting that people should stick to their appointed professional spheres and reject any interdisciplinary overtures that might threaten the existing intellectual division of labour. But there is nothing to be gained – indeed much to be lost – by a wholesale undoing of histories of thought which have laboured long and hard to separate truth from the various currencies of true-seeming fiction and consensus-belief.

"I find it bizarre," Stanley Fish writes in a recent essay, "that so many people today think that by extending the techniques of literary analysis to government proclamations or diplomatic communiqués or advertising copy you make criticism more political and more aware of its implication in extra-institutional matters; all you do (and it is nothing to sneer at) is expand the scope of the institution's activity, plant the flag of literary studies on more and more territory." I find it equally bizarre – not to say ironic – that this argument should come from a thinker like Fish, one who has pushed the neopragmatist case "against theory" to the point of denying that criticism can do anything to challenge the consensual meanings and beliefs embodied in a given "interpretive community." Fish's arguments to this effect go roughly as follows: (1) that all interpretation, whether in literature, law, philosophy or the human sciences at large, takes place within some such communal enterprise; (2) that this includes any theory, however radical, that sets out to criticise the terms of that consensus; and (3) that theorists must therefore be deluded if they think to advance any counter-hegemonic or strong revisionist argument that would somehow lay claim to an independent standpoint. This applies to positive theorists: those who adopt a value-laden rhetoric of rights, first principles, ethical absolutes or whatever, against which to measure the supposed shortcomings of a present-day consensus; and also to negative theorists: those like the Marxists and deconstructors who think to expose the mystified character of current consensual norms by pointing out the symptoms of strain, contradiction or aporia that characterize various kinds of discourse. To Fish, such claims are simply incoherent, since in order to achieve any kind of acceptance – that is, to carry weight with readers, critics, members of the relevant professional or cultural community – they *must* in the end be construed in terms of some pre-given cultural consensus. This is why Fish is quite happy with the notion of expanding the scope of literary studies into law, politics and other such fields, just so long as critics don't then delude themselves that this can make their writing more "political," or better placed to challenge the current institutional status quo. And indeed, his own work is a striking example of what might be called "travelling anti-theory"; that is, the kind of all-purpose pragmatist argument that can be used to discredit oppositional thinking in law, criticism or any other field where professional interests are in play.

All the same, it is hard to deny that some current uses of theory do make an easy target for Fish's techniques of knock-down argument. The reason – as I have said – is that they operate with a massively generalized notion of rhetoric or intertextuality which reduces all writings to a dead level of suasive or performative effect. This is why de Man, in his later essays, insists on preserving the distinction between logic, grammar and rhetoric, no matter how complex (or ultimately undecidable) their relation in any given case. For otherwise there is no possibility of tensions developing, of the text putting up the kind of localised resistance to preconceived methods or meanings that then offers a hold for critical understanding. Thus, in de Man's words, "reading is an argument . . . because it has to go against the grain of what one would want to happen in the name of what has to happen." It is only at these points of unexpected resistance – moments where the text disrupts any form of settled, consensual belief – that reading can escape what Fish conceives as the closed circle of interpretative foreknowledge. Any theory that doesn't make allowance for such possibilities, that reduces all meaning to a play of intertextual codes and conventions, or all truth to a product of vested interpretative interests, will end up as one more handy confirmation of Fish's neopragmatist views.

These arguments have an added urgency in the present political climate. After all, we in Britain are living through a period when it is vital to maintain a due sense of the difference between fact and fiction, historical truth and the various kinds of state-sponsored myth that currently pass for truth. It is not a good time to be telling students that history is only what counts as such according to some present consensus-view, and that finally it all comes down to a struggle for power between various, more or less plausible narrative fictions. The fact that many people currently believe what they are told to believe – that such distinctions may indeed become desperately blurred – makes it all the more important not to go along with this last-ditch relativist argument. The issue is posed most starkly with regard to sensitive periods like the 1930s, where a great effort is now under way to pretend that left-wing "pacifists" and appeasers were somehow responsible for Hitler's rise to power, that the left did nothing to oppose Fascism (ignoring minor episodes like the Spanish Civil War), and that only conservatives – then as now – had the wisdom to press for rearmament and a firm foreign policy stance. This latter line of argument has to pass clean over such resistant bits of evidence as Chamberlain, Munich and the widespread opposition to war with Hitler among bankers, industrialists and conservative politicians who hoped to make common cause with the Nazis in a coming anti-Soviet front. Such distortions played a significant role in Tory propaganda during the run-up to the 1987 General Election. They are more or less taken for granted across a broad section of the popular press, and will no doubt find their way into the school history textbooks if the government manages to push through its latest "core curriculum" proposals. So there might come a time when this is indeed the established consensus-view and when any opposition is marginalized to the point of becoming totally invisible. But it would still be a massively falsified consensus, brought about by the misreading or manipulative use of evidence, the suppression of crucial facts and the creation of a certain selective amnesia in those whose memory might otherwise go far enough back.

I think that these reflections should at least give pause to proponents of a sceptical historiography that regards truth as entirely a product of rhetorical or narrative contrivance. Of course this is not to suggest that the facts in any given case can be simply read off from the documents, or established in a straightforward positivist way without recourse to interpretative frameworks of any kind. Nor is it to deny that a reading of Foucault, Hayden White or other theorists of a relativizing bent may help to sharpen the student's awareness of those contests that are always being fought over the interpretation of historical texts. But there is a great difference between this sort of lesson in the critical reading of evidence, and the other form of wholesale Nietzschean scepticism which would render such lessons ultimately useless. What students need to know – by way of counterbalancing the current poststructuralist wisdom – is that there are strong arguments on philosophical, methodological and other grounds for rejecting such a desperate conclusion. These include various ways in which the criteria or truth-conditions for historical discourse differ from those that we standardly apply to fictional texts. (Causal factors, chronological constraints, ascriptions of agency and material circumstance are among the more obvious factors that would need to be taken into account). There is, to say the least, something premature and suspect about any treatment of historical texts that fastens exclusively on their narrative or tropological aspects while ignoring these other constitutive dimensions.

* * *

I have argued that current ideas in literary theory provide at best a partial and at worst an actively misleading model for the conduct of other disciplines. They lend support to a fashionable relativist trend which undermines critical reason, treats history as simply a collection of narratives or fictions, and renounces any claim to distinguish between truth and the various currencies of true-seeming ideological belief. This has come about partly through a narrow conception of "critical theory," one that derives almost entirely from French poststructuralist sources and shows small interest in the other, post-Kantian tradition of thought taken up by philosophers like Adorno and Habermas. For it is here that the claims of critical reason have received their most persistent and vigorous defence in the face of various irrationalist or relativist creeds. In Habermas this takes the form of a "transcendental pragmatics," a large-scale attempt to preserve what is essential in the Kantian enlightenment tradition while acknowledging the force of current anti-foundationalist arguments. Hence his appeal to the normative criterion of an "ideal-speech situation," one in which the discourse of various parties would no longer be subject to the pressures, distortions and misunderstandings that result from the unequal distribution of knowledge and power in present-day society. Although it exists necessarily as a kind of utopian projection, this ideal is implicit – so Habermas argues – in each and every act of communicative utterance, each attempt to make our own meaning clear or to understand what others are saying. It is Kantian in so far as it rejects the idea – common to all forms of neopragmatist thinking – that truth can be only a matter of consensus values, or what is currently "good in the way of belief." For if this were the case, then thought would be incapable of attaining any kind of critical perspective, any standpoint that questioned received ideas in the name of some better, more adequate understanding.

One need only look to the current wave of right-wing revisionist historiography to see how those assumptions are the first target of counter-enlightenment thought. Thus Jonathan Clark sets out to demolish what he takes as the old, creaky metanarrative that under-writes Whiggish or liberal-progressive accounts of British history. He rejects (among other things) the belief that constitutional reform came about through a struggle against older conceptions of divine right or royal prerogative; the idea of 1688 as marking a decisive turning-point in the progress of social-democratic institutions; and the whole "adversarial" concept of history as a field of contending forces where interests of a broadly progressive, enlightened or emancipatory character were pitched against residual forms of the old regime. Equally suspect, in Clark's view, is any use of the word "revolution" to describe events like those of the middle or late seventeenth century, events which can then be made to fit in with the "teleological" reading of history as an onward march towards present-day notions of democracy, justice and reason. *Rebellion*, not revolution, is Clark's preferred term for what he sees as merely localized symptoms of unrest against a background of largely unchanging assent to the existence of sovereign powers and a rigidly stratified social order. This change of usage helps us to appreciate "that many conflicts (like the Civil War or 1688) can better be described as reactions against innovations, a deeply rooted resistance to undesired change." For indeed, as Clark points out, the word "revolution" has itself undergone a revolution of meaning over the past two centuries, before which time it was taken to signify the end to some disruptive episode and the return full-circle to a previous, more settled and orderly dispensation.

So Clark's main object in proposing this terminological shift is to free historical discourse from the various accretions of Whiggish ideology built into its currently prevailing metanarrative stance. Even the concept of "rebellion" needs rescuing, he writes, since:

> we often take a revolution to be a successful rebellion; and by "revolution" we now understand, in addition to the political aspects, a fundamental challenge to the legitimacy of social structures, including patterns of hierarchy or stratification, and titles to economic ownership or control. . . . So to distinguish these two explanatory categories helps us to disengage ourselves from the assumption that revolutions are always "forward-looking," that they embody the progressive aspirations of "rising" social classes to speed up developments being impeded by the "forces of reaction."

In pursuit of this aim Clark offers a wholesale revisionist account of the entire period from 1640, through the Restoration and Hanoverian settlement, to the Industrial Revolution (which term he thinks highly misleading but uses as a matter of convenience) and the history of nineteenth-century socio-political change. In so far as a consensus exists on these topics it is one that he finds so deeply infected by the liberal or, worse still, the Marxist malaise that its assumptions need refuting point by point. At each stage he argues that the so-called "forces of reaction" were in fact always dominant; that any changes towards greater participant democracy or constitutional reform were short-term adjustments only; and therefore that historians go badly wrong when they overrate the importance of such episodes and ignore the more profound continuities that emerge if one abandons this false perspective. The opposing schools can be categorised roughly as "old hat" (Whiggish), "old guard" (Marxist) and "class of '68" (self-explanatory). What they share is a set of stubborn preconceptions about progress, enlightenment and the proper ends of historical understanding that have, as Clark believes, exerted a regular distorting influence on their powers of scholarly judgement.

His revisionist account of the period in question can be summarized briefly as follows. The events of 1641 and 1688 were not "revolutions" in the sense of that term proposed by liberal or left wing historians. They had little to do with the clash of opposing social forces, the rise of a disaffected merchant or "middle class" interest, the assertion of parliamentary powers against royal prerogative, or any of those "underlying" socio-economic causes that had hitherto been called upon by way of explanation. Rather, they were short-term responses to specific kinds of grievance, most often brought about by some shift in the perceived relationship between Crown, Church and State. And the result in each case was not (so Clark argues) to push on a stage towards the overthrow of Absolute Monarchy or the concept of Divine Right, but to find some new, more effective form of working compromise that would keep those institutions firmly in place. So there remained a close link between the monarchy and the legitimizing power of established religion, a link that not only survived 1688 but was in fact powerfully reinforced by the Hanoverian claim to represent the true authority of Church and State as against the now discredited Jacobite interest. Thus nothing much had changed over the past fifty years bar the advent of a so-called "Lockean consensus" which in fact merely offered a new apologetics for the *status quo ante*, and otherwise exists only as a creation of wishful-thinking subsequent historians. "The effective absolutism of the King was actually strengthened by the fiction of the King-in-Parliament within the Clarendonian constitution as implemented after 1660. Consequently, 1688–9 'did not resolve the issue of sovereignty in favour of the representative principle,' nor did it liquidate the monarchy. 'William III was no puppet. The mixture was as before'." And the same goes for the "Industrial Revolution," an event which never happened, according to Clark, or at least one whose origins, date and character remain largely undefined. In short, "the Industrial Revolution was an historical category, not an event. We may doubt whether it was even a *process*, if by that we are to understand a single, unified and thematically coherent development." In which case the historian had much better recognise that this, like other such putative "revolutions," has no reality outside the Whiggish metanarrative that interprets everything as lending support to its own providentialist thesis.

What Clark wants to do is effect a great shift in the discursive terrain of modern historiography, such that the opposing viewpoints (old-hat liberal or old-guard Marxist) no longer make any kind of sense. At times he is quite disarmingly frank about these tactical or polemical aims. Thus he presents the whole issue very often in terms of a generation-gap or war of ideas between his own (revisionist) colleagues and the defenders of an old orthodoxy. Furthermore, he concedes that "Genres of scholarship do fall into desuetude for reasons not wholly indicative of their intellectual merits," and that changes in the currency of authorized knowledge may have much to do with shifts of intellectual fashion or changes in the climate of political belief. "For reasons of which we are only now becoming aware, [this] same fate may well be overtaking the characteristic idioms of some of the schools of thought discussed here: less denounced as false, more neglected as slightly quaint." In fact his whole strategy is to speed up this process by ridiculing the positions he thinks are "old hat" and representing their exponents as so many sadly superannuated figures who have not managed to grasp the new rules of the game.

To this extent Clark fits in rather nicely with the current postmodernist or Foucauldian view that history is always a "history of the present," a discursive domain whose contours are shaped by prevailing social or political interests. Thus his work has two revisionist stories to tell, the first mainly occupied with events between 1640 and 1832, the other with the fortunes of modern historiography in the wake of the "electoral shock" of 1979. Up till then there existed a broad left-liberal consensus in history, economics and political science, a nexus of Fabian and Keynesian ideas which more or less commanded the field. But since 1979 that consensus has collapsed, and along with it the claims to serious attention of all those thinkers who have remained under its spell. In the words of Kenneth Burgin, cited approvingly by Clark: "It would be easy to list a succession of books by men who have been left like stranded whales by the ebb of the Keynesian tide. . . . Too many

existing political scientists belong to the generation of 1968 – a provenance that almost disqualifies them from comment on late 20th-century
politics."

And as Clark sees it this same condition applies to historical scholarship, since "truth" at any given time – or within any given community
of knowledge – can only be determined according to the currently
prevailing consensus.

Now clearly there is a sense in which this all goes to confirm what
Foucault, Hayden White and others have argued: namely, that history
is a field of competing rhetorical or narrative strategies, a plural discourse which can always produce any number of alternative accounts.
But it might be well to question this relativist line if it lends itself so
readily to the purposes of right-wing revisionist historians like Clark.
For the result of such thinking is not only to efface the distinction
between fact and fable but to undermine the very concept of historical
reason as aimed at a better, more enlightened or accountable version of
significant events. Clark sees nothing but error and delusion in the idea
that episodes like 1640 or 1688 might be interpreted as stages on the path
towards this kind of questioning, critical awareness. Thus he assembles
passages from the work of "old guard" historians in order to demonstrate the supposed absurdity of this way of thinking:

> educated men had been taught "to think for themselves: they could
> not easily accept the dictates of kings and bishops." "Competing
> religious ideologies shattered the unquestioning and habit-forming
> faith of the past." Orthodox theology and patrician social authority
> equals dogma produces bigotry demands unthinking acceptance or
> rational dissent: such was the pattern of prejudice which had ham-
> strung the scholarship of the Hanoverian era also.

His point is to ridicule the very idea that reason – or the power of
critical thought – can effect transformations of a social or political order
which historians are then called upon to interpret through a similar
exercise of rational intelligence. Clark's whole revisionist approach is
premised on the argument that no such understanding can ever come
about; that historical events, like historical interpretations, take rise in
response to short-term pressures of circumstance and then disappear
just as quickly when the times change. In which case historians can
only be deluded if they think to make sense of the past on assumptions
that derive from an outworn mythology of reason, progress and enlightened secular critique. For such beliefs line up all too readily with the

notion of people "thinking for themselves," and of history as offering intelligible evidence of the way this process worked itself out in socio-political terms. Hence Clark's argument that the old coercive powers of religion and monarchy never really lost their grip; that Divine Right lingered on in all but name; and that therefore we had much better recognise these deep continuities and drop all talk of "revolutions" and suchlike chimerical events.

It is not hard to see how this position might square with other current forms of right-wing revisionist thinking. Thus for instance one could take it as offering support – historical warrant – for the government's revival of Royal Prerogative as a means of enforcing its policy interests through the courts while avoiding any kind of parliamentary or public opposition. My point is that "critical theory" in the current poststructuralist mode cannot engage with such issues because it has effectively renounced any claim of distinguishing between reason and rhetoric, knowledge and power, judgements arrived at through a process of uncoerced, rational debate, and judgements resting on prejudice, dogma or the exercise of unchecked authority. What is needed is an openness to other kinds of theory that have held out against this relativising drift on account of its conservative implications. They include (as I have argued) the Frankfurt tradition of *Ideologiekritik*, especially that modified version of it – the theory of communicative action – which Habermas deploys by way of contesting present-day irrationalist trends. There is also much to be gained from a reading of those deconstructionist texts that abjure the pleasures of unlimited "freeplay" for the sake of advancing a cogent critical argument. But these issues in the sphere of textual understanding cannot be divorced from substantive questions of politics, ethics and right reason. Any attempt to counter the revisionists on their own historical ground will need to do more than offer some alternative rhetoric or some preferable story that highlights different episodes. It will have to make good the basic claim – basic, that is, to all forms of genuinely critical thinking – that truth is not a product of consensus-belief, but the upshot of an ongoing rational debate where consensus values should always be subject to question.

NOTE

The footnotes of the original have been omitted.

10 Bryan Palmer

Critical theory, historical materialism, and the ostensible end of Marxism: the poverty of theory revisited

Summary: This essay notes the extent to which poststructuralism/postmodernism have generally espoused hostility to historical materialism, surveys some representative examples of historical writing that have gravitated toward the new critical theory in opposition to Marxism, and closes with a discussion of the ironic evolution of a poststructurally inclined, anti-Marxist historiography. Counter to the prevailing ideological consensus that Marxism has been brought to its interpretive knees by a series of analytic challenges and the political collapse of the world's ostensibly "socialist" states, this essay argues that historical materialism has lost neither its power to interpret the past nor its relevance to the contemporary intellectual terrain.

It is now a decade-and-one-half since Edward Thompson penned *The Poverty of Theory: or an Orrery of Errors*, and ten times as many years have passed since the publication of Marx's *The Poverty of Philosophy*.[1] Whatever one may think about the advances in *knowledge* associated with historical materialism and Marxism, particularly in terms of the practice of historical writing, there is no denying that this sesquicentennial has been a problematic period in the making of communist society; the last fifteen years, moreover, are associated with the bleak end of socialism and the passing of Marxism as an intellectual force.

Indeed, it is a curious conjuncture of our times that the much-proclaimed end of Marxism is somehow related to the end of history as we know it. Who would have thought that history, both as an unfolding process and a set of interpretive writings, would come to an end when Marxism as a ruling ideology in what has passed for "socialist" political economies crumbled and lost its appeal to many academics? No Marxist ever accorded his or her world view the apparent force or influence – in theory or practice – that this current coupled understanding of the early 1990s end of Marxism/history suggests.[2]

For those who revel in the discursive identities and endlessly fluctuating subjectivities of poststructuralism as theory and postmodernism as condition, the instabilities of the current moment – analytical and political – are absolute advantages, realities in an age that refuses acknowledgement of "the real," substance to be celebrated and championed in times when resistance has been thankfully replaced by play and pun. To be a Marxist in these times is obviously neither easy nor pleasant, but it does offer certain securities. Among the most significant, perhaps, is the insight that what we are witnessing now, however seemingly novel and debilitating, has parallels and, perhaps, direct precedent in past struggles over questions of theory and interpretation, battles that were seldom divorced from that touchstone of the human condition, history.[3] "With man we enter *history*," proclaimed Engels.[4]

And yet if we are to appreciate current intellectual trends, it is apparent that history is precisely what is not being "entered." This essay takes as its central concern the extent to which a rather uncritical adoption of what has come to be known as critical theory has resulted in the wholesale jettisoning of historical materialist assumptions and understandings, to the detriment of historical sensitivities and the denigration of the actual experience of historically situated men, women, and children. To make this claim is not to suggest that there can be no engagement with this critical theory and that it has nothing to tell us. Rather, this ground of refusal can be claimed for Marxism and historical materialism precisely because the value of critical theory can be assimilated, enriching historical investigation and interpretation, but only if the cavalierly unthinking and patently ideological anti-Marxism so pervasive among former leftists in the 1990s is identified and rejected for what it is: the opportunism and apostasy of a particular political climate.[5]

This essay proceeds in particular directions. First, it notes briefly the extent to which poststructuralism and postmodernism have *generally* espoused a particular hostility to historical materialism[6] and, in identifying this hostility, it provides indications of what the theoretical literature in these areas espouses and contributes to a potentially analytic historiography. In this brief definitional and descriptive preface there will be occasion to comment on the nature of the relationship of poststructuralism/postmodernism and Marxism, especially the validity and quality of much of critical theory's dismissal of historical materialism. Second, contemporary developments in historiography related to the critical theory of the 1980s and 1990s will be addressed, and a critique of arguments dismissive of historical materialism elaborated. An attempt will be made to explore the contemporary relevancy of Marxist historical analysis and its capacity actually to ground the often important insights of critical theory in materially embedded social relations and experiences of struggle and subordination, power and resistance, accumulation and accommodation. Third, and finally, the essay closes with an explanation of the ironies and potency of an anti-Marxist critical theory in the context of the 1990s.

IDEOLOGY AND EPOCH

Ideology, as Terry Eagleton has recently reminded us, is a complex term with an even more complicated historical evolution.[7] It is also rather suspect in most intellectual circles at the moment, a process of denigration that Eagleton notes is not unrelated to the current fashion of poststructuralist thought and the contemporary assumptions and trends of postmodernity as a peculiarly distinct *fin-de-siècle*. It is nevertheless useful, both in terms of situating poststructuralism and postmodernism as particular meanings in the present of the 1990s and in locating them historically, to adopt a conception of ideology drawn from those who both founded historical materialism and inaugurated modern understanding of ideology as a central category in the linked projects of interpreting *and* changing the world.

At the risk of sliding over many qualifications and eliding not a few problematic writings, Marx and Engels nevertheless developed an appreciation of ideology as a material constraint on the possibility of revolution. As in much of the elaboration of the concepts of historical materialism, their method was polemical, a striking out at what was inadequate and *ideological* in the philosophical conventions of their time. Against the idealized advances of Enlightenment thought (which marked a turning point away from blind obedience to superstition, illusion, and divine authority), Marx and Engels propounded a radical-ized extension of Enlightenment reason, insisting not on the liberatory potential of dehistoricized ideas and abstractions, but rather on the powerful determination of profane social activity. In *The German Ideology* Marx and Engels assailed as ideological the idealism that refused acknowledgement of the primacy of actual humanity, the determining power of social relations over the consciousness of those relations.[8] For Marx and Engels, then, ideology was originally and fundamentally the construction of false consciousness, the obscuring of the primacy of social practice, and the reification of ideas and categories as ruling forces in history. Much muddled in later years, as the term came to be associ-ated with varied meanings associated with different movements and personalities of revolutionary opposition, ideology's tangled history as a concept parallels the history of Marxism: relatively coherent throughout the years of the Second International, it fragments in the aftermath of World War I.[9]

It is the fundamental premise of this essay that poststructuralism is the ideology of a particular historical epoch now associated with postmodernity. Alex Callinicos has recently argued, with considerable conviction and force, that postmodernity does not exist as some sharp and fundamental break from "the modern," a scepticism also at the core of Marshall Berman's exploration of the experience of modernity.[10] They may be right, although for the purposes of this essay the matter is somewhat beside the point. It is perfectly plausible to accept that the late twentieth century has witnessed a series of shifts in the cultural arena, even perhaps in the realm of political economy, without, of course, seeing this as a fundamental transformation of the mode of production. Many sites of "representation" and related fields of "design," by which the spatial and cultural aspects of our lives are ordered through the reconstruction of modernism's locale, the urban landscape, can be scrutinized in ways that suggest recent change in literary genres, art and architecture, cinema, and the technology of cultural diffusion, the case of video being undoubtedly the most dra-matic. I see no necessity to deny that all of this means something culturally and is related to material structural transformation, most markedly the rise and fall of what some social theorists designate a Fordist regime of capitalist accumulation.[11] *Contra* Callinicos (who does strike some telling blows) are the resolutely historicized and materialist recent texts of Frederic Jameson and David Harvey. Taken together,

Jameson's *Postmodernism: or, the Cultural Logic of Late Capitalism* and Harvey's *The Condition of Postmodernity: An Enquiry into the Origin of Cultural Change* present a complementary account of the remaking of a capitalist cultural order in the late twentieth century. But unlike most postmodernists, these Marxists refuse to see this restructuring of fundamental features of the non-biological reproductive realm as a remaking of the capitalist mode of production. Postmodernity, for Jameson and Harvey, whatever differences in emphases they choose to accentuate, is an epoch of *capitalism*, as fundamentally continuous with the exploitation and accumulation of earlier times as it is discontinuous in its forms of representational expression.[12] And, like the Los Angeles of Mike Davis' *City of Quartz*, this postmodernity as capitalist condition is made, not outside of history, but inside its relations of power and challenge, struggle and subordination.[13]

What a Marxist reading of postmodernism rejects, then, is not the *condition* of contemporary cultural life, which, admittedly, is open to many contending historical materialist readings, one of which might well lay stress on the cultural movement into postmodernity. Rather, Marxism rejects the *ideological* project of rationalizing and legitimating this postmodern order as something above and beyond the social relations of a capitalist political economy. In the words of the American advocate of poststructuralism, Mark Poster, this notion of postmodernism is not unrelated to the dismissal of Marxism:

> In the first half of the twentieth century marxist theory suffered three setbacks: (1) the establishment of bureaucratic socialism in Eastern Europe; (2) the rise of fascism in Central Europe; and (3) the birth of the "culture industry" in Western Europe and the United States. These massive phenomena reshuffled the dialectical deck of cards. No longer could it be said that the working class is the standard-bearer of freedom, the living negation of domination, the progressive side in the contemporary class struggles that would surely end in a utopian community.

For poststructuralists such as Poster these "truths" (which, it must be pointed out, are eminently explainable through Marxist theory and have not shaken Marxism as a project of understanding) are only reinforced by even more recent events and developments, among them the decolonization and feminist movements and the rise of an ostensible information order.[14]

The making of poststructuralism as an ideological reaction to the failures of what was once a Stalinized, actually existing, socialism is thus fairly clear. As the working class is arbitrarily and conceptually displaced as the agent of social transformation, a seemingly unassailable dismissal following logically from the degeneration of the first workers' state, Marxism is overtaken by both its own political failures and the arrival of new social forces (the feminist and decolonization movements, to which could be added other sectors: peace, ecology, aboriginal, and "national" rights) and social formations, none of which are actually situated in anything approximating an elementary relationship to *actually existing capitalism*. In the process any sense of objective "reality" and its social relations is lost in the swirl of subjectivity that forces a retreat from class and an embrace of almost any and all other "identities," which are understood as expansive, discursive, and positively plural. It is the contention of this essay that poststructuralism is thus a project of mystification and obfuscation particularly attuned to the often submerged, occasionally explicit, politics of the moment; poststructuralism as theory is to postmodernity as epoch what idealism as philosophy was to the Enlightenment. This does not mean that it contains no insights or potential, only that left to its own ultimatist trajectory it will inevitably collapse into ideology.

What is poststructuralism? What is this new critical theory? This is a large question, the answering of which demands an understanding of much of the intellectual history of the last century.[15] But, bluntly put, poststructuralism emerged out of the theoretical implosions associated with Parisian intellectual life in the 1960s, most particularly 1968. By that date a French theoretical turn had concentrated the social anthropology of Claude Lévi-Strauss, Lacanian psychoanalysis, and a textually focussed Althusserian Marxism in a paradigm known as structuralism. What united these components of the French theoretical turn was a deep commitment to a scientific explication of the structural systems of human existence. In the cases of Lévi-Strauss and Lacan, interpretation of these structural systems was explicitly scaffolded on insistence that language was the foundation of all human activity, which was therefore understandable only in terms of the laws of linguistics as propounded by Saussure. From kinship systems to the unconscious, structuralism proclaimed a linguistic apprehension of reality. "All the anthropologist can do is say to his colleagues in other branches of study that the real question is the question of language," claimed Lévi-Strauss. "If you solve the problem of the nature and origin of language, we can explain the rest: what culture is, and how it made its appearance; what art is and what technological skills, law, philosophy and religion are."[16] For his part, Lacan "Saussurianized" psychoanalysis, declaring that "the unconscious is the discourse of the other . . . the symptom resolves itself entirely in a Language analysis, because the symptom itself is structured like a Language, because the symptom is a Language from which the Word must be liberated."[17] This linguistic scientism scorched Parisian Marxism in the 1960s, culminating in what Thompson and Norman Geras dubbed "the final idealism" of Althusser.[18] In the Althusserian reading of ideology "the only interests at work in the development of knowledge are interests internal to knowledge."[19]

With the Parisian events of 1968 a curtain descended on the analytic stage of structuralism. Its players experienced a certain banishment. With them went various projects – the Lévi-Straussian imposition of classifications and order, the Lacanian stress on the historicized subject, the Althusserian insistence on ideology's rootedness in class *interest* – although the swept stage, now occupied by poststructuralism, remained littered with the residue of structuralism, most particularly language as the site of meaning, power, and resistance. Poststructuralism was thus born of structuralism's demise. It carried a part of structuralism's legacy, most acutely in terms of the stress on language, but it refused many of structuralism's assumptions and purposes. In the writings of Michel Foucault, Jacques Derrida, Jean Baudrillard, Gilles Deleuze, and Jean-François Lyotard a re-evaluation of language and its meanings culminated in an intense interrogation of "the real," a relentless exposure of the ways in which knowledge/reason masked domination, and a blunt rejection of any and all projects – emancipatory or otherwise – that sought to impose or locate centres of power or resistance. To the structuralist interpretive order was orchestrated, a conscious construction of the human mind. For the poststructuralist, however, such order/ orchestration was to be deconstructed. In the words of Derrida, drawing upon Montaigne, the poststructuralist project was "to interpret interpretations more than things," a constant unravelling of language that easily slipped into a positioning that "everything became [or was] language." History, for Derrida, has always been conceived as but "a detour between two presences."[20]

Poststructuralist thought is extremely difficult to pin down and define with clarity precisely because it celebrates discursiveness, difference, and destabilizations: it develops, not as a unified theory, but as constantly moving sets of concentric circles, connected at points of congruence, but capable of claiming new and uncharted interpretive territory at any moment. Like the architectural innovations of the post-modern age, poststructuralist theory is defiant of boundaries, resists notions of the analytic equivalent of a spatial centre in the celebration of discursiveness and proliferating subjectivities, and elevates the unity to a virtue in a principled refusal of causality. Poststructuralism thus rationalizes, legitimizes, and indeed sanctifies the postmodern condition. Its role as ideology secures the present; in the process it severs this present from the past and limits the possibilities of its future.

In its beginnings, one of poststructuralism's attractions was undoubt-edly what Callinicos has referred to as its "openness to the contingencies, the uncertainties, the instabilities of history."[21] But ideol-ogies, always dependent on their capacity to illuminate *a part* of experience at the same time as they mystify it, have a tendency to overreach themselves in moments of extremist overconfidence. Postmod-ernity, an age of excess if there ever was one, pushes ideology masquerading as theory in precisely this direction.

This point has recently been made with great force in Robert Young's insistence that history has never been anything but problematic inas-much as it has always been an outcome of imperialistic plunder and the subordination of specific peoples of colour. Drawn to the "postcol-onialist" wing of critical theory, Young regards "History" as but one expression of the Eurocentric premises of Western knowledge, a flat-tened exercise in shoring up "the concept, the authority, and assumed primacy of, the category of 'the West'." He finds great solace in post-structuralism's questioning of history – which, abstractly, poses no problem for historical materialism, engaged as it is in the same project – and, more to the point, in postmodernism's achievements in precipita-ting us into a period of dissolution:

> Contrary, then, to some of its more overreaching definitions, post-modernism itself could be said to mark not just the cultural effects of a new stage of "late" capitalism, but the sense of the loss of European history and culture as History and Culture, the loss of their unquestioned place at the centre of the world. We could say that if ... the centrality of "Man" dissolved at the end of the eighteenth century as the "Classical Order" gave way to "History," today at the end of the twentieth century, as "History" gives way to the "Postmodern," we are witnessing the dissolution of the "West."[22]

The problem with this passage, and the book of which it is a part, is *not* that it alerts us to the need to scrutinize the making of history in ways sensitive to colonialism and its immense human costs. Rather, the difficulty with Young's deconstruction of "history" is its partial, amazingly self-selecting account of what constitutes the text of a highly differentiated historical practice: Toynbee, Trotsky, and E. P. Thompson are at least alluded to once or twice (although, amazingly, Victor Kiernan merits nary a nod), but only in passing, and in ways that homogenize historiographies designated "white"; C. L. R. James, Walter Rodney, and Jean Chesneaux are absent from this account, allowing Young to bypass histories made at particular points of intersection in which First and Third Worlds meet and white, black, brown, and yellow connect.

To be sure, Young's poststructuralist assault on History contains the kernel of challenge attractive to many who want to right the wrongs of a historiography rooted in racism. But it does so in ways that actually stifle the project of emancipation, suffocating it in an ideology of illusion. For the "West," as the site of capitalism's late twentieth-century power, is not, in any meaningful sense, in the throes of dissolution. Whatever the cultural reconstructions of postmodernity as a period of capitalist accumulation, "History" has hardly been displaced. Mere months after the publication of Young's words, the carnage of the Gulf War exposed the Achilles Heel of this kind of ideological trumpeting to the unequivocal and technologically superior blows of a "West" as bellicose and militantly militaristic as other, ostensibly long-buried capitalist social formations. Small wonder that Marxists such as Ellen Meiksins Wood, attentive to the history of capitalism, have thrown up their hands in despair at what poststructuralism as ideology has accomplished in a few short years. "At the very moment when the world is coming ever more within the totalizing logic of capitalism and its homogenizing impulses, at the very moment when we have the greatest need for conceptual tools to apprehend that global totality," protests Wood, "the fashionable intellectual trends, from historical 'revisionism' to cultural 'postmodernism,' are carving up the world into fragments of 'difference'."[23]

My sympathies obviously lie with Wood, and with a host of other Marxist and feminist commentary that has grappled with the rise of poststructuralism, but that is almost universally ignored by those championing the new critical theory.[24] This is not to say that Marxists need ignore the extent to which poststructuralist thought forces our sometimes partially closed eyes open to specific problems that have received perhaps less than adequate attention within the many streams of a highly variegated Marxist tradition, including the very "difference"

Wood seems to castigate. The importance of subjectivity and the self, of identities not reducible to class, of representation and discourse, of the problematic ambivalence of "knowledge" canonized within particular social formations where thought and power are not unrelated – all of which poststructuralism alerts us to even as it overdetermines analysis of this terrain off of its material referents – need not be denigrated by Marxists. Indeed, it is possible to actually explore specific texts of historical materialism to make the point that attention to discourse, even to the point of materializing it and exploring its role in determination, is not necessarily foreign to the Marxist project.

* * *

These are not good times to be a Marxist.

Yet they are times when being a Marxist remains, arguably, of fundamental importance. For at no time in the history of the twentieth century has Marxism and the practice of historical materialism been on shakier ground; at no time has the threat to the practice of Marxism – political and theoretical – been so great. Marxist social historians will play, at best, a small role in the revival of a genuinely proletarian politics. But even a small role, in these times, is well worth playing. It will not be played, however, by adapting to the ideological climate of the moment. Historical materialism, as the post-1956 texts of Marxists historiography revealed, can indeed address silences in Marx's writing, but only if the audible accomplishments of Marx and subsequent Marxists remain. Poststructuralism is too often a reification of such silences, a reading of history and politics that throws these silences into the arena of interpretation and action the better to create a deafening din drowning out the voice of Marxism, the analytic sentences of historical materialism, the presence and capacity of class to speak. To keep the practice of historical materialism alive, to refuse to succumb to the current wave of subjectivism, but rather to reassert the necessity of historicizing and materializing both our analysis and activity as Marxists, will be no mean achievement in the years to come. Doing this cannot help but contribute, in however limited ways, to the revival of a mass class politics of resistance that is the only force capable of turning back the destructive tides evident in both the intellectual and economic histories of our time.

NOTES

1. E. P. Thompson, *The Poverty of Theory & Other Essays*, London: Merlin, 1978, Karl Marx, *The Poverty of Philosophy: Answer to the "Philosophy of Poverty" by M. Proudhon*, Moscow: Foreign Languages, n.d., original 1847.
2. Associated with the much-publicized 1989 pronouncement of Francis Fukuyama that "What we may be witnessing is not just the end of the Cold War, or the passing of a particular period of postwar history, but the end of history as such," this position has gained much credence. For a journalistic statement see Richard Bernstein, "Judging 'Post-History,' the End to All Theories." *New York Times*, 27 August 1989. Responses from the Marxist left include the essays in Ralph Miliband, Leo Pantich, and John Saville, (ed.) *The Retreat of the Intellectuals: Socialist Register 1990*, London: Merlin 1990.
3. Note, for instance, the argument in Ellen Meiksins Wood, *The Retreat from Class: A New "True" Socialism*, London: Verso, 1986.
4. Frederick Engels, "Introduction to *Dialectics of Nature*," in Marx and Engels, *Selected Works*, Moscow: Progress, 1968, p. 353.
5. Again, this has historical parallels. See E. P. Thompson, "Outside the Whale," in *The Poverty of Theory*, pp. 1–34; Thompson, "Disenchantment or Default? A Lay Sermon," in Conor Cruise O'Brien and W. D. Vanech (eds) *Power and Consciousness*, New York University Press, 1969, pp. 149–81. Note as well, Norman Geras, *Discourses of Extremity: Radical Ethics & Post-Marxist Extravagances*, London: Verso, 1990, p. 62.
6. Fredric Jameson notes "One's occasional feeling that, for poststructuralism, all enemies are on the left, and that the principal target always turns out to be this or that form of *historical* thinking . . ." Jameson, *Postmodernism: or, the Cultural Logic of Late Capitalism*, Durham, North Carolina: Duke University Press, 1991, p. 217.
7. See Terry Eagleton, *Ideology: An Introduction*, London: Verso, 1991.
8. Karl Marx and Frederick Engels, *The German Ideology*, New York: International, 1947, pp. 6–7, 14–15.
9. For an overly brief statement see the entry on "ideology" in Tom Bottomore (ed.) *A Dictionary of Marxist Thought*, Cambridge, Massachusetts: Harvard University Press, 1983, pp. 219–23.
10. Alex Callinicos, *Against Postmodernism: A Marxist Critique*, New York: St. Martin's Press, 1990, Marshall Berman. *All That Is Solid Melts Into Air: The Experience of Modernity*, New York: Simon and Schuster, 1982.
11. See, among other writings, Mike Davis, *Prisoners of the American Dream: Politics and Economy in the History of the US Working Class*, London: Verso, 1986.
12. Fredric Jameson, *Postmodernism: or, the Cultural Logic of Late Capitalism*, Durham, North Carolina: Duke University Press, 1991; David Harvey, *The Condition of Postmodernity: An Enquiry into the Origins of Cultural Change*, Oxford: Basil Blackwell, 1989. For comment on these texts see Bryan D. Palmer, "The Condition of Postmodernity and the Poststructuralist Challenge to Political and Historical Meaning," *The Maryland Historian* (1993).
13. Mike Davis, *City of Quartz: Excavating the Future in Los Angeles* London: Verso, 1990.
14. Mark Poster, *Critical Theory and Poststructuralism: In Search of a Context*, Ithaca and London: Cornell University Press, 1989, pp. 1–3.
15. I have attempted to offer a brief overview of some of the salient intellectual developments in *Descent into Discourse: The Reification of Language and the Writing of Social History*, Philadelphia: Temple University Press, 1990, pp. 3–47.
16. G. Charbonnier, *Conversations with Claude Lévi-Strauss*, London: Jonathan Cape, 1973, pp. 154–5.

17. See, for instance, Jacques Lacan, *Speech and Language in Psychoanalysis*, trans. Anthony Wilden, Baltimore: Johns Hopkins University Press, 1968, esp. pp. 7–8, 27, 32.
18. Thompson, *The Poverty of Theory*; Norman Geras, "Althusser's Marxism: An Assessment," in *New Left Review* (ed.) *Western Marxism: A Critical Reader*, London: Verso, 1978, pp. 232–72.
19. Geras, "Althusser's Marxism," pp. 266, 268.
20. Note, especially, the important article, Jacques Derrida, "Structure, Sign, and Play in the Discourse of the Human Sciences," in Derrida, *Writing and Difference*, University of Chicago Press, 1978, pp. 279–80, 291–2.
21. Alex Callinicos, *Making History; Agency, Structure and Change in Social Theory*, Ithaca, New York: Cornell University Press, 1988, p. 3.
22. Robert Young, *White Mythologies: Writing History and the West*, London: Routledge, 1990, esp. p. 20.
23. Ellen Meiksins Wood, *The Pristine Culture of Capitalism: An Historical Essay on Old Regimes and Modern States*, London: Verso, 1991, p. 93.
24. Among many exemplary texts that could be cited see Peter Dews, *Logics of Disintegration: Poststructuralist Thought and the Claims of Critical Theory*, London: Verso, 1987; Norman Geras, *Discourses of Extremity*; Kate Soper, *Troubled Pleasures: Writings on Politics, Gender and Hedonism*, London: Verso, 1990.

Part II On history in the lower case

For and against the collapse of the lower case

EDITOR'S INTRODUCTION: FOR THE COLLAPSE OF THE LOWER CASE

Because many of the arguments used to undercut lower case history are similar to those delegitimizing the upper case History, then it is something of an arbitrary decision to put, say, Roland Barthes or Michel Foucault into this Part rather than the previous one, whilst clearly Hayden White's formal analysis of narrative historiography as such (which underpins much of Hans Kellner's approach) applies to both cases: in order to turn the arguably sublime past into historiography all narrative histories have to emplot, trope, argue for and position themselves relative to whatever it is they wish "to figure out." Nevertheless, because it is taken as read that metanarratives are passé, it is the impact of postist thinking on the citadel of the lower case that is currently calling into question this still resilient and resistent ideological articulation. Accordingly, the undercutting of this genre is crucial to consider. The first extract is from Barthes' classic polemic *The Discourse of History* (1967) wherein, as Geoff Bennington and Robert Young point out (in D. Attridge *et al.* (eds) *Poststructuralism and the Question of History*, Cambridge: Cambridge University Press, 1987) Barthes attacks historians' pretentions to deliver "the facts" as guaranteed by an independently existing reality (not actuality: the actuality of the past existed alright, it is its reality that has to be "made real by representation"). As Bennington and Young put it, Barthes' essay argues that the discourse of history performs a slight of hand whereby a discursive operator, the referent, "is projected into a realm supposedly beyond signification, from which position it can be thought to precede and determine the discourse which posits it *as* referent [whereas] . . . the fact can only have a linguistic existence, as a term in a discourse, and yet it is exactly as if this existence were merely the 'copy,' purely and simply, of another existence situated in the extra-structural domain of the 'real.' [Consequently] . . . the discourse of history is guilty of reducing the three-term structure of signification (signifier-signified-referent) to a two-term structure (signifier-referent), or rather of smuggling into this ostensibly two-term structure an illicit signified, 'the real in itself surreptitiously transformed into a sheepish signified'" (p. 3). As a seminal text, Barthes' essay repays careful consideration.

Despite various critiques, Michel Foucault's works are now, due to their path-breaking suggestability and range of application, amongst the most commented upon and used corpus in the fields of historical/cultural/discourse analysis. More than any other single person Foucault is responsible for transforming our understanding of vast swathes of Western intellectuality. The passage reproduced here (from "Nietzsche, Genealogy, History," in

D. Bouchard, *Language, Counter Memory, Practice*, Oxford: Blackwell, 1987) concerns Foucault's distinction between genealogical and "effective" history on the one hand and traditional history on the other, and between histories of discontinuity and upper case "teleological" and lower case "continuity and change" histories. Because for Foucault historical knowledge is inevitably positioned and "used for cutting," his notions of effective history/genealogy take away that mask of disinterest so essential to the practitioners of the lower case, and lines him up with Nietzsche:

> Historians take unusual pains to erase the elements in their work which reveal their grounding in a particular time and place, their preferences in a controversy – the unavoidable obstacles of their passions. Nietzsche's version of historical sense is explicit in its perspective. . . . Its perception is slanted. . . . It is not given to a discrete effacement before the objects it observes and does not submit itself to their processes; nor does it seek laws. . . . Through this historical sense, knowledge is allowed to create its own genealogy.

After Foucault, the ideology of disinterest so common in the doxa of proper history is deeply problematicized.

The next two readings (Hans Kellner's, "Language and Historical Representation," and Robert Berkhofer's, "The Challenge of Poetics to (Normal) Historical Practice)" move us toward a direct engagement with proper (normal) lower case historiography. For Kellner, the injunction laid on historians to "get the story straight," to tell what happened in the past for the "past's own sake," makes two inadmissable assumptions (1) that there is a story out there waiting to be told and (2) that this story can be got straight by historians using the right (empiricist-realist) methods. For Kellner the idea that the past has stories in it just waiting to be found – that the past is already in "the shape of stories" – makes no sense, whilst historiography has no agreed, correct method. Accordingly, getting the story "crooked" means looking at the historical text in ways which reveal the problematics which have shaped its strategies, however hidden or disguised they may be, looking especially at one of the "sources" rarely considered as a source, rhetorical language. As Kellner puts it: "we must recognize that [the] . . . fundamental distinction between primary and secondary sources excludes for consideration the *other* sources of discourse, the sources that make representation in language . . . possible, credible, and ethically effective. . . . Because the sources of history include in a primary sense . . . rhetoric, we cannot forget that our ways of making sense of history must emphasize the *making*." To get the story crooked is to understand how the "straightness" of any story is a rhetorical invention, i.e., the straightness and coherence of any historical story lies not in the "events" of the past but in an aesthetic, narrative form. It is this artificial straightness that Kellner explores and exposes.

Robert Berkhofer's "The Challenge of Poetics to (Normal) Historical Practice" draws not only on the works of Hayden White (see below, Chapter 33) but on Sande Cohen's *Historical Culture: On the Recoding of an Academic Discipline* (Berkeley: University of California Press, 1986), F. R. Ankersmit's *Narrative Logic* (The Hague: Martinus Nijhoff, 1983), Paul Ricoueur's *Time and Narrative* (Chicago: University of Chicago Press, 1984) and a host of other writers who have commented on the impact of literary and linguistic theory on historiography. (See also, for the impact of what Berkhofer refers to as "poetics," P. Carrard, *The Poetics of the New History*, Baltimore: Johns Hopkins University Press, 1992). Berkhofer's article – which is reproduced here in full as Chapter 14 – summarizes so much of what the undercutting of the lower case means; his essay (complete with not-to-be-dismissed diagrams) pulls together some of the possible radical consequences of poetics to normal historical practice.

11 Roland Barthes

The discourse of History

For History not to signify, discourse must be confined to a pure, unstructured series of notations. This is the case with chronologies and annals (in the pure sense of the term). In the fully formed (or, as we might say, "clothed") historical discourse, the facts related function inevitably either as indices, or as core elements whose very succession has in itself an indexical value. Even if the facts happen to be presented in an anarchic fashion, they still signify anarchy and to that extent conjure up a certain negative idea of human history.

The signifieds of historical discourse can occupy at least two different levels. First of all, there is the level which is inherent to the matter of the historical statement. Here we would cite all the meanings which the historian, of his own accord, gives to the facts which he relates (the motley costumes of the fifteenth century for Michelet, the importance of certain conflicts for Thucydides). Into this category also fall the moral or political "lessons" which the narrator extracts from certain episodes (in Machiavelli, or Bossuet). If the lesson is being drawn all the time, then we reach a second level, which is that of the signified transcending the whole historical discourse, and transmitted through the thematic of the historian – which we can thus justifiably identify as the form of the signified. So we might say that the very imperfection of the narrative structure in Herodotus (the product of a number of *series* of facts without conclusion) refers in the last instance to a certain philosophy of history, which is the submission of the world of men to the workings of the divine law. In the same way in Michelet, we can find that particular signifieds have been structured very strongly, and articulated in the form of oppositions (antitheses on the level of the signifier), in order to establish the ultimate meaning of a Manichean philosophy of life and death. In the historical discourse of our civilization, the process of signification is always aimed at "filling out" the meaning of History.

The historian is not so much a collector of facts as a collector and relater of signifiers; that is to say, he organizes them with the purpose of establishing positive meaning and filling the vacuum of pure, meaningless series.

As we can see, simply from looking at its structure and without having to invoke the substance of its content, historical discourse is in its essence a form of ideological elaboration, or to put it more precisely, an *imaginary* elaboration, if we can take the imaginary to be the language through which the utterer of a discourse (a purely linguistic entity) "fills out" the place of subject of the utterance (a psychological or ideological entity). We can appreciate as a result why it is that the notion of a historical "fact" has often aroused a certain degree of suspicion in various quarters. Nietzsche said in his time: "There are no facts in themselves. It is always necessary to begin by introducing a meaning in order that there can be a fact." From the moment that language is involved (and when is it not involved?), the fact can only be defined in a tautological fashion . . . We thus arrive at the paradox which governs the entire question of the distinctiveness of historical discourse (in relation to other types of discourse). The fact can only have a linguistic existence, as a term in a discourse, and yet it is exactly as if this existence were merely the "copy," purely and simply, of another existence situated in the extra-structural domain of the "real." This type of discourse is doubtless the only type in which the referent is aimed for as something external to the discourse, without it ever being possible to attain it outside this discourse. We should therefore ask ourselves in a more searching way what place the "real" plays in the structure of the discourse.

Historical discourse takes for granted, so to speak, a double operation which is very crafty. At one point (this break-down is of course only metaphorical) the referent is detached from the discourse, becomes external to it, its founding and governing principle: this is the point of the *res gestae*, when the discourse offers itself quite simply as *historia rerum gestarum*. But at a second point, it is the signified itself which is forced out and becomes confused with the referent; the referent enters into a direct relation with the signifier, and the discourse, solely charged with *expressing* the real, believes itself authorized to dispense with the fundamental term in imaginary structures, which is the signified. As with any discourse which lays claim to "realism," historical discourse only admits to knowing a semantic schema with two terms, the referent and the signifier; the (illusory) confusion of referent and signified is, as we know, the hallmark of auto-referential discourses like the performative. We could say that historical discourse is a fudged up performative, in which what appears as statement (and description) is in fact no more than the signifier of the speech act as an act of authority.

In other words, in "objective" history, the "real" is never more than an unformulated signified, sheltering behind the apparently all-powerful referent. This situation characterizes what we might call the *realistic effect*. The signified is eliminated from the "objective" discourse, and ostensibly allows the "real" and its expression to come together, and this succeeds in establishing a new meaning, on the infallible principle already stated that any deficiency of elements in a system is in itself significant. This new meaning – which extends to the whole of historical discourse and is its ultimately distinctive property – is the real in itself, surreptitiously transformed into a sheepish signified. Historical discourse does not follow the real, it can do no more than signify the real, constantly repeating that *it happened*, without this assertion amounting to anything but the signified "other side" of the whole process of historical narration.

The prestige attached to *it happened* has important ramifications which are themselves worthy of historical investigation. Our civilization has a taste for the realistic effect, as can be seen in the development of specific genres like the realist novel, the private diary, documentary literature, news items, historical museums, exhibitions of old objects and especially in the massive development of photography, whose sole distinctive trait (by comparison with drawing) is precisely that it signifies that the event represented has *really* taken place. When the relic is secularized, it loses its sacred character, all except for that very sacredness which is attached to the enigma of what has been, is no longer, and yet offers itself for reading as the present sign of a dead thing. By contrast, the profanation of relics is in fact a destruction of the real itself, which derives from the intuition that the real is never any more than a meaning, which can be revoked when history requires it and demands a thorough subversion of the very foundations of civilized society.

History's refusal to assume the real as signified (or again, to detach the referent from its mere assertion) led it, as we understand, at the privileged point when it attempted to form itself into a genre in the nineteenth century, to see in the "pure and simple" relation of the facts the best proof of those facts, and to institute narration as the privileged signifier of the real. Augustin Thierry became the theoretician of this narrative style of history, which draws its "truth" from the careful attention to narration, the architecture of articulations and the abundance of expanded elements (known, in this case, as "concrete details"). So the circle of paradox is complete. Narrative structure, which was originally developed within the cauldron of fiction (in myths and the first epics) becomes at once the sign and the proof of reality. In this connection, we can also understand how the relative lack of prominence (if not complete disappearance) of narration in the historical science of the present day, which seeks to talk of structures and not of chronologies, implies much more than a mere change in schools of thought. Historical narration is dying because the sign of History from now on is no longer the real, but the intelligible.

12 Michel Foucault

Nietzsche, genealogy, history

"Effective" history differs from traditional history in being without constants. Nothing in man – not even his body – is sufficiently stable to serve as the basis for self-recognition or for understanding other men. The traditional devices for constructing a comprehensive view of history and for retracing the past as a patient and continuous development must be systematically dismantled. Necessarily, we must dismiss those tendencies that encourage the consoling play of recognitions. Knowledge, even under the banner of history, does not depend on "rediscovery," and it emphatically excludes the "rediscovery of ourselves." History becomes "effective" to the degree that it introduces discontinuity into our very being – as it divides our emotions, dramatizes our instincts, multiplies our body and sets it against itself. "Effective" history deprives the self of the reassuring stability of life and nature, and it will not permit itself to be transported by a voiceless obstinacy toward a millenial ending. It will uproot its traditional foundations and relentlessly disrupt its pretended continuity. This is because knowledge is not made for understanding; it is made for cutting.

From these observations, we can grasp the particular traits of historical meaning as Nietzsche understood it – the sense which opposes "wirkliche Historie" to traditional history. The former transposes the relationship ordinarily established between the eruption of an event and necessary continuity. An entire historical tradition (theological or rationalistic) aims at dissolving the singular event into an ideal continuity – as a teleological movement or a natural process. "Effective" history, however, deals with events in terms of their most unique characteristics, their most acute manifestations. An event, consequently, is not a decision, a treaty, a reign, or a battle, but the reversal of a relationship of forces, the usurpation of power, the appropriation of a vocabulary turned against those who had once used it, a feeble domination that poisons itself as it grows lax, the entry of a masked "other." The forces operating in history are not controlled by destiny or regulative mechanisms, but respond to haphazard conflicts. They do not manifest the successive forms of a primordial intention and their attraction is not that of a conclusion, for they always appear through the singular randomness of events. The inverse of the Christian world, spun entirely by a divine spider, and different from the world of the Greeks, divided between the realm of will and the great cosmic folly, the world of effective history knows only one kingdom, without providence or final cause, where there is only "the iron hand of necessity shaking the dice-box of chance." Chance is not simply the drawing of lots, but raising the stakes in every attempt to master chance through the will to power, and giving rise to the risk of an even greater chance. The world we know is not this ultimately simple configuration where events are reduced to accentuate their essential traits, their final meaning, or their initial and final value. On the contrary, it is a profusion of entangled events. If it appears as a "marvelous motley, profound and totally meaningful," this is because it began and continues its secret existence through a "host of errors and phantasms." We want historians to confirm our belief that the present rests upon profound intentions and immutable necessities. But the true historical sense confirms our existence among countless lost events, without a landmark or a point of reference.

Effective history can also invert the relationship that traditional history, in its dependence on metaphysics, establishes between proximity and distance. The latter is given to a contemplation of distances and heights: the noblest periods, the highest forms, the most abstract ideas, the purest individualities. It accomplishes this by getting as near as possible, placing itself at the foot of its mountain peaks, at the risk of adopting the famous perspective of frogs. Effective history, on the other hand, shortens its vision to those things nearest to it – the body, the nervous system, nutrition, digestion, and energies; it unearths the periods of decadence and if it chances upon lofty epochs, it is with the suspicion – not vindictive but joyous – of finding a barbarous and shameful confusion. It has no fear of looking down, so long as it is understood that it looks from above and descends to seize the various perspectives, to disclose dispersions and differences, to leave things undisturbed in their own dimension and intensity. It reverses the surreptitious practice of historians, their pretension to examine things furthest from themselves, the grovelling manner in which they approach this promising distance (like the metaphysicians who proclaim the existence of an afterlife, situated at a distance from this world, as a promise of their reward). Effective history studies what is closest, but in an abrupt dispossession, so as to seize it at a distance (an approach similar to that of a doctor who looks closely, who plunges to make a diagnosis and to state its difference). Historical sense has more in common with medicine than philosophy; and it should not surprise us that Nietzsche occasionally employs the phrase "historically and physiologically," since among the philosopher's idiosyncracies is a complete denial of the body. This includes, as well, "the absence of historical sense, a hatred for the idea of development, Egyptianism," the obstinate "placing of conclusions at the beginning," of "making last things first." History has a more important task than to be a handmaiden to philosophy, to recount the necessary birth of truth and values; it should become a differential knowledge of energies and failings, heights and degenerations, poisons and antidotes. Its task is to become a curative science.

The final trait of effective history is its affirmation of knowledge as perspective. Historians take unusual pains to erase the elements in their work which reveal their grounding in a particular time and place, their preferences in a controversy – the unavoidable obstacles of their passion. Nietzsche's version of historical sense is explicit in its perspective and acknowledges its system of injustice. Its perception is slanted, being a deliberate appraisal, affirmation, or negation; it reaches the lingering and poisonous traces in order to prescribe the best antidote. It is not given to a discreet effacement before the objects it observes and does not submit itself to their processes; nor does it seek laws, since it gives equal weight to its own sight and to its objects. Through this historical sense, knowledge is allowed to create its own genealogy in the act of cognition; and "wirkliche Historie" composes a genealogy of history as the vertical projection of its position.

13 Hans Kellner

Language and historical representation

PREFACE

Get the story crooked!

These are dangerous words, I recognize, to put into a book on historical discourse, especially if the author wants historians as well as literary scholars to read the book and to think about it seriously, as I certainly do. Just to get the story *straight* is the first duty of the historian, according to an influential tradition of scholarship, which presumes (a) that there *is* a "story" out there waiting to be told, and (b) that this story can be told straight by an honest, industrious historian using the right methods. On this view, to get the story "crooked" can only entail dishonesty, incompetence, or devious willfulness, none of which I endorse.

However, I do not believe that there are "stories" out there in the archives or monuments of the past, waiting to be resurrected and told. Neither human activity nor the existing records of such activity take the form of narrative, which is the product of complex cultural forms and deep-seated linguistic conventions deriving from choices that have traditionally been called rhetorical; there is no "straight" way to invent a history, regardless of the honesty and professionalism of the historian. Indeed, the standards of honesty and professionalism are to be found in precisely those conventions, both in what they permit or mandate and in what they exclude from consideration. All history, even the most long-term, quantified, synchronic description, is understood by competent readers as part of a story, an explicit or implicit narrative. The longing for the innocent, unprocessed source that will afford a fresher, truer vision (that is, the romantic vision) is doomed to frustration. There are no unprocessed historical data; once an object or text has been identified as material for history, it is already deeply implicated in the cultural system.

Getting the story crooked, then, is a way of *reading*. It means looking at the historical text in such a way as to make more apparent the problems and decisions that shape its strategies, however hidden or disguised they may be. It is a way of looking honestly at the *other* sources of history, found not in archives or computer databases, but in discourse and rhetoric. In other words, *this is a book about historical sources*. One must agree with Arnaldo Momigliano when he writes that the "whole modern method of historical research is founded upon the distinction between original and derivative authorities." At the same time, we must recognize that this fundamental distinction between primary and secondary sources excludes from consideration the *other* sources of discourse, the sources that make representation in language (as opposed to the other arts) possible...

Because the sources of history include in a primary sense the fundamental human practice of rhetoric, we cannot forget that our ways of making sense of history must emphasize the *making*. To get the story crooked is to understand that the straightness of any story is a rhetorical invention and that the invention of stories is the most important part of human self-understanding and self-creation.

PART ONE: THE OTHER SOURCES

History and Language

Continuity is the central intuitive certainty we have about history. From this moment back to the Reformation, or to the Magna Carta, or to the construction of the pyramids is an unbroken span of time, moment to moment. There is no rational reason to believe that Joshua (with God's help) could extend the length of a day in order to win a battle, nor that time would stop for decades around Sleeping Beauty's castle. However, this is only an intuition, and not provable, strictly speaking. History, furthermore, could never claim to be about the continuous past itself; at best, it is a reasoned report on the documented sources of the past, whatever form those sources may take. Yet these sources are clearly not continuous, nor is conscious human experience of time continuous.

What is the source of continuity, then? Why do we intuit and represent and defend the continuity and essential unity of history? The assumptions do not come from the documentary sources, from existing historical texts, or from our own lives. Rather, the source of the assumption that the past is in some sense continuous is a literary one. What is continuous is not so much reality, or the form in which reality exists (as artifact) in its obvious discontinuity, but the form in which our culture represents reality. Continuity is embodied in the mythic path of narrative, which "explains" by its very sequential course, even when it merely reports. A strong working suspicion arises that the intuition of historical continuity has less to do with either documentary fullness or personal consciousness than it has with the nature of narrative understanding. "This, then that" is a structure dependent on the amazing powers of the concept "then," which virtually sums up what seems to be the historical point of view. To promote "this, that" as a syntactic model of history would be to resort to the ostensibly prehistoric chronicle (or worse, annalistic) form of representation, or to espouse the catastrophic, inexplicable transformations of apocalyptic thinkers, found to some extent in the work of N. O. Brown or the early Foucault. And there is still the comma ("This, that") and the order of presentation (not "That, this") to consider. It is hard to distinguish the boundaries between the intuited continuity of reality and the relentless powers of narrative to make things continuous.

Yet no narrative can seem continuous in its beginning and ending; there the fact that a narrative, a history, is a discontinuous thing in a world of discontinuous things becomes all too apparent. As a narrative fact, a fact of language, it points to the scandal of general discontinuity. It is the source of concern . . . about sources. At the boundaries of the historical text, the general problem of presenting an image of a past presumed to be continuous becomes evident. If beginning and ending a historical text are artful, literary acts, then are not historical periods, or historical events themselves, equally literary creations, composed by the same conceptual processes?

Champions of a more textual approach to historical writing are often attacked on moral grounds. "History" – the true and verifiable story of human experience – is the guarantor of reality, of the meaning of human society and values, and of human liberties, we are told. To suggest that historical representation has an inevitable basis in the cultural forms it takes is "reductive," aiming to show that the text is nothing but a fiction, a willful creation. The results of this dangerous form of activity can be only a wanton disregard for fact, abandonment of standards of verification, loss of cultural identity, rejection of past victims and their memory. From the beginnings of the critical study of sources (wherever that beginning is assumed to be), the social and political dangers of inquiring too deeply into the sources have been repeated. A morally decent community depends upon a respect for reality; and reality for us depends on a certain notion of representability, or so the argument goes.

Rhetoric, representation, and reality, however, cannot be separated from one another. To do so is to repress that part of human reality that accounts for our understanding, convictions, and values. The moral high ground of the historical realists (who are actually less proponents of the material reality of the past than opponents of the material reality of the historical text) is always won at the expense of language and its imperatives, the "other" sources of historical representation.

THE DEEPEST RESPECT FOR REALITY

The purpose of an introductory chapter which focuses the sections that make up the book to follow is a questionable one; it is my contention from the start that *focus* is in a certain sense the enemy (albeit a valuable and necessary enemy) of any worthwhile discussion of the problems involved in historical writing and language, the problems around which all of the chapters in this book revolve. The power of the optical imagery of "focus" and "clarity" as a measure of sensible discourse and responsible thought is so great and generally unquestioned that the metaphorical status and implications of this imagery remain invisible. Sometimes we cannot see what is involved in "focusing" precisely because it is so well-focused a concept. In the summer of 1985, however, I heard an exchange that called the notion of focus into question for me.

It was the last morning of a conference in West Germany on narrative and history, sponsored by the journal *History and Theory*, a time when the conference participants sit around a vast table, having heard all the talk, read all the papers, and finally say to each other what is on their minds. An Australian philosopher of history trained in the Anglo-American school uttered at one point a phrase that, I have no doubt, he took to be innocent and self-evident, an article of faith for all who sincerely care about historical matters. To wit: "After all, what counts is to get the story straight." Across the huge table, a British historian-critic, whose historiographical work has emphasized the structural underpinnings of historical thought, shot back the report: "Oh, but you see, the point is precisely to get the story *crooked*." Around the table, the facial responses to Stephen Bann's remark seemed (in my view) to divide the international gathering in half: on the one hand were the smiles of those who had a sense that they had just heard something as true as it was clever, even if they were not quite in agreement as to how "getting the story crooked" was the point; on the other hand, the exasperated grimaces of those who, even if they could accept a fundamentally rhetorical description of the processes of historical representation, could not accept the playfulness of this response, its apparent abdication of epistemological responsibility and perhaps of reality itself.

I thought about getting the story crooked for a long time. My problem was not deciding how to make sense of it; rather, it made sense in many different ways. I thought at once, for example, of Hayden White's assertion in *Metahistory* that it is the tension between modes of explanation, emplotment, ideology, and structure that do not "naturally" align themselves that causes a work to retain that special power found in the classics of historiography, as opposed to the shorter-lived consistencies of the doctrinaires. "Getting the story crooked" in that sense is what distinguishes Michelet from Guizot even more than their differences of politics and personality, although, to be sure, politics and personality are very much involved in the kind of story they chose to tell.

A second, more personal and trivial, event happened more recently, putting Bann's remark into the perspective that I want to present here. I had dropped my opera glasses several years ago, jolting them uselessly out of alignment. They would not focus. After shopping a bit for new ones, I decided to look again at the insides of my troubled glasses. The usual lenses, prisms, and eyepieces fell victim to the tiny screwdriver, but I could not improve on the situation. Reassembling the thing, I noticed some tiny sets of holes at each side of the prism chambers, lilliputian screws therein. Proceeding empirically, I was able to adjust the sprung prisms back into alignment. At last I could focus. Whereas before there had been two images, one above and to the side of the other, now there was one – magnified eight times. Before this accidental discovery, I was all too aware that the object in my hand was an instrument of calculated distortions, bending light, bouncing it about, delivering it to my eye (which does rather the same thing, I gather) for a precise purpose, such as getting a better view of Tannhäuser and

Venus from the balcony in the opera house. After the adjustment, lenses and prisms were forgotten, the better to enjoy (or deplore) the matter at hand. My view was straight, not crooked. The glasses themselves disappeared, so to speak. Bann's point came to mind. To examine the historical text, we must see it "crooked," even if doing so makes it harder to attain the precise purpose of the text. To see the text straight is to see *through* it – that is, not to see it at all except as a device to facilitate knowledge of reality.

The case of my opera glasses is not so different, in fact, from the metaphor offered by Timothy Reiss in his book *The Discourse of Modernism*. Reiss claims that the *telescope* is the basic model for the modern "analytico-referential" way of knowing, and that such a model entails not only a semiotic (or rhetorical) shift, but also a special investment in a new notion of what reality is.

> The word, the very concept of sign, passed down the telescope with the image, so to speak, until it was conceived of as a simple mental creation, possessing a quite arbitrary relationship with the thing. The sign had been in all ways the equal of the thing. Now the word has become as it were a means of visualizing the object. It has become the mark of, but also a bridge over, a new space between the intellect and the world. It is now possible to turn an abstract system into a true knowledge of a real world, one taken as *not* ordered by man.[1]

That history and literature were once equally part of a "republic of letters," in which writers of both sorts revealed the world through mimetic language, and the poet could claim as strong a hold upon reality as the historian, is so well known that it hardly needs mention. Literature as a technique blended into history as a technique; books of rhetorical rules for the writing of history were composed as late as the seventeenth century in a form unthinkable at a later date.[2] Mimesis, the claim to represent a reality external to the representer, was the essence of letters, history included, within the classical frame. This bygone mimesis was the proper study of mankind, instilled and expressed through rhetoric, for the consideration of the reader. History in this mode (Voltaire, Montesquieu, Gibbon) presented itself as matter for active reflection and judgment, rather than as an image of a missing reality empirically proven by critical methodology. The historical narrator was as active and "visible" in his text as the fictional narrator of the eighteenth-century novel, perhaps because both narrators had a certain sort of reader in mind, a reader competent to ponder the problems and paradoxes of whatever material was at hand, a reader free from the self-incurred tutelage that Kant had warned against in his famous essay "What Is Enlightenment?" – in other words, a reader the equal of the author.[3]

The breakdown of the classical frame signaled the liberation of literature from standards of mimesis by thrusting into the foreground of literature the radical authenticity of the inner experience of romanticism, an experience that often demonstrated its authenticity by rejecting formal language, or even language altogether. As the poets cast off their mimetic heritage, historians, as though stunned by the sudden shift of ground, were forced to reclaim the terrain of realistic representation, but without the irony and self-assurance of an earlier fashion. While they did so, new techniques of realistic representation became increasingly virtuosic, but less evidently rhetorical: the silhouette, for example, or the historical diorama, or even the new science of taxidermy astonished people in the eighteenth and early nineteenth centuries with their "realism," putting the notion of mimesis, or realistic representation, on an entirely different level.[4] Mimesis, long the property of rhetoric and its tools, has left language for other parts. How could the historian compete on this new ground? For Prosper de Barante the answer was to place chunks of reality in his text as extensive quotation; for Augustin Thierry, to place numerous touches of "local color" in his work to create a multiple perspective. But neither of these relatively self-conscious responses won out.

Ranke's solution to the problem of the relation of the historical text to the documents from which it is fashioned was to separate the documentary chunks of reality from the image of reality, with the proviso that the image (the historical text "above" the gash on the page separating text from notes) is entirely verifiable below the line, showing but not presenting the past. Stephen Bann describes the process:

> The aim to "show what actually happened" is breathtakingly free of the circumspection of *mimesis*. Indeed my references to the ideal of "life-like" representation, in taxidermy, in the diorama and in the daguerreotype, have been largely devoted to establishing a representational space in which Ranke's claim could be seen to have meaning: a space in which new techniques were explicitly devoted to securing an overpowering illusion of presence. But I would wish to repeat my reservation about the "novelty" of this aim, which can appropriately be seen as the intensification through technique, of the

conditions of representation implicit in Renaissance perspective. In this light, the "colourless" virtue of Ranke can be regarded as a disavowal of language, of the historical *signifier*, and Ranke's nineteenth-century reputation (which still persists) as the mythic perpetuation of this disavowal. By comparison, the relative undervaluation of Thierry, despite his strict contemporaneity with Ranke, should be understood in the light of his determination to assert simultaneously the claims of language and of science.[5]

The claim of language disappears in the straight, "colourless" (Lord Acton's description) Rankean *showing*; the transparency of his telescope becomes "visible" only when a crooked reading reasserts that claim and the reality it embodies.

Crooked readings of historical writing are beginning to abound; these studies unfocus the texts they examine in order to put into the foreground the constructed, rhetorical, nature of our knowledge of the past, and to bring out the purposes, often hidden and unrecognized, of our retrospective creations.[6] The ideology of focused representation itself is an important subject for reflection. The narratological problem of beginnings and endings, for instance, is a special issue in historiography because it demonstrates in an obvious way how the fundamental choices made by historians affect the stories they tell and reveal the nature of their historical understanding. To begin a history of the American people with the Plymouth landing entails a plot very different from one that starts with Columbus or with the Constitutional Convention. To end a history with the outbreak of war between the North and the South frames a kind of story quite different from one that leads to Reconstruction. Beginnings and endings are never "given" in our universe of life *in* time, yet without conventionalized temporal frames – historical periods – the landmarks that prevent events in time from swirling meaninglessly would be gone. When beginnings and endings are not strongly marked by events, we find a notion of history in which discrete human events have a much reduced place; certainly, the *Annales* school exemplifies this. In Chapter 3 my discussion of historical beginnings describes some of the reasons why readers of history are never confused by always entering a story in the middle.[7]

This detour by way of beginnings and endings suggests only one of the strategies of crooked readings. The matter of metaphor, and figurative language in general, is a powerful tool for readers of history. I am not thinking primarily of the traditional praise given to "classic" historians for their vivid use of language, of "style in history". Far more important are the middle-level, regulative metaphors of history, which generate explanations rather than adorn them: the organic figures of growth, life-cycles, roots, seeds, and so on; the figures of time with their rises and falls, weather catastrophes, seasons, twilights; the figures of movement (flow of events, crossroads, wheels); the technical figures of construction, gears, chains; theatrical figures of stage, actors, contest.[8] Most of all, of course, the figure of History as pedagogue, ever "teaching" "lessons." On a more basic level than the study of middle-level metaphor is Hayden White's development of the theory of tropes (the four elementary figures of speech interpreted as fundamental modes of thinking) as "deep structural" principles that regulate historians at every step, and often appear themselves in disguise as stages of historical development. Part III of this book is devoted to these "deep" figural structures, their implications as generators of narratives, and the anxieties that such implications bring forth.

The issue of narrative has re-emerged lately in historical studies. Although the debate often sticks to the conventional question "Should historians tell stories?" the essence of the problem is better addressed in the terms of Paul Ricoeur, who suggests that all understanding of meaning in time is a narrative understanding, even if it is an understanding of a history of "long duration," within which occur those "quasi-events" that take centuries to transpire. If all historical understanding is a narrative understanding then, Ricoeur asserts, this understanding is entirely controlled and guided by the basic armature of narrative, what Aristotle called *muthos* or plot.[9] This emphasis on historical emplotment is an enormous advance over previous ways of reading history because it spotlights the innumerable choices that must be made at every turn; to emphasize the choices that must be made and rejected is to unfocus, to read crookedly, the historical text.[10]

Ultimately, however, discussions of the historical text must come down to the question of *sources*. From the beginnings of historical production down to the present maturity (or dotage) of the nineteenth-century Western professional historical consciousness, the notion that a historian is only as good as his or her sources has been an influential one. The eyewitness testimony of Thucyclides gives way to the dreamed-of "discovery" of a trove of documents (whether by Poggio Bracciolini or Robert Darnton), but the surest professional rewards go to those whose sources are the freshest and most virginal. The historian's sources are, as we have been taught, those particles of reality from which an image of the past is made; while few historians object to the idea that histories are produced, most will assert that the guarantee of adequacy in the historical account is found in the sources. If the sources are available, scrupulously and comprehensively examined according to the rules of evidence, and compiled in good faith by a reasonably mature professional, the resulting work will more or less "image" reality. Rhetoric, poetics, even dialectics (in the medieval sense) are subsidiary issues here because of the primacy of the source.

The word "source," so central to historical methodology of all sorts, deserves historical scrutiny. The use of the word in English to signify the raw materials of historical research is a late and figural one, dating from the late eighteenth century, but the word itself may be traced five centuries before that. As "the fountain-head or origin of a river or stream; the spring or place from which a flow of water takes its beginning," the word "source" appears in the fourteenth century; this meaning is still a current one. It is not difficult to understand the metaphoric transformation from a hydraulic to a documentary "source," "a work, etc., supplying information or evidence (esp. of an original or primary character) as to some fact, event, or series of these."[11] The earliest traceable source of "source" is the Latin *surgere*, "to surge."[12] As water gives life, so sources give life to history; the hydraulic metaphor reveals itself when one speaks of sources drying up. In German, the language in which much of the modern historical method was first codified, the word for "source" is *Quelle*, which has precisely the same association with water, although it stems from an entirely different etymological root.[13]

Two polar points of view confront the issues of history, sources, and language. On the one hand there is the attitude that historical substance always rests upon the materials that make up its sources, and that any significant change in our vision of the past will result from an advance in research that unearths new facts. This approach sees the research operations as the infrastructure and the written historical text as the superstructure. Another position takes just the opposite tack. On this view, it is the mental protocols, always linguistic at base, that are infrastructural, while the facts are the superstructural materials used in creating some expression of this structural vision. Quite a different picture emerges if we are to maintain that rhetoric, or more generally mental and linguistic conventions, are primary, and that consequently *they* are the actual sources of historical work. This reading suggests that history is not "about" the past as such, but rather about our ways of creating meanings from the scattered, and profoundly meaning*less* debris we find around us. This view of the past asserts a chaos, potentially terrifying in its indifference to the needs of humanity, or, perhaps, sublime in its destructive course. Such a view is found in Schiller's historical lectures and in Nietzsche (Schiller-hater that he was), and seems more a throwback to the older historical understanding because it presents history as an object of active contemplation, feeling, even reverie; contemplating history in this manner is active and creative precisely because of the essentially meaningless face behind what is contemplated. There is no story *there* to be gotten straight; any story must arise from the act of contemplation. To understand history in this way is not to reject those works which make claims to realistic representation based upon the authority of documentary sources; it is rather to read them in a way that reveals that their authority is a creation effected with other sources, essentially rhetorical in character. This, we may say, is the way of reading "crookedly."

The rhetoric of research and evidence is governed by principles of selection and patterning that seem to be hardly rhetorical at all; to read research operations as the practice of a rhetoric is to maintain that the "facts" of history (about which there is generally no dispute) are not the "givens," but rather the "takens," so to speak. These facts are "taken" in large part from the language and cultural understanding within which they must be expressed, and thus possess a literary dimension that invades the very act of research itself. The medievalist Nancy Partner notes: "Archives contain many interesting things, but Truth is not included among them." What, then, is the truth of history?

NOTES

1. Timothy Reiss, *The Discourse of Modernism*, Ithaca, 1982, 54.
2. Arnaldo Momigliano, *Studies in Historiograpy*, New York and London, 1966, 11.
3. Lionel Gossman, "History and Literature: Reproduction or Signification," in *The Writing of History: Literary Form and Historical Understanding*, ed. Robert Canary and Henry Kosicki, Madison, 1978, 23. In "Voltaire's *Charles XII*: History Into Art," *Studies in Voltaire and the Eighteenth Century* 25 (1963), 691–720, Gossman emphasizes the visual aspects of Enlightenment historiography: "The true heroes and conquerors are the intellectuals, the spectators of the great comedy. What at first appears to be their humiliation – their impotence, their non-participation in history – turns out to be their triumph. As pure see-ers they transcend both blind existence (history and the human condition) and arbitrary power (others). The reason of the intellectuals, unsullied by desire, untainted by will, becomes a pure seeing" (715). Yet because the Enlightenment historian possesses his text as an aesthetic object, he fails to "get it

crooked," so that – in Gossman's words – "[i]ts inner dynamic is never perceived and all the figures in it remain masks" (716).

4. Cf. Stephen Bann, *The Clothing of Clio: A Study of the Representation of History in Nineteenth-Century Britain and France*, Cambridge, 1984, 30.

5. Ibid.

6. F. R. Ankersmit, Stephen Bann, Roland Barthes, Lionel Gossman, Dominick La-Capra, Linda Orr, Nancy Partner, Paul Ricoeur, and Hayden White are only a few of the many scholars involved in unfocusing historical and other forms of realistic non-fictional texts.

7. In "Making Up Lost Time: Writing on the Writing of History." *Speculum* 61:1 (1986), Nancy Partner notes: "All past events, persons, and phenomena, however abstractly defined, emerge into identity only as part of a formal pattern which controls time. 'Tick' = origins, causes, predisposing factors, fundamental premises. 'Tock' = results, effects, achievements, recovered meanings. In the 'middle' our plot enables us to identify manifestations, symptoms, developments, characteristics" (93).

8. Alexander Demandt's *Metaphern für Geschichte: Sprachbilder und Gleichnisse im historisch-politischen Denken* (Munich, 1978) offers a vast catalogue of middle-level metaphors.

9. Paul Ricoeur *Time and Narrative* vol. 1, trans. Kathleen McLaughlin and David Pellauer, Chicago, 1984.

10. See Chapter 12. "Narrativity in History: Post-Structuralism and Since."

11. *Oxford English Dictionary*, Oxford, 1971, s.v.

12. Literally, *surgere* is "to lead straight up," and is composed from "*sub-*, up from below + *regere*, to lead, rule." The Indo-European root of *regere* is regi. the sense of which, "to move in a straight line," leads to a host of words signifying rectitude and law, and regalism and regime, which direct in a straight line. See *The American Heritage Dictionary of the English Language*, Boston, 1976, s.v. source.

13. Goethe, in *Faust*, exploited the multiple implications of the word for history. See the discussion of *Quellen* in Goethe's *Faust*, in Chapter 6, "Figures in the *Rumpelkammer*: Goethe, Faust, Spengler."

14 Robert Berkhofer

The challenge of poetics to (normal) historical practice

Among the challenges to the historical profession, few seem more important – and less heeded – than those concerning the poetics of normal historical practice. Contemporary literary theory defies the very intellectual foundations of current professional historical practice by denying the factuality that grounds the authority of history itself. That the past is not the same thing as history creates the methods as well as the methodology of historical practice. That the history produced is not the same thing as the past itself creates the crisis of that practice given contemporary poetics. The extent to which the past and history can be said to be quite different poses the problems of poetics for historical practice.

Why poetic analyses achieve such devastating results in the eyes of so many historians today can be understood best if we follow the process by which historians create written history from past evidence according to what we might call "normal" history, borrowing Thomas Kuhn's older terminology for the stable paradigmatic exemplar in a discipline. What, in other words, must professional historians predicate about the past in their practices so as to represent it and thereby conceive it, according to what we today call a history in specific practice and history in general.

At the heart of normal historical practice is presumed to be the processes for obtaining facts about the past from evidence or remains from the actual living past, but the combination of those facts into a coherent narrative or synthesis is even more important in actual historical practice. Thus from sources presumed to be about as well as from (past) history the historian creates generalizations assembled into a synthesis that is once again in the present called (a) history. The ambiguity of the word *history* is deliberate, for the written history is supposed to reconstruct or portray past events, behaviors, thoughts, etc., as they once occurred. In diagram, therefore, the predicated idealized process of normal history looks like this. Solid lines designate what historians generally consider "empirically grounded" conclusions while the dotted line represents "inference" according to normal historical practice.

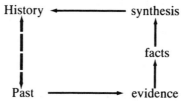

The presupposition grounding normal or traditional, historical practice is, therefore, that the historian's work is an accurate representation of an actual past, much as a map is to its terrain or a photograph to its subject. Thus the historian's written history acts as if it were a transparent medium to use a linguistic analogy between the past and the reader's mind, although both historian and reader would deny such an easy equation if raised to their consciousnesses. Nevertheless, the central presupposition of idealized, normal history production is transparency of medium, in which the exposition conveys or at least parallels factuality. Expository representation equals referentiality to use other terms, because the truthfulness or validity of such normal history productions is tested supposedly by reference to the actual past itself – a past presumed, however, to be more than the sources or remains from which it is derived.

Given this image of normal historical practice(s), then, historical methods designate the ways the historian gets from past evidence or sources to the discovery or creation of facts and then from those facts to their larger expository synthesis. The standard handbooks discuss how to validate sources as evidence and how to derive valid facts from such evidence. These standard handbooks tell little about how to connect those validated facts into a coherent narrative or synthesis beyond some propositions about style and rhetoric.[1] Since today historians believe moral and political judgements shape these steps whether in the selection of topics, synthesis of facts, or otherwise and that historians' images of basic human nature, etc., also influence these steps, let me modify the above diagram to reflect the two-way process involved in normal history production. Once again the solid lines indicate supposed empirical method and the dotted line shows inference according to normal historical practice.

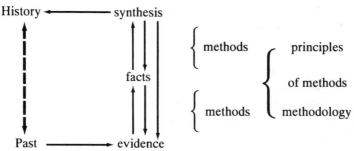

Professional historians theorizing about the nature of their task usually end their discussions at this point, because the past is not problematical beyond this point in practice. It is here that the poetics theorists begin. In other words, poetics raises issues that force a reconsideration of the entire left side of the diagram as I have represented the process.[2]

Such a conception of the historian's tasks still neglects the question we posed earlier: what must the normal historian presume about the past to conceive or represent it as history? To consider sources as evidence of the past, historians must predicate that they remain from past real events and behaviors and bear such a relationship to those past actualities that the historian can reconstruct those past events and behaviors from them. Whether documentary or other kinds of sources stand in indexical, iconic, or other semiotic relationship to the past (White 1982: 284–6) is less important to my argument at the moment than the general presupposition that present day remains and sources, no matter how numerous, are but a small part of what was once produced and, even more significant, reveal only a minute portion of full living past reality, regardless of how they are construed semiotically or otherwise.

Normal historians, as a consequence, worry about "capturing" the past in its full complexity or plenitude. Even the historical sociologist Charles Tilly argues, for example, that historical practice cannot analyze or connect all the experiences in past times, because "it is not humanly possible to construct a coherent analysis of the history of all social relationships; the object of study is too complex, diverse, and big" (1985: 12). Regardless of its difficulty, Henri Marrou makes just this effort the chief goal of normal history.

This brings us to the essential point: explanation in history is the discovery, the comprehension, the analysis of a thousand ties, which, in a possibly inextricable fashion, unite the many faces of human reality one to another. These ties bind each phenomenon to neighboring phenomena, each state to previous ones, immediate or remote (and in like manner to their results).

(1966: 192)

One need not agree with the philosophical premises of these scholars to see that each, like other historians, postulates the past as plenitude as well as real. In one sense, then, we can borrow Clifford Geertz's term "thick description" for this version of normal historical practice.[3]

For the historian the notion of "context" is both a way of comprehending past plenitude and portraying it according to thick description. It is therefore both an empirical method and a methodological premise for normal historical practice.

Contextualism is a – some would say *the* – primary method of historical understanding and practice. As a strategy it is both relational and integrative. The premise behind the strategy has been termed "colligation" by the philosopher W. H. Walsh:

> The historian and his reader initially confront what looks like a largely unconnected mass of material, and the historian then goes on to show that sense can be made of it by revealing certain pervasive themes or developments. In specifying what was going on at the time he both sums up individual events and tells us how to take them. Or again, he picks out what was significant in the events he relates, what is significant here being what points beyond itself and connects with other happenings as phases in a continuous process.
>
> (1974: 136)

The principle of historicism underlies this premise of historical practice, because what happened is described and therefore explained or interpreted in terms of when it happened and what happened around it at the same time or over time. Hayden White describes well what such an approach entails:

> The informing presupposition of contextualism is that events can be explained by being set within the "context" of their occurrence. Why they occurred as they did is explained by the revelation of the specific relationships they bore to other events occurring in the circumambiant historical space. . . . [T]he Contextualist insists that "what

happened" in the field can be accounted for by the specification of the functional interrelationships existing among the agents and agencies occupying the field at a given time.

(1973: 17–18)

Whether historians achieve true explanation by such a methodology is a matter of philosophic debate, but normal historians believe that they establish a pattern that is more than mere contiguity or contingency.[4]

Contextualism in the end copes with plenitude through seeking "unity in diversity," to use Walsh's phrase (1974: 143). As Walsh says,

> The underlying assumption here is that different historical events can be regarded as going together to constitute a single process, a whole of which they are all parts and in which they belong together in a specially intimate way. And the first aim of the historian, when asked to explain some event or other, is to see it as part of such a process, to locate it in its context by mentioning other events with which it is bound up.
>
> (1967: 23–4)

The methodological assumptions of contextual analysis tend to individualize the unit of study in terms of an overall uniqueness as the primary way of understanding history. By placing past events, behaviors, etc., in an ever-larger context – be it cultural, social or otherwise – their similarities are reduced in favor of their dissimilarities. As the context is enlarged, the overall pattern of meaning among the elements emphasizes the individuality of the total network of relationships. This principle applies to units within societies and cultures as well as between societies and cultures themselves studied as units. In all cases, the unit of study and its context become the same or coincident whether the historian posits contextualism as the basis for deducing facts from evidence or for synthesizing those facts into a written history.[5] This approach to contextualism does not raise the spurious issues of whether or not historians use generalizations, abstract from "reality," or even consume comparisons. They do. Rather contextualism presumes and produces uniqueness as its chief explanatory or interpretive mode, hence it also predicates that the past can be comprehended as a story whether on the level of synthetic exposition or as a way of evidentiary inference.

To context as plenitude, therefore, we must add the idea of narrative if we are to understand what historians presuppose about the past as history so as to produce current historical practice. The "return to narrative" discussion oversimplifies current conceptions of narrativity as applied to historical productions, because it equates all of narrative logic with simple story-telling. Thus for Lawrence Stone, who introduced the topic into the profession, "Narrative is taken to mean the organization of material into a single coherent story, albeit with sub-plots" (1979: 3). Thus, for him, narratives are "descriptive," not "analytical." The central focus is "on man, not circumstances." The historian deals with the "particular and specific rather than the collective and the statistical" (Ibid.: 3–4). Narrativity embraces more forms and pervades more aspects of history doing than Stone allows but his emphasis on the singularity of the story holds important implications for conceiving of the past as history.[6]

Just how narrative should be conceived as a form in historical practice is less important to my argument at the moment than considering at which points in the process of historical understanding the normal historian applies narrative logic. Historians apply plot and narrative logic (no matter how defined) not only to their synthetic expository efforts but also, I would argue following the reasoning of Louis Mink (1978: 129–49; 135–41), to the past itself as history. It is through postulating the past as a complex but unified flow of events organized narratively that enables normal historians to presume that their sources – as created by a past so conceived – allows (helps?) them to "reconstruct" the story of that past according to some narrative structure. Historical methods can operate only if historians conceive of contextual plenitude as a continuum of structured events organized according to the same narrative logic they employ in their own synthetic expositions, which supposedly mirror the past as homologously structured. Modern historical practice therefore only makes sense if historians predicate that the living past as contextual plenitude can be comprehended as a unified flow of events which in turn can be organized into some kind of unified exposition or story. Once again, the exposition as story and the flow of once actual events are presumed map-like or at least homologous. Whether the past is actually structured as we conceive narrative or only our understanding is structured in that manner,[7] we can see through a simple diagram how such predication of narrative structure affects historical practice and methodology. (In this and succeeding diagrams, the solid lines designate what I take to be empirically based in normal historical practice and the dotted lines represent connections made through presupposition in my opinion.)

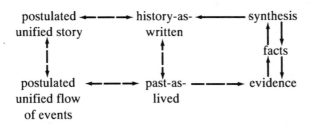

From the diagram, we can see that normal historical practice uses narrative structuring in two ways to transform the past into history. First, the paradigm of normal history presumes that there existed a total past that can be understood and constituted as history, even if only in the mind of God or an Omniscient Historian, according to narrative logic in some form. Second, each partial version of history can be organized according to the same logic both as synthesis of factuality and as the actual partial past it supposedly resembles. If we recall Stone's definition of narrative and Walsh's description of colligation, we see that they apply to both the partial and total versions of history. Only by predicating that the plenitude and context of (past) history is comprehended from the viewpoint of a third-person, omniscient narrator can normal history practice be understood: first, as the partial histories historians produce and, second, as the total historical context from which they are said to be part.

To suggest this multiple application of narrative organization to the postulated actual past as total and partial and to the representations of those pasts, I would add the notion of the "Great Story," (or what others might call the "Meta-story," the "Meta-narrative" or the "Meta-Text") of the total past that justifies the synthetic expositions of normal historians and the idea of the "Great Past" (or what others again might term the "Meta-past," "Ur-text" or "Meta-source,") that narrativizes the source material for all of the past as history.[8]

See the diagram on p. 146. I have chosen to designate the left side of this diagram the philosophy of history to indicate, first, that the nature of the Great Story was the province of classic or older, philosophy of history and, secondly, that the presuppositions of historical practice are the subject of the newer analytical philosophy of history in Anglo-American practice (as well as in later metahistory).

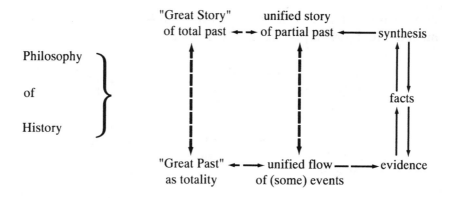

Such a view of normal historical understanding raises some obvious questions about the relation of partial stories or histories to the total or overall story of HISTORY itself. How many stories are there in the Great Story or Meta-narrative? How many pasts in the Great Past or "Ur-text?" How are variant versions or interpretations of the same partial past time period to be understood? Are variant interpretations to stand alongside each other as valid, autonomous synthetic expositions, or should all variants be reconciled by reference to the single Great Story? But, since the Great Story is nothing but a postulation of the paradigm of normal historical practice, what decides the validity of one version over another? Does measurement against the Great Past conceived as Ur-text decide between the variants? But, once again, the Great Past seems as much a paradigmatic presupposition as its synthetic equivalent, the Great Story.

To explore such questions about variant interpretations, we must turn to the issues of representation and referentiality as presumed in historical practice. The issues of representation and referentiality – or structure of interpretation as embodied in the process of synthesis versus the structure of factuality presumed as the basis of the synthesis – underlie some of the dichotomies considered basic to the historical discipline: abstraction versus concreteness, fiction versus factuality, art versus science, interpretation versus empiricism, construction versus reconstruction. The effect the normal historians try to achieve in their (re)presentations is the fusion of the structures of interpretation and factuality to impress the reader that the structure of interpretation *is* the structure of factuality, thereby reconciling and transcending the various supposed dichotomies endemic to the discipline. Rather than showing the reader how the (re)presentation is structured to *look like* total factuality, the normal historian's job is to make it appear *as though* the structure of factuality itself had determined the organizational structure of his or her account. The narrative organization, no matter what its mode or message, usually (re)presents its subject matter, in turn, as the natural order of things, which is the illusion of realism.[9]

Because normal historians try to reconcile variant interpretations by *reference* to facts rather than by arguments over the nature of narratives as such, they must presume in practice that factuality possesses some sort of coercive reality in their expositions of the partial past and their understanding of the Great Past. How can the profession's normal activities in meetings, books, and reviews be explained otherwise? If historians assumed with Roman Jakobson (1960: 350–77) or Roland Barthes (1974) that referentiality is just one mode of coding communications, just one part of a text's complex structure, then normal historical reviews, meetings, and books would take quite different forms than they do now.

According to my argument so far, history is distinguished from the past in normal disciplinary practice because historians need to divide representation from referentiality to make factuality the supposed test as well as the supposed basis of synthetic exposition in their profession. Rather than arguing this case further here, let me show what such a presupposition means in terms of an extended diagram. Without duplicating all parts of previous diagrams, I will indicate the relationship between representation and referentiality, basic to normal historical practice in general, by showing their connection to narrativity and factuality in particular. In brief, I link methods and history-as-written with the postulated unified stories through synthesis as historical construction and as narrative. Representation, then, concerns both the mode of presentation as embraced in that linkage and the nature of what that mode covers in the whole process of doing normal history. In terms of the diagram, representation covers the whole upper half of normal history practice, for it embraces both the synthesis produced and the way it is understood as "history." I also connect methods and pasts, partial and Great, as sources through evidence as historical reconstruction and as (f)actuality. Referentiality designates the mode of understanding presumed by the recourse to (f)actuality and supposedly achieved through historical reconstruction. In diagrammatic terms, once again, referentiality therefore covers the entire lower half of the process of doing normal history.

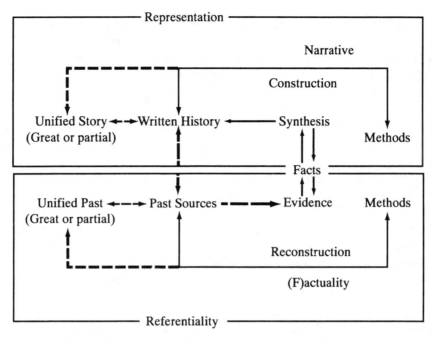

The paradigmatic presuppositional framework of normal history connects representation and referentiality through the transition from the derivation of facts from evidence to the synthesis of those facts into an exposition, as the diagram shows. Hence the statements so customary in the profession that history is both science and art, both a reconstruction and a construction. The two realms are postulated as connected but separated so that produced history can claim to be both empirical and factual but also literary in its larger sense – factual because of reference to (f)actuality, literary because of its synthetic (re)presentation of the partial and Great Stories.

It is this strict separation of representation and construction from referentiality and (re)construction that poetics, or the general theory of literary works, and contemporary literary criticism question and, therefore, in turn, challenge the basic paradigm of normal historical practice portrayed in the above diagram. In fact, poetics of history and criticism of history as literature (once again in its largest sense) take the lack of such separation as one of their basic premises.[10]

The core question that causes all the problems is quite simple: just what is the referent for the word "history"? It cannot be the past as such, because that is absent by definition. If linguistic analysts define words as signs or signifiers that denote objects in their stead, then "history" certainly fits the definition twice over. Normal history exists as a practice because of the very effort needed in the present to imagine (predicate) in the present an absent past actuality presumed to have once existed, but for that reason no one can point to the past in the same way that one can point to a horse or a tree (or even a picture of them) as the objects to which the words "horse" and "tree" refer.[11] The historian, at best, can point to actual remains that supposedly come to us from the past or to the sources historians use as evidence for their historical reconstructions. But as we know from the paradigm of normal history, those sources are employed to create pasts, whether partial or greater, that are larger than the sources themselves. Those pasts, however, depend upon still another predication or construction as observed by those interested in the poetics of historical practice.

The only referent that can be found for "history" in the eyes of such critics and theorists is the intertextuality that results from the reading of sets of sources combined with (guided by?) the readings of other historians of these same or other sources as synthesized in their expositions. "History" refers in actual practice only to other "histories," in the eyes of these critics. Thus they fail to see much, if anything, in the distinction drawn by normal historians between fact and fiction, for factual reconstruction is really nothing but construction according to the working "fictions" of normal history practice, which, in turn, are the premises of both historical realism and realistic mimesis.

Such an analysis of historical productions and practices stands normal history on its head, so to speak. Much, if not all, of what normal history presents as factuality becomes subsumed into the synthetic side of historical practice and therefore questioned as to just what it does represent. In terms of our last diagram, representation embraces the entire process of doing history with referentiality referring to, at best, the actual documentary and other remains in the present presumed to come from a past postulated passed. According to this view, then, most (all?) of what is presented as (f)actuality is a special coding of the historians' synthetic expository texts, designed to conceal their highly constructed basis.[12] In our previously used terms, the partial stories are represented as if they mapped or mirrored the partial pasts themselves.

That normal historical practice attempts to make its representations appear to present information as if it were a matter of simple referentiality indicates that the premises of realism are basic to the paradigm. Realism enters historical practice to the extent that historians try to make their structure of factuality seem to be its own organizational structure and therefore conceal that it is structured by interpretation represented as (f)actuality. This is as true of analytic as narrative expositions: art is presented as a science quite literally in the former while a supposed historical science is transformed into an art in the latter.[13]

Many contemporary scholars under such an impression of historical practice see history as just another mode of coding words and texts according to conventional presuppositions about representing the past as history. That such coding is conventional also means it is arbitrary in a technical sense to many literary and other scholars today, because they argue realism is a cultural and not a natural category of representing things. In the end, such beliefs about realism and the arbitrary coding of the past in the present as history collapse all distinction between representation and referentiality, for the latter can only be the former. The signified (the past) is naught but the signifier (history); no referent exists outside the history texts themselves (Barthes 1970: 145–55).[14]

Ultimately, the Great Past is the Great Story and nothing but the Great Story according to this view. As with the partial stories and pasts, the Great Past is coded according to the same paradigmatic presuppositions of realism. But the Great Story is no less a predication or presupposition of the historical practice paradigm than the Great Past. Its referent can no more be pointed to than that of the Great Past. It exists in the mind of God or the Omniscient Historian to test and organize the variant versions of partial stories as (hi)stories. In practice, the Great Story is extrapolated from the many partial (hi)stories and they must, in effect, be the referent for the Great Story, if it can even be said to have one part from its own wishful predication in normal history itself.[15]

Now we can modify our previous diagrams to indicate the place of meta-understanding in historical practice from the viewpoint of the poetics of history. The presuppositions that ground the synthetic constructions of historical production or the coding of the past as narrativity in its most general meaning can be labelled "meta-story," "meta-narrative" or perhaps, in some sense, "meta-text." The phrases "meta-source" and "Ur-text" would seem to do the same for the presuppositions necessary to interpret sources as intertextual evidence of the story of the past as history, as might "meta-past" to designate the premises behind the narrativization of the Great as well as partial pasts. Meta-

narrativity, in its most general sense, pervades therefore the paradigmatic presuppositions of normal history both through the connection of
referentiality to representation and through the link between the partial
and larger pasts. Metahistory embraces the whole paradigm of presuppositions that create normal historical practice, so we replace the
philosophy of history with that term on the left of the diagram.

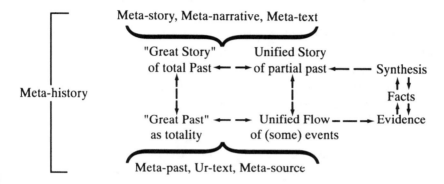

Metahistory equates meta-story with meta-past, that is, it collapses the
presuppositional framework underlying representation with the one
underlying referentiality, because the latter is considered primarily a
postulation of the former in the paradigm of normal historical practice.
Given this picture of the place of metahistorical premises in normal
history, historiography, the philosophy of history and metahistory all
integrally (inter)related, even coincident to the horror of normal historians.

One challenge of poetics to history lies in the implications of this equation of representation and referentiality, of the collapse of meta-past into
meta-story. Normal, that is, traditional, history is shown to be but a
conventional, hence arbitrary, mode of coding communication as factuality by presenting the representation as if it were entirely referential
and realistic. The transmutation of so much – some would say all – of
the referential side of history into the representational and narrative
side destroys the effect of overall factual authority claimed for historical
productions. Demystification of the historical enterprise, therefore, also
delegitimizes it as a discipline in this view.

Demystification of normal history probably also denies that any
single meta-narrative organizes either the partial or Great Stories. Thus
the story of the past cannot be read simply as a history of progress or

as decline, as cycles or as catastrophes, as class conflict or consensual pluralism, or even as change or continuity alone. No longer can any single master interpretive code be privileged over another as if one were somehow more correspondent to the (a?) "real" past than another. The denial of a single meta-narrative Great or partial story to organize history eliminates the omniscient viewpoint, probably the third person voice, and maybe the ethnocentrism so evident so long in history productions.[16]

Demystification therefore frees the historian to tell many different kinds of "stories" from various viewpoints, with many voices, emplotted diversely, according to many principles of synthesis. By denying the traditional meta-narrativity presuppositions, the historian liberates the ways of coding the past as history as well as how it is represented. For Hayden White, the demystification achieved through metahistory was intended to free the historian to emplot his narrative according to choice – or will – and therefore to move beyond the modernist stance of irony (1980: 433–34). To many normal historians, however, such a radical demystification appears to be the "end of [normal] history,"[17] because it implies that historical discourse refers to little or nothing outside itself. After all, they would ask, of what use are maps or photographs if one cannot be sure what they represent according to the usual realistic or mimetic criteria or even if they represent anything beyond their own surface configurations? By opening history construction therefore to greater possibilities of story-telling and interpretive coding than normal history allows, one appears to have eliminated the legitimating authority of factuality for history itself according to traditional premises.

But why is this a problem? Because normal history orders the past for the sake of authority and therefore power over its audience. Such power is asserted through voice and viewpoint in the paradigm of normal history. What is suppressed (repressed?) in normal historical narratives no matter what the mode of exposition, whether in so-called new or old histories, conservative, liberal or radical histories, is the personal production of the history which is claimed to map or mirror the past. By assuming a third person voice and an omniscient viewpoint, authors, be they left or right or in between politically, assert their power over their readers in the name of REALITY.

Authorial power over the reader is also asserted through the normal history presupposition of a single meta-story to organize the synthetic, representational side of history doing. Left and right seem to take similar positions on this matter. Those historians inspired by Karl Marx are no different in this search for a single metastory than those who follow Leo Marx, just to pick another Marx out of the historical hat. Those who follow Karl Marx seek a single interpretive code or master story, although they may disagree among themselves as to just what the key may be in interpreting the Ur-text according to Marx himself (Jameson 1979: 46). As with radical historians so too with liberal and conservative historians, for all must prove their cases by a single metastory, a single interpretive coding of the past; otherwise, the arbitrary nature of the produced history becomes easily evident to the audience and THE history loses its intended natural effect.

We could accept the death of normal history without declaring the death of history doing itself. Historical practice could be transformed with important implications for how the profession reads, produces, teaches and reviews what it calls "history." Poetics presents the profession with a plurality of possibilities. Rather than refusing to explore the many exciting possibilities in order to preserve old ways in the name of some metanarrative about the true nature of professional history doing, we might explore the many ways in which Clio can be clothed in garb less transparent to our humanistic colleagues and more in fashion with our late twentieth-century audience.

NOTES

1. Compare chapters 8–11 with chapters 3–7 in Louis Gosschalk, *Understanding History*, 2nd edn, New York, Alfred Knopf, 1969. See also parts two and three in Jacques Barzun and Henry F. Graf, *The Modern Researches*, New York, Harcourt, Brace and World, 1957. An exception to this generalization is Savoie Lottinville, *The Rhetoric of History*, Norman, University of Oklahoma Press, 1976.
2. Perhaps no better proof of this point may be offered than a comparison of my diagrams (1969) and the ones that follow. Readers familiar with that book will discover that some of its arguments and even some of its premises are quite different from – even contradicted by – many in this article.
3. This term, borrowed from Gilbert Ryle and popularized in the human sciences by Clifford Geertz, has its own context and therefore meaning in *The Interpretation of Cultures*, New York, Basic Books, 1973, ch. 1.
4. The argument over the nature of explanation in history and whether historical explanation achieves a true or proper explanation was a phase of a debate among philosophers and was associated with the names of Carl Hempel, William Dray and others. Many of the important articles are reprinted in Patrick Gardine (ed.) *Theories of History*, Glencoe, Ill., Free Press, (1959, pp. 344–475). Just as professional historians thought this argument irrelevant to their actual practices, so too do they feel that the New Historicism pertains to controversies internecine to the literary theory crowd and not pertinent to historians. In fact, they come away from examples of the New

Historicism feeling that these scholars establish homologies at best rather than any real (causal?) interconnections.

5. That is why the phrase "comparative history" seems an oxymoron to so many historians.
6. Compare another historian on narrative. Hayden White, "The Question of Narrative in Contemporary Historical Theory," in *History and Theory*, 23, 1, 1984, pp. 1–33. That historians might have grounds for confusion on the nature of narrative, see Wallace Martin, *Recent Theories of Narrative*, Ithaca, Cornell University Press, 1986.
7. Compare Paul Ricoeur, *Time and Narrative*, Chicago, Chicago University Press, 1984, with F. R. Ankersmit, *Narrative Logic: A Semantic Analysis of the Historian's Language*, vol. 7, The Hague, Martinus Nijhoff, 1983, on this matter.
8. I owe these insights to Louis Mink more than to any other scholar but see Peter Munz, *The Shapes of Time: A New Look at the Philosophy of History*, Middletown, Conn., Wesleyan University Press, (1977, chs. 7–8). My use of the "Great Story" is not meant to be a translation of *grand récit*. While all *grand récits* presume a great story, the great story need not presume any one master interpretive code.
9. On the presumption of realism in historical productions, see Lionel Gossman, "History and Literature: Reproduction or Signification?" in R. H. Canary and H. Kozicki (eds) *The Writing of History: Literary Form and Historical Understanding*, Madison, University of Wisconsin Press, 1978, pp. 3–40; Robert Anchor "Realism and Ideology: The Question of Order", *History and Theory*, 22, 2, 1983, pp. 107–19: and Wallace Martin, *Recent Theories of Narrative*, Ithaca, Cornell University Press, 1986, pp. 57–80. I have chosen not to distinguish between story and discourse in general, or between what is told and how it is told or between the order of events etc., as they are presented in the text as opposed to the order in which they supposedly occurred in time as represented in the text. Important as these distinctions are to historical productions, I feel they only complicate my argument without greatly affecting its main points.
10. Revealing is the entry under "Hi/story" in A. J. Greimas and J. Courtés (eds), *Semiotics and Language: An Analytical Dictionary*, trans. L. Crist and D. Patte *et al.*, Bloomington, University of Indiana Press, 1982, pp. 143–4. We do not have a work specifically aimed to help historians in their everyday production of history written from the perspective of poetics or semiotics, but see the provocative book by Sande Cohen, *Historical Culture: On the Recoding of an Academic Discipline*, Berkeley, University of California Press, 1986.
11. To use Ferdinand de Saussure's two examples (1970) to explain sign, signifier, and signified. The terms *signifier, signified* and *referent* are used differently by scholars depending upon their premises, but I believe my use here is both consistent and useful for the argument at hand. Compare the entries under "sign" and "reference" in Oswald Ducrot and Tzvetan Todorov, Encyclopedic Dictionary of the Sciences of Language, trans. C. Porter, Baltimore, Johns Hopkins University Press, 1979; and Greimas and Courtés (1982) as well as "signifier," "signification" and "signified" in the latter. Just as complicated as the relationships among these terms are the relationships involving "author" and "audience." See, for example, Michel Foucault, "What is an Author?" in J. V. Harare (ed.) *Textual Strangers: Perspectives in Poststructuralist Criticisms*, Ithaca, Cornell University Press, 1979, pp. 141–60; and William Ray, *Literary Meaning: From Phenomenology to Deconstruction*, London: Basil Blackwell, (1984). Once again, I have decided not to develop these possibilities in the interest of keeping my argument to its main points.
12. Regardless of how an historian might view the relationship between language and extra-linguistic phenomena, the factuality of an overall synthesis is not of the same order as that of the individual facts constituting it. As a result, this argument about the constructed nature of the synthesis holds, I believe, independent of one's philosophy of

language. For a sample of the debate on constructionism. See "The Constitution of the Past," *History and Theory*, XVI (no. 4 [Beiheft 16], 1977).

13. On the artistry of scientific history, see the interesting article by Donald N. McCloskey, "The Problem of Audience in Historical Economics: Rhetorical Thoughts on a Text by Robert Fogel," *History and Theory*, 24, (1985, pp. 22). That social science historians and traditional historians need not differ in their basic premises about the nature of historical "reality" is shown in Robert W. Fogel and Geoffrey R. Elton, *Which Road to the Past: Two Views of History*, New Haven, Yale University Press, 1983. Even a so-called hard social science can be read poetically: see, for example, Donald N. McCloskey (1985).

14. That *res gestae* equal *historia rerum gestarum* in normal historical practice is also the point of Munz (1977, ch. 8).

15. Even if the historians could recreate the actual past in its totality, such would still not be history as we conceive it today: historians would still have to select their themes and understandings of the past from the bewildering multiplicity of phenomena confronting them. Compare the conception of the "ideal chronicle" in Arthur C. Danto, *Narration and Knowledge*, expanded edition of *Analytical Philosoph y of History*, New York, Colombia University Press, 1985, pp. 149–82. To revert to the terms used in this article, even if the total past were reconstructed for historians, it would still not be the Great Past let alone the Great Story, without analysis and interpretation by historians – and professional ones at that – because the past as history cannot even be predicated without interpretation according to some customary presuppositional framework.

16. The ethnocentrism, indeed cultural hubris of contemporary industrial societies as embodied in normal historical practice was the main target of the well-known last chapter, "History and Dialectic," of Claude Lévi-Strauss (1966). That the discipline is organized by national histories and professional associations illustrates how deeply such ethnocentrism pervades the profession and how natural it seems to the discipline as organized academically. See the classic article by David M. Potter, "The Historian's Idea of Nationalism and Vice Versa," *American Historical Review*, 67, July 1962, pp. 924–50.

17. As some French intellectuals proclaimed for various reasons two or more decades ago. Vincent Descombes, *Modern French Philosophy*, trans. L. Scott-Fox and J. M. Harding, Cambridge, Cambridge University Press, 1980, pp. 27–32, 180–6, places the "end of history" and the "death of man" in an interesting philosophical and political context.

EDITOR'S INTRODUCTION: AGAINST THE COLLAPSE OF THE LOWER CASE

Gertrude Himmelfarb's well-known opposition to the new social history of the 1960s and 1970s turned in the 1980s and 1990s towards a new but related symptom of the recent/current turn away from traditional historiography; namely, postmodernism. In her short but succinct and thoughtful article, "Telling It As You Like It: Postmodernist History and the Flight from Fact" (*TLS* 16 October 1992) Himmelfarb accuses postmodernism of a range of sins: the deferred nature of any definitive interpretation, the deprivileging of previously valorized works, the linguistic constitution of "reality," and so on, all of which, for her, frees up historians to tell the past "any way they like." Engaging particularly with Hayden White but then turning to the use of postmodernism by various Marxists and feminists, postmodernism is yoked by Himmelfarb to the ideological left; indeed for her, postmodernism seems especially useful to – or even belongs to – the left. But it is more than that. For Himmelfarb laid-back, playful, radically innovative and creative postmodern historiography threatens the very existence of her notion of "proper" history. For unlike postmodernist histories which Himmelfarb regards in their ability to "make things up" as being "easy," traditional historiography is "hard." Herein Himmelfarb seeks – through the notion of difficulty – a way of rearticulating traditional histories. For although traditional history is hard it is "exciting precisely because it is hard." Consequently, it is this type of excitement which may prove "a challenge and inspiration for a new generation of historians." It is, she proposes, "more exciting to write true history . . . than fictional history . . . more exciting to try and rise above our interests and prejudices than to indulge them . . . more exciting to write a coherent narrative while respecting the complexity of historical events than to fragmentize history into disconnected units; more exciting to try to get the facts (without benefit of quotation marks) as right as we can than to deny the very idea of facts." And if these steps are taken, this difficult challenge accepted, so Himmelfarb concludes, "we will survive the 'death of history' – and of truth, reason, morality, society, reality, and all the other verities we used to take for granted and that have now been 'problematized' and 'deconstructed'. We will even survive the death of postmodernism."

This general approach is very similar to Geoffrey Elton's. One of the greatest champions of professional historiography, Elton has been lucidly criticizing Marxists and other ideologues for at least thirty years. His *The Practice of History* (1967) has stood as the "proper" historian's manual until today. In his 1990 Cook Lectures (published in his *Return to Essentials*, Cambridge, Cambridge University Press, 1991) Elton returns to the fray attacking now not only his old left-wing sparring partners – Christopher Hill, R. H. Tawney *et al.* – but theorists of a postmodern kind (i.e., theorists from Heidegger through Barthes, Foucault, Derrida to David Harlan and Hayden White). The selection reproduced here is taken from the declaratory first page of the Cook Lectures, and several pages from his chapter "The Burden of Philosophy," reiterating at its end, *pace* postmodernists, the proper historian's "search for truth," a truth to be found in the sources: "We historians are firmly bound by the authority of our sources (and by no other authority, human or divine)."

Gabrielle Spiegel's much cited article ("History, Historicism, and the Social Logic of the Text in the Middle Ages," *Speculum*, 65, 1990) does not demonstrate a dislike of postmodernism in the straightforward and rather polemical way in which Himmelfarb and Elton do. Spiegel's article is a persuasive, analytical dissection of what she sees as the impact of poststructuralist, textualist critiques of the lower case historian's "craft" or "practice." Yet, as I have indicated elsewhere (in *On "What Is History?": From Carr and Elton to Rorty and White*, especially Chapter One) Spiegel's critique of the textual dissolution of "the materiality of the sign" – arguably at the centre of her analysis – would perhaps only have weight if the materiality of the sign had never been "undissolved."

15 Gertrude Himmelfarb

Telling it as you like it: postmodernist history and the flight from fact

In literature, postmodernism amounts to a denial of the fixity of any "text," of the authority of the author over the interpreter, of any "canon" that "privileges" great books over comic books. In philosophy, it is a denial of the fixity of language, of any correspondence between language and reality, indeed of any "essential" reality and thus of any proximate truth about reality. In law (in America, at any rate), it is a denial of the fixity of the constitution, of the authority of the founders of the constitution, and of the legitimacy of law itself, which is regarded as nothing more than an instrument of power. In history, it is a denial of the fixity of the past, of the reality of the past apart from what the historian chooses to make of it, and thus of any objective truth about the past.

Postmodernist history, one might say, recognizes no reality principle, only the pleasure principle – history at the pleasure of the historian. To appreciate the full import of this, one should see it in the perspective of what might be called "modernist" history, familiarly known as "traditional" history.

Modernist history is not positivist in the sense of aspiring to a fixed, total, or absolute truth about the past. Like postmodernist history, it is relativistic, but with a difference, for its relativism is firmly rooted in reality. It is sceptical of absolute truth but not of partial, contingent, incremental truths. More important, it does not deny the reality of the past itself. Like the political philosopher who makes it a principle to read the works of the Ancients in the spirit of the Ancients, so the modernist historian reads and writes history in the same spirit, with a scrupulous regard for the historicity, the integrity, the actuality of the past. He makes a strenuous effort to enter into the minds and experiences of people in the past, to try to understand them as they understood themselves, to rely upon contemporary evidence as much as possible, to intrude his own views and assumptions as little as possible, to reconstruct to the best of his ability the past as it "actually was" – in Ranke's celebrated and now much derided phrase.

Historians, ancient and modern, have always known what postmodernism professes to have just discovered – that any work of history is vulnerable on three counts: the fallibility and deficiency of the historical record on which it is based; the fallibility and selectivity inherent in the writing of history; and the fallibility and subjectivity of the historian. As long as historians have reflected upon their craft, they have known that the past cannot be recaptured in its totality, if only because the remains of the past are incomplete and are themselves part of the present, so that the past itself is, in this sense, irredeemably present. They have also known that the writing of history necessarily entails selection and interpretation, that there is inevitable distortion in the very attempt to present a coherent account of an often inchoate past, that, therefore, every historical work is necessarily imperfect, tentative, and partial (in both senses of the word).

Historians have also known – they would have to be extraordinarily obtuse not to – that they themselves live and act and think in their own present, that some of the assumptions they bring to history derive from, and are peculiar to, their own culture, that others may reflect the particular race, gender and class to which they belong, and that still others (although this is made much less of today) emanate from ideas and beliefs that are unique to themselves as individuals. It did not take Carl Becker, in 1931, to discover that "everyman [is] his own historian"; or Charles Beard, in 1934, to reveal that "each historian who writes history is the product of his age." Beard pointed out that these propositions had been familiar "for a century or more" – thus antedating even Marx. Forty years before Beard delivered his famous presidential address to the American Historical Association, William Sloane, the *echt* establishment professor of history at Columbia University, inaugurated the first issue of the *American Historical Review* with a lead article announcing: "History will not stay written. Every age demands a history written from its own standpoint – with reference to its own social conditions, its thought, its beliefs and its acquisitions – and thus comprehensible to the men who live in it."

It is useful for historians to be reminded of what they have always known – the frailty, fallibility and relativity of the historical enterprise – if only to realize that these ideas are not the great discoveries of postmodernism. Yet in their familiar form, they are very different from the tidings brought by postmodernism. For the presumption of post-modernism is that *all* of history is fatally flawed, and that because there is no absolute, total truth, there can be no partial, contingent truths. More important still is the presumption that because it is impossible to attain such truths, it is not only futile but positively baneful to aspire to them.

In a sense, modernism anticipated and tried to forestall the absolutistic relativism of postmodernism by creating a "discipline" of history. Conscious of the deficiencies both of the historian and of the historical record, acutely aware of the ambiguous relationship between past and present, the profession created a discipline of checks and controls designed to compensate for those deficiencies. This is the meaning of the historical revolution that drew upon such diverse sources as Enlightenment rationalism, Germanic scholarship and academic professionalism to produce what was once called "critical history."

Critical history put a premium on archival research and primary sources, the authenticity of documents and reliability of witnesses, the need for substantiating and countervailing evidence; and, at a more mundane level, on the accuracy of quotations and citations, prescribed forms of documentation in footnotes and bibliography, and all the rest of the "methodology" that went into the "canon of evidence." The purpose of this methodology was twofold: to bring to the surface the infrastructure, as it were, of the historical work, thus making it accessible to the reader and exposing it to criticism; and to encourage the historian to a maximum exertion of objectivity in spite of all the temptations to the contrary. Postmodernists scoff at this as the antiquated remnants of nineteenth-century positivism. But it has been the norm of the profession until recently. "No one," the American historian John Higham wrote, "including the 'literary' historians, rejected the ideal of objectivity in the ordinary sense of unbiased truth; no one gave up the effort to attain it; and no one thought it wholly unapproachable." This was in 1965, well after Becker and Beard had "relativized" history but before Foucault and Derrida had "postmodernized" it.

From the postmodernist perspective, modernist, or traditional, history is as uncritical as the history it professes to transcend – as mythical and honorific as Nietzsche's "monumental" history. And it is all the more spurious because it conceals its ideological structure behind a scholarly façade of footnotes and the pretence of "facts" (in quotation marks, in the postmodernist lexicon). To "demythicize" or "demystify" this history, postmodernism has to expose not only its ideology – the hegemonic, privileged, patriarchal interests served by this history – but also its methodology, the scholarly apparatus that gives it a specious credibility. This is the twofold agenda of postmodernism: to free history from the shackles of an authoritarian ideology, and to release it from the constraints of a delusive methodology. The ultimate aim is even more ambitious: to liberate us all from the coercive ideas of reality and truth.

Theodore Zeldin was one of the first historians (as distinct from philosophers of history) to launch a serious assault upon traditional history. Traditional, or narrative, history, he argued, is dependent upon such "tyrannical" concepts as causality, chronology, and collectivity (the latter including such categories as nationality and class). To liberate it from these constraints, he proposed a history on the model of a *pointilliste* painting, composed entirely of unconnected dots. This would have the double advantage of emancipating the historian from the tyrannies of the discipline, and emancipating the reader from the tyranny of the historian, since the reader would be free to make "what lines he thinks fit for himself." More recently, Zeldin has gone so far by way of liberation as to liberate himself from the tyranny of history itself, this time by invoking a literary model. Truth, he has discovered, can be found only in "free history" – otherwise known as fiction – in testimony to which he has written a novel aptly titled *Happiness*.

Not all postmodernists go as far as Zeldin in seeking that ultimate liberation from history, but all share his aversion to the conventions and categories of traditional history. Chronology, for example, has been deconstructed by Dominick LaCapra, who explains that even so simple a fact as the date of an event depends on "what is for some historians a belief and for others a convenient fiction: the decisive significance of the birth of Christ in establishing a chronology in terms of a 'before' and 'after'."

Narrative history – "narrativity," as the postmodernist says – is the primary culprit, not only because it depends upon such arbitrary conventions as chronology, causality, and collectivity, but also because it takes the form of a logical, orderly structure of discourse that is presumed to correspond, at least in some measure, to the reality of the past, and thus communicate some truth about the past. This is the anathema of the postmodernist: the idea that there is a truth and a reality accessible to the historian, that history itself is something other than a fictional, rhetorical, literary, aesthetic creation of the historian.

The "aestheticization" of history is most evident in the work of the leading postmodernist philosopher of history, Hayden White. To the traditional historian, this kind of philosophy of history appears to be more philosophical than historical and more literary than philosophical. White's influential work, *Metahistory*, opens with a chapter entitled "The Poetics of History" outlining the strategy of the book. Each of his subjects, he explains, from Hegel to Croce, represents an aspect of the "historical imagination": metaphor, metonymy, irony, romance, comedy, tragedy, satire. (Another of his essays is called "The Historical Text as Literary Artifact.")

For White, as for postmodernism generally, there is no distinction between history and philosophy or between history and literature. All of history, in this view, is aesthetic and philosophic, its only meaning or "reality" (again, in quotation marks) being that which the historian chooses to give it in accord with his own sensibility and disposition. What the traditional historian sees as an event that actually occurred in the past, the postmodernist sees as a "text" that exists only in the present – a text to be parsed, glossed, construed, interpreted by the historian, much as a poem or novel is by the critic. And, like any literary text, the historical text is indeterminate and contradictory, paradoxical and ironic, so that it can be "textualized", "contextualized," "recontextualized" and "intertextualized" at will – the "text" being little more than a "pretext" for the creative historian.

In postmodernist history, as in postmodernist literary criticism, theory has become a calling in itself. Just as there are professors of literature who never engage in the actual interpretation of literary works – and even disdain interpretation as an inferior vocation – so there are professors of history who have never (at least to judge by their published work) done research in, or written about, an actual historical event or period. Their professional careers are devoted to theoretical speculation about the nature of history in general and to the active promotion of some particular methodology or ideology of history.

The philosopher Richard Rorty recently reported, with unconcealed satisfaction, that it is getting more and more difficult to find "a real live metaphysical prig" who believes in such outmoded ideas as "reality" and "truth." Historians may be more retrograde than philosophers, for one can still find a good number of historians who qualify as "real live historical prigs." But more and more historians, and not only philosophers of history, have come to share Rorty's contempt for such ideas. An essay in a recent issue of the *American Historical Review* casually observes that while "contemporary historians seldom believe any more that they can or should try to capture 'the truth'," this does not absolve them from passing judgment on their subjects. In support of this proposition, the author cites an earlier president of the American Historical Association, Gordon Wright, who had given it as his credo that "our search for truth ought to be quite consciously suffused by a commitment to some deeply held humane values." The quotation actually speaks against the thesis of this article, for Wright made the "search for truth" an inherent part of the commitment to "humane values." His presidential address was delivered in 1975, when it was still possible to speak respectfully of the search for truth – and, indeed, to speak of truth without the ironic use of quotation marks.

The disdain for truth, not as an ultimate philosophical principle but as a practical, guiding rule of historical scholarship, was dramatically illustrated a few years ago by a controversy that erupted in the profession and was widely reported in the press. A book on the Weimar Republic by a young Princeton historian, David Abraham, was criticized by several eminent historians for being full of errors – misquotations, faulty citations, unwarranted deductions from the sources – whereupon an equally eminent group of historians rallied to the defence of the author. The first line of defence was to impugn the political and personal motives of the critics; thus Arno Mayer and others claimed that the critics were really objecting to the Marxist thesis of the book rather than to its faulty scholarship, and were resentful of a novice who dared infringe on their turf. The second line of defence was to belittle the seriousness of the errors and the standards of scholarship that profess to make so much of them. Lawrence Stone described the mistakes as innocent faults of transcription, such as occur in any archival research and are typical of the "general messiness of life" (he did not explain how it happens that most of them support the contentious thesis); while Carl Schorske maintained that the errors, however "glaring and inexcusable," do not affect the "historical configuration" or "interpretive logic" of the book.

One of Abraham's defenders, Thomas Bender, in an article entitled "'Facts' and History," turned the argument against his critics, charging them with being so naive as to believe in "the absolute certitude of historical fact." To be sure, Bender conceded, documents should be "accurately transcribed and properly cited." But without inquiring into whether the documents in this case were so transcribed and cited, he proceeded to make his point: that the "historical imagination" is central to any historical work and that this involves a process of "imaginative creation" which goes well beyond documents and facts. Young historians, he concluded, will never learn their craft if their elders are "fact fetishists." (In the same spirit, Schorske decried as "facticity" the obsession with factuality; and Henry Turner, Abraham's main critic, anticipated that he himself would be accused of being a "vulgar factologist.")

Hard cases, it is said, make bad law. History, however, all too often consists of hard cases, and historical methods are designed to accommodate them. It is to the credit of postmodernists that they have not shirked what may be the hardest case in modern history, the Holocaust. With much sensitivity and agonizing, they have considered the implications of their theories and techniques, trying to avoid the suggestion that they are casting doubt on the narratives and "emplotments" of the Holocaust, still more on the reality of the Holocaust itself. Above all, they want to dissociate themselves from the "revisionist" school that denies both the evidence and the reality of the Holocaust. Yet committed as they are to a theory that repudiates any "realist" or "essentialist" notion of facts, that sees history (the past itself as well as the writing about the past) as inevitably "fictive," it is only by an "inordinately circuitous and abstract" mode of reasoning (as White describes it in a related context) that they can elude the most relativistic consequences of their theory – if not a denial of the fact of the Holocaust, then a denial of any objective truth about it.

On one occasion White goes so far as to retreat, for the moment at least and only for this "unique" situation, from the full import of his theory, creating a "middle voice" to express "something like the relationship to that event." "This is not to suggest," he adds, "that we will give up the effort to represent the Holocaust realistically, but rather that our notion of what constitutes realistic representation must be revised to take account of experiences that are unique to our century and for which older modes of representation have proven inadequate." A not unsympathetic historian describes the intent and effect of this compromise: "In his anxiety to avoid inclusion in the ranks of those who argue for a kind of relativistic 'anything goes,' which might provide ammunition for revisionist sceptics about the existence of the Holocaust, he undercuts what is most powerful in his celebrated critique of naive historical realism."

On less sensitive occasions, the postmodernist imagination is uninhibited and unapologetic. It is then, liberated from the delusion of "fact fetishism" and persuaded of the "fictive" nature of all history, that creative interpretation may take the form of fictional history.

This new kind of fictional history is very different from the familiar genre of historical fiction. The historical novel, as it has evolved from Walter Scott to the flourishing industry that it is today, has never been a challenge to traditional history, because it has been understood as a distinctive form of fiction, not of history – as historical fiction, not fictional history. It is only when history itself is "problematized" and "deconstructed", when events and persons are transformed into "texts," when the past is deprived of any reality and history of any truth, that the distinction between history and fiction is elided and fictional history becomes a form of history rather than fiction. History itself, all of history, is then seen as existing in a continuum with fiction, as essentially fictional. Where the late Arnaldo Momigliano deplored the "widespread tendency," as he saw it, to treat historiography as "another genre of fiction," the postmodernist applauds this tendency. White's "metahistory" has now been redefined as "historiographic metafiction."

Few historians go so far as Simon Schama, who introduced entirely fictional characters and scenes into what might appear to be a conventional work of history (*Dead Certainties*), identifying them as "pure inventions" only in an "Afterword." But many historians who shy away from any suggestion of fictional or even "metafictional" history welcome the invitation to be "inventive," "imaginative," "creative." Where once we were exhorted to be accurate and factual, we are now urged to be imaginative and inventive. Instead of "recreating" the past, we are told to "create" it; instead of "reconstructing" history, to construct or "deconstruct" it.

Formerly, when historians invoked the idea of imagination, they meant the exercise of imagination required to transcend the present and immerse oneself in the past. Today, it more often means the opposite: the imagination to create a past in the image of the present and in accord with the judgment of the historian. Schama cites Macaulay's view of historical imagination to support his own excursions into fictional history. History, Macaulay wrote, is a "debatable land" governed by two hostile powers: "Instead of being equally shared between its two rulers, the Reason and the Imagination, it falls alternately under the sole and absolute dominion of each. It is sometimes fiction. It is sometimes theory." But Schama does not quote the rest of this passage in which Macaulay places significant limits on the dominion of the imagination.

A perfect historian must possess an imagination sufficiently powerful to make his narrative affecting and picturesque. Yet he must control it so absolutely as to content himself with the materials which he finds, and to refrain from supplying deficiencies by additions of his own. He must be a profound and ingenious reasoner. Yet he must possess sufficient self-command to abstain from casting his facts in the mould of his hypothesis.

Nor does Schama quote another passage in the same essay in which Macaulay describes the "art of historical narration" as the ability to affect the reader's imagination "without indulging in the licence of invention"; nor, later still, Macaulay's comparison of the historian to the dramatist, "with one obvious distinction"; "The dramatist creates: the historian only disposes." Even Macaulay's great-nephew, G. M. Trevelyan, the most "literary" of historians, put the imagination under strict constraints:

The appeal of history to us all is in the last analysis poetic. But the poetry of history does not consist of imagination roaming at large, but of imagination pursuing the fact and fastening upon it. That which compels the historian to "scorn delights and live laborious days" is the ardour of his own curiosity to know what really happened long ago in that land of mystery which we call the past.

If postmodernism appeals to the creative imagination of the historian, it also appeals to the political imagination. Some Marxists and old-fashioned radicals are suspicious of postmodernism as being apolitical, passive, and thus conservative. Jürgen Habermas calls Foucault "neo-conservative," not only because he has been critical of Marxism, but because his "theoretical gestures" offer no positive alternative to capitalism. Yet one of Foucault's admirers describes him as "continuing the work of the Western Marxists by other means." The critic Terry Eagleton, a Marxist and "New Historicist", says of postmodernism: "Since it commits you to affirming nothing, it is as injurious as blank ammunition." But he goes on to exempt some leading postmodernists from that stricture, including Derrida himself:

Derrida is clearly out to do more than develop new techniques of reading: deconstruction is for him an ultimately *political* practice, an attempt to dismantle the logic by which a particular system of thought, and behind that a whole system of political structures and social institutions, maintains its force.

Others see postmodernism as peculiarly congenial to the post-Marxist forms of radicalism. Peter Stearns, editor of the *Journal of Social History*, notes the connection between postmodernism and the "currently-fashionable protest ideologies of the academic world" – anti-racism, anti-sexism, environmentalism. "Postmodernists," he observes, "are clearly spurred by a desire to find new intellectual bases for radicalism, given the troubles of liberalism and socialism."

Postmodernism is, avowedly and intentionally, far more radical than either Marxism or the new "isms" cited by Stearns, all of which are implicitly committed to the Enlightenment principles of reason, truth, justice, morality, reality. Postmodernism repudiates both the values and the rhetoric of the Enlightenment. In rejecting the "discipline" of knowledge and rationality, postmodernism also rejects the "discipline" of society and authority. And in denying any reality apart from language, it aims to subvert the structure of society together with the structure of language. There is nothing concealed in this agenda; it is the explicit, insistent theme of Foucault and Derrida and only slightly less insistent, but no less explicit, in the work of Hayden White.

In spite of White's plague-on-both-houses stance (repudiating conservative and Marxist historiography alike), he echoes the familiar Marxist theory in explaining traditional history as a reflection of the class interests of the bourgeoisie. His essay on the German historian Johann Droysen, subtitled "Historical Writing as a Bourgeois Science," describes history (and not only Droysen's history) "as part and parcel of the cultural superstructure of an age, as an activity that is more determined by than determinative of social praxis." Another essay, "The Politics of Historical Interpretation," strikes an equally Marxist note:

> The social function of a properly disciplined study of history and the political interests it served at its inception in the early nineteenth century, the period of the consolidation of the (bourgeois) nation-state, are well-known and hardly in need of documentation. We do not have to impute dark ideological motives to those who endowed history with the authority of a discipline in order to recognize the ideological benefits to new social classes and political constituencies that professional, academic historiography served and, *mutatis mutandis*, continues to serve down to our own time.

Provoked by the charge that his own relativism is conducive to "the kind of nihilism that invites revolutionary activism of a particularly irresponsible sort," White protests that this is not his intention: "Now I am against revolutions, whether launched from 'above' or 'below' in the social hierarchy and whether directed by leaders who profess to possess a science of society and history or be celebrators of political 'spontaneity'." His relativism, he says, is a counsel of tolerance rather than licence. Besides, in advanced countries, revolution is likely to result in the consolidation of "oppressive powers," since those who control the "military-industrial-economic complex hold all the cards." Instead of revolution, he proposes to subvert the social hierarchy by rejecting the conventional "discipline" of history – narrativity, objectivity, rules of evidence, and the rest of the "bourgeois ideology of realism" – and seeing the past as Schiller saw it, "as a 'spectacle' of 'confusion,' 'uncertainty,' and 'moral anarchy'." Only such a "utopian," "eschatological" view of history is consistent with "the kind of politics that is based on a vision of a perfected society."

In the vocabulary of postmodernism, this anarchic view of history is translated as "indeterminacy." And indeterminacy is a standing invitation to *creatio ex nihilo*. With all of traditional history discredited, the historian finds himself with a *tabula rasa* on which he may inscribe whatever interpretation he likes. This is why the principle of indeterminacy lends itself, paradoxically, to the determinacy of the race/class/gender trinity. By deconstructing both the "text" of the past and the "texts" of all previous histories, new histories can be created in accord with the race/class/gender interests of their creators – or with the political and ideological dispositions that historians conceive to be in accord with those interests.

The political potential of postmodernism has been seized most enthusiastically by feminist historians, who find the old Marxism and even some forms of the new radicalism unresponsive to their concerns. It is no accident (as the Marxist would say) that so many postmodernist historians are feminists, and that postmodernism figures so prominently in feminist history. Joan Wallach Scott explains the political affinity between postmodernism and feminism:

> A more radical feminist politics (and a more radical feminist history) seems to me to require a more radical epistemology. Precisely because it addresses questions of epistemology, relativizes the status of all knowledge, links knowledge and power, and theorizes these in terms of the operations of difference. I think poststructuralism (or at least some of the approaches generally associated with Michel

Foucault and Jacques Derrida) can offer feminism a powerful analytic perspective.

Feminist history is consciously and profoundly subversive, not only of traditional history but of earlier varieties of women's history. It belittles the kind of women's history that focuses on the experiences of women in particular events and periods. It even rejects the idea of "mainstreaming" women's history into general history – the "add-women-and-stir" recipe, as it is now called. The new feminist history, unlike the old women's history, demands that all of history be rewritten from a "consciously feminist stance," a "feminist perspective" – which is more often the perspective of the feminist historian than of the women who are the ostensible subjects of history. It is because of this ambitious goal that feminist history requires, as Scott says, a "radical epistemology" that defines all of history as essentially, irredeemably political. If traditional history is an instrument of patriarchal power, feminist history, by the same token, is an instrument for feminist power.

Thus it is that the "poetics" of history becomes the "politics" of history. Postmodernism, even more overtly than Marxism, makes of history – the writing of history rather than the "praxis" of history – an instrument in the struggle for power. The new historian, like the proletariat of old, is the bearer of the race/class/gender "war" – or rather "wars." And here lies another quandary.

What is sauce for the goose.... If the feminist historian can and should write history from her perspective and for her political purpose, why should the black historian not do the same – even if such a history might "marginalize" women? And why not the working-class historian, who might marginalize both women and blacks? (Feminist historians have criticized E. P. Thompson and other social historians on just this ground.) And why not the homosexual historian, who might marginalize heterosexuals? For that matter, why not the traditional dead-white-male (or even live-white-male) historian, who might marginalize (who has, in fact, been accused of marginalizing) all other species?

If "Everyman his own historian" must now be rendered "Everyman/woman his/her own historian" – or, as some feminists would have it, "Everywomyn her own herstorian" – why not "Every black / white / Hispanic / Asian / Native-American ...?" Or "Every Christian / Jew/ Catholic / Protestant / Muslim / Hindu / agnostic/atheist ...?" Or "Every heterosexual/homosexual / bisexual / androgynous / polymorphous/misogamous/misogynous ...?" And so on, through all the ethnic, racial, religious, sexual, national, ideological and other character-istics that distinguish people? This sounds like a *reductio ad absurdum*, but it is little more than is already being affirmed in the name of "multiculturalism."

Multiculturalism has the obvious effect of politicizing history. But its more pernicious effect is to demean and dehumanize the people who are the subjects of history. To pluralize and particularize history to the point where people share no history in common – no "generic" history, as it were – is to deny the common (generic) humanity of all people, whatever their sex, race, class, religion, and the like. It is also to trivialize history by so fragmenting it that it lacks all coherence and focus, all sense of continuity, indeed, all meaning.

From a postmodernist perspective, this is all to the good, for it destroys the "totalizing," "universalizing," "logocentric," "phallocen-tric," history that is said to be the great evil of modernity. Postmodernist history celebrates "aporia" – difference, discontinuity, disparity, contra-diction, discord, indeterminacy, ambiguity, irony, paradox, perversity, opacity, obscurity, anarchy, chaos. "We require a history," White explains, "that will educate us to discontinuity more than ever before; for discontinuity, disruption, and chaos is our lot." The modernist accuses the postmodernist of bringing mankind to the abyss of nihilism. The postmodernist proudly, happily accepts that charge.

It may be said that postmodernist history is of little importance in the profession at large, that it is confined to a self-described "vanguard" which has few disciples in theory and fewer still in practice. In sheer numbers, this may be the case, although it is difficult to make such a quantitative calculation. But the question of influence is not determined by numbers, as anyone who has followed the fortunes of Marxism in the academy and in our culture at large is aware; Marxism in the 1930s was far more influential than the number of avowed Marxists would suggest.

Postmodernism is less prevalent among historians than among lit-erary critics, although even in history it exercises a disproportionate influence because it tends to attract so many of the best and the brightest in the profession, especially among the young. How can bright, ambitious young historians resist the new, especially when it has the sanction of some of their most distinguished elders? How can they resist the appeal to be on the "cutting edge" of their profession? And how can they resist it when it carries with it not only the promise of advance-ment but the allure of creativity, imagination, inventiveness? And not only creativity but liberation from the tedium and rigour of the old "discipline" of history?

This last is a matter of more than passing importance, both in explaining the attraction of postmodernist history and its influence. In the old benighted days, an aspirant in the profession was required to go through the mandatory initiation rite known as "Historical Method-ology." That course, once the centrepiece of the graduate programme, is now obsolete because the idea of any "methodology," let alone a uniform, obligatory one, is regarded as "authoritarian" and "privi-ledged." The absence of such a course, the lack of any training in what used to be confidently called the "canon of evidence" – even more, the disrespect for any such canon – is itself a fact of considerable importance in the training (or non-training) of young historians. It has even affected some older historians, including some traditional ones, who now feel sufficiently liberated to dispense with such impediments to creativity as footnotes. This methodological liberation has done more to transform the profession, making it less of a "discipline" and more of an impressionistic "art," than any conscious conversion to postmodernism. It may, indeed, prove to be the lasting influence of postmodernism.

But what of postmodernism itself? Will it last? Is it just another of those intellectual fashions that periodically seize the imagination of a bored and fickle academia? Whatever happened to existentialism? In France, the source of most of these fashions, deconstruction is already *passé*. Can it survive much longer here? Given the volatility of intellectual and academic life, it is hard not to anticipate a not-so-distant future when postmodernism will be succeeded by something bearing the name of post-postmodernism.

In history, as in literature and philosophy, there almost certainly will be – the signs are already here – a disaffection with postmodernism, if only because the appeal of novelty will wear off. The "herd of indepen-dent minds," in Harold Rosenberg's brilliant phrase, will find some other brave, new cause to rally around. Out of boredom, careerism (the search for new ways to make a mark in the profession), and sheer bloody-mindedness (the desire to *épater* one's elders), the young will rebel, and the vanguard of today will find itself an ageing rearguard – much as the "new history" (social history) of an earlier generation has been displaced by this newer history. What is not at all clear, however, is the nature and degree of the rebellion – whether it will be a counter-revolution leading to a restoration (or partial restoration) of an older mode of history, or whether it will usher in a still newer mode, whose configuration we cannot begin to imagine.

One might think that a counter-revolution is already under way in the form of the "New Historicism," a linguistic version of Marxism which interprets "cultural productions" as the symbolic forms of "material productions" and "social relations." But while some of the members of this school (Fredric Jameson and Terry Eagleton, most notably) criticize postmodernism for being excessively aesthetic and insufficiently revolutionary, they are also attracted to those aspects of it that they recognize as truly subversive. Thus Eagleton praises feminist postmodernism not only for insisting that women have equal power and status with men, but for questioning the legitimacy of *all* power and status. "It is not that the world will be better off with more female participation in it; it is that without the 'feminization' of human history, the world is unlikely to survive." In the common cause of radicalism, structuralists and poststructuralists, new historicists and deconstructionists, have been able to overlook whatever logical incompatibilities there may be in their theories. Like the communists and socialists of an earlier generation, they have formed a "popular front," marching separately to a common goal. Thus the new historicism, so far from presenting a real alternative to postmodernism, has become an ally, if a somewhat uneasy one.

It is a cliché – and a true one – that no counter-revolution is ever quite that, that the *status quo ante* is never fully restored. In the case of history, what will stand in the way of a restoration of traditional history is not, as one might think, ideology; one can foresee a desire to return to a more objective and integrated, less divisive and self-interested history. What will be more difficult to restore is the methodology that is at the heart of that history. A generation of historians (by now, several generations as these are reckoned in academia) lack any training in that methodology. They may even lack the discipline, moral as well as professional, required for it. When Eagleton speaks of the "laid-back" style of postmodernism, he does not mean that it is casual, colloquial, or commonsensical – on the contrary, by normal standards of discourse, it is contrived, abstruse, and recondite – but rather that it is infinitely pluralistic and heterogeneous, renouncing all pretence of rational, logical, "enlightened" discourse. In the case of history, it has meant abandoning not only the conventions regarding the presentation and documentation of evidence, but the very idea of historical reasoning, of coherence, consistency, factuality. The postmodernist argument is that these are the "totalizing," "terroristic" practices of an "authoritarian" discipline. But they are also the hard practices of a difficult discipline. Gresham's law applies in history as surely as in economics: bad habits drive out good, easy methods drive out hard ones. And there is no doubt that the old history, traditional history, *is* hard.

Hard – but exciting precisely because it is hard. And that excitement may prove a challenge and inspiration for a new generation of historians. It is more exciting to write true history (or as true as we can make it) than fictional history, else historians would choose to be novelists rather than historians; more exciting to try to rise above our interests and prejudices than to indulge them; more exciting to try to enter the imagination of those remote from us in time and place than to impose our imagination upon them; more exciting to write a coherent narrative while respecting the complexity of historical events than to fragmentize history into disconnected units; more exciting to try to get the facts (without benefit of quotation marks) as right as we can than to deny the very idea of facts; even more exciting to get the footnotes right, if only to show others the visible proof of our labours.

The American political theorist William Dunning said that one of the happiest days of his life was when he discovered, by a comparison of handwriting, that Andrew Jackson's first message to Congress was actually drafted by George Bancroft. "I don't believe," he wrote to his wife, "you can form any idea of the pleasure it gives me to have discovered this little historical fact." Every historian has had this experience – the pleasure of discovering a fact that may appear in the published work in a subordinate clause or footnote, but that, however trivial in itself, validates the entire enterprise, because it is not only new but also true.

Postmodernism entices us with the siren call of liberation and creativity, but it may be an invitation to intellectual and moral suicide. Partisans and critics alike agree that postmodernism is intrinsically, radically anti-humanistic. By the same token, it is profoundly anti-historical. Hayden White commends the great historians of the nineteenth century who "interpreted the burden of the historian as a moral charge to free men from the burden of history." One may think it bizarre to attribute that intention, as he does, to Tocqueville among others, but one cannot doubt that that is indeed the aim of postmodernism. To free men from the "burden" of history is to free them from the burden of humanity. Liberationist history, like liberationist theology, is not a new and higher form of the discipline; it is the negation of the discipline.

If we have survived the "death of God" and the "death of man," we will surely survive the "death of history" – and of truth, reason, morality, society, reality, and all the other verities we used to take for granted and that have now been "problematized" and "deconstructed." We will even survive the death of postmodernism.

16 Geoffrey Elton

Return to essentials

The main theme of these lectures will revolve around the current debates on the nature of history, debates that are especially active in the United States, but I must say at once that I cannot claim to offer an exhaustive discussion. I propose to home in on a selection of the arguments that are at present running around, and I apologize from the start to all the disputants whom I shall not be able to mention. I should also like to make it plain from the start that I shall be defending what may appear to be very old-fashioned convictions and practices. My views and attitudes were formed by some forty-five years of trying to understand the historical past and write about it, and in some people's eyes I shall unquestionably appear ossified, even dead. However, I can only preach what I believe, and I do believe in those entrenched positions concerning the reality of historical studies. Perhaps there is virtue in now and again tackling the champions of innovation and new fashion from a position of mere experience.

* * *

In the study of history, a primary preoccupation with the present is thus always dangerous, a danger which appears in yet another form of the crisis which allegedly afflicts the enterprise. History has through the millennia served present-day causes of a different kind, causes which did not attempt to provide universal guidelines for action by means of predictive laws or specialize in fitting the self-centred historian within the even more self-centred milieu of the intellectual community. People have usually sought in history a justification for their convictions and prejudices; whole nations have over the centuries lived in cocoons of convenient myths the demolition of which they very much resent. I mean here by myths not those imageries and mythologies that for instance Lévi-Strauss had in mind, but supposed truths proved in historical writings which are in fact provably untrue but have gained their hold by being comforting to some ascendant political or ethnic structure or to some emotional need. Repetition has anchored them in the mind of the generality. Where would the citizen of the United States be today if he did not grow up with the comforting notion that his country is the one that invented and perfected democracy? As I write this, I recall seeing just today in the press the account of an address by one Francis Fukuyama, once of the Rand Corporation, who thinks that history (by which he means conflict) has come to an end because the whole world has settled into a contented acceptance of the American dream. He foresees an eternity of equilibrium and boredom – all existence a cross between Beverly Hills and Scarsdale. He has a lot to learn, but comes conveniently to hand to prove my point. What would the average Frenchman feel if he could not suppose that his nation had created all the civilization worth having, from literature at one end to furniture and food at the other? What is to become of the Englishman who has had to come to terms with the discovery that the supposedly upward moves of progress and perfection in power, in politics, and in government, which once he believed history told him characterized his country, were also an invention of the dream-makers? It is, after all, the myths put up by historians that have given their subject much of its general attraction.

Yet where do we stand today? Ever since historical study became professional – that is to say, systematic, thorough and grounded in the sources – it has time and again destroyed just those interpretations that served particular interests, more especially national self-esteem and self-confidence. The blatantly jingoistic imperialism of late-Victorian England quickly succumbed to historical inquests which by the 1930s had removed all unthinking satisfaction with England's imperial past. The conventional view which treated the American War of Independence as a purely idealistic assertion of principle against foreign tyranny has undergone repeated revisions that have left almost none of it standing, at least among the more serious readers of serious history. Some of the myth, interestingly enough, hung on in American public life: thus Franklin Delano Roosevelt's instinctive hostility to the British Empire, which so notably contributed to its disappearance after 1945, owed a good deal to unreconstructed views about the eighteenth century drummed into him in his schooldays. Myths can be dangerous as well as comforting. The liberal myths which have of late forwarded what is called self-government everywhere – myths which combined noble intentions with a striking ignorance about both past and present – have, since the 1960s, killed far more people in previously imperial territories than 200 years of building those empires ever destroyed. And they have powerfully assisted the emergence of tyrannies. To the historian the ironies of history have their attraction, but this one seems to me to have gone too far; it is yet another facet of the truth that the world is now in the hands of adolescents.

I am not, of course, suggesting that people must always be able to foresee the consequences of their actions, especially actions based on honest and generous convictions, which is to say myths. Admittedly, it would help if now and again they looked at the sort of history that undermines myths. When it can be shown that such actions, in the past, were misconceived because they in their turn rested on myths about that past's past, the better understanding brought by informed hindsight and sound historical investigation should not be shut out of the public mind. Of course, the demolition of comfortable myths causes pain at best and horror-struck revulsion at worst; it can lead to a dangerous over-reaction. The myth of good old Uncle Joe Stalin and the virtues of the Soviet system, carefully put together by commentators in the 1930s and given currency by the circumstances of the last Great War, lay behind many of the errors perpetrated in the settlements of the 1940s. Once historians (some historians) had exploded the myth, far too much policy came to be directed by an equally simple-minded abhorrence and fear. However, that myth seems to be decently killed and buried now that the truth about that murderous regime has been admitted by the Russians themselves, bravely replacing myth by reality in a fashion that we might term exemplary for other nations in their mistaken self-satisfaction; meanwhile, the lesson might still be learned which emerges from the refusal of so many perfectly decent and well educated people in Britain and the United States to believe the manifest truth for some forty years or more. There are times when I feel forced to regard the intellectual community not only with surprise but with horror.

One of the most interesting cases of the myth problem occurred in Germany, the original home of advanced historical science. Since the notable nineteenth-century historians there were nearly all fairly simple-minded patriots, they accepted myths about the medieval empire which they came to treat as the model and paradigm for a Germany reunited in their own day. Thus on the myth they erected interpretations which demanded profound loyalty to the nation and its expansionist state. The myth survived the First World War and played an important role in the rise of Nazism. The Second World War, assisted by new historians, destroyed it, to a point where a wholesale revulsion against the national past seemed to have set in; it has taken thirty years or so for the German educational system to return to an interest, now sober and generally sensible, in that past. Even so, this has been achieved in the main by eliminating the Middle Ages from the story altogether and, even more impressively, by forgetting Prussia at the speed of light. So far as I can tell, in West Germany, at least, history is unusually free of myths among the consumers, and it will be interesting to see whether this state of affairs can endure. Will there be new myths to absorb an interest in the past and give comfort to the present; or will Germans insist on seeing the past unclouded by myths; or will the death of myth in the end terminate anything like a serious concern with the past? That country looks likely to provide an interesting laboratory experiment.

Normally, myths enjoy tough constitutions, nor should we forget that what overthrows them may in turn partake of the nature of a myth, especially if the historical revision employs a general theory to do its work. The myth of the wonderful and beneficent British Empire was destroyed by historians such as R. H. Tawney who aimed to reconstruct society to a pattern they thought ideal – open, generous, free. Predictably this meant that the history they used to do down what they found was at least as biased, one-sided and indeed erroneous as that which it came to replace, and for some thirty years now some of us have been trying to undo the unfortunate consequences of their idealism. This does not mean restoring the earlier myth, or at least it should not and need not mean that, but the risk exists. When I have attacked Tawney it has been taken for granted that I wished to make party-political points – that I was being as Tory as he was a champion of the Labour Party. But what concerned me was the falsehood of his historical technique and the consequent creation of new myths – especially the myth that seemed to prove that political liberty was bound to be linked to social abuse. I did not, of course, expect to be read correctly by people who are committed emotionally to their myths, but I do think it is the historian's duty to put myths in their place (which is the discard) regardless of what some people may feel about it all. Nobody seems to doubt this when the myths are nasty, as for instance the lies built around the so-called Protocols of the Elders of Zion – though I might draw your attention to the current activities of an English historian, David Irving, who is actively denying the Holocaust and accusing Churchill of destroying the British Empire in the service of his own selfish glory. No myth will ever quite die, least of all in a world which believes in the truth of the Bible. When it comes to understanding the past, comfortable myths should be no more acceptable than their opposite. Some years ago, Sir John Plumb, aware of the threat both to the general mind and to the survival of his profession that the undermining of ancient convictions could pose, in effect advised historians to write the sort of history that helps people towards a contented and more cheerful life. But surely that is to back corruption: we are not to tell what for good reason we believe to be much nearer the truth if it upsets people. Besides, it cannot be done. All history upsets some people: what Plumb really called for was the sort of history that supported the social attitudes, ambitions and behaviour that he preferred.

No, it is the search for truth that must guide our labours, which is why that attack on the very possibility of discovering a truth of history is so very devastating – leaving aside the fact that it rests upon much ignorance of what seeking that truth actually means. It is only by providing as truthful an understanding of the past as we can obtain that we can offer to the present a past which can be useful to the present, a past from which it can learn. I have preached this gospel often enough, though I do not seem to have converted all that many of my fellow historians. Partly this is because I cannot pretend to bring much comfort, especially in the face of the philosophers and social scientists who question the very notion of a truth in history. They will not accept that it is there, in the events of the past, and open to investigation, even if it will never be recovered in full and beyond all doubt. That uncertainty around historical truth and a true view of the past arises from the deficiencies of the evidence and the problems it poses, rather than from the alleged transformation of events in the organizing mind of the historian. That doctrine, however dressed up, leads straight to a frivolous nihilism which allows any historian to say whatever he likes. We historians are firmly bound by the authority of our sources (and by no other authority, human or divine), nor must we use fiction to fill in the gaps. And though gaps and ambiguities close the road to total reconstruction, the challenges they pose lead to those fruitful exchanges, even controversies, among historians which do as much as anything does to advance our outworks ever nearer to the fortress of truth. That shall be the theme of my last lecture.

17 Gabrielle Spiegel

History, historicism and the social logic of the text in the Middle Ages[1]

The study of literary texts appears at the moment to stand at a decisive juncture. Trends in critical thinking over the last decades have questioned the possibility of recovering a text's historical meaning. At the same time, there is a newly insistent plea for a return to "history" in the interpretation of literature. Before a rapprochement can occur, however, we need to have a clearer understanding of how both historians and critics understand "history" and of the ways in which postmodernist thought positions history and the role of the historian with respect to issues of literary interpretation at the forefront of contemporary critical debate.

One thing is clear: the paradigms that have governed historical and literary study since the nineteenth century no longer hold unquestioned sway. The confident, humanist belief that a rational, "objective" investigation of the past permits us to recover "authentic" meanings in historical texts has come under severe attack in postmodernist critical debate. At stake in this debate are a number of concepts traditionally deployed by historians in their attempts to understand the past: causality, change, authorial intent, stability of meaning, human agency and social determination. What place, then, does history have in a postmodern theoretical climate? What, if anything, can the historian contribute to the reconfiguration of both theoretical concerns and interpretive practices signaled by the very notion of postmodernism? My purpose here is to explore some of the issues in question from the historian's point of view, paying particular attention to trends in literary criticism that suggest a reawakened interest in history.

Looking at the current critical climate from the vantage point of a historian, the dominant impression one takes away is that of the dissolution of history, of a flight from "reality" to language as the constitutive agent of human consciousness and the social production of meaning. The impulses promoting this "linguistic turn" have come from several directions.[2] Chief among them was the rise of structural linguistics, beginning with the publication in 1916 of Ferdinand de Saussure's *Course in General Linguistics* and continuing with the successive emergence of structuralism, semiotics, and poststructuralism, especially in its deconstructionist guise, whose principal impact has been felt in the period after World War II.

What unites these varieties of pre- and poststructuralisms is their common reliance upon a language-model epistemology, which views language not as a reflection of the world it captures in words, but as constitutive of that world, that is, as "generative" rather than "mimetic."[3] Despite considerable differences among the polemicists and practitioners of poststructuralism, all begin from the premise that language is somehow anterior to the world it shapes; that what we experience as "reality" is but a socially (i.e., linguistically) constructed artifact or "effect" of the particular language systems we inhabit. A belief in the fundamentally linguistic character of the world and our knowledge of it forms the core of what I would call the "semiotic challenge." As a language-based conception of reality, semiotics has disrupted traditional literary and historical modes of interpretation by undermining materialist theories of experience and the ideas of causality and agency inherent in them. To meet the challenge of semiotics, we need to understand the full range of consequences entailed in its approach to both history and literature.

Post-Saussurean theory begins "from an analysis of language as a system of differences with no positive terms."[4] Far from reflecting the social world of which it is a part, language precedes the world and makes it intelligible by constructing it according to its own rules of signification. Since for Saussure such rules are inherently arbitrary, in the sense of being social conventions implicitly understood in different ways by differing linguistic communities,[5] the idea of an objective universe existing independently of speech and universally comprehensible despite one's membership in any particular language system is an illusion. Reality does not exist "beyond" the reach of language; it is "always already" constructed *in* language, which is itself anterior to our knowledge of the world. It follows that literature, as an instance of linguistic utterance, cannot transparently reflect a world outside itself, since that "world" is only a linguistic construct, and what it reflects, therefore, is merely another articulation of language, or discourse.

Like language, literature refers not to an exterior world but only to the operation of language itself. Structural linguistics rescues literature from its lonely island of privileged being by insisting that literary language is but one instance of a much broader or, more precisely, "deeper" system of linguistic practice, a system to which Saussure gave the name *langue*. For structural linguistics, literature is but an instance or index of *langue*, a determinate speech act (in Saussure's terminology, *parole*) which, like every other sort of speech act, derives its nature from the underlying deep structures of language governing a society's linguistic praxis. What literature offers is an index of socially construable meaning rather than an image of reality; it is to the construction of social meaning, rather than the transmission of messages about the world, that the exercise of literature is directed.

As developed by semiotics and deconstruction, Saussure's investigation into the properties of language systems was to have disastrous consequences for a historical understanding of both textuality and history by severing language from any intrinsic connection to external referents. Starting from Saussure's notion of words as "signs," conceived as arbitrary (because conventional) "signifiers" capable of producing multiple significations (or "signifieds"), semiotics focused attention on the performative aspect of language as the production of meaning, dependent upon the deployment of formal signs. Semiotics further insisted that meaning is produced by the internal relations of signs to one another, rather than by reference to extralinguistic phenomena. This means, as Raymond Williams has pointed out, that language "not only [is] *not natural*, but is a form of codification."[6] Language (pre-)exists in the form of available codes, and it follows that the creation of meaning is the work of rules relating signs to one another in the manner predetermined by the code's underlying system or *langue*. In that sense, John Toews perceptively notes, "the creation of meaning is impersonal, operating 'behind the backs' of language users whose linguistics actions can merely exemplify the rules and procedures of languages they inhabit but do not control."[7] Such a view of language as constituting impersonal codes governing individual expression radically disturbs traditional notions of the author as a centered subject, in conscious control and responsible for her own utterances. It is hardly surprising, therefore, that Roland Barthes declared all authors "dead." What remains as the literary work, from a semiotic perspective, is not an autonomous expression of a centered, speaking subject, but coded texts and the multiple readings to which they are susceptible.[8] What in positivism, historicism, and even New Criticism was deemed to be a text's coherent statement or point of view, ultimately discoverable through close reading, is fractured into a series of discontinuous, heterogeneous, and contradictory codes which defy interpretive unification except at the level of allegorical recodification, itself suspect as the ideological imposition of a false coherence where none in truth exists.

More fatal for the historical consideration of literature than even this fracturing of the literary work into multiple and conflicting codes was the way in which semiotics inevitably dehistoricized literature by denying the importance of a historically situated authorial consciousness, a dehistoricization of the literary text that was tantamount to the denial of history. If authors are seen as bound by preexisting language codes rather than by social processes to which they give voice, and if those very social processes are themselves understood as linguistically constituted (are, in that sense, little more than alternative sign systems), then social life is essentially a play of discursive behavior, the interaction and combination of artificial, disembodied signs in unstable relationships with one another, cut off from any purchase on a world exterior to language and hence, in all senses of the world, immaterial.

It was deconstruction that was to carry the implications of post-Saussurean linguistics farthest in terms of the dissolution of the materiality of the sign, while at the same time moving the argument away from the consideration of speech to focus on *écriture* or textuality as the matrix of human linguistic consciousness. Once language was considered to be a system of arbitrary codification, the obvious response in the presence of codes was to decode and "deconstruct" them; to examine the specific processes at work in a given text's enactment of meaning in terms of the shifts and clashes of codes cohabiting within the literary work; to examine, that is, a text's mode of production rather than its referential content. Moreover, deconstruction came to focus on the surplus of significations produced by signs, a surplus that made it impossible to establish the stability of "intended" meaning in any act of speech or writing. The inevitable clash of codes coexisting within the text fractures at the apparently continuous, harmonious surface of the work to reveal the contradictions and pluralities of meanings that it harbors. In the course of deconstructing a text, the reader is confronted, ultimately, by its final indeterminacy of meaning, its *aporia*, in the face of which the reader fatally hesitates, unable to decide. For, once fractured, the multiplicity of differences inherent within the sign, differences that the text seeks to repress and/or negate, is exposed.[9] The aim of "deconstructing" is, precisely, to make manifest the hidden meanings which continue to lurk within the silences and absences that the text attempts, in vain, to impose. And what this unmasking reveals, ultimately, is the "inability of language to represent anything outside its own boundaries."[10] As Jacques Derrida explains it: "Through this sequence of supplements a necessity is announced: that of an infinite chain, ineluctably multiplying the supplementary mediations that produce the sense of the very thing they defer: the mirage of the thing itself, of immediate presence, of original perception."[11] Behind the language of the text stands only more language, more texts, in an infinite regress in which the presence of the real and the material is always deferred, never attainable. According to deconstruction, we are confined within a "prison house of language" (to use the fashionable Nietzschean phrase) from which there is no exit, since, as Derrida proclaimed, "il n'y a pas de hors-texte."[12] Like semiotics, to which it owes its governing conception of language, deconstruction sees the operation of language as impersonal (language uses its speakers, Derrida claims, rather than the other way around), forming and reforming itself in the play of textuality (since even speech, for Derrida, can be construed as a form of writing, an "archiécriture"), endlessly mediating, and thus deferring, the material presence towards which it appears to be destined but at which it never arrives.

This dissolution of the materiality of the sign, its ruptured relation to extralinguistic reality, is necessarily also the dissolution of history, since it denies the ability of language to "relate" to (or account for) any reality other than itself. History, the past, is simply a subsystem of linguistic signs, constituting its object according to the rules of the linguistic universe inhabited by the historian.[13] Historical being becomes for deconstruction, as Lee Patterson has shown, "not a presence but an effect of presence created by textuality. There is no *hors texte*, and in trying to discover the historically real we enter into a labyrinthine world that not only forecloses access to history in its original form but calls into question its very existence as an object of knowledge. For Deconstruction, writing absorbs the social context into a textuality that is wholly alienated from the real."[14] This is a problem not limited, moreover, to literary texts, for there is no sound epistemological reason, within a poststructuralist universe, to distinguish between literary and other uses of language. If the literary text is denied the ability to represent reality, so also are all texts, and the distinction traditionally drawn between literature and "document" becomes meaningless, since both participate equally in the uncontrolled play and intertextuality of language itself. If we cannot reach "life" through literature, we cannot reach "the past" through document.[15]

In many ways, this is a surprising outcome to the structuralist enterprise, since one might have assumed that Saussure's emphasis on the arbitrary, conventional nature of *langue* as a social phenomenon would lead naturally to a historicist perspective emphasizing the variety and historically determinate appearance of different linguistic systems. Even if one accepted Saussure's notion that reality is socially constructed, there is no implication in the *Course in General Linguistics* that it is constructed in all places and at all times in the same way; to the contrary, the Saussurean insistence on language as a system of difference without positive terms strongly militates against this conclusion. If language is an implicit social contract that binds members of the linguistic community to prescribed usages, without which communication and the production of meaning would be impossible, then any given language is necessarily a historically specific occurrence, for the investigation of which historicism would appear to hold out the best hope. It is not surprising, then, that the principal adaptations of structuralist and post-structuralist principles within the domains of anthropology and history have attempted to restore the historicist posture more or less implicit in Saussure's formulations by focusing on the social construction of meaning in historically determinate cultural discourses. But, as I shall try to argue, while cultural anthropology and cultural history, together with the New Historicism with which it entertains such rich relations, have successfully reintroduced a (new) historicist consideration of discourse as the product of identifiable cultural and historical formations, they have not been equally successful in restoring history as an active agent in the social construction of meaning.

Without doubt, the dominant figure in promoting the use of semiotic models for the study of culture and history on the Anglo-American scene has been Clifford Geertz. Although his first, enormously influential collection of essays, *The Interpretation of Cultures*, probably owed more to Northrop Frye's theory of archetypes than to semiotics proper, Geertz clearly grasped and argued for a semiotic concept of culture as an "interworked system of construable signs,"[16] which was to be the object of an interpretive, rather than functionalist, anthropology. In his classic essay, "Deep Play: Notes on a Balinese Cockfight," Geertz put to anthropological use Frye's insistence that the meaning of literary texts is expressive and formal, not instrumental, by treating the Balinese cockfight as a "sustained symbolic structure," a way "of saying something of something," whose meaning was to be understood not as a problem of social mechanics (how cockfights functioned within Balinese society to reinforce status, deploy power, advance interests, etc.) but of social semantics.[17] And he went on to propose that culture be examined as "an assemblage of texts" and that specific cultural forms "be treated as texts, as imaginative works built out of social materials."[18] Geertz's brand of interpretive anthropology, as he later claimed, was "preadapted to some of the most advanced varieties of modern opinion,"[19] which he defined as "the move toward conceiving of social life as organized in terms of symbols (signs, representations, *signifiants*, *Darstellungen* . . . the terminology varies), whose meaning (sense, import, *signification, Bedeutung* . . .) we must grasp if we are to understand that organization and formulate its principles."[20] Annexing, within this definition, hermeneutics along with semiotics, Geertz powerfully argued for the application of what he called the "text analogy" to the study of culture, in which social action would be seen as a "behavioral text" and the goal of anthropology the "systematic unpackings of the conceptual world" of other cultures.[21] That Geertz's notion of symbolic anthropology was also compatible with (if consciously distinguished from)[22] structural anthropology as practiced by Lévi-Strauss was not the least of its benefits. Where Geertz studied social behavior as symbolic texts, Claude Lévi-Strauss studied texts as symbolic action, the resolution in the structure of the imaginary of real political and social contradictions. For both, access to the processes at work in the construction of symbols came via the formal patterns which a culture employed in the creation of its social texts. Thus, although texts were described as imaginative works built out of *social materials*, it was the formal patterns, the modes of representation rather than the social conflicts whose symbolic expression and resolution they served, which tended to become the object of investigation. The result, inevitably, was an aestheticizing of culture and its absorption into the ever-widening category of "textuality" as poststructuralism came to view it.[23]

The promise of Geertz's semiotic approach to the study of culture lay in its desire to redirect anthropological explanation towards connecting "action to its sense rather than behavior to its determinants,"[24] avoiding thereby the determinisms which functionalism tended to fall into. This promise was never quite realized, as the primacy of textual modes of analysis increasingly blurred from view the active nature of the "social material" that Geertz took as his texts. As in literary criticism, so too in ethnography: discursive models of the social construction of reality effected a separation of language and "reality," and the growing concentration on language became, as Nicole Polier and William Roseberry have remarked, "a centerpiece of the postmodern ethnographic project."[25]

Perhaps it should not (and certainly would not) alarm us that cultural anthropology has become progressively saturated with poststructuralist concepts of textuality, were it not for the extraordinary impact that Geertz's "text analogy" has had on the practice of social history, and more especially on the emerging field of cultural history. In the hands of social historians, the appropriation of anthropological models, primarily by historians of early modern Europe, was a relatively straightforward affair. It was not confined to the use of Geertzian models, but drew as well from the anthropological work of Victor Turner, Mary Douglas, and French anthropologists like Marcel Mauss and Arnold Van Gennep. Led by the ground-breaking work of Natalie Davis, social historians learned to study the ritual life of past societies: charivaris, carnivals, ceremonies of social inversion, and popular cults, even the massacre of cats, were studied as symbolic expressions of a social order that was both enacted and tested through ritual life.[26] As a consequence, the historian's field of inquiry and vocabulary were enormously enlarged; terms like "liminality," "communitas," "ritual anti-structure," and the like became commonplace in the rhetoric of the new social historian. Although American medievalists were not as quick as their colleagues in early modern European history to take up the anthropological standard, the work of Peter Brown on the cult of the saints, of Stephen White on arbitration practices, and of Patrick Geary on the ritual humiliation of saints' relics, as well as Victor Turner's study of pilgrimage as a "liminoid" phenomenon, showed the potential that such work had for medieval history. At the same time, in France the group associated with Jacques Le Goff and Jean-Claude Schmitt (whose study of *The Holy Greyhound* rapidly became something of a classic in medieval ethnography) organized the resources of the Ecole des Hautes Etudes for the development of an ethnographically oriented medieval historiography.

In the main, social historians who employed ethnographic models were interested in the place of ritual in social life and were less apt to implement in any thoroughgoing sense Geertz's "text analogy."

Although ritual was treated as a form of symbolic expression, it was not subjected to a genuinely literary analysis, nor did such historians rely in any systematic way on the conceptions of language that had grown out of Saussurean linguistics. Only with the emergence of cultural history were the assumptions built into the use of a discursive model for the analysis of sociocultural phenomena consistently developed and applied. Cultural history took as its domain the study of forms of social behavior and cultural production, both of which were now consciously recast in a semiotic mode and made permeable to the influence of recent trends in literary criticism and theory, including large doses of poststructuralism.

A good example of the way in which cultural history conceives of and repositions the text within a history of society that focuses upon cultural production is provided by Jonathan Culler's essay, "Literary History, Allegory and Semiology," published in *New Literary History* in 1976.[27] Culler proposed that

> the best way of imagining a relationship between literature and society which could form the basis of cultural history and hence of literary history is to think of both literature and the culture of which it forms a part as institutions composed of symbolic systems which enable actions or objects to have meaning, among them literature and genres, whose conventions are devices for the production and organization of meaning.

For Culler and cultural historians generally, both literature and society are to be construed as systems of signs whose relationship to one another takes the form of commensurability or "homology." In such analyses, the critical foci of interpretation are directed not to the content of social life or literature but rather to the "operations which produce social and cultural objects, the devices which create a world charged with meaning."[28] These "operations" are the linguistic codes that constitute social and discursive formations. Given this, it is impossible to establish the priority of one to another, to say that society determines or "causes" in any mechanistic sense the cultural production of meaning, or that there is an ontological difference between the imaginative and the "real" (between, for instance, literature and extralinguistic events, actions, or institutions), since what is construed as the "real" is itself the product of imaginary, that is, discursive construction. Thus Geertz, with characteristic clarity, declares: "the real is as imagined as the imaginary."[29] So also Roger Chartier, arguing for the substitution of sociocultural history for more traditional forms of intellectual history, insists that "the relationship thus established [between the text and the real] is not one of dependence of the mental structures on their material determinations. The representations of the social world themselves are the constituents of social reality."[30]

It is at this point that the historian (perhaps naively) feels compelled to query: what, then, is the "real"? To this question Chartier provisionally answers: that which the text itself poses as real in constituting it as a referent situated beyond itself. But not only the reality aimed at by the text, for Chartier adds to this definition the further qualification that what is real is, in a new meaning, "the very manner in which the text aims at it [reality] in the historicity of its production and the strategy of its writing."[31] In other words, what is real are the semiotic codes that govern the representation of life both in writing and in incorporated social structures.

What cultural history achieves by this equation of the imaginary and the real within the structures of discourse is a radical foregrounding and reconceptualization of the problem of text and context. If the imaginary is real and the real imaginary and there are no epistemological grounds for distinguishing between them, then it is impossible to create an explanatory hierarchy that establishes a causal relationship between history and literature, life and thought, matter and meaning. The context in which a text is situated is itself composed of constituted meanings, as "texts of everyday life," so to speak, and the connections between them are essentially intertextual.[32] It becomes impossible, on this basis, to identify aspects of social, political, or economic life which somehow stand apart from or make up a "reality" independent of the cultural constructions which historically conditioned discourses generate; text and context are collapsed into one broad vein of discursive production. Moreover, while cultural history has proven itself adept in treating discursive production in terms of historicist perspectives of epochal variation, its historicism is not accompanied by what most historians would understand as a historical explanation of the relationship between the production of meaning and social reality. From the point of view of the traditional literary or social historian, then, the achievement of cultural history lies in its reintroduction of a historicist consideration of literature; its failure lies in its refusal to differentiate between text and context or to establish an intelligible relationship between them that does not lead to their mutual implication in a textually conceived universe. The problem becomes even more severe when we remember that so-called "documentary" representations of reality (charters, laws, fief lists, economic data, accounts of trade, or wars, not to mention cat massacres and cockfights) are equally included within the compass of the social construction of reality and equally, understood as the result of "historically contingent discursive formations."[33] To put it at its starkest: it is as if, for cultural history, there are no acts other than speech acts, no forms of being which are not assimilated to textuality and thus made accessible to the workings of the text analogy.

The consequences of this way of looking at the problem of text and context for both historians and literary critics are far-ranging and serious. To begin with, as has occurred in symbolic anthropology following Geertz, it leads inexorably to an aestheticizing of culture in which the term "society" is implicitly emptied of its normal significance and reinscribed as "social text."[34] Textuality absorbs the social into its own linguisticality; semiotic modes of literary interpretation expand their scope to include all and any manner of social texts, which now are treated as semiological systems. In this way, the deconstruction of the traditional distinction between representation and reality opens the way for the deconstruction of reality *as* text, a practice at which the New Historicists, using Michel Foucault to great effect, are expert. What began as a method of literary interpretation and grew into a generically textual interpretation has metamorphosed into social analysis. But, as Murray Krieger has cogently pointed out, it can be argued that it remains a literary mode throughout: "it is only that this interpretation now ranges far beyond the literary and even beyond the textual realm in search of objects it makes available to itself, even if it treats them as if they were literary."[35] Thus, what may have begun as an attempt to rescue literature from its privileged being and New Critical self-enclosure has paradoxically extended the boundaries of the literary to include social and material reality, thereby dissolving the material into "meaning." Paradoxically as well, what began as a revolt against formalism appears to have reinstated formalist concerns, since, if language constitutes meaning (discursively and socially), then, as Martin Jay indicates, historians of society and literature "will have to pay attention to the linguistic dimension of the texts they examine,"[36] whether those texts are purely literary/intellectual or social texts.[37] Sociocultural history begins to look not so much like a substitute for traditional intellectual history as its modulation to another key, one that makes room for the new view of textuality engendered by post-Saussurean linguistics and, in particular, deconstruction. It is New Historicism that has been most alive to the possibilities which emerge from this approach to cultural history.

Like cultural history, New Historicism takes its point of departure from a broadly symbolic and semiotic view of cultural production which seeks, in the words of Louis Montrose, "to resituate canonical literary tales among the multiple forms of writing, and in relation to the non-discursive practices and institutions of the social formation in which those texts have been produced." At first glance, this formulation of the New Historicist project would appear to rehabilitate the existence of "non-discursive" practices and institutions as autonomous material realities, but Montrose quickly goes on to acknowledge "language as the medium in which the Real is constructed and apprehended . . ."[38] Hence, as do cultural historians, New Historicists point to the culturally specific nature of texts as products of particular periods and discursive formations, while viewing reality – history – as itself mediated by linguistic codes which it is impossible for the critic/historian to bypass in the recuperation of past cultures. Characteristic of New Historicism's conceptualization of the text-context conundrum (that is, as Lee Patterson succinctly defines it, the problem that the text is at once constituted by and constitutes history)[39] are statements such as Montrose's claim that New Historicists are concerned with "the Historicity of Texts and the Textuality of History"[40] and Stephen Greenblatt's program "to examine the relation between the discourse of art and the circumambient discourses of society."[41] What such statements intend is the elaboration of a "cultural poetics," as Greenblatt calls it, in which a wide variety of social, institutional, and political practices are submitted to the same interpretive procedures as other, more recognizably discursive artifacts such as literary or nonliterary texts. Just as cultural history tacitly reinscribes society as "social text," so New Historicism treats political, institutional, and social practices as "cultural scripts."[42]

The debt here to Foucault is clear, and as with Foucault, the goal of New Historicist criticism is to demonstrate the power of discourse in shaping the ways in which the dominant ideology of a period creates both institutional and textual embodiments of the cultural constructs governing mental and social life. What perhaps differentiates the New Historicists from the practice of cultural historians with whom they are otherwise so closely allied is their skillful employment of the poststructuralist belief in the heterogeneous, contradictory, fragmented, and discontinuous nature of textuality, to which "social texts" are likewise assimilated. In this vein, New Historicism refuses unproblematical distinctions between "literature" and "history," "text" and "context," and emphasizes, instead, "the dynamic, unstable, and reciprocal relationship between the discursive and material domains."[43] But as should be all too clear by now, it is difficult to discover in what the materiality of the material domain consists, or how history is distinct from literature or context from text, in light of New Historicism's insistence on the symbolic foundation of all social constructions – textual and otherwise – and its persistent deployment of deconstructive readings in the interpretation of cultural artifacts of all kinds. Yet again, the elaboration of a (new) historicist approach to cultural production is not necessarily accompanied by a return to historical explanation as (old) historicism traditionally conceived of it. Instead, a global view of textuality and its shaping force in the constitution of social and literary formations has closed off access to a "reality" whose dubious status is figured by the persistent use of quotation marks. Yet I would argue that if we want to contextualize texts, we cannot achieve this merely by textualizing the context. New Historicism, like cultural history, appears to gloss over the problem of the text-context relationship by the adoption of a semiotic mode of analysis which occludes the issue altogether by treating culture, institutions, ideology, and power as merely interworked sets of symbolic systems or codes.[44]

It might be argued that cultural materialism, as advocated by Raymond Williams and other Marxists, successfully addresses this problem through its insistence on the materiality of thought and writing as actions-in-the-world, with real consequences comparable to those produced by what historians normally call "events." Thus Williams, in contrast to conventional Marxist views on the superstructural character of literary production, begins by seeing "language and signification from the beginning as indissoluble elements of the material social process itself, involved all the time both in production and reproduction."[45] Moreover, like the cultural historians, Williams insists that "language is not a medium [transparently communicating thought]; it is a constitutive element of social practice."[46] Just as cultural history and New Historicism seek to abolish the distinction between a reified "language" and "society" by subsuming both within textuality, so Williams rejects the same distinction in the name of an encompassing materialism, in which language is an active social agent in the workings of what he calls "practical consciousness" through and by which reality is grasped.[47] Cultural production is, therefore, one mode of material production, commensurate in its materiality with other varieties of material production by means of which societies strive to sustain and reproduce themselves. And like them, it is constitutive of social reality, a position that establishes Williams's connection to the "cultural" (semiotic) component of cultural materialism.

It is not at all clear, however, how this shift from textuality to materiality, from discourse to "practical consciousness," and from the impersonal operation of linguistic codes to the active agency of "social language" solves the problem of the relation of literature to society, that is, of text and context. To state that literature is also "real" does not answer the question of how literature is associated with reality, while remaining avowedly imaginary. Williams here comes close simply to inverting Geertz's view that the "real is as imagined as the imaginary"[48] by the counterassertion that the imaginary is as real as reality, but we are no nearer a solution to the problem of their reciprocal interaction as distinct forms of social activity. Moreover, by seeing language as constitutive of the real, Williams would appear to come full circle and rejoin the semiotic view of culture held by cultural historians against which his materialism is directed. If Marxist criticism holds some attractions for historians, even for those by no means Marxist, it is because of its recognition of a crucial difference of order between text and context, and of the necessity of theorizing their relation.

It is striking that, apart from Marxism, few strands of contemporary criticism have managed to preserve a sense of history as a relatively autonomous realm of human experience, unaffected by the prefiguration of linguistic construction. Literary theory in particular seems to have entered a labyrinth of "textuality" from which there is no exit. For most schools of critical theory, textuality has become, as Edward Said has pointed out, "the exact antithesis and displacement of what might be called history."[49] Even cultural historians and New Historicists, committed in principle to the reintegration of a contextualist perspective in the interpretation of literature and culture, have resolved the problem of how to effect such a reintegration by textualizing contexts, drawing social behavior and political power inexorably into the orbit of a critical stance that assumes the cultural construction of reality in and through language. At a time when one increasingly hears cries for a return to considerations of "history" and "power" in the interpretation of literary and cultural phenomena, it seems appropriate for the historian to ask why history as traditionally conceived appears to be so fragile.

In part, the ability of semiotics to sweep the theoretical field is testimony to the power of its challenge to traditional epistemologies, to the technical virtuosity of its practitioners, and to the underlying coherence of its theory, against which those advocating a return to history rather weakly invoke collective "common sense" or individual, subjective experience. But it is unlikely that the semiotic challenge can be met simply by an appeal to common or individual sense and experience. If recent criticism is any indication, a historically grounded view of literary and cultural production is extremely difficult to theorize in the wake of the semiotic challenge, and the obstacles to doing so have so far loomed large.

To some degree, those obstacles have arisen from the rather one-sided nature of the discussion, which has largely been in the hands of literary critics rather than historians. One of the problems has been a need on the part of literary critics for a stable term against which to play off the complexity of their textual readings. The more complex, fractured, and heterogeneous the critic's view of literary language has become, the greater the necessity has been for a "lucid" historical context against which to develop and, ultimately, adjudicate interpretive positions. The focus of structuralist and poststructuralist theory on discursive "codes," ironically, implies the existence of the same messages "in clear,"[50] and history has been cast in the role of repository for such "clear" communications from the past, offering a vast master narrative under whose aegis the occult meanings of texts can be solicited and allegorically rewritten.[51] For their part, historians have been left with the menial task of providing a lucid, accessible – above all, knowable and known – context, while critics take their leisure in exploring the productive enigmas of textuality. Literary critics have been accustomed to get their history secondhand and prepackaged and have tended, in practice if not in theory, to treat it as unproblematic, something to be invoked rather than investigated. Yet if texts bear within them layers of discursive displacements and heterogeneous meanings, so too does history. Events are not necessarily any more logical, less ridden with contradiction and hidden intentions, than speech or writing. It is interesting that the notion of play, inconsistency, and difference so subtly deployed in the analysis of textuality never seems applicable to the treatment of history, although surely this is one place where the "text analogy" might prove useful to historians and certainly would be salutary for critics. And this remains a problem, in the end, only for those literary critics and historians who have not pursued the path of the "text analogy" to its logical conclusion in the collapsing of text and context within a single, aestheticized understanding of culture.

Another difficulty has been a tendency to bracket the problem of causality. Among the indubitable attractions of anthropological models of the Geertzian sort is that they permit one to bypass issues of causality, thereby providing a way out of the reductive fallacies and determinisms that had beset positivist and old-style historicist criticism. A discursive model of culture is well suited to the needs of literary critics, for whom the complexity of causal explanation should not be underestimated. As René Wellek and Austin Warren point out, causal explanation is highly overrated as a method of literary exegesis, for in the analysis of a literary work "cause and effect are incommensurate: the concrete result of extrinsic causes – the work of art – is always unpredictable." Cause-governed, extrinsic schools of interpretation tend to be, in their cutting phrase, "ergocentric," committed to isolating a few among the host of possible social factors responsible for shaping the literary work, hence inevitably reductionist.[52] What is most striking, however, is the degree to which the rejection of causality has overtaken history done in the cultural vein as well. Thus Robert Darnton, in *The Great Cat Massacre*, proclaims that "cultural history is history in the ethnographic grain . . .; its aim is to read for meaning."[53] But it might be argued, as Toews does, that while the history of meaning has successfully asserted the reality and autonomy of its object, "a new form of reductionism has become evident, the reduction of experience to the meanings that shape it."[54] What gets lost in the concentration on meaning in place of experience is the sense of social agency, of men and women struggling with the contingencies and complexities of their lives in terms of the fates that history deals out to them and transforming the worlds they inherit and pass on to future generations. These are the questions that have always engaged historians on the deepest level of their commitment to under-standing the past, and it seems unlikely that a literary history informed by semiotic principles will be able to evade the issue of causality – of *why* and "*how* a given form of literary work appeared *as* it did, *where* it did, and *when* it did"[55] – and still satisfy even sympathetic historians' demands for a historical, and not merely historicist, conception of cul-tural production.

In the final analysis, however, the difficulties encountered in resolving the text-context conundrum do not arise from the fact that as professional scholars we are limited by or locked into disciplinary competencies that we fear to transgress. They stem, rather, from technical problems that have gone largely unacknowledged in the theoretical literature. Primarily, they are due to a series of unrecognized incommensurabilities between the objects, tasks, and goals facing historians and literary scholars that make the achievement of a genuinely integrated *literary history* extraordinarily troublesome.

There is, to begin with, an incommensurability in the object of investigation. Literary text and historical context are not the same thing, and if one should not be reduced to the other, neither should they be held up as identical foci of the scholar's gaze. While the text is an objective given, an existing artifact (in its material existence if not in its constitution as a specifically "literary" work), the object of historical study must be constituted by the historian long before its meaning can begin to be disengaged. Paradoxically, in that sense the text qua text is materially "realer" than "history," and any attempt to adjudicate the interpretive meaning of a literary text by recourse to history as "reality" begins to look like an exercise undertaken backwards. History as given chronicle or unproblematic "truth" simply does not exist and so cannot serve as a master narrative for criticism into which the enigmatic codes of literary discourse can be transcoded in clear.

Moreover, since the historical text is not given but must be constructed, the historian of texts is a writer in his or her function of constituting the historical narrative, but a reader of the already materially extant text. The task facing the one is broadly constructive, the other broadly deconstructive, and it is not hard to see why few literary critics or historians of texts have given equal attention to both undertakings. The advantage of collapsing text and context, from this perspective, emerges not only as a response to the semiotic challenge, but as a means to avoid the apparently contradictory maneuvers involved in doing literary history as the doing of history *and* literature. And this does not even begin to take account of the problems arising from the differing nature of the texts one is required to read for each enterprise, commonly distinguished as "literary" (self-reflexive) and "documentary" (in theory, transparent). No historian, even of positivist stripe, would argue that history is present to us in any but textual form. But whether the "always already" textualized character of historical data, its inevitably mediated state as made up of language, necessarily means that it is "made up," foreclosing access to any past other than that we interpretively impose on texts, remains, one hopes, an open issue. The problem, of course, is not whether there is a past "out there" (or, as Nancy Partner wittily observed in these pages, if, once we get

there, there is a "there" there),[56] but how we reach it and what procedures permit us to do so in ways that respect its integrity. A historicist
appreciation of the difference between then and now is surely a sine
qua non of historically oriented studies, but this in itself does not
vouchsafe an approach to the past that addresses explanatory issues of
primary concern to historians, as the widespread application of the "text
analogy" makes only too clear.

Arguably, as well, critics and historians will possess different goals
in their respective inquiries, even when reading the same texts. While
literary critics will perhaps be more concerned with the affective functions of a text, with its ability to startle, to confront the reader with new
aesthetic and ethical forms, the historian is possibly more interested in
a text's ideological function, the way it represents a broad complex of
social relations. The growing attention to ideological formations in the
study of literary discourse, in part stemming from the influence of
Louis Althusser and Pierre Macherey, and particularly marked (in a
Foucauldian tenor) in New Historicism, indicates that the distance separating literary critics and historians on this question is not, however,
very great. Indeed, ideology, which once occupied a somewhat modest
place in intellectual history, primarily among the sociologists of knowledge, has now become a virtual obsession with theorists of discourse,
suggesting that the absorption of history into textuality is itself an
ideological gesture with distinct ideological consequences, a byproduct
perhaps of the "hubris of word-makers who claim to be makers of
reality."[57]

How, then, are we to resolve the question of the relation of text to
context, of literature to life, while still acknowledging the full force of
the challenge which semiotics has posed to our understanding of
material and cultural production? It is clear that the massive dehistoricization to which the literary text has been subjected in recent
decades cannot be overcome simply by reverting to the methodological
status ante quo of prestructuralism, according to which "documentary"
evidence is radically protected from the vagaries of textuality and
history serves as a testing ground for vying schools of critical interpretation. Semiotics and deconstruction have too thoroughly implicated all
forms of discourse within their epistemologies and too successfully
demystified the privileged status of literary language for a simple return
to old-style historicism to be persuasive. What is needed is the elaboration of a theoretical position capable of satisfying the demands of both
literary criticism and history as separate yet interdependent disciplinary

domains with a common concern for the social dimensions of textual production in past times. Just as we rightly reject the reduction of literature to a reflection of the world, so also must we reject the absorption of history by textuality. We need to rethink the issue of text and context in terms of a critical posture that does justice equally to textual, historicist, and *historical* principles of analysis and explanation.

As a starting-point in the fashioning of this sort of critical stance, we can begin by remembering that texts represent situated uses of language.[58] Such sites of linguistic usage, as lived events, are essentially local in origin and therefore possess a determinate social logic of much greater density and particularity than can be extracted from totalizing constructs like "language" and "society." The advantage of this approach to literary history in terms of the social logic of the text is that it permits us to examine language with the tools of the social historian, to see it within a local or regional social context of human relations, systems of communication, and networks of power that can account for its particular semantic inflections and thus aid in the recovery of its full meaning as cultural history seeks to understand it. This meaning, I would argue, while it may be viewed as an instance of the larger social discourses that govern it, is not ultimately reducible to an articulation of a preexisting system of linguistic codes or *langue* in the Saussurean sense. All texts occupy determinate social spaces, both as products of the social world of authors and as textual agents at work in that world, with which they entertain often complex and contestatory relations. In that sense, texts both mirror *and* generate social realities, are constituted by *and* constitute the social and discursive formations which they may sustain, resist, contest, or seek to transform, depending on the case at hand. There is no way to determine a priori the social function of a text or its locus with respect to its cultural ambience. Only a minute examination of the form and content of a given work can determine its situation with respect to broader patterns of culture at any given time. What this means is that a genuine literary history must always to some extent be both social and formalist in its concerns, must pay attention to a text's "social logic" in the dual sense of its site of articulation and its discursive character as articulated "logos."

NOTES

1. The author would like to thank Carroll Smith-Rosenberg, Phyllis Rackin, Lynn Hunt, Stephen Nichols, David Cohen, Judith Walkowitz, Jeanne Rutenburg, Arthur Eckstein, James Henretta, J. S. Cockburn, Samuel Kinser, and members of the Mellon Seminar on the Structures of Power and Diversity of Languages at the University of Pennsylvania and the Atlantic Seminar at the Johns Hopkins University for their careful readings and acute criticisms of the following article. In particular, the University of Pennsylvania Mellon seminar, under the direction of Carroll Smith-Rosenberg, has long provided me with a congenial set of companions and a probing forum in which to explore the issues raised here. I am especially grateful to be able to participate in its meetings, from which I have taken away far more than I contribute. I would also like to thank the John Simon Guggenheim Foundation for a fellowship which supported the research and writing of this article, as well as the Rockefeller Residency Fellowship program in Atlantic History and Culture of the Johns Hopkins University, which gave me a study and a home during the tenure of my Guggenheim fellowship. The article has enormously benefited from, but does not necessarily reflect, the opinions of the scholars listed above.

2. See Martin Jay, "Should Intellectual History Take a Linguistic Turn? Reflections on the Habermas-Gadamer Debate," in Dominick LaCapra and Steven L. Kaplan (eds), *Modern European Intellectual History: Reappraisals and New Perspectives* Ithaca, 1982, pp. 86–110, and John E. Toews, "Intellectual History after the Linguistic Turn: The Autonomy of Meaning and the Irreducibility of Experience," *American Historical Review* 92 (1987), 879–907.

3. See Nancy F. Partner, "Making Up Lost Time: Writing on the Writing of History," *Speculum* 61 (1986), 95.

4. Catherine Belsey, *Critical Practice*, London, 1980, p. 4.

5. To take an example cited by Belsey, p. 39, the meanings of "river" and "stream" in English do not correspond to *rivière* and *fleuve* in French. In English, what distinguishes a river from a stream is their respective size. In French, on the other hand, a *fleuve* is a body of water that flows into the sea, while a *rivière* flows into another *rivière* or a *fleuve*. The referents of these terms change as one passes from one language to another, and what determines the referent within each language is its place within the linguistic code or rules that govern the production of meaning.

6. *Marxism and Literature* Oxford, 1977, p. 167.

7. "Intellectual History," p. 882.

8. Thus, in classic demonstrations of semiotic analysis, in S/Z Barthes shatters a Balzac novella into a random operation of multiple codes, and Hayden White analyzes *The Education of Henry Adams* in terms of the patterns of code shifting by which ideological implications are substituted for the straightforward representation of a social life which the text "pretends" to be. See Hayden White, "Method and Ideology in Intellectual History: The Case of Henry Adams," in LaCapra and Kaplan (eds) *Modern European Intellectual History*, pp. 280–310.

9. The term which Jacques Derrida uses to designate this endless multiplication and diffusion of meaning within all writing, which continually threatens to outrun the sense which the categories of the text's structure try to limit it to, is "dissemination." See his *Dissemination*, trans. with intro. by Barbara Johnson, Chicago, 1984. For Derrida, all language displays this "surplus" of meaning, not merely literary language, although it is most evident in literature. See also Terry Eagleton, *Literary Theory: An Introduction*, Minneapolis, 1983, p. 134. It is precisely this mobility of meaning, the discontinuous, fractured, and indeterminate nature of writing, that makes it impossible for us to

establish a fixed point outside of discourse which guarantees its objective reality. Thus the text is radically decentered, since there is no referent outside the play of linguistic signifiers, no ground outside language which controls its interpretive range. The interpretation of any signifying chain (or of any text) produces only another chain of signs, and we enter, as Northrop Frye foresaw, "an endless labyrinth without an outlet" (*The Anatomy of Criticism*, New York, 1969, p. 118), which is essentially what Derrida means by a decentered structure. For an excellent discussion of Frye and Derrida see Frank Lentricchia, *After the New Criticism*, Chicago, 1980.

10. Jay, "Intellectual History," p. 89.
11. Jacques Derrida, *Of Grammatology*, trans. Gayatri Chakravorty Spivak, Baltimore, 1976, p. 157. See also Lee Patterson, *Negotiating the Past: The Historical Understanding of Medieval Literature*, Madison, 1987, p. 58.
12. *Of Grammatology*, p. 158.
13. See the critique by Toews, "Intellectual History," p. 882.
14. *Negotiating the Past*, p. 59.
15. No one has been more forceful in articulating the implications of post-Saussurean linguistics for the practice of history than Hayden White, who has assessed the challenge of semiotics for historical research by recognizing that once the relationship of the classical literary text to its social environment is problematized, so too is that of putatively "transparent" texts or documents. There are no epistemological grounds, once one has accepted a post-Saussurean view of language, to bracket documentary uses of language as somehow standing apart from the self-referential play of language generally, however necessary such attempts to protect historical "evidence" might appear for the continued practice of history. See especially White's collected essays, *The Content of the Form: Narrative Discourse and Historical Representation*, Baltimore, 1987.
16. "Thick Description: Toward an Interpretive Theory of Culture," in *The Interpretation of Cultures*, New York, 1973, p. 14.
17. "Deep Play: Notes on a Balinese Cockfight," in *The Interpretation of Cultures*, p. 26.
18. Ibid., p. 27.
19. "Introduction," *Local Knowledge: Further Essays in Interpretative Anthropology*, New York, 1983, p. 4.
20. "Blurred Genres: The Refiguration of Social Thought," *Local Knowledge*, p. 21.
21. Ibid., pp. 22–3.
22. Geertz insists on distinguishing his own interpretive procedures from Claude Lévi-Strauss's structuralism, on the grounds that Lévi-Strauss takes myths, rites, etc., as ciphers to solve, but does not seek to understand symbolic forms in terms of how they function in concrete situations to organize perceptions, meanings, emotions, concepts, and attitudes. Unlike interpretive anthropology, Lévi-Strauss's structuralism, Geertz claims, is concerned only with the internal structure of myths and rituals, independent of all context. (*Local Knowledge*, p. 449, n. 38.)
23. For an excellent discussion of this tendency in Geertz's work see Lynn Hunt, "History beyond Social Theory," forthcoming. I would like to thank Professor Hunt for permission to read and cite from her unpublished paper. That this aesthetic approach to social and cultural behavior is largely an act of interpretive violence wreaked upon the ethnographic communities that come within the anthropologist's purview is a point made by the anthropologist Vincent Crapanzano, who in a critique of Geertz's "Deep Play" notes that "Cockfights are surely cockfights for the Balinese – and not images, fictions, models, and metaphors. They are not marked as such, though they may be read as such by a foreigner for whom 'images, fictions, models, and metaphors' have interpretive value": "The Hermes Dilemma: The Masking of Subversion in Ethno-

graphic Description," in James Clifford and George E. Marcus (eds.) *Writing Culture: The Poetics and Politics of Ethnography*, Berkeley, 1986, p. 73.

24. "Blurred Genres," p. 34.

25. Nicole Polier and William Roseberry, "Tristes Tropes," unpublished paper, p. 10.

26. For an excellent review of these developments see Lynn Hunt, "History, Culture and Text," introduction to *The New Cultural History*, ed. Lynn Hunt, Berkeley, 1989, pp. 1–22. I would like to thank Professor Hunt for sending a copy of the introduction before its publication.

27. *New Literary History* 7 (1976), 259–70.

28. Ibid., p. 260.

29. In *Negara: The Theatre State in Nineteenth-Century Bali*, Princeton, 1980, p. 136.

30. Roger Chartier, "Intellectual History or Sociocultural History? The French Trajectories," in LaCapra and Kaplan (eds), *Modern European Intellectual History*, p. 41.

31. Ibid., p. 40.

32. See the critique by Toews, "Intellectual History," p. 886.

33. The specific formulation is that of Hunt, "History, Culture and Text," p. 10.

34. Thus Hayden White can claim that "the best grounds for choosing one perspective on history rather than another are ultimately aesthetic and moral rather than epistemological" and that "the demand for the scientization of history represents only the statement of a preference for a specific modality of historical conceptualization, the grounds of which are either moral or aesthetic." See his *Metahistory: The Historical Imagination in Nineteenth-Century Europe*, Baltimore, 1973, p. xii.

35. "The Literary, the Textual, the Social," introduction to *The Aims of Representation: Subject/Text/History*, ed. Murray Krieger, New York, 1987, p. 18.

36. "Intellectual History," pp. 105–6.

37. As David Carroll insists: "formalism in some form or other just won't go away no matter how often and how forcefully history and politics are evoked to chase it away or at least put it in its place. Another version of formalism always seems ready to rise out of the ash can of history to take the place of previously discarded versions." "Narrative, Heterogeneity, and the Question of the Political: Bakhtin and Lyotard," in *The Aims of Representation*, pp. 69–70.

38. Louis Montrose, "Renaissance Studies and the Subject of History," *English Literary Renaissance* 16 (1986), 6.

39. *Negotiating the Past*, p. 58.

40. "Renaissance Studies," p. 8.

41. Stephen Greenblatt, "Capitalist Culture and the Circulatory System," in *The Aims of Representation*, p. 257.

42. Compare the critique of New Historicism by Myra Jehlen in "Patrolling the Borders: Feminist Historiography and the New Historicism," *Radical History Review* 43 (1989), 23.

43. "Renaissance Studies," p. 8.

44. Hence Jean Howard, in an article that both advocates and criticizes the practice of New Historicism, suggests that a requirement of the New Historicist position is to accord literature real power. "Rather than passively reflecting an external reality, literature is an agent in constructing a culture's sense of reality. It is part of a much larger symbolic order through which the world at a particular moment is conceptualized and through which a culture imagines its relationship to the actual conditions of its existence. Instead of a hierarchical relationship in which literature figures as a parasitic reflector of historical facts, one imagines a complex textualized universe in which literature participates in historical processes and in the political management of reality": "The New Historicism in Literary Study," *English Literary Renaissance* 16 (1986), 25. One can admire and share Howard's desire to reject a mimetic view of

literary discourse, but the question of precisely how literature politically manages reality goes largely unexplained. Until New Historicism, and cultural history more generally, is able to explain the supposed links between literary and social praxis in concrete and persuasive terms that can be generalized in the form of a social theory, the interpretive moves, however dazzling, of which it is capable will remain unconvincing. It is also clear that the totalizing view of culture New Historicists tend to project will sit uneasily with historians trained to an awareness of the discontinuous stages of social change, in which certain sectors of a society appear to hold quite distinct views and beliefs – to belong, in the current terminology, to a distinctive discursive regime – not necessarily shared or compatible with those held by other sectors of society. While New Historicism has used deconstruction to argue for the contradictory and fragmentary nature of textuality, it has not extended this perspective to history itself. On this, see below, p. 74.

45. *Marxism and Literature*, p. 99.
46. Ibid., p. 165.
47. Ibid., p. 37.
48. See above, n. 28.
49. *The World, the Text and the Critic*, Cambridge, Mass., 1983, p. 4.
50. A point well made by Williams, *Marxism and Literature*, p. 169.
51. Fredric Jameson, to cite one case, forthrightly proclaims that, for him, "interpretation is . . . construed as an essentially allegorical act, which consists in rewriting a given text in terms of a particular interpretive master code" (*The Political Unconscious: Narrative as a Socially Symbolic Act*, Ithaca, NY, 1981, p. 10). And for Jameson, the privileged master code is history (understood in Marxist categories), since his own rewriting of the literary text is predicated on the idea that the literary text "itself may be seen as the rewriting or restructuration of a prior historical or ideological subtext, it being understood that such a 'subtext' is not immediately present as such . . ." (ibid., p. 81). If the literary text is, in this sense, already an allegory of history, then historical criticism is devoted to recuperating the original meaning of that allegory through its reallegorization. In viewing history as the "absent subtext" of the literary work, Jameson comes close to Macherey's notion of history as the text's "unconscious," in the latter's adaptation of Freudian theory for literary criticism. Freudian psychoanalysis offers another privileged master code by which literary works can be allegorized as enactments of the hidden work of the unconscious. See Pierre Macherey, *A Theory of Literary Production*, trans. Geoffrey Wall, London, 1985.
52. *The Theory of Literature*, New York, 1977, pp. 73–4.
53. *The Great Cat Massacre*, New York, 1984, pp. 3, 5. As Lynn Hunt shows, the shift from inferring causal explanation to deciphering meaning that results from the adoption of a discursive model "throws into doubt all the conventional language of historical investigation" by denying historians the essence of their enterprise, which traditionally has been the explanation of change over time. See her "History beyond Social Theory," p. 12.
54. "Intellectual History," p. 906.
55. To quote Hayden White's cogent formulation, "The Problem of Change in Literary History," *New Literary History* 7 (1975), 99. White has moved away somewhat from this position and would now claim that the text-context problem is "resolvable from the semiological perspective to the extent that what conventional historians call the context is already in the text in the specific modalities of code shifting by which discourse produces its meaning." See his "The Context in the Text: Method and Ideology in Intellectual History," in *The Content of the Form*, p. 212. But to say this is to resolve the problem by collapsing text and context into a single textualized unit in the examination of which essentially formalist procedures (to trace the patterns of code

shifting) are called for. It is difficult to see how such an analysis will answer the set of descriptive and causal questions which White posed in 1975, how the interpretation of a single text can, in the end, address the problem of change in literary history which he then identified as crucial to the historical investigation of literature.

56. "Making Up Lost Time," p. 95.

57. In the insightful phrase of Toews, "Intellectual History," p. 906.

58. I owe this particular formulation to Dominick LaCapra, "Rethinking Intellectual History and Reading Texts," in LaCapra and Kaplan (eds), *Modern European Intellectual History*, p. 49. LaCapra, however, draws from it the conclusion that such a view of textuality implies that the context or "real world" is itself textualized in a variety of ways, and thus we must admit that one "is 'always already' implicated in problems of language use as one attempts to gain perspective on these problems . . .; for the historian, the very reconstruction of a 'context' or a 'reality' takes place on the basis of 'textualized' remainders of the past" (ibid., p. 50). LaCapra thus joins the semiotic camp, at least in his conception of the inaccessibility of a past reality in any other than a mediated, textualized form, although LaCapra does recognize that "the most distinctive issue in historiography is that of the relationship between documentary reconstruction of and dialogue with the past," and the collection of essays cited above powerfully presents the present state of this question in historical, philosophical, and literary studies.

Part III   *Nuanced or ambiguous Others*

EDITOR'S INTRODUCTION

The readings chosen for this Part: Joyce Appleby, Lynn Hunt and Margaret Jacob, *Telling the Truth about History* (1995); Tony Bennett, *Outside Literature* (1990) and his essay "Texts in History" (1987), and Susan Stanford Friedman, *Making History* (1995) are, in some ways, tips of an ever increasing iceberg: historians who can see the enormous benefits to be gained by aligning with postmodern-type historiography but who are reluctant to become postmodernists because of a desire to retain some aspects of their "old" political desires. These texts thus illustrate the magnetic pull of a postmodernism which gives writers a new creative space without totally embracing the tenets of postmodernism.

In the case of Appleby *et al.*, their desire is for a democratic, feminist, pluralist and thus potentially "totalizing" historiography. It is totalizing because, if everyone has a free, reflexive voice, then the sum of voices will reflect much more accurately the past in all its myriad ways. That this possible totality is potentially more objective if historians subscribe to a pragmatic, realist objectivity which would stop just "any old voice" being permissible. Here, in the space opened up by postmodernist deconstructionism, methodological objectivity saves the radical day. And so it does with Tony Bennett.

For many years now Tony Bennett has been trying, in the fields of literary theory and cultural studies as well as in historiography, to shed the essentialist, teleological, idealist aspects of Marxism whilst retaining his Marxist political position. In many ways Bennett could very well have been edged into two of the previous Parts (namely, those of the collapse of the upper and lower cases) except that one still detects in his position the idea that the postmodern view – that of an interpretive free-play within which an indiscriminate "anything goes" – is, because it is politically "useful" to everybody, "useless" to him. Accordingly, in a series of arguments (arguments which I have analysed a little further in "Marxism and Historical Knowledge: the Case of Tony Bennett," *Literature and History*, 3rd series, 3/1 1994) Bennett attempts to ground substantive knowledge of the past through a lower case methodology: I do not think Bennett's attempt really succeeds. Nevertheless, his essays contain some of the most economical and penetrating discussions available on the nature of historiography postmodern/post-Marxist style, and really do repay careful consideration.

The apparent dilemma of giving away much of the ground on which certainty might be based yet wanting to keep at least enough of it back to "ground" her own type of feminist historiography, arguably informs Susan Stanford Friedman's essay, reproduced here in small part. There has been, she writes, a "palpable anxiety within the feminist movement about the possibility that our activities as feminists – including the productions of our own history – run the risk of repeating the same patterns of thought and action that excluded, distorted, muted, or erased women from the master narratives of history in the first place." She shows how feminist histories in the plural (after, say, Diane Elam) need not paralyse the necessity to tell stories (presumably "trueish" ones) about feminism. This is a far cry from the disinterested history championed by Elton *et al.*, but as all the contributors to this Part variously point out or infer, those claiming such disinterest effectively do so in the name of their own interests universalized as if they were the interests of historiography *per se*. Yet the fact that there is no arguable historiography *per se* still uneasily haunts Appleby *et al.* – and hence the apparent nostalgia for at least elements of older "certaintist" discourses.

18 Joyce Appleby, Lynn Hunt, Margaret Jacob

Telling the truth about history

INTRODUCTION

More people in the United States have been to college or university than was the case in any country at any time in the past. Americans should, and indeed do, know many things. Yet confidence in the value and truth of knowledge eludes just about everyone. This is especially true of historical knowledge. Once there was a single narrative of national history that most Americans accepted as part of their heritage. Now there is an increasing emphasis on the diversity of ethnic, racial, and gender experience and a deep skepticism about whether the narrative of America's achievements comprises anything more than a self-congratulatory story masking the power of elites. History has been shaken right down to its scientific and cultural foundations at the very time that those foundations themselves are being contested.

Since the end of World War II the number of students pursuing higher education in America has more than quintupled, going from 2,338,000 in 1947 to 13,043,000 in 1988. Even more dramatic, the proportion of women in the student population has gone from 29 percent to 54 percent. By 1988, 19 percent of all college students were men and women of color.[1] Many of these new students – especially those from groups previously denied access to the higher reaches of the nation's cultural life – brought to college little confidence in the prevailing intellectual assumptions about the American past. They were also less impressed by the model of objective knowledge derived from science and dominant since the nineteenth century. Once the prerogative of a small band of philosophers, this now widespread skepticism forced teachers to become far more self-conscious about the intellectual traditions they were imparting. A mighty fissure in the philosophical foundations of Western culture was about to crack open.

We three are very much the products of the unprecedented expansion of higher education in the United States. Like others, we approached academic careers as outsiders. We have been especially sensitive to the ways in which claims to objectivity have been used to exclude us from full participation in the nation's public life, a fate shared by others of our sex, working-class people, and minorities. We also appreciate that for outsiders, skepticism and relativism offer modes of inquiry essential to redressing the wrongs of exclusion.

By the time our generation of students matured and became college teachers themselves, confidence in previous certainties had all but disappeared. No longer did people believe that any form of knowledge, including history, could be modeled on the scientific method of inquiry, or that progress in science and technology was unquestionably desirable – the more the better. Where value-free science had once made sense and offered hope of sustained progress, now neither an uncontested, edifying truth about the American past nor benign scientific advance seem possible to thoughtful people. It is as if higher education was opened to us – women, minorities, working people – at the same time that we lost the philosophical foundation that had underpinned the confidence of educated people.

Anyone who has taught in the contemporary American university and been politely told by word or gesture, "That is your opinion, prof," knows that skepticism about everything from the meaning of American history to the value of science is the order of the day. And just in case students did not get the point across, there is now a new breed of philosopher who thinks that everything is relative to where you happen to be standing, making truth what you happen to believe and hence dependent upon the "tent" in which you are encamped in your patch of social space.

This book confronts head-on the present uncertainty about values and truth-seeking and addresses the current controversies about objective knowledge, cultural diversity, and the political imperatives of a democratic education. It does so by focusing on the project of history, specifically by asking what people can know about the past that will help them elucidate the present. Our central argument is that skepticism and relativism about truth, not only in science but also in history and politics, have grown out of the insistent democratization of American society. The opening of higher education to nearly all who seek it, the rewriting of American history from a variety of cultural perspectives, and the dethroning of science as the source and model for all that is true are interrelated phenomena. It is no accident that they all occurred almost simultaneously.

In the decades since World War II the old intellectual absolutisms have been dethroned: science, scientific history, and history in the service of nationalism. In their place – almost as an interim report – the postwar generation has constructed sociologies of knowledge, records of diverse peoples, and histories based upon group or gender identities. Women, minorities, and workers populate American and Western histories where formerly heroes, geniuses, statesmen – icons of order and the status quo – reigned unchallenged. The postwar generation has questioned fixed categories previously endorsed as rational by all thoughtful men, and has denaturalized social behavior once presumed to be encoded in the very structure of humanness. As members of that generation, we routinely, even angrily, ask: Whose history? Whose science? Whose interests are served by those ideas and those stories? The challenge is out to all claims to universality expressed in such phrases as "Men are . . ." and "Naturally science says . . ." and "As we all know. . . ."

In contrast to the critics who decry the impending death of Western civilization under the impact of the democratization of education, we endorse the insights and revisions made possible by that democratization. In this book we embrace a healthy skepticism, and we applaud the research that has laid the foundations for a multicultural approach to human history. But we reject the cynicism and nihilism that accompany contemporary relativism. We seek a vision of the past and an intellectual stance for the present that will promote an ever more democratic society. To achieve this aim, we think it essential to confront the current controversies over national history, scientific integrity, and the possibility of achieving truth and objectivity in human knowledge of the past.

A host of questions present themselves. Do Americans need a knowledge of history, and if they do, whose history and for what purposes? Is history a science or an art? Is history always in some sense propaganda? The answers to these questions might once have been obvious to educated people, but they are obvious no longer. At least one thing seems clear, however: rarely has history been such a subject of controversy. In the former communist world, aroused citizens have toppled statues of Lenin and other discredited national heroes and thrown out history professors and textbooks as hopelessly contaminated by Marxist ideology. When repressive governments fall from power, whether on the left or on the right, the citizens rush to find historical evidence of the government's previous misdeeds in order to fortify the will to reconstitute their nation.

Because history and historical evidence are so crucial to a people's sense of identity; the evidence itself often becomes the focus of struggle. This is clear in the disturbing efforts of some groups to deny the reality of Hitler's final solution. The Institute of Historical Review, for instance, has taken out advertisements in college newspapers and professional organizations around the nation calling for research to contest the facts about the systematic genocide of Jews in Nazi-occupied Europe. The people behind this organization have been able to make their case public, no matter how outlandish it is, by using organizational names that imply objectivity ("Institute of Whatever" sounds more neutral than "neo-Nazi, anti-Semitic propaganda group," for example) and by manipulating laws designed to ensure free speech. Once lies are repeated in print or on the airwaves a number of times, they begin to seem like bona fide questions for debate.

This case is an extreme example of a more general set of issues about the purposes and responsibilities of history. In the United States, the recent controversy over history has centered on school textbooks. Critics have scrutinized the textbooks available for every level of education and found them Eurocentric, racist, sexist, and homophobic. They celebrate the achievements, it is alleged, of dead white European males rather than showing the contributions of women, minorities, gays, or other oppressed and excluded groups. They reinforce the worst racial and sexual stereotypes rather than helping children and young people to see beyond them. Whole new teams of writers have been hired to produce histories with perspectives thought to be more in tune with the values of a socially diverse society.

The supporters of multiculturalism, as that movement is now called, have themselves been castigated as bullying propagandizers who value a politically motivated line of interpretation more than the truth. They have been accused of deliberately exaggerating the contributions of minority groups in order to make those minorities feel good about themselves at the expense of impartiality and a common sense of national identity. State commissions, professional conferences, and government officials have issued reports, with the result that the public is alternately confused, irritated, and intrigued. Is history supposed to create ethnic pride and self-confidence? Or should history convey some kind of objective truth about the past? Must history be continually rewritten to undo the perpetuation of racial and sexual stereotypes? Or should it stand above the tumult of present-day political and social concerns? Is the teaching of a coherent national history essential to democracy? Is the attack on traditional history another sign of an insidious new barbarism at the gates, one that devalues knowledge and denies the possibility of truth?

This furor over history must be surprising to many adults who remember their history courses, if they remember them at all, as successions of names, dates, and events rather than as hothouses of debate about ethnic and national identity. The great contemporary dilemma of relativism has drawn history into the fray. Does every group or nation have its own version of the truth? Is one history as good as another? What is the role of the historian if truth is relative to the position of the author?

Let us be clear about what we, the authors, believe. Skepticism is an approach to learning as well as a philosophical stance. Since the Greeks, a certain amount of skepticism about truth claims has been essential to the search for truth; skepticism can encourage people to learn more and remain open to the possibility of their own errors. Complete skepticism, on the other hand, is debilitating, because it casts doubt on the ability to make judgments or draw conclusions.

Skepticism, in fact, is built into the very marrow of the West's cultural bones. By the time of the Enlightenment in the eighteenth century, some degree of skepticism had come to seem necessary for any true intellectual. Denis Diderot, one of the leaders of the Enlightenment, insisted, "All things must be examined, all must be winnowed and sifted without exception and without sparing anyone's sensibilities." In the new age announced by Diderot, thinkers would have to "trample mercilessly" upon all the old traditions and question every barrier to thought.[2] Nothing since that time has been taken as given or beyond questioning, not the classics, not the Bible, not the teachings of church or state.

Relativism, a modern corollary to skepticism, is the belief that the truth of a statement is relative to the position of the person making the statement. It has generated a pervasive lack of confidence in the ability to find the truth or even to establish that there is such a thing as the truth. Relativism leads directly to a questioning of the ideal of objectivity, because it undermines the belief that people can get outside of themselves in order to get at the truth. If truth depends on the observer's standpoint, how can there be any transcendent, universal, or absolute truth, or at least truths that hold for all groups for many generations? We are arguing here that truths about the past are possible, even if they are not absolute, and hence are worth struggling for.

The experience of World War II with its horrendous new weaponry and the genocidal policies of the Nazi regime temporarily forestalled the progress of skepticism and relativism. The killing of the Jews seemed to show that absolute moral standards were necessary, that cultural relativism had reached its limits in the death camps. But the lull was only temporary. Doubts spilled over the restraints of conscience and pressed against the maxims of Western philosophy. The inauguration of the atomic age in 1945 and the increasing interconnection between big science and big government impugned the disinterestedness of science itself. America's civil rights movement and the protests against the Vietnam War called into question the ability of scientists, policymakers, and professors to escape their own racial and political prejudices. Ecologists complained that modern science in the name of progress had invented the engines of mass destruction and that industry was polluting the environment. In the twentieth century, Western civilization produced the most technologically sophisticated genocide ever seen in history. Progress, democracy, objective knowledge, and modernity itself no longer seemed to march in step toward the enrichment of humankind.

We are not writing to lament the success of skepticism and relativism. We have been shaped by these attitudes as much as anyone else. Before the late 1960s and early 1970s, when we got our first jobs in the university, there were very few women teaching in the most influential history departments in the country. In that sense, we are among the barbarians whose passage into academia hostile critics lament. We have not only witnessed but also participated in the dethroning of once sacred intellectual icons. Trained to be "scientific" in our methods, we have challenged the inherited, traditional interpretations of both American and European history. We have even, perhaps ungratefully, questioned science's claims for disinterested truth and impartial objectivity. Influenced by twentieth-century philosophers, we have brought new theories to bear on older philosophical assumptions – both liberal and Marxist – about the way history works, and we have found the traditional interpretations to be wanting. If confessions are in order, we have used skepticism and relativism as tools (some would say weapons) in fashioning new understandings of the past.

We nonetheless see skepticism and relativism as two-edged swords. They can be wielded against the powers that be to promote a greater inclusiveness, but they can also wound those committed to pursuing any kind of knowledge whatsoever. These positions can imply that knowledge about the past is simply an ideological construction that serves particular interests, making history a series of myths establishing or reinforcing group identities. Skeptics and relativists boldly assert that science is only a social construction, or simply a series of linguistic conventions, an elaborate power game coded mathematically to ensure Western dominance over the earth's riches.

We want to move beyond this kind of skepticism while still embracing a pluralistic and complex understanding of ourselves as Americans and Westerners. We do this by looking closely at the ways historians have written in the past and how they write today. Because we want to affirm the achievements in the historiography of science, social change, and national purpose, we take on both the relativists on the left and the defenders of the *status quo ante* on the right.

We believe that the difficult questions in recent public debates about history can be understood by anyone willing to read a book about them. If the public is confused about the meaning of history as a subject, then historians are at least partly to blame. It is time we historians took responsibility for explaining what we do, how we do it, and why it is worth doing. Nor is just the public confused about history's status and role. Most undergraduate history majors have little sense of the historian's vocation or how their teachers learned what they lecture about. Needless to say, the situation for high school students is still more unfortunate, since history is often submerged beneath a general social studies curriculum. Moreover, history courses, at all levels, are usually conceived as conveying a specific subject matter rather than fostering a way of thinking about the past.

Finally, and perhaps most distressing, professional historians have been so successfully socialized by demands to publish that we have little time or inclination to participate in general debates about the meaning of our work. Questions about the relevance of scientific models to the search for historical truth or the role of history in shaping national identity – to name two of the central topics of this book – are often dismissed by historians as irrelevant to their work, which they define as researching in archives and writing scholarly books and articles. Questions about relativism, truth, and objectivity are relegated to the philosophy of history or left to those few historians, usually intellectual historians, with announced interests in such issues. Many historians imagine that only those with specialized knowledge can participate in the debate, even though they recognize that quarrels about history's relationship to science, to fiction, and to national identity are provoking wide public interest. We do not write out of a feeling of superiority to historians who have avoided these debates in the past; we came out of the same professional culture ourselves. But we do hope to encourage wider discussion of issues that must concern everyone.

Our aims in this book are simple and straightforward but also ambitious. We want to provide general readers, history students, and professional historians with some sense of the debates currently raging about history's relationship to scientific truth, objectivity, postmodernism, and the politics of identity. We chart a course of reflection on these issues that we hope will provide new answers. No one of us is a specialist in the philosophy of history. Each of us has been trained as a historian in particular areas of research, and we bring this training to bear on our analysis of the general debates concerning history in the late twentieth century.

We are carving out a position that is broad and inclusive. Nevertheless our arguments may give offense in some quarters. Indeed, in the current cultural climate, one made contentious by critics and caricaturists at both ends of the political spectrum, offense comes easily. Cultural conflict has been endemic to Western intellectual life since the philosophes, as the leaders of the Enlightenment are called, took on the clergy. With cultural divisiveness the norm, it is foolhardy to write books engaging cultural issues and expect a peaceful reception. There has, however, been some progress. No one, at least in the West, burns books (or their authors) anymore, although the case of Salman Rushdie mightily tests the commitment to free speech of publishers, booksellers, and governments.

What historians do best is to make connections with the past in order to illuminate the problems of the present and the potential of the future. We hope to show how historians have conceptualized their task in the past, particularly how that task has developed from telling a simple story to answering a complex array of questions about the human experience. The ambitions of history have changed over time, expanding to include general questions of historical development – itself a new idea in the eighteenth and nineteenth centuries. Yet even as the ambitions of history have grown, so too have questions about history's ability to tell a story with any certainty.

The democratization of the university has made the dilemmas posed by skepticism and relativism especially urgent. Relativism is now an issue in every branch of knowledge from science to literature. Critics of the "closing of the American mind" by the universities' new "tenured radicals" are right in at least one respect: the students welcomed in the expansion days of the 1960s are now tenured professors with positions of power to shape curricula, requirements, and the future of the university. The "barbarians" are no longer at the gates; although they may not control the budget, they sit on the most important university committees, teach many of the biggest courses, and write some of the most influential books. They have made skepticism and relativism common currency in intellectual life.

A democratic practice of history, we will argue, encourages skepticism about dominant views, but at the same time trusts in the reality of the past and its knowability. To collapse this tension in favor of one side or the other is to give up the struggle for enlightenment. An openness to the interplay between certainty and doubt keeps faith with the expansive quality of democracy. This openness depends in turn on a version of the scientific model of knowledge, based on a belief in the reality of the past and the human ability to make contact with it, which helps discipline the understanding by requiring constant reference to something outside the human mind. In a democracy, history thrives on a passion for establishing and communicating the truth.

Even in a democracy, history always involves power and exclusion, for any history is always someone's history, told by that someone from a partial point of view. Yet external reality has the power to impose itself on the mind; past realities remain in records of various sorts that historians are trained to interpret. The effort to establish a historical truth itself fosters civility. Since no one can be certain that his or her explanations are definitively right, everyone must listen to other voices. All histories are provisional; none will have the last word.

In the pages that follow, we hope to show that a democratic practice of history – one in which an ever growing chorus of voices is heard – offers the best chance of making sense of the world. We will also present a new way of thinking about objectivity, one that argues for the centrality of science to Western culture and to the search for truth. There is every reason for Americans (and indeed inhabitants of every Western nation) to expand their commitment to pluralistic education and continue their appraisal of the accounts that define them as a nation. But national histories are still necessary. So too is faith in the ultimate goal of an education: the rigorous search for truth usable by all peoples.

NOTES

1. *Digest of Education Statistics 1990 (United States Department of Education, National Center for Educational Statistics, February 1991)*, especially pp. 15, 167, 181, 199. See also *Perspectives*. American Historical Association Newsletter, Washington, DC, vol. 31, no. 4, April 1993, p. 1.
2. In his article "Encyclopedia," in the *Encyclopédie*, as translated in Keith Michael Baker (ed.) *The Old Regime and the French Revolution*, Chicago, 1987, p. 84.

19 Tony Bennett

Outside literature
Texts in history

OUTSIDE LITERATURE

Narrative, history, politics

"The history invoked as ultimate reality and source of truth," Jonathan Culler argues, "manifests itself in narrative constructs, stories designed to yield meaning through narrative ordering." Although, properly speaking, a structuralist argument given its major statements by Barthes and Lévi-Strauss, this view has since come to be associated with deconstruction in a number of secondary commentaries. It is also the aspect of deconstruction which has most exercised the attention of Marxist literary theorists. What does the argument amount to? In brief, it constitutes a rebuttal of those systems of explanation in which history is assigned the status of a metalanguage capable of furnishing the means for the explanation of social and textual phenomena. The history which is assigned such a role, it is argued, can never fulfil its obligations to the degree that it always turns out to be the product of a series of narrative and rhetorical devices. An effect of discourse itself, it is unable to function as an extra-discursive source of anything else. Historical explanation thus turns out to be a way of telling stories without any particularly convincing means, where such stories differ, of deciding between them. Of course, the objection is not limited to history but applies to any system of explanation in which a signified is granted an existence independently of the signifiers which produce it. In this sense, the argument undermines the pretensions of all would-be metalanguages in contending, as I have summarised its import elsewhere, that there is "no language which can claim an absolute or transcendental validity for its ways of 'fixing' other languages, discourses or texts as objects within itself or which can efface the traces of writing or language within itself."

So far as the literature/history couplet is concerned, this means that the latter cannot figure as an extra-discursive real in relation to which the former might find its footing. The consequences of this are particularly telling where history, conceived as a set of developmental processes with an inherent direction, is supposed to provide an objective anchorage for the meanings of literary texts – in their own time and, through a continuity of interpretative horizons guaranteed by history's inherent direction, in the present also. All that such arguments amount to, it is objected, is a narrative ordering of the relations between two series – a series of literary texts and a series of extra-literary events or structures – which cannot secure any warrant except for that provided by its own discursive manoeuvres. To paraphrase Lévi-Strauss, we might say that literary texts have their meanings vouchsafed by history only on the condition that, within the limits of a particular interpretative paradigm, we view them so. But it is then necessary to add, as Lévi-Strauss does, that *"this meaning is never the right one*: superstructures are *faulty acts* which have 'made it' socially."

The argument, it seems to me, is unassailable and it is notable that Marxist responses have been less concerned to refute it *per se* than to find some way of curtailing its implications. Usually, this leads to an attempt to negotiate some leeway between the irreconcilable views that, one, history is an effect of discourse and, two, that it is an extra-discursive real. This results in formulations such as those suggested by Jameson in *The Political Unconscious*: history (sense one) is a narrative construct but it is history (sense two) which, in the last instance, determines the narrative orderings to which history (still sense two) subjects itself. The chief difficulty with such arguments, as Geoff Bennington and Robert Young have noted, is that they are ultimately pressed to take their stand on precisely that conception of history which poststructuralists have called into question. The consequence of the various equivocations and circumlocutions which masquerade as dialectical reasoning is that the history that is shown the front door in concession to poststructuralism is ushered in through the back door where its re-entry is legitimated in the name of the nitty-gritties of last instances and the like.

What is it that motivates and sustains such counter-arguments in spite of the desperate circularities to which they are driven? Two concerns predominate – one which Marxists share with other critics of poststructuralism, and a second which is more specific to Marxist thought, and particularly to the way in which, in its classical formulations, it conceives the relations between epistemological questions and the conduct of politics.

Within the first concern, what is resisted is the threat to the very possibility of rationality which seems to be embodied in the argument that there are no metanarratives or, more generally, no metalanguages capable of resolving the differences between contending narrative and linguistic orderings of reality. If narratives are all that we can have and if all narratives are, in principle, of equal value – as it seems they must be if there is no touchstone of "reality" to which they can be referred for the adjudication of their truth claims – then rational debate would seem to be pointless. If the non-accessibility of a referent means that the theorist is "drawn into labyrinths of textual 'undecidability' where any kind of systematic truth-claim could only tell the story of its own undoing" – then why bother? The political consequence of such a radical relativism, Norris suggests, can only be quietism:

> The upshot in political terms would be a "liberal" consensus for-swearing the idea of social improvement through rational critique and relying instead on the free circulation of communal myths and values.

The danger is real enough. While Derrida's own work may be exempted from the charge, its annexation to the intellectual currents of postmodernism often results in a *jouissance*-like exultation in the pleasures of a free-wheeling relativism. However, as the painstaking argument of Norris's *Contest of Faculties* testifies, the prospect of a relativism without limits can be successfully resisted without resurrecting the concept of an extra-discursive referent as the final arbiter of competing truth claims, and certainly without seeking to reinstate history as such a referent. Ultimately, the weakness of such arguments consists in the fact that they concede too much from the outset in accepting the polar opposites proposed by the positions they oppose: truth claims must be able, under some specifiable set of conditions, to be established absolutely or they cannot be established at all; or, if there is no way of escaping the constraints of narrative and language, then all narrative and linguistic orderings of reality must be regarded as equally valid.

These are non-sequiturs. It by no means follows, because we cannot establish certain propositions as absolutely true, that we have no means of establishing their provisional truth – of determining that they meet conditions which justify our regarding them as true and so as capable of serving as a basis for both further thought and action. Nor does it follow, if we accept that there can be no escaping the constraints of language and narrative, that anything goes – that all possible narrative systems or language games are to be ranked equally with regard to their propositional content. The violent "all or nothing" logic of such polarities need hold us in its thrall only so long as we subscribe to the tenets of traditional epistemology in supposing that what is at issue in competing truth claims is the demonstration of a correspondence between thought and reality, conceived as separate realms, and, should that prove to be impossible, of accepting that all we can demonstrate is the correspondence of thought (regarded as a property of the subject) to itself.

I've already suggested why such conceptions can contribute little to our understanding of the manner in which historical knowledge is produced and validated – and in ways which allow for reasoned debate as well as for the empirical regulation of propositional statements – without the question of our access to an extra-discursive past ever arising. Marx Cousins has argued a broadly similar position. Addressing himself not to "History in the upper case" but to history "as a 'craft' with skills and rules, as a definite technique of discovery," he likens its procedures to those embodied in the law, contending that both address themselves to two primary questions: Did a specific event occur or not? If so, into what class of event does it fall? These, once answered, give rise to a similar series of further questions: Who was responsible for the event? What links of causality can be established in relation to the event and to other pertinent events? In a court of law, Cousins argues, such questions are pursued by means of definite rules governing the admissibility of, and relative credence to be given to, different types of evidence which, for an event to be legally recognized, "must be assembled into an edifice which is to be accepted as a representation of the event which is beyond all reasonable doubt." The key phrase here is "representation of the event" rather than "the event itself." As Cousins elaborates:

> It might appear that the legal process attempts to establish what really happened in the past, but "really" is used in a specialized sense. "Really" is what is relevant to the law, what is definable by law, what may be argued in terms of law and evidence, what may be judged and what may be subject to appeal. "Reality" as far as the law is concerned is a set of representations of the past, ordered in accordance with legal categories and rules of evidence into a

decision which claims to rest upon the truth. But this truth of the past, the representations of events, is a strictly legal truth.

Similarly, the past, in so far as the historian is concerned with it, is never the past as such – not everything that may be said of it – but only the past as a product of the specific protocols of investigation which characterize the discipline of history in its concern to establish, classify and order the relations between events pertinent to the inquiry in hand. In this way, Cousins argues, the practice of history may be said "to produce (uncover) events, whose representations are called historical facts." In this conception, the reality of those events – and thereby, so to speak, of the "historical past" – consists in nothing but, and certainly nothing beyond, the status of historical facts that is accorded those representations whose evidential standing has passed the test of disciplined scrutiny. Although this knowledge cannot claim to rest on any foundations other than its own procedures or to know anything other than the historical facts which those procedures produce and validate, Cousins does not see this as an occasion for any general scepticism:

> But to reject any general foundation to historical truth or any general truth of History does itself not undermine a notion of historical truth as such. There is no need to enter a form of scepticism about statements about the past. It is enough to recognize that the justification for truth claims about the past are [sic] part of the particular practice of historical investigation. Historical facts are not illusions; we may as well say they are true.

Indeed, it is these truths, the truths comprising the "historical past," which serve as a check, and as the only possible check, on the forms in which earlier epochs are represented. Of course, it is not an absolute check. Nor could it be to the degree that the "historical past" is characterized, and necessarily so, by areas of marked uncertainty and instability in consequence of the historiographical disputes concerning the forms of evidence pertinent to particular inquiries and the rules of reasoning to be applied to them. The effect of such disputes – and it is such disputes which *constitute* the discipline rather than being its accidental by-products – is to introduce a degree of indeterminacy into the "historical past." But only a degree, for this indeterminacy is located against a bedrock of what are taken to be determinate historical truths. It is true that this bedrock may be shifted in the sense that some truths may be added to it while others are subtracted as specific historio-graphical disputes are worked out. Yet such disputes never throw the totality of the "historical past" into question. Indeed, it is a condition of its intelligibility that historical debate should take place within a horizon of both determinacy and indeterminacy: it requires both – the former to supply conditions of resolution, the latter to be purposive.

Imperfect though it is, it is only to this unstable, always provisional and forever changing "historical past" that propositional statements about the past can be referred for the adjudication of their truth claims. The degree to which this enables the "historical past" to serve also as a check on the broader terrain of historical representations constituted by the public historical sphere, however, is not given by this past itself. Rather, it depends on the relations which obtain between the practice of history and the other institutional contexts and discursive regimes within which representations of the past are produced and circulated. There is nothing within the protocols of historical inquiry that can prevent historical representations which violently traduce the "historical past" from gaining an effective currency and so becoming a major social force. In such circumstances – the ascendancy of fascist myth, for example – it is not a general crisis of reason that is at issue but the failure of the specific form of reasoning embodied in the procedures of history to establish their pertinence or carry much weight in the general political arena.

It is, then, the ratio of determinacy/indeterminacy within the "his-torical past" and the degree of weight accorded this past in relation to other spheres of historical representation which effectively limits what can be said about the past with any degree of warrantability in a particular set of circumstances. And if this is not an absolute check, neither is it one which can be imposed on the future. As the past which is produced by the social labour of historians may change in unforeseeable ways, it must be allowed that it may one day furnish a support for statements which it currently provides no warrant for.

This is a far cry from any transcendental guarantees. It amounts to neither more nor less than saying that the discipline of history – like a court of law – constitutes a particular institutionalised form for the social regulation of statements about the past. As such, it never goes beyond referring such statements to those representations comprising the "historical past" which function as history's truths. But what other kind of regulation could be applied to such statements? A higher order of certainty could only be obtained by reaching back beyond the past produced by historical inquiry to the notional referent of the past as it really was and as revealed to some ideally situated observer. It is only where the demand for such transcendental certainties prevails that when it is disappointed – as inevitably it must be – its all-or-nothing logic asserts itself. Since the practical forms that are available to us for the regulation of historical truths cannot satisfy this demand, the only alternative seems to be a radical relativism in which, since nothing can be absolutely secured, anything must be allowed to go. The paradox here is that the only condition which could stop this slide – that is, knowledge of the past *as such* – would, at the same time, put an end to history conceived as a specific type of inquiry governed by definite protocols of reasoning. One might say that historical inquiry is kept open because the gap between what functions as if it were its referent (records, primary sources, etc.) and, so to speak, that referent's referent (the past "as it really was") is never closed down.

It is this demand for transcendental certainties that is present in "History in the upper case": that is, philosophies of history which purport to assign events their objective significance by identifying their place and function within a general schema of historical development. It is clear, of course, that the boundary line between history, thus understood, and "the historian's craft" is not a rigorous one. In practice, the procedures of historical inquiry are often too visibly governed by the assumptions of some general theory of history. Yet, as it is equally clear that this need not be so, the distinction – understood as a theoretical one – remains useful. It is thus primarily the philosophical sense of the term that Derrida has in mind when he argues that "if the word 'history' did not carry with it the theme of a final repression of différance, we could say that differences alone could be 'historical' through and through and from the start". For philosophies of history must reduce all differences to the identity of History as an objectively known process which, since it assigns all events their significance, closes off – or promises to close off – that infinite deferment of ultimate meanings which Derrida intends by the concept of *différance*.

It is usually conceptions of history of this kind that Marxist critics have been concerned to defend in resisting the "incisive acid of deconstruction." The actual procedures of historical inquiry seem scarcely to have entered into the matter. This is regrettable for, as I have tried to show, an argument which takes these as its point of departure can arrive at a means of specifying how historical truths are produced and socially deployed which satisfies many of the requirements of Marxist thought. The adjudication of statements about the past effected by the disciplined procedures of history consists in a particular institutionalized set of social processes whose relations with other social practices are historically variable and contingent. This may not be what Marx meant when he said that men make their own history, but on the basis of determined conditions. Nonetheless, the phrase will serve nicely as a summary of the position I have been arguing.

TEXTS IN HISTORY

In recent discussion, "poststructuralism" has, for the greater part, been equated with the work of Derrida or, more generally, with the ever mobile and flexible strategy of deconstruction. Whilst not entirely shifting this centre of gravity, my concerns tend rather in the direction of a poststructuralist Marxism. I mean, by this, a Marxism which comes after structuralism, which is responsive to its criticisms – and, indeed, to those of other poststructuralisms – and which seeks to take account of them in reformulating its theoretical objectives and the means by which it should both represent and pursue them. I also want to tilt the balance of the discussion slightly in another respect. So far, poststructuralism has been posed largely as a set of tendencies inimical to Marxism and problematic for it in the sense of calling into question a good many of its founding premises and theoretical procedures. That's obviously right so far as the major currents of interaction between the two traditions are concerned. Still, it seems to me to be misleading in at least two respects. First, it tends to neglect the degree to which the anti-metaphysical and de-essentializing orientation of poststructuralist deconstruction has been paralleled by – in turn fuelling and being fuelled by – related tendencies within Marxism. Admittedly, this has often resulted in forms of Marxism which have been so thorough-goingly revised theoretically that they bear scarcely any recognizable relationship to their classical antecedents. This need not in itself, however, occasion any embarrassment. It is only by being ongoingly revised that a body of theory retains any validity or purchase as a historical force. To construe the relations between the formulations of classical Marxism and those which have been developed in the wake of structuralism as if the latter could be assessed in terms of the degree of their fidelity to or compatibility with the former would be unduly restricting. That way, a body of theory could never be allowed to develop other than via the germination of the seeds of development sown during the crystallizing phase of its inception – a profoundly unhistorical conception of the ways in which theoretical ideologies are adapted to changing theoretical and political circumstances. Rather than testing the value of theoretical innovations via such backward-looking glances, the acid test should always be: What do they enable one to do? What possibilities do they open up that were not there beforehand? What new fields and types of action do they generate?

It is in view of considerations of this kind that the construction of relations of *necessary opposition* between poststructuralism and Marxism is not only misleading but counter-productive. This is not to suggest that Marxism could or should even want to ingest deconstruction whole-sale. But it is to suggest that poststructuralism confronts Marxism not just with a series of negative problems (although it does that), but with a field of positive possibilities also. I want, therefore, to suggest that, through a critical sifting of the diverse elements of poststructuralism, Marxism may be able to reformulate its problems and objectives – not because it has to in order, so to speak, to keep its theoretical credentials in good condition but because, by doing so, it may open itself into a differently constituted field of political possibilities. Such "revisionism," that is to say, may contribute to the urgent task of re-thinking Marxism's conception of its relationship to the spheres of political action it consti-tutes for itself and of the strategies by which it seeks to intervene within them.

I want, then, to consider the relations between poststructuralism, as a general tendency, and poststructuralist Marxism, largely in their potentially positive aspects. First, however, some brief comments on those aspects of poststructuralism which have widely been regarded as posing a series of negative problems for Marxism. What are these prob-lems? "The work of Derrida and others," Terry Eagleton argues, has " . . . cast grave doubt upon the classical notions of truth, reality, meaning and knowledge, all of which could be exposed as resting on a naively representational theory of language." Why is this a problem? (The question is rarely put, but it's well worth asking.) The reason it has been *felt* to be a problem – indeed, has sometimes been conceived, and very often perceived as an explicit challenge to Marxism – is that it calls into doubt all those mechanisms (theories of knowledge; metaphysical conceptions of meaning; eschatological or historicist versions of History) which purport to provide a warrant, a certainty of rightness (epistemological, ethical or historical), in the light of which our orientation to and practice within the present might be validated, secured in and by means of some set of criteria that transcends our local, limited and irremediably muddied calculations.

Obviously, acceptance of such criticisms entails that Marxists should critically review all those economistic, scientific and historicist conceptions by means of which Marxism has traditionally sought to supply itself with such warrants. But need this be a problem? Again, the question is worth asking if only because the major theoretical developments within Marxism over the past two decades have been pushing in precisely this direction. It's singularly odd to expect that Marxists should feel placed on the defensive by the "discovery" that there neither are nor can be any transcendental guarantees, any absolute certainties or any essential truths since, in recent years, they have devoted some considerable effort to expunging from Marxist thought precisely such residues of nineteenth-century theologies, philosophies of history or ideologies of science. Nor has this been a process of theoretical self-criticism undertaken purely for its own sake. Such essentialising tendencies have been opposed, above all, because of their political effects – the quietism produced by the scientism of the Second International, for example, or the class essentialism which informed the political strategies of the Third International.

To the degree that such tendencies within Marxism have proved politically unhelpful, the only fitting Marxist response to the discovery that there can be no transcendental guarantees is: who needs them, anyway? If it is further argued that Marxism cannot secure its own relation to reality as a knowledge relation, if it must accept its own discursivity and acknowledge that it is submitted to the effects of language and writing: so be it! How could it be otherwise? Still, such acceptance should be accompanied by a demand: that deconstruction prove its worth by showing that it can do more than stand on the side-lines and undermine the terms in which every and any body of theory constructs itself. To argue that Marxism "is shot through with metaphors disguised as concepts" or that it is dependent on a whole battery of rhetorical and figurative devices is all very well but, in itself, hardly matters a jot. What would matter, what would count as helpful, would be to show that the existing stock of metaphorical, rhetorical and figurative devices used in Marxism had disabling theoretical and political consequences which could be remedied by the use of another set of similar devices. If this is not the point at issue, then deconstruction seems likely to do no more than to lock itself into a historical cul-de-sac in which it keeps alive the demand for transcendence simply by never-endingly denying its possibility – a criticism of essentialism which can rapidly become a lament for its loss, a consolation for the limitations of the human condition which is simultaneously a recipe for political quietism.

To put this another way, it has been argued that one of the major critical effects of deconstruction consists in the claim: "There is no metalanguage." That's not true of course. If by "metalanguage" is meant a language which constitutes other languages or discourses as objects of analysis within itself, then the world is full of them. What, then, does this claim amount to? Simply that there is no meta-metalanguage, no language which can claim an absolute or transcendental validity for its ways of "fixing" other languages, discourses or texts as objects within itself or which can efface the traces of writing or language within itself. Fine. God is dead and there's no such thing as an Absolute Science which escapes the constraints of its own discursivity. Meanwhile, the struggle between metalanguages – the struggle as to which discursive framing or other discourses is to predominate – continues. What matters for Marxism, as a party to such struggles, is not that it should be able to secure its discursive construction of the "real" and its framing of other texts and discourses within that "real" *absolutely*; rather, it is a matter of securing such constructions and framings *politically* in the sense of making them count above contending ones in terms of their ability to organize the consciousness and practice of historical agents.

If it is objected – "But what can the justification for such a practice be?" – the answer must be "None" if it's a case of looking for absolute justifications, be they epistemological, ethical or historical. In *Language, Semantics and Ideology*, Michel Pêcheux tells the story of Baron von Munchausen who rode into a bog only to extricate himself from this predicament by dragging himself – and his horse – out "by pulling with all the strength of one arm on a lock of my own hair". Pêcheux likens this to the way in which an individual, in being hitched into a subject position within ideology, is also subjected to a "phantasy effect" whereby, once in place, such a subject represents himself to himself as "cause of himself." Whilst I intend the argument only analogically, it seems to me that socialism can extricate itself from the mire of an epistemological and ethical relativism only by means of a political desire which functions as cause and justification of itself (although it is, of course, produced by and within the complex play of social forces and relationships) and which supplies the criteria – always contested – for the determination of the ends to which political and theoretical practice are directed. If that's not felt to be enough, I would ask: what other foundation could there be which is not a demand for transcendence and which – in order to preserve things as they are – simultaneously denies the possibility that such a demand might ever be realized?

NOTE

The footnotes of the original have been omitted.

20 Susan Stanford Friedman

Making history: reflections on feminism, narrative, and desire

> women have always been making history, living it and shaping it.
>
> Gerda Lerner

> The dream of a "total history" corroborating the historian's own desire for mastery of a documentary repertoire and furnishing the reader with a vicarious sense of – or perhaps a project for – control in a world out of joint has of course been a lodestar of historiography.
>
> Dominick LaCapra

> With these stories of ours
>   we can escape most anything,
> with these stories we will survive.
>
> Leslie Marmon Silko

> What has surfaced is something different from the unitary, closed, evolutionary narratives of historiography as we have traditionally known it: . . . we now get the histories (in the plural) of the losers as well as the winners, of the regional (and colonial) as well as the centrist, of the unsung many as well as the much sung few, and I might add, of women as well as men.
>
> Linda Hutcheon

My reflections begin with the contradictory desires within contemporary American feminism revolving around the question of history, particularly what is involved when feminists write histories of feminism. On the one hand, a pressing urgency to reclaim and hold on to a newly reconstituted history of women has fueled the development of the field of women's history, as well as the archaeological, archival, and oral history activities of feminists in other areas of women's studies outside the discipline of history, inside and outside the academy. On the other hand, there has been a palpable anxiety within the feminist movement about the possibility that our activities as feminists – including the productions of our own history – run the risk of repeating the same patterns of thought and action that excluded, distorted, muted, or erased women from the master narratives of history in the first place. The first impulse is outer-directed; it has chanelled phenomenal energy into the interrelated projects of the deformation of existing history and reformation of new histories of women, examining the place of gender in all cultural formations as they change over time. The second impulse is inner-directed and has applied the brakes to the new enthusiasms and in sober self-reflexivity insisted on problematizing the project of feminist history writing. With some exceptions, the reflexive impulse has found expression not so much in the field of women's history itself as in the discourses of feminist theory and activism. Feminism, particularly as it attempts to construct the stories of its own production, is caught between the desire to act and the resistance to action that threatens to reproduce what poststructuralists, like Luce Irigaray, call the economy of the same.

In this essay, I intend to explore the political necessity and creative possibilities of both the outer- and inner-directed activities. As well, I hope to show how the insight of one involves a blindness to the insight of the other, how ultimately both are necessary to the larger agenda of feminists "making history." I will first examine the underlying epistemological issues and then defend both the problematization of feminist history writing and the political necessity of this enterprise. Additionally, I will discuss how the competing needs to narrate and problematize the history of feminism reflect the desire for empowerment and fear of the will-to-power, the one affirming women's agency, the other muting it. Finally, I will suggest that feminists can be engaged in a dialogic, not monologic, project of writing feminist histories – in the plural – in which the politics of competing histories need not paralyze the need to tell stories about feminism.

FEMINIST EPISTEMOLOGIES AND MAKING HISTORY

The contradictory desires of feminists "making history" reflect the epistemological issues embedded in the double reference of the term *history* itself: first, to history as the past; and second, to history as the story of the past. The first meaning of history – what has happened – posits a base reality whose totality can never be fully reconstituted. The second meaning of history – the narrative of what has happened – foregrounds the role of the narrator of past events and consequently the nature of narrative as a mode of knowing that selects, organizes, orders, interprets, and allegorizes. These two dimensions of *history*, in turn, reflect the double reference in my title, "making history." The feminist desire to "make history" entangles the desire to effect significant and lasting change with the desire to be the historian of change. As a heuristic activity, history writing orders the past in relation to the needs of the present and future. The narrative act of assigning meaning to the past potentially intervenes in the present and future construction of history. For feminists, this means that writing the history of feminism functions as an act in the present that can (depending on its influence) contribute to the shape of feminism's future.

The heuristic and interventionist dimension of history writing – historiography as an act in the present on behalf of the future – raises the question of epistemology, central to understanding the inner-and outer-directed energies of feminist history writing, whether inside or outside the academy, whether within the field of women's history or more broadly within women's studies in general. For those working out of a positivist epistemology, the goal of history writing is to construct an objective account of the past based on thorough immersion in the empirical data and an unbiased assemblage of that data into an accurate sequence. The positivist belief in history writing as the production of objective truth may no longer be very prevalent in its purest form, although it once served as the philosophical bases for the formation of history as a discipline in the nineteenth and early twentieth centuries. However, the notion of history writing as the best possible reconstruction of the past – in a seamless narrative by an omniscient, invisible narrator – nonetheless continues to underwrite many projects, including feminist ones. Within this framework, the heuristic and interventionist dimension of history writing tends to be unacknowledged or overtly denied, and thus covertly operative.

For those working out of a subjectivist epistemology, the Real of history is knowable only through its written or oral textualizations. The past is therefore triply mediated – first, through the mediations of those texts, which are themselves reconstructions of what "really" happened; second, through the fragmentary and partial survival of those textualizations which are dependent upon the politics of documentation and the luck, skill, and persistence of the historian-as-detective who must locate them; and third, through the interpretive, meaning-making gaze of the historian. From this perspective, the excellence of history writing depends not upon the level of objectivity but rather upon the cogency of interpretation. And interpretation, as Hayden White and Dominick LaCapra pre-eminently theorize, introduces the mediations of language: the meaning-making of tropes, rhetoric, and narrative. Within the subjectivist epistemology, this dimension of historical discourse is often openly acknowledged as a source of speculation or even commitment.

Both epistemologies have been at work in women's studies, as feminists from a variety of fields engage in "making history" – in the writing about feminism's past and the performance of feminism's present and future. Some feminists work within a positivist framework, emphasizing the "truth" of what has been recovered; others function within a subjectivist framework, foregrounding the interpretive dimension of their narratives; and still others combine aspects of each epistemology. This diversity of historiographic assumption reflects, I believe, the contradictions built into the foundations of women's studies itself, contradictions that continue to underlie and permeate most work in the field, whether acknowledged or not. On the one hand, women's studies developed out of the need to counter hegemonic discourses about women that ignored, distorted, or trivialized women's history, experience, and potential. Women's studies consequently formulated compensatory and oppositional histories that told the "truth" about women – whether it was about women's status in the so-called Renaissance, the production of women's writing in the nineteenth century, or the sexual brutalization of black women slaves. This search to discover the "truth" of women's history that could shatter the "myths" and "lies" about women in the standard histories operates out of a positivist epistemology that assumes that the truth of history is objectively knowable.

On the other hand, the early insistence in women's studies that hegemonic knowledge was produced out of and in the service of androcentrism necessitated a subjectivist epistemology that insisted on all knowledge as value-based, emerging from a given perspective or standpoint. No knowledge is value-free, many feminists claimed, including feminist knowledge. Thomas Kuhn's *The Structure of Scientific Revolutions* (1962) was widely used to promote women's studies as a "paradigm shift" of dramatic and revolutionary proportions within the institutions of knowledge. The goal of writing history within this epistemological framework was not to discover the true history, but rather to construct the story of women's experience out of a feminist paradigm. Feminist histories countered hegemonic histories not with the objective truth, but with stories produced from a feminist perspective.

Both feminist epistemologies developed out of and have continued currency because of the urgently felt *political* agenda of women's studies: to engage in the deformation of phallocentric history and the refor- mation of histories that focus on or integrate women's experience and the issue of gender. Why political? Because what we know of the past shapes what becomes possible in the future. Because the repositories of human knowledge constitute the building blocks of the symbolic order. Because knowledge is power, ever more increasingly so in what is coming to be called the Information Age. As much as my own work and sympathies operate primarily out of the subjectivist epistemology, I believe that both epistemologies are necessary to the enterprise as moderating influences on the potential excesses of each. On the one hand, the positivist epistemology can lead toward fundamentalist assertions of truth that obscure the interpretive perspective of historical narrative. On the other hand, the subjectivist epistemology can lead toward the paralysis of complete relativism in which the Real of history vanishes into the play of story and discourse.

It would be easy, but misleading, to align the positivist epistemology with the outer-directed, action oriented desire to "make history" and the subjectivist epistemology with the inner-directed, self-reflexive prob- lematizing of feminist history writing. Certainly, the anxiety about the potential for replicating the master narratives of hegemonic discourse assumes the subjectivist model and foregrounds the role of the narrator in an interpretive ordering of the past. But to associate feminist history writing (whether in women's history or other fields of women's studies) with positivism would obscure the diversity of epistemologies present in these histories – some of which are positivist, some subjectivist, and some a combination, with the contradictory presence of both epistem- ologies underlying the endeavor as a whole. Moreover, it would too simply replicate the dismissive gesture that consigns everything but the act of poststructuralist problematizing to a bankrupt and naive humanism. Instead, the epistemologies underlying feminism should aim for a negotiation between objectivism and subjectivism, between the search for the Real and a recognition that all access to the Real is mediated through discourse. As LaCapra writes, "extreme documentary objectivism and relativistic subjectivism do not constitute genuine alternatives. They are mutually supportive parts of the same larger complex." He insists that his critique of positivist historiography does not mean that he abandons the empirical. He argues instead for a "dialogic and mutually provocative" relation between the empirical and the rhetorical as equally necessary parts of history writing.

This interplay encompasses the kind of dialogue Shoshana Felman and Dori Laub advocate in *Testimony: Crises of Witnessing in Literature, Psychoanalysis, and History.* They use the Holocaust as touchstone for theorizing a kind of history writing that acknowledges history as a form of representation and a testimony to the Real. On the one hand, history writing bears witness to "the encounter with the Real" (xvi). On the other hand, this Real is not transparently present, but is rather "reinscribed, translated, radically rethought and fundamentally worked over by the text" of history (xv). The "empirical context," they argue, "needs not just to be *known*, but to be *read*" (xv). The Real to which we have access only through texts of various kinds must be read with an eye to the processes of textualization and interpretation. If the Real of the past is always mediated, then history writing should not only "encounter the real" but also reflect upon those forms of mediation.

In spite of the risks of pluralism, however, I believe that negotiating the active and reflective modes of feminist historiography opens up the potential for feminists to engage in constructing histories *in the plural*, for recognizing that no single history can encounter the full dimensionality of the Real, and for reflecting upon our own process of mediation. I have defended two positions that are all too often set up as mutually exclusive oppositions: the need to make history by writing history as a political act; and the need to problematize that activity so as to avoid the creation of grand narratives that reproduce the totalizing histories of winners in which the stories of losers are lost. Instead of either/or, I promote both/and, where the active and reflective supplement each other in creative negotiation. Feminist histories (in the plural) of feminism (in the plural) are essential for negotiating the interplay between action and reflection and between the Real and its textualizations.

NOTE

The footnotes of the original have been omitted.

Part IV *Debates from the journals*

EDITOR'S INTRODUCTION

The journals I have chosen to take extracts from – *Past and Present*, *History and Theory* and *Social History* (some of the articles from *History and Theory* being allied to the volume edited by Saul Friedlander, *Probing the Limits of Representation*, regarding the Holocaust Debate) are those in which a series of "engaged" debates – around particular "actualities" – have appeared. This will enable readers to consider the points raised in Parts I to III in the context of specific historical contestation: here some of the positions taken up in the earlier Parts, often in isolation, are "connected." Readers will not only therefore see what is at stake in "general" postmodern versus modernist/traditionalist positions, but will be able to develop their own position regarding specific historical issues. At the same time, of course, the reproduction of extracts from journals wherein there are very specific engagements between historians (and, of course, the above journal debates are not at all exhaustive – thus the famous series of articles by Harlen, Megill, Scott and Himmelfarb *et al.* in the pages of the *American Historical Review* – as listed below under "Notes for Further Reading") are not in this volume. Again, the inclusion here of contested debates means that single articles which may be quite brilliant "on their own" have also been omitted, articles which have appeared in journals such as *Critical Practice*, *Gender and History*, *New Formations*, *Diacritics*, *New Left Review*, *Speculum*, *Central European History*, *The American Historical Review*, *Journal of American History*. These omittences are obviously regrettable, but such is the range of history journals now beginning to carry the occasional article on postmodernism – and such are the constraints imposed upon the length of a *volume* such as this – that I hope readers will gain, from the engagements reproduced here, a sense of what is going on in these areas and thus be desirous of following up other discussions to be found in the wider literature.

EXTRACTS FROM *PAST AND PRESENT*

In May, 1991, the journal *Past and Present* published a four-hundred-word Note by Lawrence Stone – "History and PostModernism" – warning that history as "we" have known it was being so seriously questioned that it was throwing the profession "into a crisis of self-confidence about what it is doing and how it is doing it," such that "we" might wonder if history may be "on the way to become an endangered species." It was a call to arms against a postmodernism apparently composed of three elements: linguistics, cultural and symbolic anthropology, and the New

Historicism. It was a postmodernism that could perhaps be rebutted if one read and presumably worked the kinds of anti-postmodernist approaches advocated by Gabrielle Spiegel in her "History, Historicism, and the Social Logic of the Text in the Middle Ages" (reprinted above as Chapter 17). Two issues later, Patrick Joyce and Catriona Kelly contributed replies to Lawrence Stone from social(ist) and feminist positions, to be followed, another two issues later, by a reply to Joyce and Kelly by Stone and Gabrielle Spiegel herself. In an Editorial Note appended to the contribution by Joyce and Kelly, the editors of the journal indicated that they were happy to receive substantial historical articles "engaging with these or other methodological debates," but that invitation has not yet been responded to by historians other than Stone and Spiegel – or at least no "substantial" articles have been published. In his article, Patrick Joyce had welcomed Stone's intervention, whilst wondering whether a "one-and-a-half page polemical 'note' [was] . . . the best way to have initiated debate" in a major journal that had been laggardly in registering discussions and scholarly work linked to postmodernism, and looked forward to the Editor's invitation for further articles. The fact that such articles have not really been forthcoming, the fact that Stone *et al.* have not been joined "theoretically" by others gives rise to two comments. The first is that although these short exchanges in *Past and Present* were pretty much the mere staking out of positions, this somewhat aborted debate has, nevertheless, become much referred to in other articles and books so that there is now almost an obligation to cite this debate as indicating that at least some "real" historians have been getting involved . . . to that extent this present *Reader* "reflects" that situation. The second point, however, is to underline a comment I have already made: namely, that this debate is perhaps a little "early" as debates go. I think this has got something to do with the position of Patrick Joyce. By virtue of his reply to Stone, Joyce has become something of a champion of postmodern perspectives on historiography, the problem being that possibly Joyce's digestion of postmodernism was, in 1991, at a fairly early stage as well as being perhaps skewed towards helping him "win" some old "social history" battles fought out not least in the pages of the journal *Social History*. It is therefore fortunate that since then Joyce has gone on to a much more interesting and engaged "postmodernist" position. The *Past and Present* debate is thus, for him, an early riposte and readers can now profitably turn, in this text, to some of his radical contributions in the journal *Social History* (below Chapters 29 and 31).

In the following pages the five contributions by Stone (two) Joyce, Kelly and Spiegel (Chapters 21–25), are given in full. In terms of the status of these articles, they seem to me to stand as indicative of the arrival in mainstream journal form of postmodernism and history not least because of their citation influence... they have indeed become very much part of the "postmodern history debate" in the UK and elsewhere.

21 Lawrence Stone

History and postmodernism

During the last twenty-five years, the subject-matter of history – that is events and behaviour – and the data – that is contemporary texts – and the problem – that is explanation of change over time – have all been brought seriously into question, thus throwing the profession, more especially in France and America, into a crisis of self-confidence about what it is doing and how it is doing it. The first threat comes from linguistics, building up from Saussure to Derrida, and climaxing in deconstruction, according to which there is nothing besides the text, each one wide open to personal interpretation irrespective of the intentions of the author. Texts thus become a mere hall of mirrors reflecting nothing but each other, and throwing no light upon the "truth," which does not exist. (For a damaging exposure of the many logical flaws in this form of argument, see John Searle, "The Storm over the University," *New York Rev. Books*, 6 Dec. 1990, pp. 34–42.)

The second development, at first enormously liberating and finally rather threatening, comes from the influence of cultural and symbolic anthropology as developed by a brilliant group of scholars headed by Clifford Geertz, Victor Turner, Mary Douglas and others. Their work has influenced many of the best historians of the last decade, especially in America and France. But the cultural historian and the symbolic anthropologist part company where the latter says "the real is as imagined as the imaginary." This presumably means that both are merely a set of semiotic codes governing all representations of life; that the material is dissolved into meaning; and that the text is left unconnected with the context.

The third threat comes from New Historicism. At first sight a welcome return to a study of the text in its geographical, temporal, social, economic and intellectual context, it has turned out to be a variant of the symbolic and semiotic view of cultural productions, in which language is "the medium in which the real is constructed and appre-hended." As a result, New Historicism treats political, institutional and social practices as "cultural scripts," or discursive sets of symbolic systems or codes.

These matters are the subject of a penetrating article by Gabrielle M. Spiegel, "History, Historicism and the Social Logic of the Text in the Middle Ages," *Speculum*, lxv (1990), pp. 59–86. In it she has taken up the challenge of these three modes of looking at history and historical texts, and has offered a way out of the ever-narrowing trap in which we historians find ourselves. This is an article which should be read by any historian, no matter what his or her field, period or methodology, who has been sufficiently disturbed by rumblings from adjacent disci-plines to wonder if history might be on the way to becoming an endangered species.

22 Patrick Joyce

History and postmodernism

Lawrence Stone appears to have elected himself as the defender of "history" against the threefold threat of "postmodernism," namely, in Stone's terms, structuralist and poststructuralist "linguistics," cultural anthropology and the New Historicism. These have brought "seriously into question" the subject-matter of history, its data, and the problem it deals with, the "explanation of change over time." The result is a crisis of self-confidence in the profession, and a call to action on the part of those who sufficiently feel this threat as to fear that history may be becoming "an endangered species."[1]

It is good that postmodernism has at last been brought into open view in the pages of *Past and Present*. Whether a one-and-a-half page polemical "note" is the best way to have initiated debate is another matter. In fact Stone is not interested in debate, but in denunciation. Aside from his opening sentence, he does not condescend to explain or defend the epistemological basis of "history." His opening words tell us that the subject-matter of history is "events and behaviour," the data "contemporary texts," and the purpose the explanation of change. Even by the standard of the undigested empiricism that does service as a philosophy of history in so many history departments this is pretty thin gruel. *Only* events and behaviour? *Only* texts that are "contemporary," whatever "contemporary" means? Clearly there is no crisis of confidence for Stone.

However, "the profession" is held to experience such a crisis, more especially in France and America. This may be so. Readers will judge best. In both countries my impression is that the force of what Stone calls the "ever-narrowing trap" of postmodernism is grossly exaggerated: far from the historian being beleaguered, the commanding heights of academy history seem secure against the skirmishing bands outside, though some notable walls have fallen, chiefly in the United States. In

Britain and Germany those unhappy with the philosophical realism that seems to underpin Stone's account have a still leaner time, in Britain, certainly, rank indifference rather than outright hostility being the dominant response.

If the "threat" that so exercises Stone seems far less substantial in practice than in his imagination, there is a real danger that the tone of his remarks will help turn indifference into hostility. Similarly, the form of the very brief, *ex cathedra* "note" does not suggest a receptivity to debate: is this really the way for a major journal to initiate discussion of such profoundly important matters? The question may be put still more insistently when it is considered how laggard *Past and Present* has been in registering debates and scholarly work linked to the so-called "linguistic turn." However, no doubt Stone's war cry is not the war cry of *Past and Present*.

For a war cry it does seem to be, Stone citing with approval John Searle's *New York Review of Books* article, "The Storm over the University."[2] This piece is in fact a diatribe against the "cultural leftism" deemed to threaten the American academy. Not unexpectedly, a major element in Searle's phantasmagoria is postmodernism, in particular the satanic rite of deconstruction. For Stone, the "threat" to history seems to be part of a larger conspiracy. It is no service to his argument that he seeks support from such intemperate sources.

The same cannot be said of Stone's second recommendation to his beleaguered readers, Gabrielle M. Spiegel's "History, Historicism, and the Social Logic of the Text in the Middle Ages."[3] This is measured, rational and constructive, and may serve as the basis of a very brief discussion of some of the points at issue. The gist of her argument is that while cultural anthropology and cultural history, together with New Historicism, "have successfully reintroduced a (new) historicist consideration of discourse as the product of identifiable cultural and historical formations, they have not been equally successful in restoring history as an active agent in the social construction of meaning."[4] She is of the opinion that the historicization of discourse has led to the "text analogy" subsuming the "real" or the "social" in the discursive: in place of a necessary distinction between the real and representations of it, is the "intertextuality" of "text" and "context."

At the end of her piece Spiegel aims to reassert traditional dualisms by attention to the example of vernacular historical writing in thirteenth-century France, in such a way as to show the social or "situated" contexts of language use, the "determinate" social locations texts occupy.[5] She offers what she calls a "relational" reading of text and context, in which suppressed meanings are considered beside overt ones, and implied beside articulated purposes. The suppressed and implied, she argues, are often not located with reference to the text alone, but must be sought in the social, beyond the text. Whether her examples support the idea of the autonomy of the social seems to me doubtful. None the less she has at the same time a firm grasp of the mutuality of the discursive and the social, citing Mikhail Bakhtin with approval to the effect that verbal discourse is always a social phenomenon: language constitutes the social world of meaning, but language only has meaning within specific historical and social settings. While resisting it, she acknowledges the force and the advances of the "semiotic challenge."[6] Indeed she recognizes that the object of historical study is always "constituted by the historian long before its meaning can begin to be disengaged." She notes, paradoxically, that "the text qua text is materially 'realer' than 'history'," and that "any attempt to adjudicate the interpretive meaning of a literary text by recourse to history as 'reality' begins to look like an exercise undertaken backwards."[7] Spiegel extends traditional perspectives in a productive way, moving beyond Stone's pieties.

Whether this position is all that different from many she assails is not too clear (one must register in passing a considerable unease, especially in regard to Stone's note, with the way in which often quite divergent ideas are yoked together under the term "postmodernism')."[8] Bakhtin's work, for example, has long been in the mainstream of cultural history. His work on literary conventions, such as genre, as *social* conventions, representing understandings between writers and readers, has a definite social location. Spiegel points to the social nature of language, and sociolinguistics, social and cultural history are now establishing quite firm links.[9] There are many other instances where the relationship between the social and the discursive is at the centre of concern. In cultural history itself it is open to question whether the "text analogy" does in fact collapse language and reality to "the same phenomenological order" in the way Spiegel suggests.[10] Take Roger Chartier's work, which is held up as an example. In declaring his definition of "the real" to be discursive only Spiegel neglects to show how he utilizes Pierre Bourdieu to explore the relationships between the text and social life.[11] This exploration has been especially marked in those areas where social and cultural history overlap most, especially in the history of class and "class consciousness."[12] While useful, the "text analogy" is somewhat restrictive here, and it has been supplemented by what may be termed the "language analogy": institutions and events, groups and movements, being investigated by means of their verbal and extra-verbal communicative practices, modes and strategies. The literature on class presents in a particularly urgent way the search for new understandings of the social that go beyond the old dualisms, though it must be said that this search has yet to be translated into elaborated theoretical positions.

At one level we may of course posit a dualism between the "real," or the "social," and representations of it. The "real" can be said to exist independently of our representations of it, and to affect these representations. But this effect is always discursive, and it must be insisted that history is never present to us in anything but a discursive form, here taking "discursive," of course, to denote all forms of communication, including those beyond the verbal alone. If true, these statements by themselves lead to a pointlessly circular logic. They are also banal. In order to break out of this circularity and banality it seems to me vital to take the "linguistic turn" seriously and go beyond the reassertion of the old dualistic understanding, the tactic employed by Stone and Spiegel. Moving forwards in this way involves questioning received categories of the "social." When these are questioned, so is the claim of historians like Stone that they are its guardians, and that the practice of "history" is its essential guarantee.

The major advance of "postmodernism" needs to be registered by historians: namely that the events, structures and processes of the past are indistinguishable from the forms of documentary representation, the conceptual and political appropriations, and the historical discourses that construct them.[13] Once this is conceded the foundations of the "social history" paradigm are greatly weakened, the paradigm that arguably informs much of the rationale of *Past and Present*. A recognition of the irreducibly discursive character of the social undermines the idea of social totality. There is no overarching coherence evident in either the polity, the economy or the social system. What there are are instances (texts, events, ideas and so on) that have social contexts which are essential to their meaning, but there is no underlying structure to which they can be referred as expressions or effects. Thus with the notion of social totality goes the notion of social determination, so central to "social history." The certainty of a materialist link to the social is likewise broken. Gone too are the grand narratives that historicized the notion of social totality. Responding to the anti-reductionist logic of postmodernism means, therefore, thinking about new versions of the social, ones that require historians to be the inquisitors and perhaps the executioners of old valuations. Whatever the outcome, what must be questioned is the sanctity of "history" as a distinct form of knowledge predicated upon the autonomy of the social. Stone's pre-emptive strike on "postmodernism" is not a defence of history *per se*, but of one particular approach to the past. New approaches and new kinds of history are now on the agenda.

NOTES

1. Lawrence Stone, "History and PostModernism," *Past and Present*, no. 131, May 1991, pp. 217–18.
2. John Searle, "The Storm over the University," *New York Rev. Books*, 6 Dec. 1990, pp. 34–42.
3. Gabrielle M. Spiegel, "History, Historicism, and the Social Logic of the Text in the Middle Ages," *Speculum*, lxv (1990), pp. 59–86.
4. Ibid., p. 64.
5. Ibid., pp. 78–83.
6. Ibid., pp. 76–7.
7. Ibid., p. 75; cf. p. 76.
8. Obviously, "postmodernism" extends far beyond linguistics, literary theory and anthropology. In turn it has been shaped by a wide range of influences, perhaps the most notable of which has been feminism. If the result has been a transformation in the way intellectual activity is now conceived, this has not resulted in any uniformity in the theoretical positions, areas of writing, and political views involved.
9. See R. Porter and P. Burke (eds) *The Social History of Language*, i, Cambridge, 1987, ii, Cambridge, 1991; see also P. Joyce, *Visions of the People: Industrial England and the Question of Class, 1848–1914*, Cambridge, 1991, chs 8, 11, 12.
10. Spiegel, "History, Historicism, and the Social Logic of the Text," p. 85.
11. Ibid., p. 68; R. Chartier, "Intellectual History or Sociocultural History? The French Trajectories", in D. LaCapra and S. L. Kaplan (eds), *Modern European Intellectual History: Reappraisals and New Perspectives*, Cambridge, 1982, pp. 40–1; P. Bourdieu, *Distinction: A Social Critique of the Judgement of Taste*, trans. R. Nice, London, 1984, esp. pp. 466–84.
12. For often very different approaches, see G. Stedman Jones, *Languages of Class: Studies in English Working Class History, 1832–1982*, Cambridge, 1983; W. H. Sewell Jr., *Work and Revolution in France: The Language of Labour from the Old Regime to 1848*, Cambridge, 1980; J. Rancière, *The Nights of Labor: The Workers' Dream in Nineteenth-Century France*, trans. J. Drury, Philadelphia, 1989; W. M. Reddy, *Money and Liberty in Modern Europe: A Critique of Historical Understanding*, Cambridge, 1987); Joyce, *Visions of the People*. See also the prize-winning essay, notice of which ironically enough follows the Stone piece, James Epstein, "Understanding the Cap of Liberty: Symbolic Practice and Social Conflict in Early Nineteenth-Century England," *Past and Present*, no. 122 (Feb. 1989), pp. 75–118. On the language model of culture, see the introduction and essays in L. Hunt (ed.) *The New Cultural History*, Berkeley, 1989. On the relationship between class and gender, see J. W. Scott, *Gender and the Politics of History*, New York, 1988. Class is obviously only one area where the "linguistic turn" has been registered. Religion

is another. See, for example, M. Rubin, *Corpus Christi: The Eucharist in Late Medieval Culture*, Cambridge, 1991.

13. I am indebted to Geoff Eley for a view of his spirited and informed defence of the "linguistic turn": G. Eley, "Is All the World a Text? From Social History to the History of Society Two Decades Later," in T. McDonald (ed.) *The Historical Turn in the Human Sciences*, Univ. of Michigan Press, 1992.

23 Catriona Kelly

History and postmodernism

It was the wording of Lawrence Stone's note that first attracted my attention.[1] By speaking of recent conceptual developments which have affected the historical field as "threats" and "traps," he was, to my mind, himself falling into the snares of textual absolutism: for it is arguable that it is not ideas and methodological strategies, but the ineluctable exigencies of social and economic – or even demographic – processes, that currently most "threaten" the humanities as traditionally practised.

To say this is not to aim a cheap debating trick at a thoughtful and stimulating piece, but to work towards the nub of the controversy. As Gabrielle M. Spiegel, author of the article recommended by Stone, puts it: "No historian, even of positivist stripe, would argue that history is present to us in any but textual form."[2] The debate, then, is about whether it is of greater value to read through texts towards something else, or to look at them. The latter strategy seems to Stone to make reality and the imaginary "merely a set of semiotic codes," while to Spiegel it renders "social life . . . in all senses of the word, immaterial."[3]

Here a linguist might respond that there is nothing "mere" or "immaterial" about language, a Derridean that historians would naturally be reluctant to surrender the authority which they vest in the "metaphysics of presence," making "social life" their equivalent of the literary historian's "the author." To some extent the situation reflects Susan Sontag's well-known axiom that "there are tastes in ideas"; tastes here hinging around the problem of deciding which particular set of ideas, or intellectual constructs, are most appropriate to the depiction of societies where materiality has often been understood in terms of bodies and objects, and where the concept of economic forces might well seem as immaterial as that of linguistic differentiation.

I doubt whether there is, or even ought to be, a final resolution to the dispute. But I shall attempt to deal very briefly with some of the points raised by Spiegel and Stone from a particular perspective: that of women's history. I agree that it is essential to retain a notion of extra-textuality, but I have some reservations about the definition of the extra-textual which they offer (or rather, which Spiegel offers). I should also be reluctant to surrender all the insights which have been afforded by the antagonistic, combative and counter-intuitive strategies of textual reading which have developed in the wake of deconstructionism.

A major task of women's history at the moment is to explain the different significances and operations which may be adopted by patriarchal, that is gender-based, systems of power relations. As Toril Moi has put it: "Only a concept of ideology as a *contradictory* construct, marked by gaps, slides and inconsistencies, would enable feminism to explain how even the severest ideological pressures will generate their own lacunae."[4] This does not mean advocating the sort of over-assimilative relativism criticized by Stone and Spiegel. It would, no doubt, be possible to identify "lacunae" even in such an unpromising document as Andrei Zhdanov's notorious 1946 denunciation of Anna Akhmatova as "half-nun, half-whore." But such an investigation of textual fluidity *per se* would sacrifice any notion of "ideological pressures" – recognition of which can only emerge through consideration of factors outside an individual text.

It is here that the notion of context becomes crucial. Rather than emphasizing text as an expression of context (mimesis), or seeing context as a product of text, Spiegel advocates allowing equal weight to matters textual and extra-textual, and to the complex relations between these. Like many recent commentators, she looks to the Russian theorist Mikhail Bakhtin's model of discourse as dialogue between utterance and social environment. Thus far her suggestions accord with, indeed have been anticipated by, those made by feminist historians and cultural critics, who have long accepted the idea that texts are both constructed by, and construct, an external context. The formulation was recently restated by Janet Wolff: "Art, literature and film [i.e., cultural texts] do not simply represent given gender identities, or reproduce already existing ideologies of femininity. Rather, they participate in the very construction of these identities . . . consequently, culture is a crucial area for the contestation of the social arrangements of gender."[5] But how should the context and the process of construction be defined? Spiegel sees it in the transcription of power relations, arguing that "texts inscribe the variegated motives and interests, material desires and imaginary dreams that motivate human behavior" – elements already inherent in their siting, for "involved in this positioning of the text is an examination of the play of power, human agency, and social experience as historians traditionally understand them."[6] She illustrates these theoretical formulations with two pieces of practical criticism, analyses of the genealogical history whose author is the Anonymous of Béthune, and of the *Pseudo-Turpin Chronicle*.[7]

Arguing that the former piece was produced as an affirmation of the agnatic family, Spiegel demonstrates a very straightforward set of relations between "text" and "reality," in which the ideology of producers and users is in seamless overlap; in the latter case she illustrates how "prose" (presumably meaning a form not open to classification in terms of repeated metrics) was used to suggest a narrative which appeared "true" by contrast with epic.

There is no doubt that the central idea of "context" is formulated by Bakhtin in sufficiently ambiguous terms to allow for such appropriations. But the sense of dynamism and fluidity essential to gender history, well expressed in the word "contestation," is better suited by Ken Hirschkop's recent post-Bakhtinian re-definition of context in the following terms: "It might be more sensible to think of context as a set of largely invisible pressures and purposes, stemming from the social creation of a speech act, which are often conflicting or contradictory."[8] Such "conflicting pressures and purposes" would only become obvious were one to site the text chosen by Spiegel in a less obvious "context," tracing its effects on those not sharing its ideological presuppositions, who did not themselves control the representations, and who played a passive rather than an active role in their dissemination. (It would be interesting to know, for example, how the emphasis on genealogy and patrimony might have affected women: did they or did they not sense that their property rights and family status might be under threat?)

For the historian of women's lives, an understanding of the link between text and context often requires a considerable sensitivity to negative relations. This does not only mean asking questions which texts themselves do not ask; some notion of textual redundancy, such as can be substantiated only with reference to a considerable range of material, is also requisite. Linguistic patterns do not invariably exist out of context; it is, however, essential to have some appreciation of how they *may*, of how texts may be parasitical one on the other, of how, in the words of Eve Kosofsky Sedgwick, "one of the functions of a tradition *is* to create a path-of-least-resistance (or, at the last resort, pathology-of-least-resistance) for the expression of previously inchoate material."[9] Only when the persistence of certain incentive or disincentive stereotypes in a manner independent, or apparently independent, of their context has been recorded, can the process of registering shifts in beliefs and desires begin.

An aggressive attitude may have to be adopted to the sources themselves, concentrating not on the most obvious interpretation, but on secondary layers of meaning. Reading historical material for information about women automatically means reading against the grain, since many sources share Stone's conviction that "events and behaviour" are the proper subject of history, relegating the repetitive and everyday matters in which most women were involved to the margins, if their existence is acknowledged at all. Rather than painting historical texts in Romantic colours, and seeing them as "the violent coupling of cocks" (in Spiegel's self-consciously bizarre Geertzian formulation),[10] one may have to consider them as an over-flavored broth of dubious provenance, whose precise quantities of ingredients must be established, and process of culinary preparation determined.

Such a determining process is impossible without a sophisticated attention to stylistics in the sense of lexicon and narrative order; the textual material has necessarily to be placed in a "context" which, while not in any sense excluding the events, behaviour, power, human agency and social experience which Stone and Spiegel nominate as the historian's concern, may not necessarily accommodate these factors in precisely the manner, or give them precisely the weight, that might be expected by "traditional understanding." Some recent studies belonging to the directions catalogued by Stone seem self-indulgent in their literary aspirations, and irritating in their concern with the explosively picturesque. But others, such as Natalie Zemon Davis's analysis of women's pardon tales in *Fiction in the Archives*, are to my mind considerably more subtle, insightful and stimulating than Stone and Spiegel's assessments might suggest.[11]

NOTES

1. Lawrence Stone, "History and PostModernism," *Past and Present*, no. 131 (May 1991), pp. 217–18.
2. Gabrielle M. Spiegel, "History, Historicism, and the Social Logic of the Text in the Middle Ages," *Speculum*, lxv (1990), p. 76.

3. Stone, "History and PostModernism," p. 217; Spiegel, "History, Historicism, and the Social Logic of the Text," p. 62.
4. Toril Moi, *Sexual/Textual Politics: Feminist Literary Theory*, London, 1985, p. 26.
5. Janet Wolff, *Feminine Sentences: Essays on Women and Culture*, Oxford, 1990, p. 1.
6. Spiegel, "History, Historicism, and the Social Logic of the Text," pp. 86, 85.
7. *Ibid.*, pp. 78–83.
8. Ken Hirschkop and David G. Shepherd, *Bakhtin and Cultural Theory*, Manchester, 1989, p. 16.
9. Eve Kosofsky Sedgwick, "The Beast in the Closet: James and the Writing of Homosexual Panic," in Elaine Showalter (ed.) *Speaking of Gender*, New York, 1989, p. 243.
10. Spiegel, "History, Historicism, and the Social Logic of the Text," pp. 85–6.
11. N. Zemon Davis, *Fiction in the Archives: Pardon Tales and their Tellers in Sixteenth-Century France*, Stanford, 1987.

24 Lawrence Stone

History and postmodernism

I am sorry that Patrick Joyce is so cross with me.[1] The purpose of my brief note was not to start a quarrel, or crush a rebellion, or issue a *diktat*, but merely to draw attention to the very interesting – and to me persuasive – article by Gabrielle M. Spiegel.[2] The note was brief since I had nothing to say which had not been better said by her and John Searle (the latter, by the way, is not a right-wing inquisitor, nor is the *New York Review of Books* famous for its reactionary views).[3]

When I was very young, now forty or fifty years ago, I was taught the following things, none of which bore much relation to the crude positivism of the late nineteenth century:

1, that one should always try to write plain English, avoiding jargon and obfuscation, and making one's meaning as clear as possible to the reader;

2, that historical truth is unattainable, and that any conclusions are provisional and hypothetical, always liable to be overturned by new data or better theories;

3, that we are all subject to bias and prejudice because of our race, class and culture; and that in consequence we should follow the advice of E. H. Carr and before we read the history, examine the background of the historian;

4, that documents – we did not call them texts in those days – were written by fallible human beings who made mistakes, asserted false claims, and had their own ideological agenda which guided their compilation; they should therefore be scrutinized with care, taking into account authorial intent, the nature of the document, and the context in which it was written;

5, that perceptions and representations of reality are often very different from, and sometimes just as historically important as, reality itself;

6, that ritual plays an important role as a vehicle for religious expression and as a demonstration of power: that is why we admired Marc Bloch's *Les rois thaumaturges* (1924) and later Ernst Kantorowicz's *The King's Two Bodies* (1957).

In view of all this, I suggest that, with some notable exceptions, we did not at all resemble the positivist troglodytes that we are often accused of being.

I do not entirely understand Joyce's position. First he admits that "The 'real' can be said to exist independently of our representations of it, and to affect these representations." With this I heartily agree, and this was the *only* point I was trying to make. But he then seems to take it all back, by insisting that "history is never present to us in anything but a discursive form." Moreover, if he really believes that "there is no overarching coherence evident in either the polity, the economy or the social system," then I am baffled to understand how he, or anyone else, can write history at all.[4]

If we look on the bright side, and take Joyce's first statement as overriding the second and third, then my and his views about history do not differ very much from those adopted by many anthropologists, sociologists and specialists in discourse and language. Where we part company, as I pointed out, is at the extreme stage, when reality is defined *purely* as language. This is because if there is nothing outside the text, then history as we have known it collapses altogether, and fact and fiction become indistinguishable from one another.

So long as it stays on the right side of this breakpoint, the "linguistic turn" in history has great merits. It has taught us to examine texts with far more care and caution than we did before, using new tools to disclose covert beneath overt messages, to decipher the meaning of subtle shifts of grammar and so on. These new techniques have been used to great effect by scholars of English literary history, as in Stephen Greenblatt's witty "Fiction and Friction," or Annabel Patterson's devastating demolition of Milton on divorce, and also by historians like Miri Rubin, in her illuminating study of Corpus Christi.[5] It is noticeable, however, that Patterson is very much a traditional scholar, who openly deplores "the depersonalizing and antianthropomorphical premises of postmodernism, denying us for nearly two decades the commonsense categories of author, *oeuvre*, and intention."[6] Thus what Joyce calls my "pieties," Patterson calls "common sense." More severe criticism of the wilder shores of postmodernism has recently come from Perez Zagorin.[7] Moreover it can surely be no accident that it is impossible to think of a major historical work written from a thoroughly postmodernist perspective and using postmodernist language and vocabulary. But it is, I believe, now possible to find a common ground between most historians of my generation and the more cautious of the postmodernists.

My objection to the work of historians bedazzled by the lures of "discourse" arises only when they push their argument about the autonomy of "discourse" to the point of making it a historical factor in its own right. This blocks off explanations of change over time based on more complex interactions of material conditions, culture, ideology and power. The objections to this procedure in dealing with the French Revolution have recently been brought out by Robert Darnton.[8] As for the use of symbolic and social anthropology, influenced largely by my friend Clifford Geertz, I can only repeat what I have said before. It has already had, and is continuing to have, a stunning effect upon historical scholarship. One has only to look at the work of Darnton, Natalie Davies, Keith Thomas, Carlo Ginzburg, Emmanuel Le Roy Ladurie and others to see the spectacular results. Moreover it is still at work, powerfully affecting two recent but very different books, Inga Clendinnen's brilliant *Aztecs* and David Harris Sacks's remarkable study of Bristol.[9] I myself have also been deeply influenced by Geertz's writings.

Where I part company with the anthropologists of ritual is when they try to persuade us that there are states which do little or nothing but conduct rituals, and that rituals alone are sufficient to create meaning. Thus on close inspection the states in *Negara* turn out to be doing many of the things that states do: raising taxes, making war on their neighbours, punishing criminals, and other such normal exercises in brute force, as well as laying on elaborate rituals for the burning of wives and so on.[10] This is not to deny that ritual has a very significant effect in bonding, boundary-setting, or hierarchy-enforcement. This is something we have learnt from the anthropologists.

To sum up, my Note was merely intended to draw attention to Spiegel's astute criticism and apt example of how to avoid the extreme position that there is no reality outside language. This threat to historical scholarship has moved a step closer today with my admired friend Simon Schama's deliberate obliteration of the difference between archival fact and pure fiction in his book *Dead Certainties*. The strong objections to this new model of historical writing have been well laid out by Gordon S. Wood in his review of Schama's book.[11]

However, it seems as if at least some of the leaders of the "linguistic turn" are backing away from this radical elimination of the reality principle. If so, a path to a common position of moderation is opening up, just at the moment when Schama's book reveals the perilous chasm looming directly ahead of us. Not only do we now have Spiegel's article, Joyce Appleby has already also joined in the fray on the side of history, arguing that a text is merely a passive agent in the hands of its author. It is human beings who play with words; words don't play with themselves. To establish their meaning we historians therefore need to search for the authorial intention; to study the social and political context which created the contemporary form of language; and to steep ourselves in the traditions of the culture. By these historical means, we will be able to recapture a provisional truth, at least sufficiently plausible to command assent for a while from most well-informed readers.[12]

No less a figure than Stanley Fish, a prominent leader of the radical movement in literature, has recently brought reassurance from the camp of literary criticism. He now tells his followers that they should cease to bully historians and to "brandish fancy theories that declare all evidence suspect and ideological." He goes so far as to say: "If you set out to determine what happened [in England] in 1649, you will look at the materials which recommend themselves to you as the likely repositories of knowledge, and go from there." He quotes with approval a statement by a historian, Henry Horwitz: "Arguments about history are not finally epistemological, but empirical, involving disputes about the content of knowledge, about evidence and its significance."[13] This position has been reinforced even more recently by another distinguished literary critic, Geoffrey Hartman. He is a strong advocate of the current stress on language, but "not to the point of being forced to think that reality is merely an affair of words." If this is the final position of the postmodernists, then the battle is all over, and a truce can be declared. Hartman's gloomy prophecy that "new days of rage are upon us" will thankfully go unfulfilled.[14]

A debate over this issue was important, healthy and long overdue. But mud-slinging does nobody any good and is bad for the profession as a whole. What I should have made clearer in my brief statement was the enormously stimulating effect upon historical scholarship of a wide variety of new ways of seeing the world, mostly associated with language and relativism, all of which are nowadays rather sloppily housed under the broad canopy of postmodernism. My only objection is when they declare not that truth is unknowable, but that there is no reality out there which is anything but a subjective creation of the historian; in other words that it is language that creates meaning which in turn creates our image of the real. This destroys the difference between fact and fiction, and makes entirely nugatory the dirty and tedious archival work of the historian to dig "facts" out of texts. It is only at this extreme point that historians have any need to express anxiety. But since nearly everyone, except perhaps Schama, seems to be retreating from this position, there is now at last a common platform upon which we can all, without too much discomfort, take our stand.

NOTES

1. P. Joyce, "History and Postmodernism," *Past and Present*, no. 133, Nov. 1991, pp. 204–9.
2. Lawrence Stone, "History and Postmodernism," *Past and Present*, no. 131 (May 1991), pp. 217–18; Gabrielle M. Spiegel, "History, Historicism, and the Social Logic of the Text in the Middle Ages," *Speculum*, lxv (1990), pp. 59–86.
3. John Searle, "The Storm over the University," *New York Rev. Books*, 6 Dec. 1990, pp. 34–42.
4. Joyce, "History and Post-Modernism, I", p. 208.
5. S. Greenblatt, "Fiction and Friction," in his *Shakespearean Negotiations: The Circulation of Social Energy in Renaissance England*. Oxford, 1988; A. Patterson, "No Meer Amatorious Novel," in D. Loewenstein and J. Turner (eds), *Politics, Poetics and Hermeneutics in Milton's Prose*, Cambridge, 1990; M. Rubin, *Corpus Christi: The Eucharist in Late Medieval Culture*, Cambridge, 1991.
6. Patterson, "No Meer Amatorious Novel," p. 87.
7. P. Zagorin, "Historiography and Postmodernism: Some Reconsiderations," *History and Theory*, xxix (1990).
8. Robert Darnton, "An Enlightened Revolution?," *New York Rev. Books*, 14 Oct. 1991, pp. 33–6.
9. I. Clendinnen, *Aztecs*, New York, 1991; D. H. Sacks, *The Widening Gate: Bristol and the Atlantic Economy*, 1450–1700, Berkeley, 1991.
10. C. Geertz, *Negara: The Theater State in Nineteenth-Century Bali*, Princeton, 1980.
11. S. Schama, *Dead Certainties (Unwarranted Speculations)*, New York, 1991; rev. by Gordon S. Wood, *New York Rev. Books*, 27 June 1991, pp. 12–16.
12. J. Appleby, "One Good Turn Deserves Another: Moving Beyond the Linguistic: A Response to David Harlan," *Amer. Hist. Rev.*, xciv (1989).
13. S. Fish, "Commentary: The Young and the Restless," in H. A. Veeser (ed.) *The New Historicism*, New York, 1989, pp. 308, 317.
14. G. Hartman, *Minor Prophecies: Literary Essays in the Culture Wars*, Cambridge, Mass., 1991; rev. by D. Donoghue, *New York Rev. Books*, 15 Aug. 1991, p. 54.

25 Gabrielle Spiegel

History and postmodernism

> Language, like economics and love, is wonderful in practice, but just won't work out in theory.[1]

Poststructuralism, we know, has boldly pronounced all authors "dead." Being still among the living, however, I would like to thank the editors of *Past and Present* for their thoughtful invitation to speak for myself in the debate that has arisen as a consequence of Lawrence Stone's recommendations of my article "History, Historicism, and the Social Logic of the Text in the Middle Ages."[2] Despite the polemical tone of both recommendation and responses, I suspect there is actually less disagreement over fundamental issues than appears. Indeed one of the problems in the ongoing controversy concerning the implications of poststructuralist theory for historical study has been a tendency to polarize positions taken, thus falling into precisely the binary modes of thinking from which poststructuralism, in principle, seeks to liberate us.[3] This is not to deny the very real tensions that the debate over postmodernism has generated, tensions that are symptomatic of contemporary discontents with history as presently practised (of which this debate itself can perhaps be said to partake).

Areas of formal study, Hans Kellner recently argued, are complexes of defences against particular anxieties.[4] I would like to suggest that history's anxiety now hovers over the status and meaning of the word "reality," whose power to signify – to stand for and mean something – is thought to be radically diminished, and whose dubious status is figured by the persistent use of quotation marks. This is, of course, simply another way of posing the postmodern dilemma, the hallmark of which has been a growing awareness of the mediated nature of perception, cognition and imagination, all of which are increasingly construed to be mediated by linguistic structures cast into discourses of one sort or another – the famed "linguistic turn" that has raised such troubling problems for the study of history and literature alike. As a language-based conception of reality, poststructuralism has disrupted traditional literary and historical modes of interpretation by its denial of a referential and material world, a material reality we once believed could be known and written about scientifically. Until recently the writing of history depended on a concept of language which, as Nancy Partner puts it, "unhesitatingly asserts the external reality of the world, its intelligibility in the form of ideas, concepts, phenomena or other mental things and a direct connection between mental things and verbal signs." But poststructuralism has shattered this confident assumption of the relation between words and things, language and extralinguistic reality, on the grounds, as she states, that language is the "very structure of mental life, and no meta-language can ever stand outside itself to observe a reality external to itself."[5] This dissolution of the materiality of the verbal sign, its ruptured relation to extra-linguistic reality, entails the dissolution of history, since it denies the ability of language to "relate" to (or account for) any reality other than itself. Such a view of the closed reflexivity of language – its radically intransitive character – necessarily jeopardizes historical study as normally understood. Hence, Jean E. Howard aptly queries, "if literature [or, more generally, language] refers to no ground exterior to itself, what can be the nature of its relationship to a historical context or to material reality? In fact, if one accepts certain tendencies in post-structuralist thought, is the possibility of a historical criticism even conceivable?"[6]

Although almost everyone (myself included) who enters the debate over postmodernism frames their argument in epistemological terms, it has long seemed to me that the unstated issue is often one of ethics rather than epistemology. That is to say, epistemological and methodological questions are frequently employed in the historian's discourse as ways of coding ethical principles of behavior: how do we proceed ("behave") in order to "know" as historians; what is correct, true, "virtuous" even, in our praxis; what, ultimately, legitimizes history as a disciplinary body of knowledge?

For historians the ethical core of their professional commitment has always been a belief that their arduous, often tedious labour yields some authentic knowledge of the dead "other," a knowledge admittedly shaped by the historian's own perceptions and biases, but none the less retaining a degree of autonomy, in the sense that it cannot (putatively) be made entirely to bend to the historian's will.[7] This belief (some would say illusion) in the irreducible alterity of the past confers on history its proper function, which is to recover that alterity in as close an approximation of "how it actually was" as possible. In the interest of preserving this alterity, the historian practises modesty as a supreme ethical virtue, discreetly holding in abeyance his or her own beliefs, prejudices and presuppositions.

Historians have accurately sensed that the "linguistic turn" challenges this ethical foundation for the practice of history by problematizing not merely the methods historians have traditionally used to study it, but the very notion of the past as a recuperable object of study. If texts – documents, literary works, whatever – do not transparently reflect reality, but only other texts, then historical study can scarcely be distinguished from literary study, and the "past" dissolves into literature. Since I discussed the variety of ways in which postmodern thought arrived at this notion of both the textuality and intertextuality of history and historical investigation in "History, Historicism, and the Social Logic of the Text," I will not rehearse those arguments here. We would do well, however, to refocus our attention on the question of mediation, for it both stands at the crux of the "linguistic turn" and yet may offer a way of connecting our current preoccupation with language to theories of historiography and the historian's function as conventionally understood. At the same time the obvious links between the notion of mediation and the intermediate may lead us to a theory of the middle ground as the place of mediation – the only ground on which, I believe, history and postmodernism can hope productively to interact with one another.

Patrick Joyce and Catriona Kelly both concede (albeit in passing) that "the 'real' can be said to exist independently of our representations of it" (Joyce) and that "it is essential to retain a notion of extra-textuality" (Kelly).[8] Whether our continued belief in reality needs such authorization is an open question,[9] but I submit that these concessions logically entail a view of mediation that the remainder of their critiques appear to wish to deny. If one of the major moves in poststructuralist thought has been to displace the controlling metaphor of historical evidence from one of reflection to one of mediation (that is, has been a shift from the notion that texts and documents transparently reflect past realities, as positivism believed, to one in which the past is captured only in the mediated form preserved for us in language), then we need to think carefully about how we understand mediation and how that understanding affects our practice.

The classical concept of mediation views it as an analytical device that seeks to establish a relationship between two different orders or levels of phenomena that are the object of scrutiny: between, say, a work of literature (or any linguistic artefact) and its social ground. Because the objects of analysis are phenomenologically distinct, they can only be compared against the background of some more general identity, and mediation, as Frederic Jameson explains, represents "the intervention of an analytic terminology or code which can be applied equally to two or more structurally distinct objects or sectors of being."[10] In that sense, mediation is a term that describes, in Raymond Williams's definition, "an indirect connection or agency between separate kinds of act."[11] And this definition holds both for the operation of mediation in the past (that is, for example, as embodied in a discourse that mediates between a social world and its literary or discursive consciousness of its own nature) and for the historical analysis that we undertake of that world, allowing historians to comprehend historical experience via the linguistic evidence – whether literary or documentary – by which we come to know and understand the past. The critical aspect of the classical notion of mediation is that it keeps analytically separate the dual phenomena that at the same time it seeks to relate; that it functions, therefore, as a middle term that mediates *between* two disparate, yet analytically relatable, domains of inquiry.[12]

The modern concept of mediation, such as articulated by the Frankfurt school, insists, to quote Theodor Adorno, that "mediation is in the object itself, not something between the object and that to which it is brought," a concept of mediation that attempts to abolish (or overcome) dualism altogether.[13] In this view, mediation is an active process that constructs its objects in precisely the sense that poststructuralism conceives of the social construction of reality in and through language. Rather than functioning as a middle term relating two disjunct phenomenal orders from which it stands apart, mediation is intrinsic to the existence and operation of the reality that it actively produces. In studying history, then, what we study are the mediatory practices of past epochs (in effect, discourses) which, then as now, constructed all being and consciousness.[14] Moreover the performative nature of such discourses – preserved and thus available to us only in texts of a literate, if not precisely literary, nature – prohibits our access to any reality other than the codes inscribed in such texts.

To be sure, for historians and literary critics alike, whichever definition of mediation one chooses, the mediating function will be constituted by language because language, by definition, is that which mediates human awareness of the world we inhabit. Moreover it is late in the day to have to insist that all historians, even of positivist stripe, live and breathe in a world of texts, or that knowledge of the past is primarily present to us in textual form. But our understanding of the implications of this "always already" textualized character of historical data, its inevitably mediated state as made up of language, depends to a high degree on what concept of mediation we adopt and, by logical inference, what view of language we deploy. Just as there are multiple models of mediation, so also are there various ways of viewing language: the fashionable, postmodern performative idea of language as constitutive of the world, hence inherently self-reflexive; or an instrumentalist or constative view of language, in which language is seen to describe and explicate as well as to "invent" reality and, in that sense, to constitute an "instrument of mediation between human consciousness and the world it occupies."[15] This second concept of language is normally employed in scientific discourse or in any discipline concerned with purveying information about the world rather than with the construction of social meaning. One of the features of the "linguistic turn" in the humanities has been to replace the classical notion of mediation with the modern, and to undermine our faith in the instrumental capacity of language to convey information about the world.

Joyce and Kelly, in conceding the existence of extra-textual reality, appear to admit that language can function instrumentally by mediating *between* us as perceiving, knowing subjects and the absent past that we wish to describe (how else could they know of the existence of this reality in the past?). But both almost immediately take back what they seem to have granted by insisting on the discursively mediated character of our knowledge of the past and, in Kelly's case, on what I take to be an essentially deconstructionist view of language represented by the "antagonistic [agonistic?], combative [ideological?] and counter-intuitive [aporetic?] strategies of textual reading" that she is loath to surrender.[16] But must we really choose between these two conceptions of language and mediation? Must we limit language's power to the reflexive, or is there not room in our historiographical practice, as there clearly is in our everyday linguistic habits, for a constative (i.e., descriptive) as well as performative use of language, even when that language is embodied in past texts (including documents) and thus possesses something of the literary character that poststructuralism has taught us to apprehend? The choice between seeing language as either perfectly transparent or completely opaque is simply too rigidly framed.[17] One might add here that Joyce, in registering the major advance of postmodernism as the recognition that "the events, structures and processes of the past are indistinguishable from the forms of documentary representation, the conceptual and political appropriations, and the historical discourses that construct them," appears to conflate two horizons of knowledge and action, namely what happened and how we know about it or, more broadly, the difference between production and reception.[18] However, because our knowledge of the past comes to us in documentary representations, we need not confuse the problems entailed in our access to the past with the past itself. Moreover, as Martin Jay points out, "because certain social forms can be read as if they were languages, there is no reason to suppose their linguisticality exhausts their being."[19] The duality of perspectives that I am arguing for would allow us to maintain these distinct issues in a more clearly delineated and fruitful tension with implications for our understanding of the character of representation as well as of "reality."[20]

I do not wish to contest the "linguistic" character of even instrumental language as preserved in documentary records. The archive, as Dominick LaCapra has asserted,[21] is as much the repository of written traces as the literary text. I do want to insist, however, that language functions in many registers and in many modes (often at the same time), not all of which are *mis-en-abîme*. The polarized character of the debate over poststructuralism has tended to insist that we align ourselves on one or another side of the semiotic divide, as if we were somehow in a zero-sum linguistic game. But in opting for the middle ground, I would also opt for a mixed and potentially richer understanding of language and its mediatory possibilities in the interests of a more highly differentiated analysis of past texts and their social contexts.[22] The middle ground that I am seeking to demarcate would allow both concepts of mediation and language to be put into play simultaneously.

Obviously the question of instrumental language is more of an issue for historians than for literary critics, whose positive knowledge of their material is given to them ready-made, as it were, in the form of literary texts. Historians, however, have no givens – no ready-made chronicle of events or histories – and must construct their narratives on the basis of some degree of positive (if ideologically impressed)[23] vision of the past. It is precisely this incommensurability in the objects of investigation distinguishing historical and literary study that I sought to signal in "History, Historicism, and the Social Logic of the Text," and which seems to me to require a much more highly differentiated analysis of their respective aims and obstacles than has so far appeared in debates on postmodernism. The goal of this analysis would not be to return to or reproduce traditional dualisms, as Joyce asserts,[24] but to create a more productive and reciprocal duality in our approach to the past and a keener sense of the heterogeneous nature of the material available for its study.

A duality of perspectives in the investigation of texts (*both* literary and documentary) and their social contexts is what I tried to convey by the phrase "the social logic of the text", a term that seeks to combine in a single but complex framework a protocol for the analysis of a text's social site – the social space it occupies, both as a product of a particular social world and as an agent at work in that world – and its own discursive character as "logos", that is, as itself a literary artefact composed of language and thus demanding literary (formal) analysis.

My emphasis on the text's social site stems from my belief that the power and meaning of any given set of representations derives in large part from its social context and its relation to the social and political networks in which it is elaborated. Even if one accepts the poststructuralist argument that language constitutes the social world of meaning, it is possible to maintain, as Carroll Smith-Rosenberg has written, that "language itself acquires meaning and authority only within specific social and historical settings. While linguistic differences structure society, social differences structure language".[25] Texts, as material embodiments of situated language-use, reflect in their very materiality the inseparability of material and discursive practices and the need to preserve a sense of their mutual implication and interdependence in the production of meaning.

Implicit in the notion of the "social logic of the text", then, is the belief that we are capable of recovering some sense of the material world of the past, a belief that in turn commits us to at least a partial acceptance of language's instrumental capacity to convey information about historical forms of life, for without that capacity we could never know in even a partial sense anything about history. This is not an attempt to smuggle positivism in through the back door, as Joyce seems to be suggesting when he accuses me of reasserting "*traditional* dualisms". It *is* an attempt to argue for an understanding of semiotics that retains a conception of the sometimes referential (if always "arbitrary" because conventional) function of signs as part of socially shaped systems of human communication organized by languages, as Saussure himself understood semiotics. It is only by acknowledging the irreducibly semiotic character of our historical practice, I believe, that we can respond to the challenge semiotics has posed to traditional historiography. But a semiotic conception of language does not commit one to a belief in the intransitively self-reflexive character of *all* linguistic acts and artefacts. Indeed it was over this very point that Derrida ultimately broke with Saussure's theory of language, accusing him of a lingering nostalgia for a "transcendental signified."[26] As successor to semiotic theory, Derrida wishes to install a view of the endlessly ludic and mediatory play of language unconnected to any ground exterior to itself. In granting the force of semiotic conceptions of language, we do not necessarily have to concede the Derridean spin that deconstruction places on it.

In saying this, I do not intend to protest against the use of deconstructive strategies in reading historical texts, as Kelly implies in avowing her allegiance to them, for I believe that they have proven to be powerful tools of analysis in uncovering and dismantling the ways in which texts perform elaborate ideological mystifications of which it is proper to be suspicious and which texts themselves inevitably betray through their fracturing of meaning, once we have learned to read them deconstructively. Even more so has deconstruction taught us to heed the silences within language, to search out the unsaid as well as the spoken, and to understand the constitutive force of silence in shaping the texts we read.

The acceptance of a semiotically based view of language and of deconstructive modes of reading, as I will try to demonstrate in a forthcoming book on vernacular historiography in thirteenth-century France entitled *Romancing the Past*,[27] does not compel us to abandon our effort to enrich our understanding of the past as more than a complex of discursive strategies and events. *Romancing the Past* seeks to elaborate the ways in which Old French prose chronicles encode the historical experiences of thirteenth-century French nobles through a displacement in the past. In order to do this, it was necessary to know what those experiences – economic, social, political – were, and how they proved problematic for the class that patronized vernacular histories. This "context" (to use the traditional term) could not be derived directly from the historiographical texts themselves, since the chronicles in no way transparently reflect those experiences. On the contrary. Like all literary works, these histories are the site of multiple, often contradictory historical realities that are both present and absent in the works and in both capacities are constitutive of their form and inscribed meaning. Rather than incorporating or "reflecting" current social and political realities, thirteenth-century vernacular chronicles, I contend, sought to deny and mask the consequences of recent transformations in the political power and social status of the nobility responsible for their creation through its patronage. Moreover it is precisely this attempt to mantle adverse historical change beneath the calm and deproblematized surface of prose narrative that alerts us to the social uses of historiography in thirteenth-century France, even as it sought to disavow the very changes from which it was born.

In writing *Romancing the Past*, I employed the tools of both social historians and literary historians. I turned to the first because I wanted to situate the texts within a social world that they themselves do not bear witness to (for which reason, I might add, they have been generally misunderstood as "royalist" in orientation, a demonstrably mistaken social "siting" that an exploration of the phenomenon of patronage makes evident). I resorted to the second because I wished to investigate the ideological manipulation of the past that occurs in these writings, to which end I submitted them to close, essentially deconstructive, readings, and attempted to display the ways in which they tacitly inscribe through a variety of literary techniques the very social context that I inferred, from *other* sources, to be relevant in understanding their literary character and the motives for their creation. It is for reviewers to determine whether this attempt to investigate historical contexts and literary texts in a single work, and to practise a form of reading that seeks to maintain a dual perspective on the production of history in the Middle Ages as a socially motivated but specifically literary endeavour, is ultimately successful. My point here is that it is only possible given a differential analysis of the various materials available for study. Inextricably related within these histories are a wide range of social and discursive practices, of material and linguistic realities that are interwoven into the fabric of the text, whose analysis as determinate historical artefacts in turn grants us access to the past. It is this kind of relational reading of text and context, of overt and suppressed meaning, of implied and articulated purposes, together with the variety of literary and discursive modes in which they are given voice, that I believe we need to pursue if we are to achieve a genuinely historical understanding of textual production. This means occupying a theoretical "middle ground" and practising a "mixed" kind of reading, attentive to the differential linguistic practices and registers of past languages.

Postmodernism challenges us to develop such complex strategies of research and reading, despite the fact that they are not easily theorized. Moreover it is clear that many historians have already taken up this challenge and are implementing it in practice, even if they have not yet fully voiced their theoretical stances. In addition to the broadly diverse works that range themselves under the label of cultural history, feminism in particular has been at the forefront of an attempt to meld traditional forms of social history with strategies of reading and analysis borrowed from critical theory, not least from deconstruction. Because it has always been important to feminists to retain a sense of women's distinctive historical experience, yet at the same time to deconstruct the conventional implications of sexual difference by demonstrating how gender is itself a socially and culturally constructed category of experience, feminist historiography has produced some of the most sophisticated studies combining both perspectives in recent years. One thinks, for example, of Judith Walkowitz's book on *Prostitution and Victorian Society*, and even more so of her forthcoming *City of Dreadful Delight*, both of which investigate Victorian discourses on sexuality in relation to the regulation of women's social lives and the social and public space they occupied in London at the end of the nineteenth century.[28] In American history, a comparable, and exemplary, combination of social and discursive analyses can be found in Smith-Rosenberg's *Disorderly Conduct*,[29] but these are only a few among a host of studies that could easily be cited. They have shown that a historiographical practice located in the middle ground can be at once innovative, coherent and telling, enriching our understanding of the intricate dance of discourse and experience in past times.

Although the precise links between thought, language and action may be difficult to explain, it is not helpful to deal with them in terms of what Brian Stock has called "textual gnosticism".[30] A flexible appreciation of the ways postmodernism can aid in redefining the nature of historical investigation and enhance historiographical practice would surely represent a healthy appropriation of its tenets, without necessarily consigning us to its more extreme, and polarizing, forms.[31] We can never return to the confident, humanistic assumptions of nineteenth-century positivist historiography, even if we wanted to (and not many of us do). While we should, I believe, reject the tendencies of an extreme poststructuralism to absorb history into textuality, we can – and should – learn to appreciate and employ what it teaches us by and in its enactment of the complex tensions that shape the postmodern world.

As historians we are constantly engaged in attending, Paul Zumthor wrote recently, "to the discourse of some invisible other who speaks to us from some deathbed, of which the exact location is unknown. We strive to hear the echo of a voice which, somewhere, probes, knocks against the world's silences, begins again, is stifled." Our most fundamental task as historians, I believe, is to solicit those fragmented inner narratives to emerge from their silences. In the final analysis, what is the past but a once material existence, now silenced, extant only as sign and as sign drawing to itself chains of conflicting interpretations that hover over its absent presence and compete for possession of the relics, seeking to inscribe traces of significance upon the bodies of the dead?

NOTES

1. Richard Powers, *The Gold Bug Variations*, New York, 1991, p. 518.
2. Gabrielle M. Spiegel, "History, Historicism, and the Social Logic of the Text in the Middle Ages," *Speculum*, lxv (1990), pp. 59–86; Lawrence Stone, "History and Post-Modernism," *Past and Present*, no. 131, May 1991, pp. 217–18. For critiques of Stone's note and of my article, by Patrick Joyce and Catriona Kelly, see "History and Post-Modernism," *Past and Present*, no. 133, Nov. 1991, pp. 204–13.
3. Thus Jacques Derrida claims that the general goal of deconstruction is "to avoid both simply neutralizing the binary oppositions of metaphysics and simply residing within the closed field of these oppositions, thereby confirming it." The first phase of a deconstructive strategy is to overturn the hierarchies which rest upon such binary oppositions, and then to release the dissonances (the *aporia* or indeterminacies) within any act of speech or writing and thereby to disorganize the entire inherited order of thought. See J. Derrida, *Positions*, trans. and annotated Alan Bass, Chicago, 1981, p. 41. In this, deconstruction participates in what Ihab Hassan has described as the much broader pattern of postmodernism, which he defines as "indeterminacy and immanence; ubiquitous simulacra, pseudo-events; a conscious lack of mastery, lightness and evanescence everywhere; a new temporality, or rather intemporality, a polychronic sense of history; a patchwork or ludic, transgressive or deconstructive approach to knowledge and authority; an ironic, parodic, reflexive, fantastic awareness of the moment; a linguistic turn, semiotic imperative in culture; and in society generally the violence of local desires diffused into a terminology of seduction and force." In short, what Hassan sees as "a vast revisionary will in the Western world, unsettling/resetting codes, canons, procedures, beliefs – intimating a post-humanism": I. Hassan, *The Postmodern Turn: Essays in Postmodern Theory and Culture*, Ohio, 1987, p. xvi.
4. H. Kellner, "Triangular Anxieties: The Present State of European Intellectual History", in Dominick LaCapra and Steven L. Kaplan (eds) *Modern European Intellectual History: Reappraisals and New Perspectives*, Cambridge, 1982, p. 112.
5. N. Partner, "Making Up Lost Time: Writing on the Writing of History," *Speculum*, lxi (1986), p. 95.
6. Jean E. Howard, "The New Historicism in Literary Study," *Eng. Lit. Renaissance*, xvi (1986), p. 19.
7. Hence Michel de Certeau asserts, "the function of the past is to indicate alterity": M.

de Certeau, *The Writing of History*, trans. Tom Conley, New York, 1988, p. 85. And for de Certeau, this "alterity," which is that of the real world, is never merely a figment of language, but a *réel* that resists full intelligibility and therefore cannot be remade entirely according to the historian's desire. It is here that the much maligned notion of "objectivity" in historiography may retrieve some utility. As Dominick LaCapra argues, "objectivity implies an injunction to face facts that may prove embarrassing for these one would like to propound or the patterns one is striving to elicit. It is reciprocally related to a 'coefficient of resistance,' both in the 'textual' material one is interpreting and in the modes of empirical reality one is inferring from that material or its cognates": see D. LaCapra, *Soundings in Critical Theory*, Ithaca, NY, 1989, pp. 37–8.

 8. Joyce, "History and Post-Modernism, I," p. 208; Kelly, "History and Post-Modernism, II," p. 210.
 9. As Frederic Jameson observes, "one does not have to argue the reality of history; necessity does that for us": F. Jameson, *The Political Unconscious Narrative as a Socially Symbolic Act*, Ithaca, NY, 1982, p. 82.
10. Jameson further stipulates that "it is not necessary that these analyses be homologous, that is, that each of the objects in question be seen as doing the same thing, having the same structure or emitting the same message. What is crucial is that, by being able to use the same language about each of these quite distinct objects or levels of an object we can restore at least methodologically the lost unity of social life and demonstrate that widely distant elements of the social totality are ultimately part of the same global process": *ibid.*, pp. 225–6.
11. R. Williams, *Marxism and Literature* (Oxford, 1977), p. 98.
12. An example of how this works is afforded by Michael Baxandall's use of the "Bougier principle", which states that "in the event of difficulty in establishing a relation between two terms, modify one of the terms till it matches the other, but keeping note of what modification has been necessary". Thus Baxandall, acknowledging that "art and society are analytical concepts from two different kinds of categorization of human experience" – are, therefore, "unhomologous systematic constructions put upon interpenetrating subject matters" – shows how some strands of modern criticism have modified the term "society" into the term "culture" in order to establish an analysable, homologous relationship between the two. See M. Baxandall, "Art, Society and the Bougier Principle", *Representations*, x (1985), pp. 40–1. For a discussion of Baxandall, see also Stephen Greenblatt, "Towards a Poetics of Culture", in H. A. Veeser (ed.), *The New Historicism* (New York, 1989), pp. 11–12.
13. Quoted in Lee Patterson, *Negotiating the Past: The Historical Understanding of Medieval Literature* (Madison, 1987), p. xi. See also Williams, *Marxism and Literature*, pp. 98–9; R. Williams, *Keywords: A Vocabulary of Culture and Society*, rev. edn. (New York, 1985), pp. 204–6. Mediation in its "classical" sense here corresponds to Williams's definition (ii), while Adorno's version falls within his category (iii).
14. One could restate this in simpler fashion by arguing that what we study in the past are discourses, which represent identifiable units of a given society's mediated and mediating practices and beliefs. The result of this focus on discourse, I have argued, is to collapse text and context into a single, aestheticized understanding of culture, a procedure characteristic of New Historicist criticism, with its self-avowed elaboration of a cultural "poetics", and, to a lesser extent, of new forms of cultural history, both of which tend to treat texts and their contexts as equally part of one broad vein of discursive production characteristic of a given epoch. See Spiegel, "History, Historicism, and the Social Logic of the Text", pp. 67–74. Thus Lynn Hunt, herself an exemplar and advocate of the new cultural history, poses what seems to me to be the relevant and trenchant question that arises from New Historicist and cultural history's

focus on the social practices of any given society as discursively homologous artifacts: "where will we be when every practice – whether it is economic, intellectual, social or political – has been shown to be culturally determined? Or, to put it another way, can a history of culture work if it is shorn of all theoretical assumptions about culture's relationship to the social world, if indeed, its agenda is conceived as the undermining of all assumptions about the relationship between culture and the social world?": Lynn Hunt, "History, Culture and Text", in Lynn Hunt (ed.), *The New Cultural History* (Berkeley, 1989), p. 10.

15. To borrow the formulation of Hayden White, "The Problem of Change in Literary History", *New Lit. Hist.*, vii (1975), p. 109. I derive the term "constative" for language that is instrumental or descriptive from LaCapra's use of it in his *Soundings in Critical Theory.*

16. Kelly, "History and Postmodernism, II," p. 210.

17. See Martin Jay, "Should Intellectual History Take a Linguistic Turn? Reflections on the Habermas-Gadamer Debate," in LaCapra and Kaplan (eds.), *Modern European Intellectual History*, p. 110.

18. Joyce, "History and Postmodernism, I," p. 208.

19. Jay, "Should Intellectual History Take a Linguistic Turn?", p. 108.

20. Thus, Judith Newton insists, "Taking the 'material' seriously, a material always apprehended within representation, changes the way that representation itself is represented": Judith Newton, "History as Usual? Feminism and the 'New Historicism'," in Veeser (ed.); *New Historicism*, p. 166.

21. LaCapra, *Soundings in Critical Theory*, p. 55.

22. This accords, in fact, with Joyce's own practice in his recent book, *Visions of the People: Industrial England and the Question of Class, 1848–1914* (Cambridge, 1991), even if it does not appear exactly to cohere with his present polemic. In *Visions of the People,* Joyce, while contesting traditional notions of "class", by no means abandons the idea of a social reality that conditions the specific inflections of working class culture. Thus although he begins by advocating "an expanded sense of language as a sign system – of what might be called the semiology of the social order" (p. 17), he concludes by arguing that "conceptions of the social order were [themselves] related to attempts to bring order and decency to the experience of poverty, insecurity and labour" (p. 330). That "experience" included, notably, the harsh realities of poverty and hunger that *as experience*, he further argues (p. 338), shaped popular culture in its effort to construct a social identity for poor and labouring people. What Joyce appears to be proposing here is that equal weight be given to the experience of poverty as to the experience of work in understanding working-class culture, thus attenuating "class" as the constitutive aspect of popular identity. It is unclear from Joyce's book whether he believes that poverty itself was discursively constructed, but his belief that "poverty twisted aspiration into resignation, but also served as a spur to visions of a better life and a juster world" (p. 341) would seem to argue against it, as would his further qualification that "discourses actively structured perceptions, but did so only because they articulated the needs and desires of their audiences". Both statements suggest a relative degree of autonomy (or, to put it another way, relational interdependence) between experience and culture as distinct orders of phenomena. Thus, unless I am reading him incorrectly, I see in these statements the same attempt to enfold discursive and material realities in an analysis of the production of culture that I sought to articulate in my work on thirteenth-century historiography. I am grateful to Richard Price for discussing Joyce's work with me.

23. I have set aside in this discussion the hermeneutic problem of our reading of both categories of texts and the myriad ways in which we construe and misconstrue them, primarily because it is so fundamental to historical "reading" that it goes virtually

without saying. I am not arguing for a return to a positivist belief in our capacity to recover a "true" account of *wie es eigentlich gewesen* or making a common-sensical appeal to the authenticity of "experience". But I do wish to open up an epistemological space that allows a degree of positive perception of the past, however imperfect and distorted by present ideological lenses.

24. Joyce, "History and Post-Modernism," p. 208.
25. C. Smith-Rosenberg, "The Body Politic", in Elizabeth Weed (ed.), *Coming to Terms: Feminism, Theory, Politics* (New York, 1989), p. 101.
26. Derrida, *Positions*, p. 19.
27. Gabrielle M. Spiegel, *Romancing the Past: The Rise of Vernacular Prose Historiography in Thirteenth-Century France* (Berkeley, forthcoming 1992).
28. J. Walkowitz, *Prostitution and Victorian Society: Women, Class and the State*, Cambridge, 1980; J. Walkowitz, *City of Dreadful Delight: Narratives of Sexual Danger in Late Nineteenth-Century London*, Chicago, forthcoming 1992.
29. C. Smith-Rosenberg, *Disorderly Conduct: Visions of Gender in Victorian America*, Oxford, 1985.
30. Brian Stock, "History, Literature and Medieval Textuality", *Yale French Studies*, lxx (1986), p. 17. Similarly, Edward Said, in arguing for a "secular criticism", maintains that "even if we accept . . . that there is no way to get past texts in order to apprehend 'real' history directly, it is still possible to say that such a claim need not also eliminate interest in the events and circumstances entailed by and expressed in the texts themselves": E. Said, *The World, the Text and the Critic*, Cambridge, Mass., 1983, p. 4.
31. Thus I agree basically with LaCapra's desire to "elaborate a critical and self-critical historiography that remains opens to the risks Derrida explores but also insists upon certain constraints in a manner that engages the disciplinary conventions of professional historians": LaCapra, *Sounding in Critical Theory*, p. 6. These "disciplinary conventions" comprise a respect for empirical-analytic techniques of research (i.e., a belief in the referential, constative possibilities of language) along with a new, and theoretically informed appreciation of the literary nature of all historical documents and their mediating and supplementary role in all historiography.

EXTRACTS FROM *HISTORY AND THEORY*

History and Theory is perhaps the foremost philosophy of history journal in existence. Originally an analytical-type journal, and much engaged in its earlier days with debates about the possible scientific nature of historiography (on this see Richard Vann's excellent article, "Turning Linguistic: History and Theory and *History and Theory* 1960–1975," in F. R. Ankersmit and H. Kellner (eds) *A New Philosophy of History*, Reaktion, 1995), over the years it has turned increasingly towards considerations of poststructural problematicizations of the real, the "idea" of the referent, and arguments on narratology – the latter largely inspired by the seminal works of Hayden White. It is difficult to select from the many first-class articles published by *History and Theory* those of most relevance to this volume, but it might be useful to mention the following, all of which contain extensive footnotes for "further reading." Thus, F. R. Ankersmit, "The Dilemma of Contemporary Anglo-Saxon Philosophy for History," *Beiheft*, (1986) 25, pp. 1–27; H. Kellner, "Narrativity in History: Poststructuralism and Since," Beiheft, (1987) 26, pp. 1–29; A. P. Norman, "Telling It Like It Was: Historical Narratives on their own Terms" (1991), 30, 2, pp. 119–35; M. Bevir, "Objectivity in History," (1994) 33, 3, pp. 328–44 and W. Kansteiner, "Hayden White's Critique of the Writing of History," (1993) 32, 3 pp. 273–95.

It was F. R. Ankersmit – a contributor to and sometime guest editor of *History and Theory* – who first addressed explicitly the impact of postmodernism and historiography in its pages in 1989 ("Historiography and Postmodernism" (1989) 28, 2, pp. 137–53). Ankersmit's article ranges widely: from the over-production of historiography to the philosophy of science, from the aestheticization of historiography in its narrative form ("narrative substance") to psychoanalysis, and from any notion of a narrative/metanarrative structure unifying the past in ways translatable into corresponding historicizations, to postmodern nostalgia for the pre-Socratics. It was a *tour de force*, Ankersmit welcoming the "freed-up" nature of historiography under the workings of the postmodern whilst not entirely abandoning – at least at the level of the statement – historiography as an "epistemology."

A year later, in Vol. 29, (3) of *History and Theory*, Ankersmit was taken to task by Perez Zagorin. Beginning by placing Ankersmit in a wider context than the narrowly circumscribed one of historiography (the metahistory of White, the anti-humanism of Foucault, the "stagism" of Fredric Jameson), Zagorin went on to a piecemeal critique of the main points of Ankersmit's argument, finally charging him with a postmodernism which would take away from historiography its "real" function: "It could no longer perform its principal intellectual obligation in education and culture [an actually present-centred obligation] which must be to give to each living generation the broadest and best possible knowledge of its own society and civilisation as well as of the larger human past of which it is a part." Postmodernism, goes on Zagorin, represents "the abnegation of this obligation which is the ultimate cultural responsibility of historiography and one that remains indispensable . . .".

This "exchange" was not the end of the matter. In the same issue as Zagorin's critique of Ankersmit there appeared Ankersmit's response to Zagorin. This was a long reply – of about 10,000 words – at the end of which Ankersmit commented that he fully expected that, after reading Zagorin's perceptive reply to his original article, most readers might well have con-cluded that "I had manoeuvred myself into a pretty hopeless position," hoping that his own response would, however, convince such readers that "my case is not quite so hopeless as they [may have] initially thought." And in his penultimate paragraph, Ankersmit summed up his case for a postmodern historiography in an almost manifesto type way:

> That narrative language has the ontological status of being an object that is opaque; that it is self-referential; that it is intensional and, hence, intrinsically aestheticist; that the narrative meaning of an (historical) text is undecidable in an important sense of that word and even bears the marks of self-contradiction; that narrative meaning can only be identified in the presence of *other* meaning (intertextuality); that as far as narrative is concerned the text refers but not to a reality outside itself; that criteria of truth and falsity do not apply to historiographical representations of the past; that we can only properly speak of causes and effects at the level of the state-ment; that narrative language is metaphysical (tropological) and as such embodies a proposal for how we should see the past; that the historical text is a substitute for the absent past; that narrative representations of the past have a tendency to disintegrate . . . all these postmodern claims so amazing and even repulsive to the mod-ernist can be gives a formal or even a "modernist" justification if we are prepared to develop a philosophical logic suitable for dealing with the narrative substance.

(*History and Theory*, 29, 3, pp. 295–6)

I reprint here two-thirds of the Ankersmit–Zagorin debate; namely, Ank-ersmit's original article and Zagorin's reply (both given in full, Chapters 26 and 27). Because of the length of Ankersmit's response to Zagorin's critique – and the difficulty in cutting it given Ankersmit's detailed refer-ences back to Zagorin throughout – that response is not given here.

However, there is little doubt that, not least in the pages of *History and Theory*, – the Ankersmit–Zagorin debate was a seminal moment, and that the issues raised therein are still at the top of the current "postmodern v proper history" discussions. Readers are thus urged to complete the exchange given here by going themselves to Ankersmit's further contribution, not least because this intellectually challenging discussion, though now some six or seven years old, still has contemporary pertinence.

26 F. R. Ankersmit

Historiography and postmodernism

My point of departure in this chapter is the present-day overproduction in our discipline. We are all familiar with the fact that in any imaginable area of historiography, within any specialty, an overwhelming number of books and articles is produced annually, making a comprehensive view of them all impossible. This is true even of the separate topics within one and the same specialty. Let me illustrate this with an example from political theory, a field with which I am fairly familiar. Anyone who some twenty years ago wanted to go into Hobbes's political philosophy needed only two important commentaries on Hobbes: the studies written by Watkins and Warrender. Of course, there were more even then but after reading these two books one was pretty well "in the picture." However, anyone who in 1989 has the courage to try to say anything significant about Hobbes will first have to read his way through a pile of twenty to twenty-five studies which are as carefully written as they are extensive; I will spare you an enumeration of them. Moreover, these studies are usually of such high quality that one certainly cannot afford to leave them unread.

There are two aspects to the unintended result of this overproduction. In the first place, the discussion of Hobbes tends to take on the nature of a discussion of the *interpretation* of Hobbes, rather than of his work *itself*. The work itself sometimes seems to be little more than the almost forgotten reason for the war of interpretations going on today. In the second place, because of its evident multi-interpretability, Hobbes's original text gradually lost its capacity to function as arbiter in the historical debate. Owing to all the interpretations, the text *itself* became vague, a watercolor in which the lines flow into one another. This meant that the naive faith in the text itself being able to offer a solution to our interpretation problems became just as absurd as the faith in a signpost attached to a weathervane. The paradoxical result of all this is that the text itself no longer has any authority in an interpretation and that we even feel compelled to advise our students not to read *Leviathan* independently; they are better off first trying to hack a path through the jungle of interpretation. To put it in a nutshell, we no longer have any texts, any past, but just interpretations of them.

When I read the reviews and notices announcing new books in the *Times Literary Supplement*, the *New York Review of Books*, or in the professional journals which are increasing in number at an alarming rate, I do not doubt that things are very much the same in other areas of historiography. The situation which Nietzsche feared more than a hundred years ago, the situation in which historiography itself impedes our view of the past, seems to have become reality. Not only does this flood of historical literature give us all a feeling of intense despondency, but this overproduction undeniably has something uncivilized about it. We associate civilization with, among other things, a feeling for moderation, for a happy medium between excess and shortage. Any feeling for moderation, however, seems to have been lost in our present-day intellectual alcoholism. This comparison with alcoholism is also very apt because the most recent book or article on a particular topic always pretends to be the very last intellectual drink.

Of course, this situation is not new and there has therefore been no lack of attempts to retain some reassuring prospects for the future for disheartened historians. The Dutch historian Romein saw in this overproduction a tendency towards specialization; he therefore called for a theoretical history which would undo the pulverization of our grasp of the past which had been caused by specialization. Theoretical history would be able to lift us to a more elevated view-point from which we would again be able to survey and to bring order to the chaos caused by specialization and overproduction.[1] But Romein's book on the watershed of two ages is proof that this is easier said than done. Above all, the problem seems to be that on this higher level postulated by Romein a real interaction among the various specialises remains difficult to realize. Integral historiography leads to enumeration rather than to integration.

Another way out of the dilemma is the strategy adopted by the *Annales* school. They have devoted their attention chiefly to the discovery of new objects of inquiry in the past; with this strategy they do indeed allow themselves the chance of once again finding history in an unspoiled state. Of course, this offers only temporary solace: before too long, countless other historians, French or not, will pounce upon these new topics and soon they, too, will be covered by a thick and opaque crust of interpretations. There is, however, more to be said about how resourceful the *Annales* school is in finding new and exciting topics. In the course of this article I shall return to this matter.

The crucial question now is what attitude we should take with regard to this overproduction of historical literature which is spreading like a cancer in all fields. A reactionary longing for the neat historical world of fifty years ago is just as pointless as despondent resignation. We have to realize that there is no way back. It has been calculated that at this moment there are more historians occupied with the past than the total number of historians from Herodotus up until 1960. It goes without saying that it is impossible to forbid the production of new books and articles by all these scholars presently writing. Complaining about the loss of a direct link with the past does not get us any further. However, what *does* help and *does* have a point is the defining of a new and different link with the past based on a complete and honest recognition of the position in which we now see ourselves placed as historians.

There is, moreover, another reason to make an attempt in that direction. The present-day overproduction of historical literature can indeed be called monstrous if our point of departure is *traditional* ideas about the task and the meaning of historiography. Historiography today has burst out of its traditional, self-legitimating, theoretical jacket and is therefore in need of new clothes. This is not in order to teach the historian how he should set about his work as an historian, nor to develop a theory *Vom Nutzen und Nachteil der Historie für das Leben*. With regard to the first half of this statement, there is no point outside historiography itself from which rules for the historian's method of work can be drawn up: if historians consider something to be meaningful, then it is meaningful and that is all there is to it. As for the second half of the statement, I do not believe that historiography is useful or has a recognizable disadvantage. By this I do not mean that historiography is useless, but that the question concerning the usefulness and disadvantage of historiography is an unsuitable question – a "category mistake," to use Ryle's expression. Along with poetry, literature, painting, and the like, history and historical consciousness belong to culture, and no questions can meaningfully be asked about the usefulness of culture. Culture, of which historiography is a part, is rather the background *from which* or *against which* we can form our opinion concerning the usefulness of, for example, certain kinds of scientific research or certain political objectives. For that reason science and politics do not belong to culture; if something can have a use or a disadvantage or enables us to manipulate the world it is not a part of civilization. Culture and history define use, but cannot themselves be defined in terms of usefulness. They belong to the domain of the "absolute presuppositions,"[2] to use Collingwood's terminology. This is also the reason that politics should not interfere with culture.

That is why, if we were to try to find a new jacket for historiography, as was considered necessary above, the most important problem would be to situate historiography within present-day civilization as a whole. This problem is of a cultural-historical or an interpretative nature, and could be compared with the sort of problem which we sometimes pose ourselves when we are considering the place and the meaning of a particular event within the totality of our life-history. In general, it is strange that historians and philosophers of history have paid so little attention over the last forty years to parallels between the development of present-day historiography on the one hand and that of literature, literary criticism, printing – in short, civilization – on the other. Apparently, the historian did not see any more reason to suspect the existence of such parallels than did the chemist or the astronomer.

It is not my goal to determine here the place of historiography in this way. Instead, I will move further away to ascertain whether the overproduction in historiography has its counterpart in a considerable part of present-day civilization and society. Who does not know the cliché that we are living in an age of an information surplus? In the course of all this theorizing about information – which is more profound at some times than at others – two things stand out which are of importance for the rest of my article. In the first place, it is strange that one often talks about information as if it is something almost physical. Information "flows," "moves," "spreads," "is traded," "is stored," or "is organized." Lyotard speaks of the State as a body which restrains or disperses information flows.[3] Information appears to be a sort of liquid with a low viscosity; we are flooded by it and are in imminent danger of drowning in it. Second, when we talk about information, information as such has assumed a conspicuously prominent place with respect to the actual subject matter of that information. This relationship was usually the other way around. Take a statement giving information, such as "In 1984 Ronald Reagan was elected President of the US." This informative statement itself is hidden by the state of affairs described by it. However, within our present-day way of speaking about information, the reality which that information concerns tends to be relegated to the background. The reality is the information itself and no longer the reality behind that information. This gives information an autonomy of its own, a substantiality of its own. Just as there are laws describing the behavior of things in reality, there would also seem to be a scientific system possible to describe the behavior of that remarkable liquid we call information. Incidentally, I would like to add at this point that, from the perspective of Austin's speech act theory, information could just as well be said to be purely performative as not at all performative. This is certainly one of the fascinating aspects of the phenomenon of information.[4]

In recent years, many people have observed our changed attitude towards the phenomenon of information. Theories have been formed about it and the theoreticians concerned have, as usually happens, given themselves a name. In this context we often talk about postmodernists or poststructuralists and they are, understandably, contrasted with the modernists or structuralists from the recent past. In 1984, a very interesting conference in Utrecht was devoted to postmodernism, and anyone who heard the lectures read at the conference will agree that it is not easy to define the concepts postmodernism or poststructuralism satisfactorily.[5] Nevertheless, it is possible to discern a general line, as did Jonathan Culler in a recent book.[6] Science was the alpha and omega of the modernists and the structuralists; they saw science as not only the most important given but at the same time the ultimate given of modernity. Scientific rationality as such does not pose a problem for postmodernists and poststructuralists; they look at it, as it were, from outside or from above. They neither criticize nor reject science; they are not irrationalists, but they show the same aloofness with respect to science as we observed above in our present attitude towards information. This is not a question of metacriticism of scientific research or scientific method as we are used to in philosophy of science. Philosophy of science remains inherent in the scientism of the modernists; philosophers of science follow the line of thought of scientists and study the path they have covered between the discovery of empirical data and theory. For postmodernists, both the philosophy of science and science itself form the given, the point of departure for their reflections. And postmodernists are just as little interested in the sociological question of how research scientists react to one another or what the relation is between science and society. The postmodernist's attention is focused neither on scientific research nor on the way in which society digests the results of scientific research, but only on the functioning of science and of scientific information itself.

For postmodernism, science and information are independent objects of study which obey their own laws. The first principal law of postmodernist information theory is the law that information multiplies. One of the most fundamental characteristics of information is that really important information is never the end of an information genealogy, but that its importance is in fact assessed by the intellectual posterity it gives rise to. Historiography itself forms an excellent illustration of this. The great works from the history of historiography, those of a de Tocqueville, Marx, Burckhardt, Weber, Huizinga, or Braudel, proved repeatedly to be the most powerful stimulants for a new wave of publications, instead of concluding an information genealogy as if a particular problem had then been solved once and for all: "Paradoxically, the more powerful and authoritative an interpretation, the more writing it generates."[7] In the modernist view, the way in which precisely interesting information generates more information is, of course, incomprehensible. For modernists, meaningful information is information which does put an end to writing; they cannot explain why precisely what is debatable is fundamental to the progress of science, why, as Bachelard said, it is the *debatable* facts which are the *true* facts.

It is important within the framework of this chapter to look in greater detail at this postmodernism which is ascientistic rather than antiscientistic. In the first place, it can teach us what we should understand by a postmodernist historiography and, in the second place, that historiography, remarkably enough, has always had already something postmodernist about it. A good example of a postmodernist criterion of science is Nietzsche's "deconstruction" – to use the right term – of causality, which many consider to be one of the most important pillars of scientific thought. In causalistic terminology, the cause is the source and the effect the secondary given. Nietzsche then points out that only on the basis of our observation of the effect are we led to look for the causes and that therefore the effect is in *fact* the primary given and the cause the secondary given. "If the effect is what causes the cause to become a cause, then the effect, not the cause, should be treated as the origin."[8] Anyone who puts forward the objection that Nietzsche has confused the order of things in research and reality respectively is missing the point of Nietzsche's line of thought; for the point is precisely the artificiality of the traditional hierarchy of cause and effect. Our scientific training has, so to speak, "stabilized" us to adhere to this traditional hierarchy, but beyond this intellectual training there is nothing that forces us to continue to do so. Just as much, albeit not *more*, can be said in favour of reversing this hierarchy.

This is the way things always are in postmodernism. Science is "destabilized," is placed outside its own center, the reversibility of patterns of thought and categories of thought is emphasized, without suggesting any definite alternative. It is a sort of disloyal criticism of science, a blow below the belt which is perhaps not fair, but which for that very reason does hit science where it hurts most. Scientific rationality is not *aufgehoben* in an Hegelian way to something else, nor is it true to say that every view automatically evokes its antithesis; it is rather the recognition that every view has, besides its scientifically approved inside, an outside not noticed by science. In his *Tractatus*, Wittgenstein had already suggested something similar with respect to every valid line of reasoning. It is in fact the valid line of reasoning which aims at making itself superfluous, which therefore is always a journey over the territory of the untrue – that is, the journey from initial misconception to correct insight. Consequently, what is true always remains tainted by what is untrue.

Both a logical and an ontological conclusion can be attached to this insight; together they give an idea of the revolutionary nature of postmodernism. Let us first look at logic. For the postmodernist, the scientific certainties on which the modernists have always built are all as many variants on the paradox of the liar. That is, the paradox of the Cretan who says that all Cretans lie; or, to put it more compactly, the paradox of the statement "this statement is untrue," where this statement is a statement about itself. Of course, all the drama of postmodernism is contained in the insight that these paradoxes should be seen as unsolvable. And here we should bear in mind that the solution to the paradox of the liar which Russell, with his theory of types and his distinction between predicates and predicates of predicates, proposed in the *Principia Mathematica*, is still recognized today as one of the most important foundations of contemporary logic.[9] The postmodernist's aim, therefore, is to pull the carpet out from under the feet of science and modernism. Here, too, the best illustration of the postmodernist thesis is actually provided by historiography. Historical interpretations of the past first become recognizable, they first acquire their identity, through the contrast with *other* interpretations; they are what they are only on the basis of what they are *not*. Anyone who knows only one interpretation of, for example, the Cold War, does not know any interpretation at all of that phenomenon. Every historical insight, therefore, intrinsically has a paradoxical nature.[10] No doubt Hayden White in his *Metahistory* – the most revolutionary book in philosophy of history over the past twenty-five years – was thinking along the same lines when he characterized all historiography as fundamentally ironic.[11]

Let us now turn to ontology. In his deconstruction of the traditional hierarchy of cause and effect, Nietzsche was playing off our way of speaking about reality against processes in reality itself. The current distinction between language and reality thus loses its *raison d'être*. In particular, scientific language is no longer a "mirror of nature" but just as much a part of the inventory of reality as the objects in reality which science studies. Language as used in science is a thing,[12] and as Hans Bertens argued at the Utrecht Conference on postmodernism,[13] things in reality acquire a "language-like" nature. Once again, historiography provides the best illustration for all this. As we will see presently, it is historical language which has the same opacity as we associate with things in reality. Furthermore, both Hayden White and Ricoeur (whom I certainly do not mean to call a postmodernist) like to say that past reality should be seen as a text formulated in a foreign language with the same lexical, grammatical, syntactical, and semantic dimensions as any other text.[14] It is equally characteristic that historians in their theoretical reflections often show a marked tendency to speak about historical language as if it were part of reality itself and vice versa. Thus, Marx spoke of the *contradiction* between the production forces and production relations as if he were discussing *statements* about reality instead of *aspects* of this reality. Similarly, historians very often would like to see the same uniqueness realized for historical language as is characteristic of historical phenomena.[15] In short, the latent and often subconscious resistance to the language/reality dichotomy which historians have always displayed in fact had its origin in the unconsidered but nevertheless correct insight of historians into the fundamentally postmodernist nature of their discipline.

When the dichotomy between language and reality is under attack we are not far from aestheticism. Does not both the language of the novelist and of the historian give us the illusion of a reality, either fictitious or genuine? More important still, Gombrich has in various works taught us that the work of art, that is to say, the language of the artist, is not a *mimetic reproduction* of reality but a *replacement or substitute* for it.[16] Language and art are not situated *opposite* reality but are themselves a pseudo-reality and are therefore situated *within* reality. As a matter of fact, Megill in his brilliant genealogy of postmodernism has shown to what extent postmodernists from Nietzsche up to and including Derrida want to extend aestheticism over the entire domain of the representation of reality.[17]

This aestheticism is also in harmony with recently acquired insights into the nature of historiography – that is, the recognition of the stylistic dimension of historical writing. To the modernists, style was anathema or, at best, irrelevant. I quote from a recent lecture by C. P. Bertels: "fine writing, the display of literary style, does not add an iota of truth to historical research nor to any other scientific research."[18] What is important is the content; the way, the style in which it is expressed, is irrelevant. However, since Quine and Goodman, this pleasant distinction between form or style and content can no longer be taken for granted. Their argument can be summarized as follows. If various historians are occupied with various aspects of the same research subject, the resulting difference in *content* can just as well be described as a different *style* in the treatment of that research subject. "*What* is said . . . may be a way of talking about something else; for example, writing about Renaissance battles and writing about Renaissance arts, are different ways of writing about the Renaissance."[19] Or, in the words of Gay, "manner," style, implies at the same time a decision with regard to "matter," to content.[20] And where style and content might be distinguished from one another, we can even attribute to style priority over content; for because of the incommensurability of historiographical views – that is to say, the fact that the nature of historical differences of opinion cannot be satisfactorily defined in terms of research subjects – there remains nothing for us but to concentrate on the style embodied in every historical view or way of looking at the past, if we are to guarantee the meaningful progress of historical debate. Style, not content, is the issue in such debates. Content is a derivative of style.

The postmodernist recognition of the aesthetic nature of historiography can be described more precisely as follows. In analytical philosophy, there is the phenomenon of the so-called "intensional context." An example is the statement "John believes that p" or "John hopes that p" (where p stands for a particular statement). The point is that in an intensional context like this, p can never be replaced by another statement even if this other statement is equivalent to p, or results directly from it. After all, we do not know whether John is in fact aware of the consequences of his belief or hope that p. It is possible that John believes that the water is boiling, to give an example, without his believing that the temperature of the water is a hundred degrees Centigrade. In other words, the exact form in which a statement in an intensional context was formulated is one of the prerequisites for the truth of this statement. The sentence attracts, so to speak, attention to itself. Thus, the *form* of the statement is certainly just as important here as the *content*. In a particularly interesting book, Danto has pointed out that this intensional nature of statements and texts (or at least some of them) is nowhere clearer than in literature: "we may see this [this intensional element] perhaps nowhere more clearly than in those literary texts, where in addition to whatever facts the author means to state, he or she *chooses the words* with which they are stated" and the literary intention of the writer "would fail if other words were used instead."[21] Because of its intensional nature, the literary text has a certain opacity, a capacity to attract attention to itself, instead of drawing attention to a fictitious or historical reality behind the text. And this is a feature which the literary text shares with historiography; for the nature of the view of the past presented in an historical work is defined exactly by the language used by the historian in his or her historical work. Because of the relation between the historiographical view and the language used by the historian in order to express this view – a relation which nowhere intersects the domain of the past – historiography possesses the same opacity and intensional dimension as art.

Art and historiography can therefore be contrasted with science. Scientific language at least has the pretension of being transparent; if it impedes our view of reality, it will have to be refined or elucidated. It is true that some philosophers of science, such as Mary Hesse, want to attribute even to science the abovementioned aesthetic and literary dimensions. That would, of course, lend some extra plausibility to my claim regarding historiography, but I see the differences between the exact sciences and historiography as *more* than a question of nuances. Where the insight provided in a discipline is far more of a syntactical than of a semantic nature – as is the case in the exact sciences – there is comparatively less room for intensional contexts. After all, only from the perspective of semantics is it meaningful to ask the question whether there is synonymy or not (and that is the most important issue in intensional contexts).

If we are in agreement with the above, that is to say, with the applicability of postmodernist insight to historiography, I would like to draw a number of conclusions before rounding off this article. For the modernist, within the scientific world-picture, within the view of history we all initially accept, evidence is in essence the evidence that something happened in the past. The modernist historian follows a line of reasoning from his sources and evidence to an historical reality hidden behind the sources. On the other hand, in the postmodernist view, evidence does not point towards the *past* but to other *interpretations* of the past; for that is what we in fact use evidence for. To express this by means of imagery: for the modernist, the evidence is a tile which he picks up to see what is underneath it; for the postmodernist, on the other hand, it is a tile which he steps on in order to move on to other tiles: horizontality instead of verticality.

This is not only an insight into what actually happens but just as much an insight into what historians should concentrate on in the future. The suggestion could best be described as the contemporization of the historical source. Evidence is not a magnifying glass through which we can study the past, but bears more resemblance to the brush-strokes used by the painter to achieve a certain effect. Evidence does not send us back to the past, but gives rise to the question what an historian here and now can or cannot do with it. Georges Duby illus-trates this new attitude towards evidence. When his intelligent interviewer Guy Lardreau asks him what constitutes for him, Duby, the most interesting evidence, he says that this can be found in what is not said, in what a period has *not* said about itself, and he therefore com-pares his historical work with the developing of a negative.[22] Just as the fish does not know that it is swimming in the water, what is most characteristic of a period, most omnipresent in a period, is unknown to the period itself. It is not revealed until a period has come to an end. The fragrance of a period can only be inhaled in a subsequent period. Of course, Hegel and Foucault have already made many interesting comments about this. However, the point here is Duby's observation that the essence of a period is determined by the *dessinataire*, to use the term of the French postmodernists, by the historian who has to develop here and now his negative of a period from that which was not said or was only whispered, or was expressed only in insignificant details. The historian is like the connoisseur who recognizes the artist not by that which is characteristic of him (and consequently imitable) but by that which, so to speak, spontaneously "escaped" him. "Le style, c'est l'homme" and our style is where we are ourselves without having thought about ourselves. That is why so few people still have style in our narcissistic era. In short, the way of dealing with the evidence as suggested by Duby is special because it points not so much to something that was concealed behind it in the past, but because it acquires its point and meaning only through the confrontation with the mentality of the later period in which the historian lives and writes. The mentality of a period is revealed only in the difference between it and that of a later period; the direction in which the evidence points thus undergoes a shift of ninety degrees. As has so often been the case, this, too, had been anticipated by Huizinga. Writing about the historical sensation, he says: "this contact with the past, which is accompanied by the complete conviction of genuineness, truth, can be evoked by a line from a charter or a chronicle, by a print, a few notes from an old song. It is not an element introduced into his work by the writer [in the past] by means of certain words: . . . *The reader brings it to meet the writer*, it is his response to the latter's call."[23]

It is not surprising that Duby and Lardreau point out in this connection the relation between historiography and psychoanalysis.[24] In both historiography and psychoanalysis, we are concerned with interpretation in the most fundamental sense of the word. In historiography, this way of dealing with traces of the past as suggested by Duby compels us to refrain from searching for some initially invisible machine in the past itself which has caused these traces discernible on the surface. In the same way, psychoanalysis, in spite of the positivist notes struck by Freud himself, is in fact a repertory of interpretation strategies. Psychoanalysis teaches us to understand what the neurotic *says* and does not draw our attention to the causal effects of a number of elementary and undivided homunculi in his mind.[25] Both the psychoanalyst and the historian try to project a pattern *onto* the traces and do not search for something *behind* the traces. In both cases, the activity of interpretation is understood strictly nominalistically: there is nothing in historical reality or in the mind of the neurotic that corresponds with the content of interpretations.[26]

However, there is a still more interesting parallel to psychoanalytic interpretation. Of course, Duby's thesis that the historian should pay attention to what is not said and to what is suppressed – madness, untruth, and taboo, to use Foucault's criteria – is obviously related to the analyst's method of work. Just as we are what we are not, or do not want to be, in a certain sense the past is also what it was not. In both psychoanalysis and history, what is suppressed manifests itself only in minor and seemingly irrelevant details. In psychoanalysis, this results in the insight that man does not have an easily observable being or essence on the basis of which he can be understood, but that the secret of personality lies in what only rarely and fleetingly becomes visible behind the usual presentation. Our personality is, as Rorty put it, a collage rather than a substance: "the ability to think of ourselves as idiosyncratically formed collages rather than as substances has been an important factor in our ability to slough off the idea that we have a true self, one shared with all other humans. . . . Freud made the paradigm of self-knowledge the discovery of little idiosyncratic accidents rather than of an essence."[27]

This is also the case in historiography, at least in what I would like to call postmodernist history (of mentalities). To formulate this in the paradoxical manner so popular among postmodernists: the essence of the past is not, or does not lie in, the essence of the past. It is the scraps, the slips of the tongue, the *Fehlleistungen* of the past, the rare moments when the past "let itself go," where we discover what is really of importance for us. I suspect that at least a partial explanation can be found here for what Jörn Rüsen referred to as the "paradigm change" in present-day historiography, a paradigm change which in his opinion consists mainly of exchanging *makrohistorische Strukturen* for *mikrohistorische Situationen und Lebensverhältnisse* as the object of the historian's attention.[28] What we are witnessing could perhaps be nothing less than the definitive farewell for the time being to all the essentialist aspirations which have actually dominated historiography as long as it has existed. Historians have always been searching for something they could label as the essence of the past – the principle that held everything together in the past (or in a part of it) and on the basis of which, consequently, everything could be understood. In the course of the centuries, this essentialism in historiography has manifested itself in countless different ways. Of course, essentialism was conspuciously present in the various speculative systems which have directed the thinking of Western man about his past. The Augustinian theological concept of history and its secularized variants,[29] the idea of progress, with its blind faith in the progress of science and the social blessings it was expected to bring, were always the "metanarratives," to use Lyotard's term, by means of which not only historiography but also other fundamental aspects of civilization and society were legitimated.[30]

Then came historism which, with a strange naiveté,[31] saw the essence of the past as embodied in a curious mixture of fact and idea. The epistemological naiveté of the historist doctrine of historical ideas was only possible in a time when the belief and faith in the perceptibility of the essence of the past were so easily taken for granted that nobody had an inkling of his own ontological arrogance. The social history discussed by Rüsen was the last link in this chain of essentialist views of history. The triumphant note with which social history made its entry, particularly in Germany, is the most striking proof of the optimistic self-overestimation on the part of these historians, who feel they have now found the long sought-after key which will open all historical doors. Anyone who is aware of the essentialist nature of this social history and of the traditional enmity between essentialism and science cannot fail to notice the ludicrous nature of the pretensions of the social historians. But the worst modernists are still to be found among philosophers of history – which, incidentally, is not so surprising; they cheer any pseudoscientific ostentation even more readily than do historians, as soon as they think they see in it the confirmation of their worn-out positivist ideas.

I would like to clarify the movement in historical consciousness indicated above by means of the following image. Compare history to a tree. The essentialist tradition within Western historiography focused the attention of historians on the trunk of the tree. This was, of course, the case with the speculative systems; they defined, so to speak, the nature and form of this trunk. Historism and modernist scientific historiography, with their basically praiseworthy attention to what in fact happened in the past and their lack of receptiveness towards apriorist schemes, were situated on the branches of the tree. However, from that position their attention did remain focused on the trunk. Just like their speculative predecessors, both the historists and the protagonists of a so-called scientific historiography still had the hope and the pretension of ultimately being able to say something about that trunk after all. The close ties between this so-called scientific social history and Marxism are significant in this context. Whether it was formulated in ontological, epistemological, or methodological terminology, historiography since historism has always aimed at the reconstruction of the essentialist line running through the past or parts of it.

With the postmodernist historiography found in particular in the history of mentalities, a break is made for the first time with this centuries-old essentialist tradition – to which I immediately add, to avoid any pathos and exaggeration, that I am referring here to trends and not to radical breaks. The choice no longer falls on the trunk or on the branches, but on the leaves of the tree. Within the postmodernist view of history, the goal is no longer integration, synthesis, and totality, but it is those historical scraps which are the center of attention. Take, for example, *Montaillou* and other books written subsequently by Le Roy Ladurie, Ginzburg's *Microstorie*, Duby's *Sunday of Bouvines* or Natalie Zemon Davis's *Return of Martin Guerre*. Fifteen to twenty years ago we would have asked ourselves in amazement whatever the point could be of this kind of historical writing, what it is trying to prove. And this very obvious question would have been prompted then, as it always is, by our modernist desire to get to know how the machine of history works. However, in the anti-essentialist, nominalistic view of postmodernism, this question has lost its meaning. If we want to adhere to essentialism anyway, we can say that the essence is not situated in the branches, nor in the trunk, but in the leaves of the historical tree.

This brings me to the main point of this article. It is characteristic of leaves that they are relatively loosely attached to the tree and when autumn or winter comes, they are blown away by the wind. For various reasons, we can presume that autumn has come to Western historiography. In the first place, there is of course the postmodernist nature of our own time. Our anti-essentialism, or, as it is popularly called these days, "anti-foundationalism," has lessened our commitment to science and traditional historiography. The changed position of Europe in the world since 1945 is a second important indication. The history of this appendage to the Eurasian continent is no longer world history.[32] What we would like to see as the trunk of the tree of Western history has become part of a whole forest. The *meta-récits* we would like to tell ourselves about our history, the triumph of Reason, the glorious struggle for emancipation of the nineteenth-century workers' proletariat, are only of local importance and for that reason can no longer be suitable meta-narratives. The chilly wind which, according to Romein, rose around 1900 simultaneously in both the West and the East,[33] finally blew the leaves off our historical tree as well in the second half of this century.

What remains now for Western historiography is to gather the leaves that have been blown away and to study them independently of their origins. This means that our historical consciousness has, so to speak, been turned inside out. When we collect the leaves of the past in the same way as Le Roy Ladurie or Ginzburg, what is important is no longer the place they had on the tree, but the pattern we can form from them *now*, the way in which this pattern can be adapted to other forms of civilization existing now. "Beginning in the days of Goethe and Macaulay and Carlyle and Emerson," wrote Rorty, "a kind of writing has developed which is neither the evaluation of the relative merits of literary productions, nor intellectual history, nor moral philosophy, nor epistemology, nor social prophecy, but all of these mingled together in a new genre."[34] In his commentary on this statement of Rorty's, Culler points out the remarkable indifference with regard to origin and context, historical or otherwise, which is so characteristic of "this new kind of writing":

> the practitioners of particular disciplines complain that works claimed by the genre are studied outside the proper disciplinary matrix; students of theory read Freud without enquiring whether later psychological research may have disputed his formulations; they read Derrida without having mastered the philosophical tradition; they read Marx without studying alternative descriptions of political and economic situations.[35]

The right historical context has lost its traditional importance, function, and naturalness as background, not because one is so eager to take up an ahistorical position or lacks the desire to do justice to the course of history, but because one has "let go of" the historical context. Everything now announces itself unannounced and in this lies the only hope we still have of being able to keep our heads above water in the future. Just as the leaves of the tree are not attached to one another and their interrelation was only guaranteed by the branch or the trunk, it was the above mentioned essentialist assumptions which used to ensure the very prominent role played by this reassuring "historical context."

Don't misunderstand me. I am not talking about the candidacy of a new form of subjectivity, the legitimation of imposing contemporary patterns on the past. Legitimating anything at all can best be left to the modernists. The essence of postmodernism is precisely that we should avoid pointing out essentialist patterns in the past. We can consequently have our doubts about the meaningfulness of recent attempts to breathe new life into the old German ideal of *Bildung* for the sake of the position and the reputation of historiography.[36] I would, incidentally, like to add immediately that I am nevertheless much more in sympathy with these attempts than with the scientistic naiveté demonstrated by social historians regarding the task and the usefulness of historiography. However, going into the hopes raised by a socioscientific historiography would be flogging a dead horse. The resuscitation of the ideal of *Bildung*, on the other hand, is indeed a meaningful reaction to the map-like nature of our present-day civilization. Whereas civilization in the past showed more resemblance to a direction-indicator which provided relatively unambiguous directions for social and moral behaviour, present-day civilization does not teach us where we have to go any more than a map does; nor, if we have already made our choice, does it teach us whether we should travel by way of the shortest route or by way of a picturesque detour. Realization of the ideal of *Bildung* would at most give us a good picture of the road we have traveled up until now. The ideal of *Bildung* is the cultural counter-part of Ernst Haeckel's famous thesis that the development of the separate individual is a shortened version of that of the species. *Bildung* is the shortened version of the history of civilization on the scale of the separate individual, through which he can become a valuable and decent member of our society.

However, within the postmodernist historical consciousness, this shortened ontogenetic repeat of our cultural phylogenesis is no longer meaningful. The links in the evolution of this series of historical contexts of which our cultural phylogenesis consists have after all been broken apart. Everything has become contemporary, with the remarkable correlate, to use Duby's expression, that everything has also become history. When history is reassembled in the present, this means that the present has taken on the stigma of the past. *Bildung* consequently requires the orientation on a compass that is rejected by postmodernism. We must not shape ourselves according to or in conformity with the past, but learn to play our cultural game with it. What this statement means in *concrete terms* was described by Rousseau for the separate individual in the following way in his *Les rêveries du promeneur solitaire*: there is an

> état où l'âme trouve une assiette assez solide pour s'y reposer tout entière et rassemble là tout son être, sans avoir besoin de rappeler le passé ni d'enjamber sur l'avenir; où le temps ne soit rien pour elle, où le présent dure toujours sans néanmoins marquer sa durée et sans aucune trace de succession.[37]

And Rousseau subsequently points out that such a way of dealing with time awakes a feeling of complete happiness in our lives – "un bonheur suffisant, parfait et plein, qui ne laisse dans l'âme aucun vide qu'elle sente le besoin de remplir."[38]

History is no longer the reconstruction of what has happened to us in the various phases of our lives, but a continuous playing with the memory of this. The memory has priority over what is remembered. Something similar is true for historiography. The wild, greedy, and uncontrolled digging into the past, inspired by the desire to discover a past reality and reconstruct it scientifically, is no longer the historian's unquestioned task. We would do better to examine the result of a hundred and fifty years' digging more attentively and ask ourselves more often what all this adds up to. The time has come that we should *think* about the past, rather than *investigate* it.

However, a phase in historiography has perhaps now begun in which meaning is more important than reconstruction and genesis; a phase in which the goal historians set themselves is to discover the meaning of a number of fundamental conflicts in our past by demonstrating their contemporaneity. Let us look at a few examples. An insight such as Hegel's into the conflict between Socrates and the Athenian State may conflict in a thousand places with what we now know about the Athens of about 400 B.C., but it will nevertheless not lose its force. A second example. What Foucault wrote about the close link between power and discourse aiming at truth or about the very curious relation between language and reality in the sixteenth century was attacked on factual grounds by many critics, but this does not mean that his conceptions have lost their fascination. I am not saying that historical truth and reliability are of no importance or are even obstacles on the road to a more meaningful historiography. On the contrary: examples like Hegel or Foucault show us, however – and that is why I chose them – that the metaphorical dimension in historiography is more powerful than the literal or factual dimensions. The philological Wilamowitz, who tries to refute Nietzsche's *Die Geburt der Tragödie*, is like someone who tries to overturn a train carriage singlehanded; criticizing metaphors on factual grounds is indeed an activity which is just as pointless as it is tasteless. Only metaphors "refute" metaphors.

And that brings me to my final remarks. As I have suggested, there is reason to assume that our relation to the past and our insight into it will in future be of a metaphorical nature rather than a literal one. What I mean is this. The literal statement "this table is two meters long" directs our attention to a particular state of affairs outside language itself which is expressed by it. A metaphorical utterance such as "history is a tree without a trunk" – to use an apt example – shifts the accent to what is happening between the mere *words* "history" and "tree without a trunk." In the postmodernist view, the focus is no longer on the past itself, but on the incongruity between present and past, between the language we presently use for speaking about the past and the past itself. There is no longer "one line running through history" to neutralize this incongruity. This explains the attention to the seemingly incongruous but surprising and hopefully even disturbing detail which Freud in his essay on the *Unheimliche* defined as "was in Verborgenen hatte bleiben sollen und hervorgetreten ist"[39]; in short, attention to everything which is meaningless and irrelevant precisely from the point of view of scientific historiography. For these incongruous, *Unheimliche* events do justice to the incongruity of the historian's language in its relation to the past.

Just as postmodernism since Nietzsche and Heidegger has criticized the whole so-called logocentric tradition in philosophy since Socrates and Plato, that is, the rationalistic faith that Reason will enable us to solve the secrets of reality, postmodernist historiography also has a natural nostalgia for a pre-Socratic early history. The earliest historiography of the Greeks was epic; the Greeks told one another about the deeds of their ancestors in the past in narrative epics. The stories they told one another were not mutually exclusive, despite their contradicting each other, because they inspired above all ethical and aesthetic contemplation. Because war and political conflict stimulated a more profound social and political awareness and because the written word has much less tolerance for divergent traditions than the spoken word, the "logocentric" uniformization of the past was introduced after and by Hecataeus, Herodotus, and Thucydides.[40] With this, the young trunk of the tree of the past appeared above ground. I certainly do not mean to suggest that we should return to the days before Hecataeus. Here, too, it is a question of a metaphorical truth rather than a literal one. Postmodernism does not reject scientific historiography, but only draws our attention to the modernists' vicious circle which would have us believe that nothing exists outside it. However, outside it is the whole domain of historical purpose and meaning.

Rijksuniversiteit Groningen,
Instituut voor Geschiedenis

NOTES

1. J. Romein, "Het vergruisede beeld," and "Theoretische geschiedenis," in *Historische Lijnen en Patronen* (Amsterdam, 1971).
2. R. G. Collingwood, *An Essay on Metaphysics* (Oxford, 1940).

3. J. F. Lyotard, *La condition postmoderne* (Paris, 1979), 15.

4. Information is performative, has purely "illocutionary" and "perlocutionary" force, because the constatory element has been lost; information is not performative, because it is subject to its own laws and not to those of interhuman communication – communication is only a part of the life of information.

5. W. van Reijen, "Postscriptum," in *Modernen versus Postmodernen*, ed. W. Hudson and W..van Reijen (Utrecht, 1986), 9–51; W. Hudson, "The Question of Postmodern Philosophy?," *ibid.*, 51–91.

6. J. Culler, *On Deconstruction: Theory and Criticism after Structuralism* (London, 1985), 18ff.

7. *Ibid.*, 90.

8. *Ibid.*, 88.

9. J. van Heijenoort, "Logical Paradoxes," in *The Encyclopedia of Philosophy*, ed. P. Edwards, (London, 1967), 45–51.

10. F. R. Ankersmit, *Narrative Logic: A Semantic Analysis of the Historian's Language* (The Hague, 1983), 239, 240.

11. H. White, *Metahistory: The Historical Imagination in Nineteenth-Century Europe* (Baltimore, 1973), 37.

12. F. R. Ankersmit, "The Use of Language in the Writing of History," in *Working with Language*, ed. H. Coleman, Berlin, 1989.

13. H. Bertens, "Het 'Talige' Karakter van de Postmoderne Werkedijkheid," in *Modernen versus postmodernen*, 135–53. Bertens's position is actually still modernist: his thesis that language can never represent the fullness of reality makes him choose a position *within* the polarity of language and reality, instead of outside it as would be required by the postmodernists.

14. White, *Metahistory*, 30. P. Ricoeur. "The Model of the Text: Meaningful Action Considered as a Text," in *Interpretative Social Science*, ed. P. Rabinow and W. M. Sullivan, London, 1979, 73.

15. Von der Dunk, *De Organisatie van het Vertleden* (Bussum, 1982): see for example 169, 170, 344, 362, 369.

16. E. H. Gombrich, "Meditations on a Hobby Horse, or the Roots of Artistic Form," in *Aesthetics Today*, ed. P. J. Gudel, New York, 1980.

17. A. Megill, *Prophets of Extremity: Nietzsche, Heidegger, Foucault, Derrida*, Berkeley, 1985; see in particular 2–20.

18. C. P. Bertels, "Stijl: Een Verkeerde Categorie in de Geschiedwetenschap," in *Groniek* 89/90 (1984), 150.

19. N. Goodman, "The Status of Style," in N. Goodman, *Ways of Worldmaking*, Hassocks, 1978, 26.

20. P. Gay, *Style in History*, London, 1974, 3.

21. A. C. Danto, *The Transfiguration of the Commonplace: A Philosophy of Art*, Cambridge, Mass., 1983, 188.

22. G. Duby and G. Lardreau, *Geschichte und Geschichtswissenschaft: Dialoge* (Frankfurt am Main, 1982), 97, 98.

23. J. Huizinga, "De Taak der Cultuurgeschiedenis," in *J. Huizinga Verzamelde Werken 7*, Haarlem, 1950, 71, 72; italics mine.

24. Duby and Lardreau, 98ff.

25. This is the *Leitmotif* in D. P. Spence, *Narrative Truth and Historical Truth: Meaning and Interpretation in Psychoanalysis*, New York, 1982.

26. Lardreau expressed this for historiography as follows: "Somit gibt es nichts als Diskurse über eine Vergangenheit, die wiederum aus nichts anderem als aus diesen Diskursen besteht, in denen jeweils gegenwärtigen Interessen mobilisiert werden. Ein präzis inszeniertes Ballert von masken, die die Interessen und Konflikte der Gegenwart

darstellen, mis wechselnden Rollen, aber gleichbleihenden Standorten – die Geschicht als Kleiderkammer imaginärer Inskriptionen, der Historiker als Kostuümbildner, der Verkleidungen arrangiert, die nie neu gewesen sind: die Geschichte ist aus dem Stoff unserer Träume gewebt, unser Kurzes Gedächtnis von einem Schlummer umhüllt." Lardreau is speaking explicitly of nominalism in this context. See Duby and Lardreau, 10.

27. R. Rorty, "Freud and Moral Reflection," 17. (I was given a photocopy of this article by the author; unfortunately, I have no further information on it.)

28. *Programmaboek Congres "Balans en Perspectief"* (Utrecht, 1986), 50.

29. This, of course, refers to K. Löwith's thesis in his *Meaning in History* (Chicago, 1970).

30. Lyotard, 49–63.

31. F. R. Ankersmit, "De Chiastische Verhouding Tussen Literatuur en Geschiedenis," in *Spektator* (October, 1986), 101–20.

32. Striking proof of the sharply decreased significance of the European past is offered by M. Ferro, *Hoe de Geschiedenits aan Kinderen Wordt Verteld* (Weesp, 1985).

33. J. Romein, *Op het Breukvlak van Twee Eeuwen* (Amsterdam, 1967), I. 35.

34. Culler, 8.

35. *Idem.*

36. In November 1985, a forum on *Bildung* was organized by the arts Faculty in Groningen. Among the speakers were M. A. Wes, E. H. Kossmann, and J. J. A. Mooij. See also E. H. Kossmann, *De Functie van een Alpha-Faculteit* (Groningen, 1985): Kossmann also observes that the *Bildung* ideals of the late eighteenth and the nineteenth century can no longer be realized in our time: "It is, after all, self-evident that an ideal of *Bildung* in today's situation cannot be a homogeneous, prescriptive pattern of ethical and aesthetical standards and set erudition. Rather, it will be in the form of an inventory of possible ethical and aesthetic standards, of objectives which are possible and which have at the same time in history been realized by mankind. The present ideal of *Bildung* is not prescriptive but descriptive, it is not closed but open"(23).

37. J. J. Rousseau, *Les rêveries du promeneur solitaire* (Paris, 1972), 101.

38. *Idem.*

39. S. Freud, "Das Unheimliche," in *Sigmund Freud: Studienausgabe IV. Psychologische Schriften* (Frankfurt, 1982), 264.

40. For these remarks on the origins of Greek historical consciousness I am greatly indebted to Mrs. J. Krul-Blok.

27 Perez Zagorin

Historiography and postmodernism: reconsiderations

Historiography today has become so pluralistic and subject to the play of fashion that it need come as no surprise to find F. R. Ankersmit recommending in a recent essay in *History and Theory* that historians should now adopt the perspective of postmodernism as the new, superior form of understanding of their discipline.[1] Such a move was only to be expected, considering the current influence of postmodernism in some of the arts as well as in literary theory and other fields through its affiliation with deconstructionism. Ankersmit may not even be the first to have extended an embrace to postmodernism on behalf of historiography, though he is perhaps the first to do so explicitly. The same tendency is evident among the disciples of Foucault. Some of the essays collected in a lately published volume arguing for the predominantly rhetorical character of history and the human sciences may also be taken as implying a similar position.[2]

Until now Ankersmit has been best known to readers of *History and Theory* as a contributor to a recent collection of essays dealing with current issues in Anglo-American discussions of the philosophy of history.[3] In his own article in this collection he appeared as an ardent advocate of the narrativist-rhetorical conception of historiography which Hayden White put forward in his *Metahistory* (1973) and subsequent writings. He has stressed the revolutionary import of White's ideas ascribing primacy in historical thinking to literary tropes and verbal structures, and has hailed his work as the wave of the future. It is therefore noteworthy that in contrast to literary theorists, who have provided the majority of supporters of White's view, most philosophers and philosophically-inclined historians have been decidedly critical of it, when they have not simply ignored it. Many historians in particular seem as resistant to it as they were previously to the Hempelian positivist covering-law doctrine of historical explanation. Just as they opposed

Hempel's scientism as a damaging misconception of the character of historical knowledge, so they have likewise tended to reject White's linguistic turn and its rhetorical approach for its disregard and distortion of certain essential characteristics of historical inquiry and writing.[4]

In his espousal of postmodernism, Ankersmit acts as a philosophic trend-spotter who has his eye out for the latest thing. No doubt some merit may be granted to an author who strives to discern the newest fashion in his discipline and bring out its implications. Ankersmit, however, is not only intent on recognizing what is new, but also identifies with it. He does not want to resist it as fallacious or harmful. Rather, like other historicists (although I know he would reject his designation, I believe it is justifiable in this context), he greets its novelty as an inevitable development and makes its cause his own.

Ankersmit's postmodernism may be regarded as an extension of his earlier commitment to White's narrativist principles. It represents a further step in the attempt to aestheticize history and sever it from its formerly accepted grounding in conditions of truth and reality. Although he offers no definition of postmodernism, he relates the latter to certain new situations and necessities that he believes leave us no choice but to accept it. In the following remarks I want to examine the validity of some of the claims and reasons he advances on behalf of his position.

At the outset, however, it is important for the sake of clarity to stress several features generally associated with the theory or idea of postmodernism. First, it must be recognized as an essentially historicist conception. Those who announce the advent of postmodernism regard it as an inevitable stage of present-day culture and a break with the past that, owing to the conditions of contemporary society, cannot be withstood. Thus, a strong sense of fatality and the irresistible hovers over the notion.

Second, the basic impulse of postmodernism lies in its repudiation of the values and assumptions of the preceding high modernist movement which revolutionized the arts of the twentieth century, along with an equal repudiation of the philosophy it calls logocentrism – the belief in the referentiality of language, in the determinacy of textual meaning, and in the presence of a meaningful world to which language and knowledge are related. Yet it is striking that these postmodernist themes are unsustained by any feeling of *élan* or conviction of advance or progress. On the contrary, postmodernism, as its name implies, carries with it strong connotations of decline, exhaustion, and of being at the end rather than the commencement of an era.

Finally, a central element in postmodernism is its hostility to humanism. Foretelling, as Foucault wishfully predicted, the end of man, it rejects humanism as an outmoded relic and illusion of bourgeois ideology: the illusion of individuals creating their history through their free activity, which it sees as merely a cover for bourgeois society's oppression of women, the working class, non-whites, sexual deviants, and colonized natives. As a corollary, it also criticizes as elitist and oppressive the idea of a canon, which both modernism and humanism hold strongly in common, with its necessary discrimination and hierarchization among the creations of culture. The consequence is that postmodernism lends itself to a marked relaxation of cultural standards and sanctions an extreme eclecticism and heterogeneity without any critical or ordering principle. In the cultural domain as a whole it implies a total erasure of the distinction between high or elite culture and mass popular culture largely shaped and dominated by advertising and the commercial media, a distinction that both modernism and humanism accepted as axiomatic.

Some of the features I have just noted are touched upon, albeit in a much more favorable way, by Frederic Jameson, a Marxian literary theorist, in a wide-ranging survey entitled "Postmodernism, or the Cultural Logic of Late Capitalism." In considering the bearings of postmodernism upon historiography, it will be useful to look briefly at his account in order to enlarge our understanding of the concept of the postmodern.

The first thing to observe about his discussion is the typically historicist character it imputes to postmodernism as a periodizing category. Jameson asks himself whether postmodernism is merely a passing fashion or only one of a number of alternative styles or trends, and concludes that it is neither. Whether our attitude toward it is one of celebration or moral revulsion, we must recognize it, he contends, as a fundamental mutation in the sphere of culture reflecting the new multinational phase of world capitalism and its concomitant level of advanced technology which others have described in such terms as the post-industrial or consumer society, media society, electronic society. Moreover, despite the fact that capitalist society in its earliest appearance in the west is still less than two hundred years old, and therefore much younger than other types of society that have preceded or coexisted with it, Jameson simply takes it for granted that it is in its *late* stage. But how does he know this? Needless to say, he does not. Nevertheless, he believes it because his Marxist faith assures him of it, just as it (falsely) assured Lenin before and after 1917 that imperialism was the final stage of capitalism and that European socialist revolutions were imminent. Postmodernism and late capitalism are thus alike, subject in Jameson's historicist logic to the same inevitability. This causes him to argue that Marxists and radicals who seek the transformation of society must abandon their moralizing condemnation of postmodernism and accommodate their theorizing and political strategy to its presence as the dominant cultural force in today's world.

The most striking part of Jameson's treatment, however, is its analysis of the postmodern as exemplified in a variety of contemporary cultural products drawn from a spectrum of the arts. The fact that he ascribes to some of these, like Andy Warhol's paintings or the architecture of John Portman's Bonaventure Hotel in downtown Los Angeles, not only a representative and symptomatic importance, but also an artistic value which is highly debatable need not concern us. What is significant, rather, is the constellation of generic traits his scrutiny of these works leads him to identify as synonymous with postmodernism. They include the following: a new depthlessness and superficiality; a culture fixated upon the image; the warning of affect and disappearance of or liberation from emotion; abandonment of the concept of truth as useless metaphysical baggage; disappearance of the autonomous individual and the death of the subject; loss of historicity and the past; disintegration of the time sense into a series of pure, unrelated presents; the prevalence of pastiche and imitation and cannibalization of past styles. Such, according to Jameson's perceptive observation, are among the leading characteristics and thematics of the postmodern as the inevitably ascendant style of the culture of late capitalism.[5]

Ankersmit would no doubt be unwilling to accept every one of these features as indicative of what he advocates as postmodernism. Nevertheless, the affinity between them and his own point of view is unmistakable. The historicist fatalism implicit in the theory of the postmodern is reflected in his belief that "autumn has come to Western historiography," which no longer has a theme or metanarrative, now that Europe since the end of World War II has ceased to be identical with world history and declined to an appendage of the Eurasian continent (150). The turning away from the past is apparent in his rejection of the importance of historical origin and context and in his conviction that evidence has nothing to do with a past reality but points only to the interpretations given by historians (145–146, 150). The similarity between the two is further manifest in the conception of historiography

Ankersmit proposes. According to his postmodernist philosophy, the historian would renounce the task of explanation and principle of causality, along with the idea of truth, all of which are dismissed as part of a superseded "essentialism." Instead, he would recognize historiography as an aesthetic pursuit in which style is all-important (141–142, 144, 148–149).

What stands out in Ankersmit's postmodernist concept of historiography is its superficiality and remoteness from historical practice and the way historians usually think about their work. It trivializes history and renders it void of any intellectual responsibility. The logic and factual judgments which bring him to this conclusion, moreover, are far from convincing.

His point of departure is the present overproduction of historical writings, which he tells us is spreading like a cancer and fills him with intense despondency. Perhaps it is not very important that he fails to mention the reasons for this condition, which are largely sociological in nature. They lie, as we all know, in the great postwar expansion of higher education and university faculties, plus the necessity of publication imposed on academics as a prerequisite of career advancement. In any case, however, taking the literature on the philosopher Hobbes as an example, he notes that it has become so voluminous that Hobbes's text no longer possesses any authority and vanishes before its many interpretations. From this instance he infers that "we no longer have any texts, any past, but just interpretations of them" (137–138).

Many things might be said about the troubling problem of the ever-growing quantity of historical publications without succumbing to the pessimistic opinion to which Ankersmit's spectacular illogic has led him. For one thing, the situation as J. H. Hexter pictured it in 1967 is even more the case today:

1. Never in the past has the writing of history been so fatuous as it is today; never has it yielded so enormous and suffocating a mass of stultifying trivia, the product of small minds engaged in the congenial occupation of writing badly about insignificant matters to which they have given little or no thought and for which they feel small concern.

2. Never in the past have historians written history so competently, vigorously, and thoughtfully as they do today, penetrating into domains hitherto neglected or in an obscurantist way shunned, bringing effectively to bear on the record of the past disciplines

wholly inaccessible to their predecessors, treating the problems they confront with both a catholicity and a rigor and sophistication of method hitherto without precedent among practitioners of the historical craft.[6]

I am sure most historians would agree with this appraisal. What it means is that despite the burden of an increasing amount of mediocre and ephemeral historical work, there likewise exists in contrast a considerable body of work of exceptional originality, learning, and insight which has not only widened our intellectual horizons but deepened and even transformed our knowledge of many areas of the past.

For another thing, while the phenomenon of historical overproduction may sometimes depress us and seem unmanageable, we may also take some comfort from the fact that its effect is usually counteracted over time by a selective process which relegates trivial publications to obscurity and insures that the more significant contributions will in due course become known to specialists and, if they merit it, to a large part of the historical profession.

But how, in any event, can the condition of historical overproduction deprive us both of the text and the past, leaving us only with interpretations? As it happens, like Ankersmit, I too have had Hobbes as one of my special interests on which I have occasionally written. In a recent essay I have attempted to survey the literature concerning Hobbes which has appeared in the last several years.[7] Contrary to Ankersmit's assertion, even twenty years ago it would not have been sufficient for someone desiring to orient himself in the discussion of Hobbes's political philosophy to have read only Warrender and Watkins. At the least he would also have had to know the classic work by Leo Strauss, Oakeshott's introduction to his edition of *Leviathan*, and MacPherson's *The Political Theory of Possessive Individualism*. For any claim to expertise, he would have needed to be familiar as well with other important contributions such as A. E. Taylor's article on Hobbes's ethical doctrine, and David Gauthier's study of *Leviathan*, not to mention still other works that would be pertinent.

By now, of course, the literature on Hobbes has indeed become very large. Yet, as is almost too obvious to state, in both previous and more recent writings, the relationship between the text of Hobbes's political theory and its interpretations remains extremely close. Far from being displaced or lost, the text is always scrutinized and discussed as the foundation for any proffered interpretative conclusion. Among the students of Hobbes, moreover, some, like Quentin Skinner, in their aim of recovering Hobbes's meaning and intention, insist on a reading fully grounded in the historical context, by which is meant an understanding of the intellectual tradition, ideological and political situation, and conventions of political language within which Hobbes wrote. For those in particular who see the study of political philosophy as an essentially historical discipline, interpretation does not eclipse the past; rather, the latter, comprehended as history, serves as a crucial test of the former's validity.

It is also plain that interpretations may stand or fall on textual and historical grounds. Two of the most widely discussed interpretations of Hobbes in the past generation have been Warrender's and Macpherson's. The first sought to explain Hobbes's theory of moral and political obligation as ultimately founded on the command of God; the second argued that Hobbes's conception of both the state of nature and the political order was a reflection of the nascent capitalist market society of competitive possessive individualism. Neither of these interpretations, it is fair to say, has commended itself to the majority of Hobbes scholars, who have judged them incompatible either with the meaning of Hobbes's text and the character of his beliefs or with a proper understanding of his society.

What I have said about Hobbes is no less true of the other areas of early modern British and European history with which I am familiar as part of my principal field of study. Wherever in any of these a revisionary interpretation has been offered, textual evidence (in which I include not only literary sources and philosophical texts, but archival documents of all kinds) and contextual considerations are invariably central to the discussion. It would be superfluous to emphasize this point were it not for Ankersmit's curious discovery that in our postmodern age interpretation has abolished the text and the past.

Although the work of Gadamer, Ricoeur, and other thinkers has helped to reinstate the problem of interpretation and hermeneutic understanding as a major issue in the philosophy of history. Ankersmit's essay throws no light on this subject. Instead, he concentrates some of his remarks on the claim that interpretation has acquired a new status in postmodern historiography. Observing that in contemporary society information and interpretations continually increase as if by a law of their being, he stresses what he calls the paradox that powerful new interpretations do not put an end to writing but only generate more of it. This allegedly paradoxical fact is supposed to be explicable only from a postmodernist perspective (140–141). But why should it be considered a paradox? Historical interpretations are similar in some respects to scientific theories and hypotheses. Like them, any original new interpretation will have both adherents and opponents. The former will attempt to apply, strengthen, and extend it so as to demonstrate its superiority over its competitors. The latter will seek out its weaknesses and try to refute it. If an historical interpretation comes to be widely accepted, it may even cease to be the subject of debate and take its place as an established part of our understanding of the past. Of course, this may not last. The subsequent emergence of another interpretation may force it to undergo renewed challenges which throw it into question and perhaps displace it. There is nothing paradoxical, however, or unique to the present, in the fact that significant new interpretations stimulate rather than close off discussion.

The lack of substance in Ankersmit's position is further illustrated in his comments on postmodernist historiography's attitude to science, which he describes as one of apartness and detachment but not opposition, hence "ascientistic" rather than "antiscientistic." This is scarcely consistent, though, with his claim that postmodernism has succeeded in destabilizing science and hitting it where it hurts most by deconstructing the concept of causality, one of the main pillars of scientific thought. How does it accomplish this remarkable feat? The ensuing demonstration is the same as the one given in Jonathan Culler's *On Deconstruction* and derives from the latter's inspirer, Nietzsche. It runs as follows. When we consider an effect, it makes us look for the cause; the effect thus precedes or becomes the cause of the cause; hence the effect is the origin of the cause. This accordingly reverses the traditional hierarchy of cause and effect and proves its artificiality (141–142).

This verbal juggling is a transparent confusion, as John Searle has already pointed out in his critical review of Culler's book.[8] While an effect may be the epistemic source of an inquiry into its cause, this cannot mean that it is temporally prior or that it produces or originates the cause. If my car stops running for want of gas, I look for the cause. It is the empty tank, however, not my curiosity about why it will not run, that caused it to stop. The effect, in short, is the origin of my interest, but not of the cause. There is no question here, moreover, of conceiving cause and effect as a hierarchy, a point that is entirely irrelevant. The two are simply correlatives, each entailing the other.

In making these criticisms, I have not committed myself to any particular meaning which the historian should attach to the notion of causality as he uses it. Whether "cause" in the historian's language always signifies a reason or motive on the part of historical agents, or the subsumption of an event, action, or phenomenon under a general causal law, or perhaps neither, depending on the subject under consideration, continues to be a disputed question in the philosophy of history.[9] It is an illusion, nevertheless, to assume that historiography can dispense with the concept of causality. As long as it includes explanation as one of its objectives, causal attribution will remain a necessary ingredient of historical thinking.[10] Postmodernism's revelation to the contrary is not only mistaken, but futile.

One of the principal aims of Ankersmit's discussion is to bring out "the revolutionary nature of postmodernism" which enables it to perform its subversive function. As a manifestation of the latter he adduces not only its alleged deconstruction of the principle of causality, but its view that all our scientific certainties are logically implicated in the liar's paradox. As a succinct version of this paradox, he instances the statement, "this statement is false." By means of this logical weapon, he imagines, postmodernism pulls the carpet out from under science and modernism. Historiography is supposed to provide an illustration of this operation in the intrinsically paradoxical character of interpretation (142–143).

The looseness and absence of clarity in these assertions make it hard to deal with them seriously as argument. One could say the following, however, about their proposed conclusion. The liar's paradox poses a problem of reflexivity in which a statement is logically included in its own verdict of falsity on a class of statements of which it is itself a member. But how does such reflexivity apply to historiography or the theories of science? Ankersmit presents no reason for his contention that the interpretations or factual statements of historians are paradoxical in this way. Apart from this failure, it is also doubtful whether the paradox he has chosen as an example is really a paradox. This is because the sentence does not actually state anything and is thus not a proposition. To be a proposition, it would need to entail a truth value or particular truth conditions, and this it is unable to do. It can hardly yield, therefore, the subversive result Ankersmit would like to assign to it.

The most important insight Ankersmit credits to postmodernism is its recognition of the aesthetic nature of historiography. He relates this insight to the new understanding in contemporary thought that the distinction between language and reality has lost its *raison d'être*. With the disappearance of this distinction, he points out, aestheticism extends its sway over all forms of representation. Historiography is thereby finally perceived to be a literary product in which the historian does not produce a representation of reality (or we may also say, of the past), but a replacement or substitute for it. Style is seen as prior to content and content as a derivative of style. Historical differences likewise prove to be due to differences of style (143–145).

One of the characteristic moves of postmodernist and deconstructionist theory has been to try to obliterate the boundaries between literature and other disciplines by reducing all modes of thought to the common condition of writing. So it maintains that philosophy, like historiography, is merely another kind of writing and subject to its laws, rather than a separate species of reflection concerned with distinctively philosophical questions.[11] Putting aside, however, the identification of language and reality, a thesis construable in different ways (which in any case is well beyond the subject of my discussion). I venture to say that few historians would agree with Ankersmit's consignment of historiography to the category of the aesthetic. Nor would they be likely to approve a characterization that gives preeminence to its literariness. As the Russian formalists and Roman Jakobson have told us, the quality of literariness consists in the way it thrusts language and expression into the foreground and grants them an independent value and importance. Although Ankersmit holds that literary and historical works are similar in this respect, this is surely not the case. In historiography, the attempt by language to draw attention to itself would commonly be regarded as highly inappropriate and an obtrusive breach of the rules of historical writing. In history language is very largely subservient to the historian's effort to convey in the fullest, clearest, and most sensitive way an understanding or knowledge of something in the past.

To sustain the opinion that style is the predominant factor in historiography, Ankersmit emphasizes the intensional character and context of the words and statements in historical works, which entail that they cannot be replaced by other equivalent statements. This opinion seems to me to be equally mistaken. If it were true, it would be impossible to paraphrase or summarize a work of history without altering its substance or meaning. But such summaries are possible; we can very well give a description of something as distinctive in style as Gibbon's narration of the origin and triumph of Christianity in the Roman Empire which effectively conveys not only his understanding of how and why this development occurred but also the irony that pervades his account of it.

Generally it must be said that Ankersmit fails to provide any explanation of how style can determine or engender the content of historical works. Like the notion that interpretation has eliminated the text and the past, this is another of those extreme claims which, despite its inherent implausibility, postmodernists like to put forward as proof of the revolutionary import of their ideas. Certainly it runs counter to some of the strongest convictions and intuitions historians feel about their discipline. Their comment on it would most likely be that content derives from the critical study of sources and evidence, from the critical consideration of other writings dealing with their subject, and from their perception of the interrelationships that exist among the indefinite multiplicity of facts pertaining to the object of their inquiry.

Ankersmit's postmodernist attempt to absorb historiography into the literary and aesthetic domain ignores features that are central to the very concept of history. One of these is the difference history presumes between fact or truth and fictionality, for which the aesthetic perspective makes no provision. Unlike the work of literature, the historical work does not contain an invented or imaginary world. It presents itself as consisting, to a great degree, of facts and true or probable statements about the past. Many of its sentences are propositions with truth-conditions attached to them. If this were not so, the reader would take no interest in it. The distinctive significance that history asserts for itself, therefore, is entirely dependent on its claim to veridicality. Even though historical writing may contain many false or erroneous statements and propound debatable interpretations resting on very complex evidential considerations, veridicality in the widest sense is generally taken to be among its basic regulatory principles.

Another feature, for which the aesthetic domain contains no place, is the role occupied by evidence. Historians operate within definite constraints, of which they are fully conscious, arising from the nature and limitations of their evidence. While it is for them to determine that something is evidence and what it is evidence for, when they have done so the evidence exerts a continuous force upon them. They are not free to ignore it or make of it whatever they please. Its pressure acts as a major determinant in giving shape to the historical work.

Connected with the preceding is yet another intrinsic feature of historiography, the necessity for justification of its specific knowledge-claims, a requirement it shares with other types of inquiry. Historians know that they may be called upon to justify the veridicality, adequacy, and reliability of particular statements, interpretations, and even of their entire account. Their form of writing is apt to incorporate many justifications for the judgments they make, the opinions they express, and the descriptions and analyses they present in their treatment of the past. Even the purest narrative history is unable to dispense with the necessity of justification if it is to be acceptable to critical readers and students.

The aestheticizing of historiography which Ankersmit conceives as a major postmodernist insight inevitably results in the trivilization of history through its failure to acknowledge features that both define history as a form of thought and give it its significance. The same effect is apparent in the prescriptions for historiography which form the conclusion of his article. One of them is that historians should concentrate, as psychoanalysis does, on the unconscious aspects of the past that have been repressed and come to light only involuntarily through "slips of the tongue" (147–148). Although I do not deny that this aim may possess a certain value, it is of much less consequence than the attempt to discover and understand the values, beliefs, assumptions, conventions, rules, and social practices that constitute a large part of the conscious life of past societies. The study of these is not only a task of extreme difficulty, requiring exceptional insight and imagination, but one of fundamental importance of which the priorities of postmodernism take no account.

Another of Ankersmit's prescriptions tells historians that they can no longer deal with big problems or seek to reconstruct or discover patterns in the past, as modern scientific historiography once aspired and pretended to do. All that now remains for them to be concerned with are micro-subjects and "historical scraps," as exemplified in the work of some contemporary social historians, despite the fact that writings such as the latter produce may seem to have little point. In the postmodernist view, he states, "the goal is no longer integration, synthesis, and totality," and small topics now come to occupy the center of attention (149–150).

Needless to say, few historians would look with favor on this formula for a new antiquarianism which springs from a trivialized, tired, and defeatist conception of historical inquiry. Contrary to Ankersmit's belief, the expansion and fragmentation of historiography in our time through the simultaneous growth of specialization and extension of our historical horizons has made the need for integration and synthesis greater and more important than ever before. It is a need, moreover, that is widely recognized. The point is not whether it is possible to attain a total conception of world history or the historical process, for it almost certainly is not. This does not preclude the feasibility, nevertheless, of focusing on large-scale subjects at a quite general level and on questions that transcend specialist and disciplinary boundaries in order to provide an understanding of whole societies and civilizations and of broad areas and aspects of the past. Not only does modern historical literature contain numerous examples of works of this kind, but there will always be historians with the intellectual ambition to tackle subjects of exceptional breadth and significance.

In the course of his article Ankersmit touches on the question of the usefulness of historiography, only to dismiss it as impertinent and a category mistake. As historiography is a part of culture, he explains, the question of its usefulness cannot meaningfully arise any more than it can about culture itself (139).[12] While we may concede this point, we can nevertheless ask what the function of history is and what purpose it serves or should serve in culture and society. Although Western society is sometimes said to be fast losing its connection to its past, that it still values history and believes it important is apparent from the considerable resources it provides to support historical research and teaching. Why does it or should it do so?

An indirect answer to this question was once given by Ankersmit's compatriot, Huizinga, a scholar humanist of distinctive mind and sensibility, who defined history as "the intellectual form in which a civilization renders account to itself of its past." This definition also implies a description of history's function. Huizinga went on to say that "our civilization is the first to have for its past the past of the world, our history is the first to be world-history." To this observation he added that

> a history adequate to our civilization can only be a scientific history. The instrument of modern Western civilization for the intellectual understanding of the world is critical science. We cannot sacrifice the demand for scientific certainty without injury to the conscience of our civilization. Mythical and fictitious representations of the past may have a literary value as forms of play, but for us they are not history.[13]

In this statement Huizinga was not speaking of science as a positivist. By scientific history he understood precisely what Collingwood did by the term, namely, the rigorous cognitive standards, exigent critical methods, and global sense of the past that became characteristic of western historiography in the course of its development during the nineteenth and twentieth centuries.

Of course, historiography serves a number of functions, including several practical ones, but Huizinga was looking at the question from the general standpoint of society as a whole. Whether we agree entirely with him or not, his vision of historiography is probably not far different from the way many Western historians today would conceive their craft. Ankersmit disparages this vision as modernist, but his alternative postmodernist view seems woefully impoverished by comparison. If it were to prevail – though there is little likelihood of this happening – history would no longer have a real function. It could no longer perform its principal intellectual obligation in education and culture, which must be to give to each living generation the broadest and best possible knowledge of the past of its own society and civilization as well as of the larger human past of which it is part. Postmodernism represents the abnegation of this obligation which is the ultimate cultural responsibility of historiography and one that remains indispensable as the rapidly changing world moves faster into the future than ever before.

The University of Rochester

NOTES

1. F. R. Ankersmit, "Historiography and Postmodernism," *History and Theory* 28 (1989), 137–153.
2. John S. Nelson, Allan Megill, and Donald N. McCloskey, *The Rhetoric of the Human Sciences* (Madison, Wisc. 1987).
3. F. R. Ankersmit, "The Dilemma of Contemporary Anglo-American Philosophy of History," *Knowing & Telling History: The Anglo-Saxon Debate, History and Theory, Beiheft* 25 (1986).
4. See some of the papers in *Metahistory: Six Critiques, History and Theory, Beiheft 19* (1980), particularly Maurice Mandelbaum's "The Presuppositions of *Metahistory*," as well as Frederick A. Olafson's comments in his "Hermeneutics: 'Analytical' and 'Dialectical,'" in *Knowing & Telling History*, 40–41. See, too, the critical observations and cautions regarding White's views in Paul Ricoeur, *The Reality of the Historical Past* (Milwaukee, Wisc. 1984), 33–34, and William H. Dray, "Narrative and Historical Realism," in *On History and Philosophy of History* (Leiden, 1989), chapter 7. I have also observed from conversations with historians and discussions with doctoral students in seminars on the philosophy of history that their response to White's *Metahistory* and *Tropics of Discourse* is generally unfavourable.
5. Frederick Jameson, "Postmodernism, or the Cultural Logic of Late Capitalism," *New Left Review*, 146 (1984), 53–92. The literature on postmodernism is by now considerable; for further discussion of what it stands for and its relationship to deconstructionism,

see Terry Eagleton, *Literary Theory* (Minneapolis, 1983), and the essays in *Postmodernism*, ed. Lisa Appignanesi (London, 1986).

6. J. H. Hexter, "Some American Observations," *Journal of Contemporary History* 2 (1967), 5–6, cited in Peter Norvick, *That Noble Dreams, the "Objectivity Question" and the American Historical Profession* (Cambridge and New York, 1988), 377.

7. Perez Zagorin, *A History of Political Thought in the English Revolution* (London, 1954), chapter 13; "Thomas Hobbes," *International Encyclopedia of the Social Sciences*, "Carendon and Hobbes," *Journal of Modern History* 57 (1985), 593–616: "Cudworth and Hobbes on is and Ought," in *Philosophy, Religion, and Science in the Later Seventeenth Century*, ed. Richard Ashcraft, Richard Kroll, and Perez Zagosin, Cambridge University Press; "Hobbes on Our Mind," *Journal of the History of Ideas* 51 (1990), 317–335.

8. See Searle's review of Jonathan Culler, *On Deconstruction: Theory and Criticism after Structuralism* (Ithaca, New York, 1983), in *New York Review of Books* 27 (October, 1983), 74–79.

9. See the recent discussion in W. G. Runciman's *A Treatise on Social Theory* (Cambridge, 1983), 1, chapters 1, 3, in which the author tries to resolve the problem by first distinguishing reportage, description, evaluation, and explanation from one another, and then suggesting that historical or sociological explanation consists of subsuming the *explanandum* as a case of some general causal law or connection.

10. I agree, however, with those critics, including Ankersmit, who hold that in its virtually exclusive preoccupation with the problem of explanation, analytical philosophy of history neglected other significant features of historical thinking and practice.

11. For a discussion, see Christopher Norris, *Deconstruction, Theory and Practice* (London, 1982), and *The Deconstructive Turn: Essays in the Rhetoric of Philosophy* (London, 1983).

12. It is typical of the superficiality of Ankersmit's approach that he is willing to permit the question of the usefulness of science because unlike historiography, science does not belong to culture. One may wonder how any reflection on modern western civilization, in which, in contrast to other civilizations past and present, science has been a uniquely powerful force and in which scientific thought has exerted an incalculable influence on philosophy and other disciplines, could possibly exclude science from the realm of culture.

13. J. Huizinga, "A Definition of the Concept of History," in *Philosophy and History*, ed. Raymond Klibansky and H. J. Paton [1936] (New York, 1963), 8–9.

EXTRACTS FROM *SOCIAL HISTORY*

There is no doubt that the journal *Social History* is one of the foremost publications of its type in the world. Because of its interest in histories of labour, popular culture, the politics of the workplace, social class, and so on, and because of the influence on such social history of Marxist-type analyses, the journal has always provided an arena for radical discussions and engagements on a theorized historiography. For these reasons one might have expected the journal to have published many articles on postmodern-type concerns. And in a way it has, but much in the guise of what is referred to within the journal (and more widely) as "the discontents of social history debate"; in effect, to analyses of older Marxist (modernist) categories of the "social," the "economy" and the cognate notion of class.

As a result, the invitation put to historians by Thomas Patterson ("Poststructuralism, Postmodernism: Implications for Historians," *Social History*, 14, 1, 1989, pp. 83–7) to attend in generally positive ways to the spectre raised by a poststructuralist and postmodernist presence which will "probably not go away," has been responded to rather obliquely, through a series of articles gravitating around the discursive analyses of "the social" by Gareth Stedman-Jones and Patrick Joyce especially. These analyses have given rise to articles by, for example: D. Mayfield and S. Thorne, "Social History and its Discontents: Gareth Stedman-Jones and the Politics of Language," *Social History*, 17, 2, 1992, pp. 165–88; J. Lawrence and M. Taylor, "The Poverty of Protest: Gareth Stedman-Jones and the Politics of Language – A Reply," *Social History*, 18, 1, 1993, pp. 1–15; P. Joyce, "The Imaginary Discontents of Social History . . .," *Social History*, 18, 1, 1993, pp. 81–5; D. Mayfield and S. Thorne, "Reply to 'The Poverty of Protest' and 'The Imaginary Discontents'," *Social History*, 18, 2, 1993, pp. 219–33; and, J. Vernon, "Who's Afraid of the 'Linguistic Turn'? . . .," *Social History*, 19, 1, 1994, pp. 81–97, articles to which might be added Bryan Palmer's "Critical Theory, Historical Materialism, and the Ostensible End of Marxism . . .," *International Review of Social History*, 38, 1993, pp. 133–62 – included amongst the readings in Part II above (Chapter 10). It was therefore not until 1994 that Patterson's challenge was picked up very directly and postmodernism faced full-frontal by Neville Kirk and Patrick Joyce (although in 1993 Anthony Easthope's "Romancing the Stone: History-Writing and Rhetoric," *Social History*, 18, 2, 1993, pp. 235–49 had advocated rhetorical approaches to historiography as associated with Hayden White, Derrida and Rorty *et al.*).

I reproduce here, as Chapters 28–31, the bulk of Neville Kirk's challenging article, the whole of Patrick Joyce's radical postmodern reply, the detailed response to Patrick Joyce by Geoff Eley and Keith Nield, "Starting

Over: The Present, The Post-Modern and the Moment of Social History," *Social History*, 20, 3, 1995, pp. 355–64 and Joyce's short response to them, "The End of Social History? A Brief Reply to Eley and Nield," *Social History*, 21, 1, January 1996.

These pieces express the perceived impact of a problematicizing post-modernism in the area of social history. Though Kirk, Joyce, Eley and Nield are in some ways conducting what has obviously been a fairly incestuous debate amongst a limited number of historians, that debate has rippled across the practices of social historians more generally – as the lengthy footnotes to the articles attest. This is therefore a crucial area of not just theoretical interest but one tied to a very specific "historical debate" and it is hoped that the readings offered here will serve to introduce new readers to it.

28 Neville Kirk

History, language, ideas and postmodernism: a materialist view[1]

This article makes a contribution to recent and current debates concerning the discipline of history, the "linguistic turn" and postmodernism.[2] Four main arguments are presented. First, I suggest that the very categories, assumptions and tenets of postmodernism and its frequently related phenomenon, poststructuralism, are far more problematical and contested than often assumed by those historians embracing the "linguistic turn." As such, postmodernism and poststructuralism constitute sites of critical investigation rather than self-evident truth. Second, I maintain that the crucial defects of subjectivism and idealism, as seen above all in the conflation of reality and language, greatly weaken the cases of poststructuralism and postmodernism. A core part of the article is accordingly devoted to a consideration of these defects, as manifested in the work of two champions of language and discourse, Gareth Stedman Jones and Patrick Joyce. Given their leading role in the English historiographical shift to language and the rejection of the determining role of the "social" in the historical process, Joyce, Stedman Jones and their various writings are subjected to scrutiny. Third, I contend that many "social determinists" have been far more attentive in their practices to the issues of complexity and diversity and the importance of language, agency and ideas than claimed by discourse theorists and other critics. My final thesis is that a non-reductionist historical materialism, as manifested in the work of David Montgomery, Edward Thompson and others, continues to provide an extremely fruitful means of historical investigation. The materialism endorsed in this article both posits the existence of a reality beyond consciousness and simultaneously explores the dialectic between, on the one hand, agency and consciousness (embracing many forms of language) and, on the other hand, the unintended, unrecognized and material determinations of life.

POSTMODERNISM: DEFINITIONAL PROBLEMS AND CHARACTERISTICS

We may usefully begin with a short discussion of the problematical nature of the term postmodernism. In their exchanges in the pages of *Past and Present and Social History*, contributors to the debates about history, language, discourse theory and postmodernism have largely taken for granted the existence, features and meanings of postmodernism. Yet the latter is a complex, disputed and elusive concept, and could beneficially have been indicated as such by its central enthusiast in debate, Patrick Joyce. It is important for us to demonstrate briefly the main ways in which postmodernism has been characterized in recent debates in the arts, humanities and social sciences. We will then be in a better position to consider the specific issues which have engaged the minds and excited the passions of historians.

As observed by David Harvey in his incisive and lucid book, *The Condition of Postmodernity*, "No one exactly agrees as to what is meant by the term, except, perhaps, that 'postmodernism' represents some kind of reaction to, or departure from, 'modernism'." However, as Harvey continues. "Since the meaning of modernism is also very confused, the reaction or departure known as 'postmodernism' is doubly so." Harvey does, nevertheless, enlist the aid of Terry Eagleton and Frederic Jameson in detailing key features of both modernism (a cultural movement contentiously claimed to span the period between *c.* 1850 and 1950) and postmodernism (arguably dating from the late 1950s).[3]

As shown in Table 1, Harvey presents the features of modernism and postmodernism as being fundamentally oppositional. Postmodernism is thus set against the allegedly totalizing, system-building and social engineering schemes of modernism. And in its antipathy to the global claims of Marxism and other "grand narratives," to "total" history, to objective realities of an external kind, and to absolute truths and unitary structures, postmodernism can be seen to hold an appeal to (especially younger) scholars living in the fragmented, decentred, uncertain and yet flexible and exciting contemporary "scene." Postmodernism's embrace of the notions of complexity, diversity, relativity, discursively

Table 1. *Selected characteristics of modernism and postmodernism*

Modernism	Postmodernism
Elitism, closure, authoritarianism and social engineering ("Fordism")	Popular consumerism, flexibility, choice, openness, opportunity
High culture and tradition, profundity	Popular culture and the commodification of leisure and culture, "irreverent pastiche", "contrived depthlessness"
Austerity and discipline	Playfulness, "laid back" hedonism
Fixed meanings, centres, absolute laws and truths ("meta narratives," such as Marxism and Freudianism)	Relativity, indeterminacy, contingency, fragments of being, decentring, life (or "petite") histories
Holism	Individualism
Planning	Experimentation, pragmatism
Homogeneity	Heterogeneity
Signified	Signifier
Certainty, unitary structures, e.g. class and systems, synthesis, externality (i.e. reality "out there")	Scepticism, deconstruction, discursive reality

constructed realities, and the significance of the "Other" exerts similar attractions.

Much of the discussion concerning the characteristics of modernism and postmodernism is, however, flawed by the highly dubious nature of the terms themselves. As Harvey observes, the extremely subjective character of modernist and postmodernist categories and characteristics, combined with the contradictions within and strong overlaps and continuities between allegedly modernist and postmodernist periods of history, render precise and useful analysis and description very hazardous. For example, "Fordist" structures of management and business have not, as teachers, lecturers, health workers and others in the public sector are only too well aware, been cast into the dustbin of "modernist" history in "postmodern" Britain! Indeed, the very adequacy of the extremely vague and elusive terms of modernism and postmodernism, especially as useful tools of historical investigation, and the validity of a sharp rupture between "modernist" and "postmodernist" periods of history, must be seriously questioned.[4]

We must emphasize from the outset, therefore, that we are dealing with highly contested, rather than consensually given, terms and characteristics. This point of emphasis has been unduly neglected in the debates which have featured in *Past and Present* and *Social History*. The manifold confusions and problems surrounding the terms modernism and postmodernism should, therefore, immediately alert historians as to the potential pitfalls of seeking instant "postmodernist" cures for the "ills" of their discipline. So forewarned, we may proceed to a discussion of some of the tenets and strengths and weaknesses of poststructuralism and postmodernism as seen in the work of Gareth Stedman Jones and Patrick Joyce.

GARETH STEDMAN JONES, PATRICK JOYCE AND THE CASES OF POSTSTRUCTURALISM AND POSTMODERNISM

Among historians of modern English society the poststructural "turn to language" has been most closely identified with Gareth Stedman Jones and Patrick Joyce. But before moving to a consideration of the work of these two historians, a brief note of clarification concerning the term poststructuralism and its relationship to postmodernism is in order.

The "linguistic turn" has been a key feature of poststructuralism – a body of ideas commonly, if in some cases problematically, associated with Foucault, Derrida and other French thinkers of the 1960s. Poststructuralism marks a reaction against the notion of structural determination, against the view that (often hidden) structures matter most in the construction of reality. Many poststructuralists proceed to deny the existence of a reality independent of thought and language, and emphasize the fragmented, relative and largely autonomous nature of people's personal and social lives. *Discourse, decentring* and *deconstruction* constitute key words in the poststructuralist lexicon. For many scholars, including Patrick Joyce, the tenets of poststructuralism constitute an integral part of the wider postmodernist reaction against modernism and its "totalizing" characteristics listed in Table 1.[5]

The work of Stedman Jones and Joyce does undoubtedly illustrate a number of poststructuralist and postmodernist assumptions and aims. In recent years both historians have expressed growing dissatisfaction with the notions of social structure and class interest/structure as existing prior to, outside of, and thus beyond language. Joyce and Stedman Jones have, as their first shared characteristic, the poststructuralist emphasis upon the key significance of language and discourse in the construction of social reality.

The argument in support of the centrality of language might be developed in the following way. Much in the manner of the metaphysical tradition within philosophy, Stedman Jones and Joyce place great weight upon the role of thought in the formation of knowledge and social reality.[6] And in their poststructuralist framework of reference, thought is intimately bound up with its expression in language. Language, in turn, consists of written, spoken and symbolic utterances and means of communication. Joyce thus considers language "in the broad sense of a sign system, embracing verbal and non-verbal forms, and both literal and symbolic meaning."[7] As the representative of thought, language is therefore of key importance to the creation and understanding of reality.

Examples of the latter proposition abound in the writings of Joyce and Stedman Jones. In *Languages of Class* Stedman Jones describes his movement away from "any simple prejudgement about the determining role of the 'social'" and towards an embrace of language.

> In particular, I became increasingly critical of the prevalent treatment of the "social" as something outside of, and logically – and often, though not necessarily, chronologically – prior to its articulation through language. The title, *Languages of Class*, stresses this point: firstly, that the term "class" is a word embedded in language and should thus be analysed in its linguistic context; and secondly, that because there are *different* languages of class, one should not proceed upon the assumption that "class" as an elementary counter of official social description, "class" as an effect of theoretical discourse about distribution or production relations, "class" as the summary of a cluster of culturally signifying practices or "class" as a species of political or ideological self-definition, all share a single reference point in an anterior social reality.

This embrace has also moved Stedman Jones to treat class

> as a discursive rather than as an ontological reality, the central effort being to explain languages of class from the nature of politics rather than the character of politics from the nature of class.[8]

Similarly, Joyce writes in the January 1993 issue of *Social History*:

> The salutary effect of post-modernist thought might be said to lie in its invitation to question the idea of a clear distinction between representation and the "real." The result of so doing is to upset the sacred categories of so much social history, especially those with which historians have aimed to police their version of the real, categories such as "experience" (which Joan W. Scott has so effectively questioned recently), or the "social" (as in the continuing historiography of class of which myself and Stedman Jones are part), or . . . the body (a category, of course, so effectively questioned by much feminist history and theory).

And in the introduction to *Visions of the People* we are variously informed that: class is "increasingly, and rightly, seen less as objective reality than as a social construct, created differently by different historical actors"; that the category of "experience" (so central to the Thompsonian project) is "in fact not prior to and constitutive of language but is actively constituted by language"; and that class and other "interests" are "not somehow given in the economic condition of workers, but are constructed through the agency of identities."[9]

To the extent that they emphasize the importance of language to the reconstruction of the historical past, and challenge an absolute separation between "reality" and representation, Joyce and Stedman Jones do not, at least initially, appear to be elevating the "linguistic" to positions of total domination and sole determination in the nature and construction of society. Indeed, both Joyce's reply to Mayfield, Thorne, Taylor and Lawrence in *Social History*, and Taylor and Lawrence's defence of Stedman Jones, have centrally rejected the charge of "linguistic determinism." Throughout *Visions of the People* Joyce makes references to language *and* the social order, language *and* economic and social conditions, and so on. Similarly, denials of wishing to replace the "social" with the "linguistic," as the key to unlocking the door of history, are present in Stedman Jones's *Languages of Class*?[10]

As I will demonstrate in more detail later in this article, this matter of "linguistic determinism" in the work of Stedman Jones and Joyce is not, however, so easily resolved. For example, at other points in their works Joyce and Stedman Jones do, as already implied in quotations cited in this article, questionably collapse or dissolve *any* distinction between the "representational" and "real" levels (a vanishing act which, at the level of general historical practice, has met with justifiable opposition from Lawrence Stone). Indeed, both historians appear at times to be saying that there is *no* reality beyond language and discourse – for example, no economy, no society, no cultural or political systems and structures, but only economic, social, cultural and political discourses.[11] We may surely pose the question that, if reality does not extend beyond representation in language and discourse, then how can we logically and practically investigate (as urged by Stedman Jones, Joyce, Taylor and Lawrence) the links between the "linguistic," the "social," the "political" and the "economic"? The extent of our investigations would surely be confined to an identification and characterization of different discourses and their shifting patterns of overlap and communication. Reality would become the narrow cul-de-sac of language, and *nothing more*. In such ways does a crucial contradictory weakness appear in the arguments of Joyce and Stedman Jones, as does a major flaw in the claim made by Lawrence and Taylor that Stedman Jones has consistently sought to pull together and explore the complex relations between the "linguistic/political" on the one hand and the "social" on the other.[12] We will return later to a discussion of this confusion and lack of clarity in Joyce and Stedman Jones's treatment of language and social reality.

Stedman Jones's and Joyce's refreshing and important explorations of the "popular" languages of nineteenth-century England have yielded several significant and controversial conclusions. First, Stedman Jones's study of Chartist language and Joyce's more general attention to workers' languages have strongly suggested to both historians that "class" (as a point of identification, and as synonymous with internal unity and hostile actions and thoughts towards the claims and rights of capital) enjoyed far less purchase upon workers' loyalties than the conventional wisdom of E. P. Thompson, Dorothy Thompson, Eric Hobsbawm and other "determinists" would suggest. Second, that languages of "the people" and "political exclusion and oppression" (as opposed to the economic language of exploitation in production) prevailed, in largely non-class-based ways, in Chartism (Stedman Jones). Third, that the languages of radicalism and radical-liberalism provided an extremely important and resilient point of continuity throughout the nineteenth century (Joyce, Stedman Jones and Jon Lawrence).[13] Fourth, that, generally speaking, political languages and political continuities were far more important to nineteenth-century workers than allowed by a variety of "social determinists". Fifth, as expressly, and in some instances, pioneeringly argued by Patrick Joyce in *Visions of the People*, that general notions of "the people" and "populism" (with their extra-class, i.e. extra-economic characteristics) were at the very heart of popular culture, especially in Lancashire. According to Joyce, "class" was present in people's lives, but in many cases it was challenged, indeed overshadowed, by "populism."[14] And, finally, that such findings effectively end the previously hegemonic influence of "Marxism" within the field of modern English social history (a claim made most vociferously by Joyce).[15]

The death knell of Marxism as an intellectual system (and by implication as a defensible political practice) is also clearly assumed in the manifestly poststructural emphases of Joyce and Stedman Jones upon deconstruction and decentring.

In terms of the latter issue, both historians oppose the "modernist" belief that the social world and individuals' lives are rooted or "centred" in a determining or "essential" structure or presence. It is in this context that the question of "social determinism" becomes crucial. In opposition to "determinists" of a historical-materialist persuasion, Joyce and Stedman Jones have come to reject the position that societies are centrally influenced by economic and social forces existing "out there." Even the notion of "determination in the last instance" (Althusser) is firmly rejected. Rather, in true poststructuralist and postmodernist fashion, societies are seen as consisting of largely autonomous discursive (and other?) formations operating within their own spaces, patterns of articulation and chronologies.

Decentring has many useful features. It acts as a safeguard against crude "essentialisms" and "reductionisms", and it rightly alerts us to the operation of many different levels, practices, chronologies and complexities within societies. But there are many dangers inherent in decentring. For example, opposition to a strict hierarchy of causation *can* lead to a refusal to admit any sense of causative priority, to a mere description of "free-floating," relatively valid and equally significant forces. Moreover, in some of the more extreme forms of poststructuralism, as epitomized by Barry Hindess and Paul Hirst's *Pre-Capitalist Modes of Production*, social forces are wholly constructed in theory/language, thus leading to a "theoreticism" lacking external, empirical controls, and to an unsatisfactory idealism (in which, notes E. P.

Thompson, "a self-generating conceptual universe . . . imposes its own identity upon the phenomena of material and social existence, rather than engaging in a continual dialogue with them").[16]

As seen in their attention to the complexities of the empirical world, Stedman Jones and Joyce do not share the extreme idealism of *Pre-Capitalist Modes of Production*. But there are signs, especially on the part of Joyce, of an ill-tempered impatience with "old-fashioned" empirical history, "the pieties of the same old bland social history", and of an unduly uncritical acceptance of postmodernism.[17]

Furthermore, in their opposition to the "centred" position of "social determinism," Stedman Jones, Joyce and their associates in Cambridge, Manchester and elsewhere, also tend to present very narrow and caricatured pictures of the broad traditions of Marxism and historical materialism. For example, largely unitary and revolutionary models of class are erroneously attributed to an unchanging "Marxism", duly demolished and "new and exciting" historical discoveries made.[18] But as recently suggested in conversation by David Howell, many historical-materialist or left-inclined "dinosaurs" do not recognize themselves in this picture. I fully agree with Howell's sentiments.

Thus Howell himself, and many of the former students of Raymond Williams, Edward and Dorothy Thompson, David Montgomery, Herbert Gutman and Eugene Genovese (such as Eagleton, Epstein, Rule, Behagg, Sykes, Kirk, Fink, Levine, Kealey and Linebaugh) have, since the 1960s, taken issue with mechanistic models of society and with reductionism as practised by the right, left or centre. Inspired by the "old dinosaurs themselves," this second generation of historians have busied themselves in exploring the limits and pressures (rather than necessary and lawed effects) of the "economic" on other practices and structures, the complex interactions between agency and conditioning, the extent to which structures exist and are part of cognition, degrees of "relative autonomy," and the nature, construction, meanings and social contextualization of language.[19]

Much of this work may not, of course, strongly register with and count for a great deal among pillars of the British historical establishment. But it is only fair that Stedman Jones, Joyce, their students and like-minded colleagues do at least acknowledge the *anti-reductionist practices* of these two generations of "dinosaurs." To utilize, in blanket fashion, the labels "reductionism" and "determinism," and to announce gleefully the death of intellectual Marxism and historical materialism (as Joyce does in *Social History*) is to do scant justice to the complexity and accuracy of the historical record (does it exist beyond discourse?) and the endeavours of a large and, in some ways quite diverse, body of historians. Accurate description of, and attention to the complexities and nuances of other historians' work is surely a matter of "first principles" among practitioners of the *discipline*.

We may now proceed, with less indignation, to consider the notion of decentring, as applied to individuals rather than societies. In place of the transcendent, sovereign and unified subject standing at the very core of the historical process, poststructuralism has identified the decentred human "effect," in large measure the prisoner of discursive structures, and the possessor of multiple characteristics, relationships and experiences. Emphases upon diversity, complexity, relativity and bearer have come to contest the "modernist" categories of unity, fixed centre and creator.

As Eagleton has noted, in some strains of discourse analysis "valuable attention to the split, precarious, pluralistic nature of all identity slides at its worst into an irresponsible hymning of the virtues of schizophrenia".[20] Thankfully, Joyce and Stedman Jones have avoided such a slide. They have also commendably demonstrated that, in the face of the fragmentary, transitional and multifaceted nature of much of reality, working people in nineteenth-century England did impose agency, determination, needs, choices, desires, purpose and coherence upon life. People were thus both the bearers and the agents of patterns of discourse, rather than being largely unconscious and "ideological" Träger (bearers) of discursive and non-discursive structures (these structures being the cognitive, indeed creative preserve, of Althusserian theoreticians). People thus had, notes Joyce, "agency in the use of discourse."[21]

Joyce and Stedman Jones could, nevertheless, have usefully pursued the agency-effect dialectic further in relation to two questions. First, how did agents modify and change the meanings and character of those politico-linguistic formations and continuities (e.g. the radical tradition relating to the rights of the "freedom Englishman") of which they were a part? And, second, to what extent were discontinuities and ruptures in discursive formations, and especially politically discursive formations, occasioned by economic and social forces in addition to the political factors identified particularly by Stedman Jones (e.g. the allegedly softened roles of the state and the political parties in the decline of Chartism)? To explore such issues would shed new light on our understandings of agency and the conscious/unconscious personality split, and more fully engage discourse and material reality.

Discursive and decentring emphases in Joyce's and Stedman Jones's work are accompanied by a third shared emphasis upon the importance of deconstruction. Within postmodernism, deconstruction may be seen as part of the decentring process. Instead of unitary structures (such as class), complete with shared experiences and patterns of "consciousness," postmodernism places a premium upon difference, diversity, complexity, nuance and fragmented (if, at least in the practices of Joyce and Stedman Jones, overlapping and patterned) thoughts and actions. To give a concrete example, Joan Scott, recently at the forefront of the poststructuralist "linguistic turn", has argued that E. P. Thompson's allegedly unitary and male-centred notion of the early nineteenth-century British working class obscures the roles and views of working-class women and gender-based differences and divisions within the class.[22] And within modern English history there is currently increased attention devoted to the issues of ethnicity, race and gender.[23]

This attention is to be welcomed. But it is highly doubtful as to whether such interest is as novel as often claimed. As observed in relation to the notion of decentring, I would suggest that many of the so-called determinists have *not* entertained uniform and undifferentiated views of the working class. Thompson himself (in *The Making of the English Working Class* and in *Customs in Common*), Engels and Marx (on the Irish and "labour aristocrats"), Genovese (on slavery, race and class in the United States), Hobsbawm (on modern workers' cultures and politics), and most recently Montgomery (whose masterpiece, *The Fall of the House of Labor*, explores much of the richness and complexity of American workers' lives between the 1860s and 1920s) constitute classic examples of a so-called determinist tradition which has long explored the interplays between sources of fragmentation and unity, competition and co-operation, individualism and mutuality, and conflict and comradeship within working-class life. In the same vein we may also cite the ("determinist"?) work of Dorothy Thompson and Angela John (on gender and class), Herbert Gutman (on ethnicity, mobility, race and class in the United States), John Belchem (on the "making," "unmaking" and "remaking" of class in nineteenth-century Britain) and my own work on class and fragmentation in Britain and the United States.[24]

This list could be multiplied several times over. The points to note are twofold. First, to have any real meaning the term "determinist" must be framed in far more rigorous, precise and less cavalier ways than has frequently been the case. Second, it has often been the "determinists" (operating both within and outside historical materialism) who have been most attentive to complexity and diversity, and to the overall assessment of class and fragmentation both within specific contexts and over time.

STEDMAN JONES AND JOYCE: DIFFERENCES

The reader's attention has so far mainly been drawn to the shared practical commitments of Stedman Jones and Joyce to discourse, decentring and deconstruction. These commitments should not, however, mask the significant differences which exist between these two historians. These differences may be said to manifest themselves in relation to the issues of the focus and overall direction of their work, to style, tone and temperament, to shaping traditions and influences, and to approaches to, and usages of, language and ideas. Before moving to an assessment of the strengths and weaknesses of the "turns to language" of Stedman Jones and Joyce, it is accordingly important for us to briefly consider these differences.

In terms of focus, direction, tone and temperament it is important to record that it is Patrick Joyce who has offered a loud, evangelical and triumphal, if insufficiently critical endorsement of postmodernism (which is not defined by Joyce). Joyce's dismissal of empirical social history has tended to be unqualified, irritable, impatient and, one might add, somewhat lacking in consideration and careful criticism. By way of contrast, Stedman Jones's turn to a Saussurean approach to language, and the investigation of "non-referential" forms of language in relation to Chartism and the Labour party, were couched in far more conditional, considered and provisional ways (see, for example, p. 24 of his *Languages of Class*). One tends to come away with the conclusion that Joyce's embrace of "populism" lacks something of the considered complexity and patience of Stedman Jones's experimentation with the issues of class and discourse. In contrast to *Visions of the People, Languages of Class* did not offer an instant cure-all for history's ills.

It is also important to point out that, notwithstanding the many attempts to "read" his "post-modernist" discourse, Stedman Jones's endorsement of a Saussurean approach to the study of language properly belongs to a poststructuralist rather than a postmodernist problematic. As Easthope informs us, in Britain poststructuralist concerns with deconstruction, discourse and decentring largely arose out of engagements with Althusserian structuralism and a renewed interest in phenomenology.[25] Stedman Jones's "turn" was made in part engagement with the work of Althusser. (To the best of my knowledge, Patrick Joyce was not similarly engaged.) And his "linguistic" interpretations of Chartism and the Labour party were presented during the late 1970s and early 1980s. In effect, we await Stedman Jones's word as to whether he interprets his specific concerns with Althusserianism and post-Althusserian issues as being in harmony with the wider and ironically totalizing endeavours of Joyce's postmodernism.

The question of poststructuralist and/or postmodernism problematics leads us into a consideration of the wider, and in some ways different, traditions which have shaped the work of Joyce and Stedman Jones. In many ways the logic and patterns of Stedman Jones's intellectual development are easier to chart. Involvements in *New Left Review*, unorthodox Marxism and the "social" problematics of casual labour, relations between classes and the issues and processes of "formal" and "real" control at the point of production, were increasingly subordinated during the 1970s to an interest in the relationship between politics and culture. The shift to language was to take place in the later 1970s and early 1980s.

A strong continuity in Stedman Jones's work has been an interest in politics. This interest has also been prominent in Joyce's writings, stretching from his doctorate (which focused upon popular Conservatism) to *Visions of the People*. But the influences upon Joyce's work have been far more electric than has been the case with Stedman Jones, ranging from John Vincent, to the *Annalistes*, to Gramsci. To the best of my knowledge, Joyce has not been part of a left tradition and culture, and rooted in historical-materialist problematics, to anything like the same extent as Stedman Jones. *Work, Society and Politics* did make use of the Marxist sections of formal and real control over production (and owed much to Stedman Jone's usage of these notions), if only to arrive at the anti-Marxist conclusion of paternalistic employers and deferential operatives developing at the very heart of modern industry. The study of language was not central to *Work, Society and Politics*, published in 1980. It has been during the past decade that Joyce's focus upon language has originated and matured. Joyce's "turn" has thus come later than that of Stedman Jones, and probably owes far less to an engagement with Althusser than to contact with the work of Derrida (in line with the "American" route to postmodernism). More speculatively, it would appear to me that Joyce's break with the notion of class is far more complete than may prove to be the case with Stedman Jones.

A final difference concerns approaches to, and usages of, language. Stedman Jones's focus has rested upon relatively formal *political* languages, largely restricted to the printed word and political ideas. For example, as suggested by Dorothy Thompson, Stedman Jones's concern with Chartism has been in the area of political ideas rather than with the Chartists' construction and communication of language in its widest sense. And a number of scholars have criticized Stedman Jones's somewhat formalistic and decontextualized approach to the study of language, the latter's interests residing far more in the observance of continuities in political discourses over time than in changing linguistic contexts and meanings.[26] Patrick Joyce's approach, as seen most effectively in *Visions of the People*, has embraced language as a much broader system of signs and means of communication.

Notwithstanding the significant differences indicated above, it is the similarities and points of agreement in the work of Joyce and Stedman Jones which are of central concern to this article. And it is now time to return to these points of agreement in order more sharply to illustrate the strengths and weaknesses of the work of our two historians and of poststructuralism and postmodernism.

STRENGTHS

The embrace of language has produced several healthy effects upon the discipline of history and the practices of historians in Britain. Above all else, the writings of Stedman Jones and Joyce have acted as a timely reminder that language and systems of discourse play active rules in the creation of aspects of social reality, rather than being mere expressions and reflections of a *totally* given, or pre-existing external reality. An empiricist/positive view of reality – which assimilates social reality to nature and which posits an external reality to be studied and counted largely without reference to the active and formative characteristics of thought and language – has rightly been taken to task. Knowledge and interpretation are not automatically given in "reality/ experience." As Stedman Jones has argued, it is not adequate to "treat . . . language as a more or less immediate rendition of experience into words." And, to quote Roy Bhaskar, people are not "passive sensors of given facts and recorders of their given conjunctions". Rather, as the "agents" of history – in the sense of being "active initiators" rather than "passive instruments" – people do shape, in part by means of language, their inherited and determined conditions of existence.[27]

In taking seriously the languages of "ordinary people," in terms of both their epistemological importance and their socially constitutive role, Stedman Jones and Joyce have also offered useful correctives to crude notions of "false consciousness" and popular thought as being inherently "ideological." Above all, perhaps, Althusserian and some other forms of structuralism, with their forever hidden structures, and their all too hasty dismissals of the validity of the claims of popular "consciousness" to the status of "real/true" knowledge, have been exposed as deficient. To put the matter plainly, Joyce and Stedman Jones have said that any adequate account of modern British social history must take due account of the thoughts and languages of people. In "Rethinking Chartism" Stedman Jones writes:

> An analysis of Chartist ideology must start from what Chartists actually said or wrote. . . . It cannot simply be inferred . . . from the supposed exigencies, however plausible, of the material situation of a particular class or social group.[28]

This is a view to which I would subscribe.

But we must surely go further – to explore the *links* and *tensions* between what the Chartists said and did, and between the intended and unintended consequences of their thoughts and actions. The contexts of saying and doing should also be explored as fully as possible. To proceed to such matters is to raise, once again, questions concerning the nature of reality itself and its appropriation in thoughts and language. Indeed, at various points in this article, we have implied that, authorial and defenders' protests to the contrary, Mayfield and Thorne's criticism of "linguistic determinism" cannot easily be shrugged aside. It is now important for us to reach a definite conclusion concerning the validity or otherwise of this criticism. In order to arrive at a conclusion we must attend to the following matters: authorial intention and practice; the epistemological adequacy of Stedman-Jones's and Joyce's "turn to language"; the very nature of reality; and the materialist or critical-realist notion that reality extends beyond thought and language. This discussion will be conducted within a general focus upon the limitations of the work of our two subjects.

WEAKNESSES

As earlier noted, Joyce's and Stedman Jones's views and practices at times lack clarity and consistency, and exhibit ambiguity. There also seem to develop, in relation to the practices of both historians, confusions and contradictions between stated intentions and actual practices. We will first consider the intentions and practice of Stedman Jones, and then move to a discussion of Patrick Joyce's work. More general criticism and suggestions will finally be made.

As I have suggested elsewhere, as expressed in his essays on Chartism and in *Languages of Class*, Gareth Stedman Jones's stated aims concerning, on the one hand, political languages and, on the other, the "social" are far from clear and consistent.[29] In "The language of Chartism" (6), Stedman Jones argues:

> if the interpretation of the language and politics is freed from *a priori* social inferences, it then becomes possible to establish a far closer and more precise relationship between ideology and activity than is conveyed in the standard picture of the movement.
>
> In adopting this approach, however, it is not intended to imply that the analysis of language can provide an exhaustive account of Chartism . . . *It is not a question of replacing a social interpretation by a linguistic interpretation, it is how the two relate, that must be rethought.* (My italics)

Similarly, *Languages of Class* does not appear to effect a rupture between the "political" and the "social." Stedman Jones thus writes on p. 24:

> between the changing character of social life and the order of politics there is no simple, synchronous or directly transitive line of connection, either in one direction or the other. *To begin at the other end of the chain does not obliterate the significance of the work of the social historian, but locates its significance in a different perspective.* (My italics)

So far there would thus appear to be no basis to the charge of "linguistic determinism." Stedman Jones seems to be tackling, as argued by Taylor and Lawrence, the problems of "how to relate social and political change to one another," demonstrating (along with Robbie Gray, Michael Sonenscher and Joan Scott) "the complex and ambiguous interaction of language and social structure," and social history's neglect of politics and the latter's "relative autonomy".[30]

Matters are, however, much less straightforward than either the above-mentioned quotations from, or Lawrence and Taylor's somewhat selective and partial reading of, Stedman Jones's work would suggest. For example, at other points in his utterances on Chartism and language in general Stedman Jones variously seems to doubt: the very nature of material determination; the existence of the "social" outside of and prior to "its articulation through language" (*Languages of Class*, p. 7): the degree to which material forces exerted any significant influence upon the language of popular radicalism ("Rethinking Chartism," p. 95); and, as noted earlier, the existence of class as an ontological (as opposed to a discursive) reality. Contrary to the claim made by Lawrence and Taylor, it thus appears to be the case that Stedman Jones would endorse Joyce's claim that notions of the economy, society and the polity lack "overarching coherence" and underlying structures beyond their expressions in language and discourse.[31]

As I argued in my 1987 article, "In defence of class," Stedman Jones's *practice* amounts to an unconvincing idealism. The political languages and concepts of the Chartists are improperly wrenched loose from their material and other influences. The overall character and aims of the Chartists are derived, far too selectively, from a particular strand of the many languages and ideas informing the movement. And, as attention to the language of McDouall, O'Connor and other Chartists suggests, a (non-socialist) language of class and exploitation (both within and outside production) certainly co-existed alongside (and frequently prevailed over) Stedman Jones's preferred language of economic and social "producerism" (complete with its connotations of class harmony within production) and political exclusion. Indeed, Dorothy Thompson, the leading authority on the subject, has made a very strong case in support of the class-based character of the movement. And, according to Thompson, class was to be located not only in economic matters (Stedman Jones and Joyce identify class, in improperly "determinist" ways, far too narrowly with the "economic"), but also in politics, culture, ideology and social relations in general.[32] In fact, it is the "experiential determinist" (my phrase) Thompson who has made the most important and detailed attempt so far to link the "social", the "political" and the "linguistic" in Chartism.[33] In his opposition to economism, and in his "non-referential" usage of language, Stedman Jones effectively ignores (or denies?) the "social" and inflates the autonomy enjoyed by political language and ideas within Chartism. *The* Chartist reality becomes, in fact, a discursive reality.

As mentioned earlier, in *Visions of the People* Patrick Joyce does explicitly retain notions of the social order and economic and social conditions. And in the introduction to his book Joyce clearly alerts us to the fact that his primary concern rests with (16) "social identities and . . . discourses concerning the social order," rather than with "putting social structure, organizations and identities back together again." Nevertheless, we have seen that in his eagerness to question simplistic distinctions between the "real" and its "representations," Joyce, much in the manner of Stedman Jones, bends the stick much too far in an idealist direction. Reality and its constituent parts become inseparable from, indeed defined by, language.

Furthermore, Joyce's practice often betrays his stated commitments to the contextualization of language and the exploration of complexity and nuance in relation to meaning. Two examples may serve to demonstrate this point. First of all, while Joyce usefully identifies the language(s) of "populism," he nowhere proceeds in *Visions of the People* sufficiently to investigate the extent to which class-based meanings can be expressed within a "populist" framework and the wider overlaps of usage and meaning between class and populism; or to engage and assess the relative appeals of the two languages within specific contexts and over periods of time. That process of *contextualized engagements and linkages* and attention to *complexity* and *nuance*, which lies at the heart of Thompsonian and other examples of "best practice" within historical materialism, is sadly lacking in *Visions of the People*.[34] Indeed, Joyce could very usefully have paid attention to the works of two American historians of American labour history, Sean Wilentz and Bruce Laurie (heavily influenced by, respectively, E. P. Thompson and David Montgomery) who have sensitively traced the complex internal histories and meanings of, and (by no means necessarily antagonistic) relations between "producerism" and "class" in mid-nineteenth-century New York City and Philadelphia.[35]

Second, Joyce all too often simply accepts language, and especially the language of self-representation, at face value. There is also the strong tendency to divorce saying from doing and self-presentation from the ways in which one is seen and represented by others. Thus John Bright's claim to be the "standard bearer of the people" and liberalism's assumed purchase upon the enlightened, progressive, rational and democratic needs and desires of "the people" are taken to be largely self-evident truths.[36] Unlike *Work, Society and Politics*, *Visions of the People* makes little attempt to "look behind" such claims. John Bright's role at work, and especially his long-standing memory in Rochdale (persisting into the

1990s) as a "tyrant" is not investigated, nor are other possible contradictions between self-image and public perception. Similarly, the tensions
within mid-Victorian liberalism, identified by Cole for Rochdale, Taylor
for Bolton and Tiller for Halifax are not pursued. As in much of the
current "Cambridge School's" work on popular politics, it is the consensual, inter-class and enduring features of liberalism and radicalism
which are emphasized by Joyce.[37] The result is a partial approach to
reality. Individuals and social groups are not situated within the *ensemble*
of social relations and practices. Subtle attention to agency and conditioning, and to the complex range of factors which lie between
structure/interest and consciousness and action is conspicuous by its
absence.[38] In effect, Joyce's practice in *Visions* marks a retreat into the
narrow cul-de-sac of language – away from the broad and open vistas
of *Work, Society and Politics*. Subjectivity has now become of the essence.
Fragmented, multifaceted and largely free-floating life histories, in effect
descriptive narratives lacking fixed points of reference, playful, and
choosing their "realities," may well mark Joyce's next step within the
field of postmodernist history writing.

In sum, the considerable gains registered during the post-1950s
radical phase in social history are in danger of being lost in the current
linguistic return to, or restoration of (to adopt the term used by Mayfield
and Thorne) "traditional values": to the importance of ideas and political
concepts at their "natural" Cambridge home; and to the central importance of narrative and description at pragmatic, "no nonsense"
Manchester.

CONCLUSIONS

We can therefore conclude that both Joyce and Stedman Jones do effectively dissolve reality/being into the processes of thought and language.
In so doing, they preclude, by definition, any real engagement between
language, politics and the "social." We are left simply with idealist
engagements between discourses of politics, discourses of society and
discourses of the economy. In resurrecting the importance of languages
of "the people" against Althusserian theoreticism of the intellectuals,
Stedman Jones and Joyce have nevertheless fallen into the same epistemological trap as Hindess and Hirst and Joan Scott. Shifting languages
and discourses circulate and sometimes overlap, but any real external
(i.e. empirical) controls are conspicuous by their effective absence. Circu-

larity and self-confirmation become the idealist norm. There is no way off this discursive merry-go-round, apart from the option of making and breaking concepts against complex evidence, the "real" task of social history. But the latter represents far too bland and mundane a purpose for Joyce's postmodernist juggernaut.

In conflating being and thought/language, Joyce and Stedman Jones fail to make the necessary distinction between *existence* and *interpretation/ understanding*. These are two distinct, if interrelated, areas of life. As the materialist Eagleton has written in relation to the "inflation of discourse" (Anderson) in the ideas of Laclau and Mouffe:

> Heretically deviating from their mentor Michel Foucault, Laclau and Mouffe deny all validity to the distinction between "discursive" and "non-discursive" practices, on the grounds that a practice is structured along the lines of a discourse. The short reply to this is that a practice may well be organized like a discourse, but as a matter of fact it is a practice rather than a discourse. It is needlessly obfuscating and homogenizing to subsume such things as preaching a sermon and dislodging a pebble from one's left ear under the same rubric. A way of *understanding* an object is simply projected into the object itself, in a familiar idealist move. In notably academicist style, the contemplative analysis of a practice suddenly reappears as its very essence.... The category of discourse is inflated to the point where it imperializes the whole world, eliding the distinction between thought and material reality. The effect of this is to undercut the critique of ideology – for if ideas and material reality are given indissolubly together, there can be no question of asking where social ideas actually hail from. The new "transcendental" hero is discourse itself, which is apparently prior to everything else. It is surely a little immodest of academics, professionally concerned with discourse as they are, to project their own preoccupations onto the whole world, in that ideology known as (post-) structuralism.[39]

On a less abstract level, it is important to note that, as a result of many years of hard theoretical and empirical labour, historians and others have clearly *demonstrated* that socio-economic, political and cultural systems and processes have emerged and changed over time. People have been observed to move up and down social ladders, populations to rise and decline, social classes to coalesce and fragment, and econ-omies to "move" and "work" in patterned, if far from "lawed" ways. It has furthermore been demonstrated that social forces and changes often take place "behind people's backs" and in unintended and partly unrecognized ways (this is not to suggest that structural determinations are necessarily hidden from view). Language can be present in the construction and comprehension of social life. But, as brilliantly argued by social anthropologist Maurice Bloch, language is not necessarily present, and exists alongside a variety of non-linguistic influences. Scholars have convincingly shown that the presence of class structures, demographic trends and even concepts in society is ultimately not dependent upon their registration in language. Language confers meaning and understanding upon realities which both embrace and extend beyond the kinds of popular languages and discourses examined by Joyce and Stedman Jones.[40]

The validity of the notion of reality reaching beyond language has been usefully demonstrated by the critical-realist philosopher, Roy Bhaskar. While emphasizing the interaction between agency and inherited structure in the creation of social life, Bhaskar convincingly argues that structures are not solely consciousness-dependent. Thus:

> while social structures are dependent upon the consciousness which the agents who reproduce or transform them have, they are not reducible to this consciousness. Social practices are concept-dependent; but, contrary to the hermeneutical tradition in social science, they are not exhausted by their conceptual aspect. They always have a material dimension.

And, in contrast to "subjective idealism," Bhaskar's philosophical "realism" thus

> stands for the idea that material objects exist independently of our perceiving them, and in the domain of social science for the idea that the conceptual and the empirical do not jointly exhaust the real.[41]

If the formation and processes of social reality amount to more than the poststructuralist and postmodernist subjectivities of particular kinds of language, then, as suggested by Lawrence and Taylor, we must shoulder our debt to generations of historians and social scientists by accordingly refining our conceptual tools, engaging theory and evidence, and attempting to explore the *ensemble* of forces at work in people's lives. And this is intellectual labour which does not equate with blandness, blind defence of tradition or the exhaustion of the empirical project of social and labour history.

As a very brief acquaintance with twentieth-century history has taught me, there remains so much to be conceptualized, interrogated and explored. Furthermore, the opposition of "determinists" such as Wilentz, Fink, Epstein and Belchem to absolute or "true" notions of class consciousness (part of a widespread "determinist" opposition which does not seem to have registered upon the absolute practices of Joyce and Stedman Jones themselves),[42] their treatment of class as it actually was rather than as it ought to have been according to some ideal model of development, and their linkages between language, material reality, culture and politics will fortify me in my voyage into the history of the twentieth century. But, as Lawrence and Taylor observe, social history's renewal and future development will benefit from toleration, due regard for competing views, and frank, comradely exchanges.

In opposition to the claims of Joyce, I maintain that an important role in social history's future will continue to be played by those historians who tackle the materialist programme of work set by Edward Thompson, David Montgomery and other examples of "best practice." These historians will be obliged to oppose reductionism, idealism and subjectivism and, in the manner of Thompson and Williams, to incorporate the study of language into a wider framework of analysis which embraces agency and structure, saying and doing, the conscious and the unconscious, and the willed and unintended consequences of individual and social action and thought.[43] We will also then be in a strong position to assess critically Terry Eagleton's conclusions that

> the neo-Nietzschean language of post-Marxism, for which there is little or nothing "given" in reality, belongs to a period of political crisis – an era in which it could indeed appear that the traditional social interests of the working class had evaporated overnight, leaving you with your hegemonic forms and precious little material content. Post-Marxist discourse theorists may place a ban on the question of where ideas come from; but . . . the whole theory is itself historically grounded in a particular phase of advanced capitalism. . . . What is offered as a *universal* thesis about discourse, politics and interests, as so often with ideologies, is alert to everything but its own historical grounds of possibility.[44]

NOTES

1. I would like to thank John Saville, Janet Blackman, Keith Nield, Pat Lacy, John Walton, David Howell, Karen Hunt, and Dorothy and Edward Thompson for their comments upon drafts of this article. Sadly, Edward Thompson has recently died. I wish to dedicate this piece to his memory. Edward was a tremendous inspiration, a dear friend, and a superb and generous historian.

2. See the contributions by P. Joyce, L. Stone, C. Kelly and G. M. Spiegel to "History and Postmodernism," *Past and Present*, cxxxi (May 1991); cxxxiii (November 1991); cxxxv (May 1992); R. Samuel, "Reading the signs," *History Workshop Journal*, xxxii (Autumn 1991) and "Reading the signs: part II." *HWJ*, xxxiii (Spring 1992); G. M. Spiegel, "History, historicism and the social logic of the text in the Middle Ages," *Speculum*, ixv (1990); G. Stedman Jones, Introduction and "Rethinking Chartism" in his *Languages of Class: Studies in English Working Class History 1832–1982* (Cambridge, 1983); D. Mayfield and S. Thorne, "Social history and its discontents: Gareth Stedman Jones and the politics of language," *Social History*, xvii, 2 (May 1992); J. Lawrence and M. Taylor, "The poverty of protest: Gareth Stedman Jones and the politics of language – a reply," *Social History*, xviii, 1 (January 1993); P. Joyce, "The imaginary discontents of social history: a note of response to Mayfield and Thorne, and Lawrence and Taylor," *Social History*, xviii, 1 (January 1993); T. C. Patterson, "Post-structuralism, postmodernism: implications for historians." *Social History*, xiv, 1 (1989).

3. D. Harvey, *The Condition of Postmodernity: An Enquiry into the Origins of Cultural Change*, Oxford, 1991. 7; T. Eagleton, "Awakening from modernity." *Times Literary Supplement*, 20 February 1987 and *Ideology: An Introduction*, 1991, ch. 7; F. Jameson, "Postmodernism or the cultural logic of late capitalism," *New Left Review*, cxi.vi (1984) and "The politics of theory: ideological positions in the postmodern debate," *New German Critique*, xxxiii (Fall 1984).

4. Harvey, op. cit., ch. 6; A. Huyssen, *After the Great Divide: Modernism, Mass Culture and Postmodernism* (1986), ch. 10. I am grateful to Pat Lacy for pointing me in the direction of Huyssen's important work. See also P. Anderson, "Modernity and revolution," *New Left Review*, cxliv (1984).

5. For introductions to poststructuralism see J. Sturrock (ed.), *Structuralism and Since: From Levi-Strauss to Derrida*, (Oxford, 1986; I. Craib, *Modern Social Theory: From Parsons to Habermas*, Brighton, 1984, ch. 9. For the "turn" to language see P. Joyce, *Visions of the People: Industrial England and the Question of Class 1848–1914* Cambridge, 1991; G. Stedman Jones, "Rethinking Chartism," op. cit. and "The language of Chartism" in J. Epstein and D. Thompson (eds), *The Chartist Experience: Studies in Working-Class Radicalism and Culture 1830–1860*, 1982. For a forceful critique of discourse theory and its applications to social history, see B. D. Palmer, *Descent into Discourse: The Reification of Language and the Writing of Social History*, Philadelphia, 1990, especially 1, 2 and conclusion.

6. D. W. Hamlyn, *The Penguin History of Western Philosophy*, 1990, especially pp. 65–70, 218–21, 304–7; G. P. Baker and P. M. S. Hacker, *Wittgenstein: Meaning and Understanding*, 1984 edn pp. 265–70.

7. Joyce, *Visions*, op. cit., pp. 17–18.

8. Jones, *Languages of Class*, op. cit., pp. 7–8.

9. Joyce, "Imaginary discontents", op. cit., p. 84 and *Visions*, op. cit., pp. 9, 16.

10. Jones, *Languages of Class, op. cit.,* 95.

11. *Ibid.*, 22–3; Joyce, "History and post-modernism", *Past and Present*, cxxxiii (November 1991), 206–8; L. Stone and G. M. Spiegel's comments in "History and post-modernism", *Past and Present*, cxxxv (May 1992), especially 190, 197, 200.

12. Lawrence and Taylor, *op. cit.*, 5–6.
13. See J. Lawrence, "Popular radicalism and the socialist revival in Britain", *Journal of British Studies*, xxxi (April 1992); Joyce, *Visions, op. cit.*, 54–5.
14. Joyce, *Visions, op. cit.*, 5–6, 11, chap. 2.
15. Joyce, "Imaginary discontents", *op. cit.*, 83.
16. E. P. Thompson, *The Poverty of Theory and Other Essays* (1978), 205, quoted in P. Anderson, *Arguments Within English Marxism* (1980), 6.
17. Joyce, "Imaginary discontents", *op. cit.*, pp. 82–4.
18. Thus class is often presented as a purely economic construction. According to an assumed historical-materialist model, only revolutionary socialist consciousness fully qualifies as class. However, as John Belchem notes, this "vision" of class has long been "purged from the historiography of industrial England": J. Belchem, "A language of classlessness", *Labour History Review*, I.VII, 2 (1992), p. 43. See also N. Kirk, "In defence of class," *International Review of Social History* (1987), especially pp. 37–8, for the view that Stedman Jones's employment of a "true view of class" blinds him to the actual existence of class among the Chartists. For Joyce's excessively narrow equation of class with socio-economic factors see *Visions, op. cit.*, 3. pp. 10–11. Alastair Reid and Duncan Tanner, sharing Stedman Jones's opposition to "social determinism" and in part his central emphasis upon politico-linguistic factors in the historical process, also tend to construct an erroneous model of class (of workers more or less totally unified by economic and cultural factors and largely frozen in time), misleadingly attribute this model to advocates of class, and then proceed to the process of demolition. See D. Tanner, *Political Change and the Labour Party 1900–1918*, Cambridge, 1990; especially pp. 2–4, 6, 7, 8, 319, 419–20, 431; A. J. Reid, "The division of labour and politics in Britain, 1880–1920" in W. J. Mommsen and H.-G. Husung (eds), *The Development of Trade Unionism in Great Britain and Germany 1880–1914*, 1985.
19. See, for example, J. Epstein, "Understanding the cap of liberty: symbolic practice and social conflict in early nineteenth-century England", *Past and Present*, cxxii (February 1989); R. Sykes, "Popular Politics and Trade Unionism in South-east Lancashire, 1829–1842" (D. Phil., Univeristy of Manchester, 1982); N. Kirk, *The Growth of Working Class Reformism in Mid-Victorian England*, 1985, especially, p. 1; C. Behagg, *Politics and Production in the Early Nineteenth Century*, 1990; I. Fink, *Workingmen's Democracy: The Knights of Labor and American Politics*, Urbana, 1983; S. Levine, *Labor's True Woman: Carpet Weavers, Industrialization and Labor Reform in the Gilded Age*, Philadelphia, 1984.
20. Eagleton, *Ideology, op. cit.*, p. 198.
21. Joyce, "Imaginary discontents," *op. cit.*, p. 81.
22. J. W. Scott, *Gender and the Politics of History*, New York, 1988, chs. 2, 3 and 4. See also the criticisms of Scott's arguments concerning gender and language made by Bryan Palmer and Christine Stansell in *International Labor and Working Class History*, xxxi Spring 1987.
23. See, for example, K. Lunn (ed.), *Race and Labour in Twentieth Century Britain* (1985); C. Hall, *White, Male and Middle Class: Explorations in Feminism and History*, 1992, Karen Hunt's forthcoming book to be published by Cambridge University Press on women and the S.D.F.; S. Fielding, "A separate culture? Irish Catholics in working-class Manchester and Salford, c. 1890–1939" in A. Davies and S. Fielding (eds), *Workers' Worlds: Cultures and Communities in Manchester and Salford 1880–1939*, Manchester, 1992; A. Davies, *Leisure Gender and Poverty: Working Class Culture in Salford and Manchester 1900–1939*, 1992; J. W. Scott, "Deconstructing equality-versus-difference: or, the uses of poststructuralist theory for feminism," *Feminist Studies*, xiv, 1, Spring 1988; and for a balanced evaluation of the strengths and weaknesses of postmodernism for feminists, see S. Jackson. "The amazing deconstructing woman," *Trouble and Strife*, xxv, winter 1992. I am grateful to Karen Hunt for these references.

24. See, for example, E. P. Thompson, *The Making of the English Working Class*, 1968, Preface and *Customs in Common*, 1991, pp. 305–30 for women's roles in food riots, the household economy and labouring communities; J. Belchem, *Industrialization and the Working Class: The English Experience 1750–1900*, Aldershot, 1990, A. V. John (ed.), *Unequal Opportunities: Women's Employment in England 1800–1918*, Oxford, 1986; D. Thompson, *The Chartists*, Aldershot, 1984, ch. 7; H.-G. Gutman and I. Berlin, *Power and Culture*, New York, 1987; N. Kirk, *Labour and Society in Britain and the United States, 1780–1939*, Aldershot, 1994.

25. A. Easthope, *British PostStructuralism since 1968*, 1991 edn, pp. xii–xiv, 16–22.

26. See also in this context J. Foster, "The declassing of language" *New Left Review*, 1985; R. Gray, "The deconstructing of the English working class," *Social History*, xi (1986); J. W. Scott, 'On language, gender and working-class history," *International Labor and Working Class History*, xxxi, Spring 1987.

27. Jones, *Languages of Class*, op. cit., p. 94; R. Bhaskar, *Reclaiming Reality; A Critical Introduction to Contemporary Philosophy* 1989, p. 51; Anderson, *Arguments Within English Marxism*. op. cit., ch. 2 for an excellent discussion of agency.

28. Jones, *Languages of Class*, op. cit., p. 94.

29. See Kirk, "In defence of class", *op. cit.*, pp. 6–7.

30. Lawrence and Taylor, *op. cit.*, pp. 5–6; Lawrence, "Popular radicalism and the socialist revival," *op. cit.*, p. 186.

31. Jones, *Languages of Class*, op. cit., pp. 7–8, 17–24; Joyce, "History and post-modernism," *op. cit.*, p. 208.

32. Thompson, *The Chartists*, op. cit., ch. 10; Kirk, "In defence of class," *op. cit.*, pp. 37–43.

33. As demonstrated, for example, in the excellent range and depth of Chartist material presented in Dorothy Thompson's *The Early Chartists*, 1971.

34. J. Belchem, "A language of classlessness," *op. cit.*

35. S. Wilentz, *Chants Democratic: New York City and the Rise of the American Working Class 1788–1850*, New York, 1986; B. Laurie, *Working People of Philadelphia, 1800–1850*, Philadelphia, 1850, and *Artisans into Workers: Labor in Nineteenth Century America*, New York, 1898. See also Leon Fink's sophisticated treatment of the language of the Knights of Labor: I. Fink, *Workingmen's Democracy*, op. cit.

36. Joyce, *Visions*, op. cit., ch. 2.

37. J. Cole, "Chartism in Rochdale", M.A. dissertation, Manchester Polytechnic, 1986, and *Rochdale Revisited: A Town and its People*, vol. 2, Rochdale, 1990, pp. 37, 41–4; K. Tiller, "Late Chartism: Halifax 1847–58" in J. A. Epstein and D. Thompson (eds), *The Chartist Experience*, op. cit., pp. 337–41; P. F. Taylor, "Popular Politics and Labour-Capital Relations in Bolton, 1825–1850; D. Phil., Lancaster University, 1991, especially Introduction and ch. 3. See also T. Koditschek, *Class Formation and Urban-Industrial Society: Bradford 1750–1850*, Cambridge, 1990, ch. 18; E. F. Biagini and A. J. Reid (eds), *Currents of Radicalism: Popular Radicalism, Organized Labour and Party Politics in Britain, 1850–1914*, Cambridge, 1991, especially p. 1.

38. For the retention of class-based analysis which is also very sensitive to those manifold factors – such as agency, capacities and institutions – lying between structure and consciousness/action see M. Savage, "Two Paradigms on the Urban History of Social Class," unpublished MS., 1992. I am very grateful to the author for a copy of this paper. See Savage's earlier *The Dynamics of Working Class Politics: The Labour Movement in Preston 1880–1940*, Cambridge, 1987, especially Introduction.

39. Eagleton, *Ideology*, op. cit., p. 219.

40. Thus Bloch, "contrary to what anthropologists tend to assume, we should see linguistic phenomena as a *part* of culture, most of which is non-linguistic." M. Bloch, "Language, anthropology and cognitive science," *Man* (new series), xxvi June 1991, p. 192. I am

grateful to Steve Sapolsky and Jim Maffie for drawing Bloch's important work to my attention.

41. Bhaskar, *Reclaiming Reality, op. cit.*, pp. 4, 190.

42. See S. Wilentz, "Against exceptionalism: class consciousness and the American labor movement," *International Labor and Working Class History*, xxvi, Fall 1984. In his approach to the issue of the languages of Chartism (see *Visions, op. cit.*, pp. 95–6), Joyce most definitely suggests that: (i) class is economic in character; (ii) that, in order to qualify as class based, Chartist language would have to have assumed a socialist/ Marxist form, and (iii) that a "stages" model of consciousness ("primitive," "more developed," etc.), is appropriate. In employing this methodology Joyce largely fails to recognize the *actual* class nature of Chartist language, as expressed by McDouall and others. See Kirk, "In defence," *op. cit.*, pp. 37–8; J. Epstein, "The populist turn," *Journal of British Studies*, xxxii, 2, April 1993.

43. In an excellent review and commentary ("The wanderings of the linguistic turn in Anglophone historical writing," *Journal of Historical Sociology*, vi, 2, June 1993, Lorna Weir alerts us to the works of Fowler and Bourdieu which link language and social practice, and which constitute important alternatives to "the meaning-centred analyses of language/discourse present among historians today" (p. 230).

44. Eagleton, *Ideology, op. cit.*, pp. 219–20.

29 Patrick Joyce

The end of social history?

Historians are with some justice suspicious of the concepts of "modernity" and "postmodernity." These terms employ a history, yet in their use – most often by those who are not historians – they often seem curiously far from history as most of its academic practitioners would understand it. In order for "postmodernism" to exist it must project a "modernism" by means of which its own image can be made. Ironically, in much postmodernist thought, there is a tendency to invent a modernism which acts as postmodernism's founding concept. The result is a history which historians rightly criticize, one often without the sense of the particular and the conjunctural, or the sense of the alterity of the past, senses which have recently been identified as the hallmarks of "history".[1] The suspicions of historians have therefore led to their failing to engage with contemporary academic discourse on the nature of modernity and postmodernity. Yet engage they must, if for no other reason than that an intellectual agenda is being set in their absence, one that is shaping the nature of the future by reshaping the understanding of the past. The intellectual history of the last quarter of the twentieth century is not something historians can for ever continue to ignore. Yet the need to engage with contemporary discourse on modernity arises as much, and indeed I would argue more, from what this discourse can bring to history than from what history can bring to it. One is far from a sense of wisdom being brought to a history-less present by an enlightened profession. Indeed, the self-confidence and unity of "history" have been fissured as never before, precisely by the postmodernist critique (but of course not only by this critique). The response to this challenge need not be to reject it but to engage in a positive exchange with it.

This exchange will be especially necessary if it can be shown that contemporary history, in this case social history, is itself in fact the offspring of modernity. This is the argument made here. A postmodern view would identify modernity as a normative project. If social history is the child of modernity, then it is seen to be part of this project, not innocently naming the world but creating it in its own political and intellectual image. If this is so, or even if it can be entertained at all, it follows that historians need to engage with contemporary debates, for these entail reflection on the very founding propositions, and the history, of their discipline itself. From this perspective, the "discontents" of social history are those of a modernity at last coming to reflect upon itself.[2] If social history comes to be seen as the outcome of the project of modernity then this may be the signal of its end. Once innocence is lost it cannot be regained. However, while marking an end, a self-reflective and historicized understanding of "social history" may point beyond this end, to a reconfigured social history, to something new.

For, far from being anti-historical, as so many antagonistic responses to postmodernist thought have painted it,[3] its relativism and scepticism are deeply historical. These characteristics, in recent skirmishes between historians and postmodernism, have been chiefly viewed in terms of epistemology. However, it is the history behind the epistemology that matters just as much, the history of power and of the regimes of knowledge that have produced ways of knowing the world. It is this history that what has been called the anti-foundationalism of postmodernism helps us address, its radical scepticism being an invitation to a radical historicization of those "naturalized" or reified categories of thought that have served as the basis of our knowledge. The "foundations" that have been attacked are many, as will later be apparent. Two that have been critical in the foundation of social history are "the material" and "the social," and with them the cognate idea of class.

I

The importance of these various foundations has been registered in Eley and Nield's forthcoming account of the challenge of postmodernism and the "linguistic turn" to social history. The initial form of this account is a conference paper on class, given in 1993, and it is to this I refer in what follows.[4] This positive and constructive engagement with postmodernism is doubly welcome, coming as it does from two historians who have been so important in guiding the development of social history, in the form of the journal *Social History* (along with *Past and Present* perhaps the chief exemplification of contemporary social history, at least in Britain). Eley and Nield have drawn attention to the materialist assumptions of what, for the sake of argument, can be called the old social history.[5]

They chart the emergence of social history in the desire to transcend the narrowness of an older political history: there was a shift in accounts of politics from the state to "society." This move was powered by Marxism, "history-from-below" populism, and social science idealizations of "structural history." The case was made for the analytical priority of "social context" and "social forces." As they suggest, by the early 1970s the trend was very definitely in the direction of a foundational materialism in which "social causality," indeed "social determination" in some cases, carried the day. It is worth emphasizing more than Eley and Nield the liberal and whig antecedents of social history, especially the discourses of class and the social, though they are perhaps right to emphasize how Marxism formed this history's common sense. The basic repertoire of concepts in social history was (and remains) identifiably Marxist, though this conceptual undergirding was usually obscured by the predominating "empirical idiom" of this history, "theory" being implicit even while it was in many instances publicly spurned. However "culturalist" this history became, the basic idea remained that class and politics were rooted in the realities of material life.

Eley and Nield's account helps us to situate some of the ways in which class and the "social" were seen in social history. The "social," and "society," served as the origin of culture and politics, all the more effective because they also functioned as a kind of explanatory connective tissue, linking the substratum of the material to the cultural, for instance the economy to politics (the function of a "social context" is thus apparent). Books with titles like *Work, Society and Politics* tended to be published.[6] "Society" was therefore conceived of as a system, or a totality, something decidedly thing-like in its systemic nature. The concept of class served similarly as a "junction concept," linking the ideational to the material, and so revealing in the open court of "culture" the logic of what were conceived to be "underlying" social, or economic, processes. However indirectly, and the indirection of Gramsci was influential, classes in the end were seen to arise from economic relationships and to determine the fundamental nature of culture, and what – very characteristically – was known at the time as "consciousness" (the model of the unconscious mind echoing the model of the social). The social was the vast, neutral background in which everything was registered and everything connected. If society was the system, or the machine, class was the motive force, and historical principle, which drove the machine. To Eley and Nield's account also needs to be added the aspiration to write a totalizing history, the influence of *Annales* claims to "total history" also being influential. The ambition was to write a "total history," truly reflecting the reality of society's totality. Of course, totalizing narratives like Marxism were best placed to write this history of totalities.

The challenge of postmodernism to all this will be apparent, and is clearly evident in Eley and Nield's account. The categories of the material and the social are revealed to be idealized or essentialized "foundations," unable to bear the weight resting upon them. The narratives that write the history of these foundational categories – the liberal ones as much as the Marxist – stand revealed for the modernist "grand narrative" project they are. The political challenge is of equal moment: knowledge in the old dispensation was about transforming the object of its attention (women, classes, the oppressed). The political aim was clear. Knowledge in the new dispensation is seen to reveal the operations of power, and not itself to confer power through access to objective truth. The political aim is now no longer clear. Eley and Nield's own position here is to look to the past of social history as a way of looking to the future. But whether one can go back to the future like this is unclear. Obviously, there is great room for debate here. The stakes are high. It is to be hoped this debate will be forthcoming, especially among younger scholars.

A particularly thoroughgoing rejection of the materialist assumptions of social and labour history is evident in William H. Sewell's recent work.[7] In this Sewell takes issue with the idea of the "materiality" of the economy, and argues against the dualism of the physical and the "ideational" that marks so many accounts of the human body. He therefore reminds us of two other "founding" categories, those of the economy and the body, whose influence has been eroded by recent cultural history, and the "linguistic turn," whether or not we wish to label these developments postmodernist and their quarries modernist. Much feminist history would not be shy about describing its anti-foundationalism as postmodernist: the foundations it has dissolved, under the influence of poststructuralist thought in particular, are the naturalized categories of gender, including "man" and "woman" themselves.[8] In attacking the foundational status of gender, the body and in turn the material have themselves been historicized, and so de-essentialized. The relativism, and historical locatedness of "science," also stand revealed, in a by now enormous literature. In the hands of figures like Donna Haraway this approach to the history of science is presented in the light of an explicitly postmodern ethics and politics.[9] "The social" and "the material" are therefore only two of the building blocks of what can arguably be described as modernism.

Sewell's chief interest lies, however, in his brief but pungent aside on the history of the material,[10] for this in turn suggests the possibility of a history of "the social." It is this possibility which strikes me as one of the more productive ways forward for a reconfigured social history, and it is the one that I will give most attention to in what follows. Sewell is concerned to show where present-day notions of materialism come from, especially the idea that production and exchange are somehow uniquely material. The split between the spiritual and the material emerged out of traditional Christian and aristocratic discourse. In the nineteenth century the ethics and aesthetics of representations of the material were reversed: the ordering principles of human life – as found, for example, in political economy – were seen to lie in the material, free now of the pejorative associations of baseness and disorder. In fact, the material became tractable, the stuff of laws and "sciences," which were now extended from the physical to the "social" and the "economic," both of which were the creations of Enlightenment discourse. Ironically, therefore, the historical materialism of Marxism is seen to originate in this nineteenth-century exaltation of the "material" as the stuff of law. The irony is not lost on Sewell, who remarks,[11]

> Marxists proudly proclaim their radicalism by employing an arbitrary identification of the economic as material, never realizing that they have inherited the idea intact and uncriticized from traditional Christian and aristocratic discourses. Would-be friends of the proletariat hence believe they are being progressive when they denounce as "idealists" historians who actually take seriously what past proletarians thought. The claim that the economy is uniquely "material" always was arbitrary, misleading and tendentious: that it continues to be clung to by purportedly leftist scholars is an embarrassing anachronism.

It is, however, above all the figure of Michel Foucault which stands at the beginning of any new history of the social,[12] for it is Foucault who has done most to identify the emergence of human subjectivity in the west. One of the principal ways in which this subjectivity was defined was through discourses on the body, especially discourses on sexuality. The object of these, and other discourses shaping subjectivity became the "individual."[13] However, the subject as individual was inseparable from the creation of the social. The individual, and ultimately liberal freedom itself, were located in terms of a social that defined his or her conduct and being. In turn, "the social" aimed to facilitate the full emergence of the individual.[14] "Man," the "self" and "society" are thus identified as key elements in the emergence of modernity. The origins of "sciences" and "histories" centred upon the social are therefore insep-arable from modernity's project, not least social history itself.

However, before outlining the contours of a new history of the social it is necessary to step back a little, and relate this activity to the problem-atic of which it is a part, namely the troubled relationship of history and postmodernist thought. The hard words of Sewell provide a cue here: the indifference, and often the hostility, of historians to this thought do, unhappily, give much cause for concern at the anachronisms of thought evident in academic history far beyond an, anyway, by now rapidly retreating Marxism.

II

It is, however, the ghost of Marx that unites the extremes of right and left in the most intemperate denunciations of the postmodernist scourge. Elton and Himmelfarb may stand for the former,[15] Kirk and Palmer for the latter.[16] The instinctual anti-Marxism of the one mirrors the fundamentalism of the other. Aside from the predictable, and totally inapposite defence of "objectivity" against the menace of relativism, Elton and Himmelfarb's responses amount to little more than an – equally predictable – discovery of reds under the bed of postmodernism and poststructuralism. Espousing E. P. Thompson as their standard bearer, Kirk and Palmer profess a so-called "historical materialism" which is at once sectarian and sanctimonious. This approach reproduces all the failings of the old social history at its worst: for instance, in true reductive fashion, poststructuralism is seen as the ideological represen-tation, or superstructure, of the structure of postmodern society.[17] The least said of these positions the better, perhaps, though it is unfortu-nately the case that this kind of apologia for a decaying social history is still given credence in some areas of labour and social history, particularly in the UK. It is also unfortunate that Thompson himself cannot be absolved from the sectarian spirit of these defences: his intemperate rejection of "theory" is evident in these defenders, and, like them, it must be said that inseparable from the passion of conviction in Thompson was the creation of enemies needed to fuel the fires of this passion.[18]

The material and the social come in turn to be coded terms for "the real", and courts of appeal against those who would seek to controvert the distinction between representation and reality. In recently published work I have considered this "ideology of the real," and how historians have invoked it in defence of "history" against postmodernism.[19] What is at issue is not the existence of the real, but – given that the real can only ever be apprehended through our cultural categories – which version of the real should predominate. In fact, just as a realist epistemology and ideology were built into history from its professionalization in the late nineteenth century,[20] so in the present "history" is itself invoked not just as the defender of the real, but as the incarnation of the real itself, as if the past silently bore witness to its own truth. This is very much apparent in the recent *Past and Present* exchanges, where both Stone and Spiegel have done this. Very characteristically as well, Spiegel tends to equate the real with the social, and this equation can be seen to extend very widely indeed.[21]

It is apparent in labour and social historians like Kirk and Palmer, but also in left-inclined feminist historians, uneasy about postmodern conceptions of identity, and about a feminist politics developing from this decentred understanding of identity. The social also tends to overlap with "experience," "social experience," in one account, being mobilized against the so-called idealism of a putative "linguistic determinism."[22] "Experience" is indeed another of those foundations constantly invoked in the social history project, especially by E. P. Thompson. Joan W. Scott, herself so much the focus of the anxieties of this social-historical feminism, has recently, and powerfully, argued against this "essentializing" of "experience."[23]

Of more positive responses to postmodernist thought, Patrick Curry's recent argument for a post-Marxist social history involves a particularly telling critique of traditionalist Marxist defences of social history, and of the basic repertoire of social history itself.[24] Much more ambivalent is the response of History Workshop, understandably so as its *Journal* has been a major conduit for new kinds of thought, while at the same time the hold of the Marxist legacy is still strong. This ambivalence can be seen in Samuel's recent account of "Reading the signs," a generic term for the turn to representation in history, but a term that loses in discrimination what it gains in comprehensiveness in showing the many tributaries of the turn to semiotics and hermeneutics.[25]

The kind of broad perspective evident in Samuel's work is none the less useful if the real nature of contemporary anti-positivism is to be understood. The turn to hermeneutics and semiotics is one factor, itself made up of many different, and sometimes conflicting traditions. The terms "poststructuralist" and "postmodernist" would, of course, not be accepted by many working in these traditions. They would certainly not be accepted by right revisionist history in Britain; but if we are to understand the forces at work undermining the old liberal-left consensus of social history, and indeed of history more widely in Britain, then it is to diverse currents like the anti-positivism of right revisionism, and "Cambridge School" discourse analysis, that we need to attend.[26] J. C. D. Clark's critique of the liberal-left consensus in British history, for instance, applies equally to social history,[27] for that is a characteristic expression of this consensus.

And consensus it has become, marked less by antagonism to outside ideas, usually, than complacency about such ideas, or indeed about any ideas, with the exception of those extruded by the "discipline" itself. In its heyday, however empirical its idiom, social history had the cutting edge of a youthful academic Marxism, and the ebullience of social science's optimism. It was challenging, open to other disciplines and new ideas, present-minded, and political. In short, it was anti-establishment. Now it *is* the establishment, or a good part of it. One speaks of the "end of social history" somewhat ruefully, therefore, in the knowledge of the hegemony of this establishment in our academic culture (and of the hegemony of an anti-heterodox history in our culture more broadly). Zygmunt Bauman describes the processes at work well, in noting how the "advent of postmodernity" may turn out to have little effect on the academy (though the same points could be made with reference to any other heterodox thought):

> There is nothing to stop one from doing just that (pursuing "objective" knowledge and declaring "postmodernity" to be a sham). In the vast realm of the academy there is ample room for all sorts of specialized pursuits, and the way such pursuits have been historically institutionalized renders them virtually immune to pressures

untranslatable into the variables of their own inner systems; such pursuits have their own momentum; their dynamics subject to internal logic only, they produce what they are capable of producing, rather than what is required or asked of them; showing their own, internally administered measures of success as their legitimation, they may go on reproducing themselves indefinitely.[28]

But if the "end of social history" is not to be expected in one sense it is easily imaginable in another, an ending evident in intellectual ossification, one in which an intellectual hegemony is lost even as an institutional hegemony is retained. The journal *Past and Present* is a good example of this, as it is of the poacher turned gamekeeper. The elders of social history remain in station still, supported by a younger generation of scholars largely immune to the intellectual history of our own times. In shifting this complacency new intellectual maps will have to be drawn, ones, for instance, in which the common anti-positivism of a "leftist" postmodernism and a "rightist" revisionism might make common cause. The political correlates of intellectual positions are, anyway, fairly free floating. As Clark himself has recently observed, positivist history in the UK has been centre left, but in the US much more to the right.[29] Critiques of positivist history will be correspondingly complex in their political orientation. Whatever possibilities become evident, something is needed to shake the hold of a history which continually reproduces itself, in the process sucking the erstwhile heterodox into its consensus, in much the way that "cultural history" is slowly but surely becoming routinized as more methodology, yet one more subdiscipline in the house of history.

Apart from feminist history, post-colonial history evinces the one other area of robust critique of modernity, and of the historical orthodoxy that helps to underpin it. The work of Edward Said, and the body of poststructuralist theory, have been influential, especially on Indian historians writing about India. There the Marxism of *Subaltern Studies* has been shifted in a decidedly postmodern direction, which results in the identification of history itself as the sign of a Europe-centred modernity. As Dipesh Chakrabarty has recently argued,[30] the Western idea of history, emanating from the time of the Renaissance, involved conceptions of time that were absolutely central to notions of "progress" and the "modern." The nation came to represent the modern, becoming in itself the distinctively modern sign under which "history" was written.[31] From the viewpoint of this post-colonial history the colony represented not merely the location of domination and resistance, but of all manner of complex interrelations and "hybridization," which were integral to the mode in which modernity was instituted.[32] Modernity was reproduced through this process, and neither unilaterally ordained by the coloniser nor unilaterally resisted by the colonized: in this the colonizer was not immune, for the history of modernity was produced from the colony, as well as from the West. It is in the light of this understanding that the sort of history of the social proposed here needs to be seen. For instance, forms of the social like the "public sphere," and "civil society," were produced outside the west as well as in it. However, it is with the Western dimensions of the history of the social that I am concerned here, well aware as I am of an incomplete story.

III

As a contribution to finding a way out of the current impasse of social history I would like to propose the outlines of a history of the social, as well as some very brief and preliminary points concerning the question of "social structure," a concept that has of course been of great importance for social history. The importance of postmodernist thought for social history can be described in terms of a challenge, or a series of challenges. These I will describe in terms of the understandings of identity, of modernity and of structure. New understandings in these three areas involve a challenge to, and critique of the founding categories of social history, above all class and the social.

In regard to identity, poststructuralist conceptions have been of crucial importance, especially feminist appropriations of them. Feminist theory has offered a new subject for analysis, and new conceptions of identity for our understanding, in the shape of gender. More than simply offering a new category, to contradict or complement old ones, such as class, feminist theory has helped problematize the whole question of what identity is. Gender identities are seen as historically and culturally formed. They are not the product of an external "referent" which confers meaning on them. Identity is seen as a product of conflicting cultural forces, and viewed as relational, composed of systems of difference.[33] The debt to poststructuralist theory is apparent, and its conception of language not as the mirror of a world external to it, but as a conventional and arbitrary structure of relations of difference, the eventual shape of which is produced through cultural and power relations.

The implications for understandings of class will be apparent: if gender cannot be derived from an external referent, then the same follows for class. It cannot be referred to an external "social" referent which is its foundation or cause. This referent, the "social," is itself a "discursive" product of history. The relevant questions then become, "how have the links between language and its object – the wrongly assumed social referent – become established, and how have the conventional operations of discourse been produced?" These, eminently historical, questions produce a rather different agenda from more orthodox understandings of the social and of class. The search now is for how meanings have been produced by relations of power, rather than for "external" or "objective" class "structures," or other "social" referents. It also follows that if identity is composed through the relations of systems of difference, then it is marked by conflict, and is plural, diverse and volatile. The view of identity is one in which many "identities" press in and react with one another (we are men and women, parents and children, members of classes and nations, modernists and postmodernists, and so on). It is a view rather at odds with many accounts of class, which tend to deal in fairly uniform and coherent identities (the very idea of a class having a consciousness of itself puts a high premium on this view of identity as stable and uniform). "Class" is indeed regularly stacked up with other, similarly stable identities (race, nation, gender, and so on). Out of these rough-hewn blocks sociologies and histories continue to be made. Perhaps it is time for a more credible notion of identity, one which considers the systems by which relations of difference work, including those means by which differences are composed into unities, however conditional these unities may sometimes be.

Let me move next from identity to the question of modernity. Considerations of identity involve notions of the human subject itself, and ultimately of modernity. Instead of a human subject conceived as the centre and organizing principle of multiple identities, human subjectivity is itself an historical creation. As Foucault has argued, the idea of a "centred," controlling human subject is a product of the "classical age," particularly the eighteenth century when the emergence of "man" in his true grandeur becomes evident. In this argument the Western subject has been constructed as an "individual." However, inseparable from this creation, and simultaneous with it, was the construction of "the social". The individual's rights, obligations and conduct were measured in terms of a "social" that both guaranteed their integrity and policed their excesses.[34] Strategies for the implementation of the individual – such as the constitution of the "private sphere" – were inseparable from strategies implementing the social – such as the constitution of the "public sphere" and "civil society."[35] Thus it is the case that the radical questioning of identity and subjectivity indicated here poses further fundamental problems for the concept of class: that concept is one of the consequences of the implementation of "the social" considered here. "Society" is the ground upon which the figures of class have been placed, figures that in some readings of class have become not only social "facts" but collective actors on the historical stage. It is necessary to go back and look at the history of this ground if the figures that are its consequence are to be understood.

The implementation of the human subject and of society may be seen as the implementation of "modernity." From this point of view "modernity" describes a subject and a society which, though while eminently real in their consequences, are in fact themselves elements in a project. The project of modernity disguises the fact that "individual" and "society" are not real, "objective" entities, but historical and normative creations, designed to handle the exigencies of political power and political order. This perspective on modernity, one of critique, can be understood as the perspective of postmodernity, though many of those involved in the critique would not describe themselves thus. From a postmodern viewpoint, "class," alongside categories like "society" and "economy," but also "reason," "the self," and so on, are all seen as exemplifications of a modernity that, as we have seen, takes them to be the "foundations" of knowledge. Modernism is therefore conceived of as writing the "grand narratives" of history in which these various essences play leading roles, for instance the narratives of science and progress, and of liberalism, socialism and conservatism.

If modernity is a project in these senses then sociology, and social theory more widely, can be said to be implicated directly in it, at once its progenitors and its products. Postmodern sociologies have increasingly asked whether the terms of nineteenth-century sociology are really satisfactory in describing the nature of twentieth- and twenty-first-century society. This suggests the possibility of a radical rethinking of the founding propositions of sociology, and social theory more generally, "society" and "class" among them. There is a further, and equally searching question to be asked of nineteenth-century sociology: if it does not describe present reality, can we be so sure it describes the reality of the times in which it grew up? The work of Bauman and

Touraine, for example, offers categories of analysis which they regard as better able to interpret present reality than existing ones, class among them. Aiming to describe a world moving beyond the modern phase of society, they find the tools of a "modernist" sociology inadequate.[36] The new tools they offer involve the attempt to transcend the old dualism of structure and agency (the emphasis, as will be seen, is broadly processual, "society" in Bauman being replaced by "sociality" for instance).[37] However, it is distinctly possible that such tools may help us understand the past as well as the present, especially as the old ones – among them class – are indeed seen to be part of a normative, historically situated "project." Both writers see the ideas of sociology, and the idea of society, to be modelled on the nation state, and in this mode conceived of as a system or a totality. The notion of society is also seen to be related to the problem of how political order might be secured in a period of what was held to be unparalleled change (a period described in the term "progress", or the more neutral "modern").[38] Classes were integral to this understanding of "society" as a structure: they were the content of which it was the form, or – conceived more actively – they were the motors by which this structure was changed. This is not to say that the terms of classical sociology did not sometimes, indeed often, well describe the society that produced them, but the point, precisely, is that they were an historical product and not a neutral analytic. So, it is productive to think about a history of the social which conceives of this category as the product of modernity.

Finally, and briefly, the third challenge to orthodox accounts concerns the central problem of structure and agency, or structure and action (there are many terms for a dualism that has been a central concern of sociology and history). If these new sociologies are right it becomes very difficult to conceive of a structure of class relationships, or a structure of any set of "social" variables (occupation, income, etc.), as lying objectively outside the agent or observer. This goes for the historical agent in the past, or the sociological one in the present, *and* for the observer who is employing a concept of structure in order to explain how society is organized or how people feel or behave. Agents in these accounts might usefully be seen as involved in creating or reproducing structure; observers as implicated in producing the knowledge they purport to be simply reporting on. Some of the more recent critiques of sociologized notions of structure will be considered later.

These various challenges to social history, and to the concepts of society and class, have many implications for historical work itself.

Once these concepts are viewed as historically produced conventions it becomes necessary to trace their origins and development. And once a more credible notion of the formation of identity is forthcoming, in which we are led to examine the principles of unity and difference which compose personal and collective identity, it becomes possible to explore more productively the sources of identity and of different sorts of collective mobilization, political and otherwise. Here we are decidedly in the area of the operation of hegemonies: in social history the concept of hegemony has been very important, not least in the journal *Social History*, representing as it did in Gramsci and his powerful influence the attempt to square the traditional social-structural concerns of social history with a recognition of the indeterminacy of culture. The resulting intellectual gymnastics of the attempt to square this particular circle were never very convincing; the desire to ground culture in the structures of class resulted in the baroque complexities of "hegemonic power blocks," "elite ruling fractions," and so on. Releasing the understanding of hegemony from class, as Curry has recently suggested, enables us to think more productively about the operations of power.[39]

How, then, do we trace the history of the discursivities of the social, including the ways in which they are produced by, and produce, power? The new history of class is of course one such way. Accounts of the operation of "languages of class" have developed in the work of scholars like William H. Sewell, Gareth Stedman Jones, Joan W. Scott, Jacques Rancière and myself.[40] The forthcoming work of Dror Wahrman is a further contribution to this,[41] and the approach can be extended in many ways.[42] It promises to substantially rewrite the traditional narratives of social history, which still continue to be plotted in terms of classes as collective actors, and of the "underlying" structural processes of capitalism. The language of class itself, as opposed to more populist forms, for instance, is in fact a good example of how one element in the discourse of the social has achieved hegemonic status: in Britain, until recently, the language of class was so firmly anchored in academic and popular common sense as to become naturalised, and invested with a spurious facticity it still retains today. In this process the presence of other collective subjects of the discourse of the social was forgotten, subjects such as "the people," indeed "people" and "humanity" and "humanity" themselves, the absolutely central collective subject of liberal democratic regimes.[43] These achieved hegemonic status in their own manner. Whatever the collective subjects involved, the "linguistic turn," in looking at *how* such subjects are put in place, is pointing to the manner and mode in which hegemony is achieved: for instance, collective identity and political mobilization can be very valuably reinterpreted in terms of the narrative patterns that enunciated them.[44] The example instanced earlier, drawn from the "hybridized" operation of modernity in India, similarly points to new possibilities. Attention to the creation of subjectivity, to new "social" subjects and to the manner in which subjectivity is produced, all suggest a new agenda for a reconfigured "social history."

However, there has been relatively little direct attention among mainstream historians to the history of the ground upon which these various subjects of the social may be said to move, namely "society" and "the social" themselves. Tracing the history (and hegemony) of the social directly has been left to other traditions, and is most notably evident in the work and influence of Foucault. The influence of Habermas has certainly been felt among historians concerned to write the history of "civil society" and the "public sphere," though this has tended to be simply grafted upon traditional approaches, and is in fact itself quite far removed from the perspective on the social developed here.[45] While the influence of both men, and Elias, will no doubt continue to be productive, it seems to me that Foucault is the most suggestive figure, particularly in the form of the recent development of his work by a range of scholars working for the most part outside history.[46]

Of these approaches, that of Habermas may be regarded as the most conventional. The argument against it, and of many of its appropriations by historians, would be that it posits as an explanation of the public sphere that which should in fact be the subject of an explanation (namely, the "bourgeoisie"). From a "languages of class" perspective, one could view the discourse and practice of the public sphere and civil society as that which enabled people to view themselves as "bourgeois" in the first place (rather than a bourgeois class creating the public sphere). However, this might be to connect the public sphere too completely with the bourgeoisie: as Eley has recently pointed out, the public sphere was always gendered, and one can talk of many public spheres, not one, including a plebeian or "working class" one (though this is open to the same counter-argument as above).[47]

It is Foucault's work that most emphatically releases us from the limits of traditional approaches to society and the social, the discourses and practices organized around conceptions of society becoming the means by which different groups, individuals and institutions identify and organize themselves, and handle power. It is Foucault's later work on the nature of rule that is the most apposite, where attention is given to its most expressly political forms, found, for example, in modes of "governmentality" and in the role of the modern state. In this work, and its later extensions, liberalism is seen as a means, a "technology," of rule. It is the mode of "governmentality" that has marked the transition to the modern world in the West. The operation of "the social," in the liberal mode of governmentality, is hence regarded as one of the major means by which identity and politics have historically evolved. Whereas Habermas, however critically, writes from within an ideology of liberalism, Foucault can be said to write outside one.

Foucault's own lecture on "governmentality," or the "art of government," charts the eighteenth-century eclipse of sovereignty and the family as – respectively – the justification and the model of rule.[48] He then describes the emergence of a new justification and model, in the form of governmentality and "population." "Population" reveals entities with their own regularities and characteristics, accessible through statistics. "Society" and "economy" come to be thought of in modern ways, ways now amenable to technologies of rule. Gordon and Burchell offer later points in this history (a history, it should be said, only beginning to emerge).[49] In their accounts liberalism cannot be viewed as the expression of class interest. Rather, it is a mode of governmentality, which cannot be given a class origin. Nonetheless, the articulation of "political economy" is quite central in the liberal development of governmentality. What both writers describe is the movement from "sovereignty" to "population," and thence to liberalism. Liberalism itself involves a shift from a knowable object of governmentality to an unknowable one, rule now not being exercised over populations but ceded to them in the form of individuals. Liberalism, paradoxically, is a form of governmentality which is at once an interrogation of governmentality: rule is ceded to a self which must constantly monitor the civil society and political power which are at one and the same time the guarantee of freedom and its threat.

Donzelot describes the emergence of a more systemic "social."[50] In nineteenth-century France a new sort of social emerged from the rethinking of the bases of social and political order that followed the revolution of 1848. This involved a new view of the relationship of state and society. The previous treatments concentrate mostly on political thought: Donzelot shows how the social is always a matter of practice as well as of "thought." What is also particularly interesting in this work is the instance of how sociological notions of society and the social, in the form of Durkheim and French sociology, can be closely related to "society" as a mode of political legitimation.

Rose's work develops this history of the social, revealing its practical impact across Western society more widely. It considers an emerging, and important, body of work describing the rationalizing project of "civility" and civil society in nineteenth-century liberalism,[51] pointing to the importance in this of the town,[52] the home and the family,[53] and the school.[54] As I have recently argued, for much of the nineteenth century a full-blown, systematic "social" was kept at arm's length by the moralizing and individualizing tendencies in liberalism.[55] The sovereignty of the social was delimited by notions of the self and the individual as sources of identity and rule (the "social," however, still functioned, for instance as a means of securing the full independence of the moral self). In the course of the century the state and civil society drew closer together, and the legitimation of rule in the name of this social became more marked. The social began to take on a life of its own, becoming an objective "thing," the source of both political and moral legitimation. Rose considers the full-blown "social" of the late nineteenth century, that of "sociology" and of state intervention and new models of community.[56]

It is within this trajectory of the social, this nascent history of the social, that the history of social history urgently needs to be placed. This placing would certainly involve consideration of the early and mid-nineteenth-century understandings of the systemic nature of "the social" and "the economic" evident in Marx. It would also consider the effect of the full-blown social of the late nineteenth and early twentieth centuries, which was amply apparent in the work of radical liberal social and political thinkers in Britain. The influence of both versions of the social, those of Marx and radical liberal thought, has of course been of fundamental significance for the development of British social history.

Rose also describes twentieth-century developments, pointing to the slow decline of the social, and the reinscription of authority and freedom on new versions of the self, ones involving the capacity of autonomous individuals to establish an identity internally and externally, "as a depth within us to be deciphered," and "as an individuality to be expressed in our dealings with the everyday world"[57] (particularly in the area of consumption). This condition of liberal freedom some have termed the postmodern condition of society. This long history of the social has been severally addressed by Baudrillard, after his own fashion,[58] and by

Denise Riley, who has emphasized how the "social", like the "public sphere", is always gendered.[59]

Now a number of objections can be raised to this, as to any other Foucault-influenced history. Some of these objections seem to me more relevant than others, but on balance the initiative is an extremely suggestive way forward. The familiar, often-expressed view that this approach only conceives of power as one-way, "top-down," does not seem relevant: power only makes sense as a concept if it acts upon a subject who was previously unaddressed by it. It is only necessary where it has not accomplished its task. The concept of "governmentality" in this work extends to "all means for the calculated administration of life, for the conduct of conduct", as Rose puts it. "Governmentality" properly involves, therefore, the almost numberless projects of conduct, for example those emanating from "the self", which may counter as well as complement the various "dominant" centres of power and understandings of conduct. The very idea that liberalism is a form of governmentality that interrogates governmentality, itself permits space for a history that allows for conflict and contradiction.

However, work in this neo-Foucauldian tradition does not always occupy this space: interest in paradigms of rule, and rationalities of conduct (as in "the calculated administration of life") results in an overemphasis on the neatness and coherence of "structures" of such rule and conduct. At its worst, what is involved is a glorified history of public policy. What "calculated administration" is, how strategies of rule become "paradigms" at all, what "conduct" itself means, cannot be known unless traced in the full details of their eventuation, down to the smallest detail of "everyday life." It is here that the breadth of the concept of governmentality creates problems, extending as it does from the rule of the state to the conduct of conduct in everyday life. The notion that the state is diffused in the conduct of the self and of the everyday is enormously important and suggestive, but once we enter upon the history of conduct we encounter many accounts of what subjectivity is and how it is created. Foucauldian approaches tend to be of little help in this encounter. Above all, they do not help us discern why some forms of conduct are taken up and not others. For instance, psychoanalytic or phenomenological accounts of what affects such outcomes are not usually considered.

What affects outcomes can properly be called "the social," in a sense other than the Foucauldian one so far chiefly emphasized. This is the sense of the whole sphere of human interaction and the inter-subjective, and the many schools of thought bearing upon this sphere, not least those that have gone to make up sociology and social history. The social can, and should, be understood as a mode of rule and conduct, in however wide a context. Indeed, it is only when the schools in question pursue it in this way that they can provide a properly historicized and reflective account of their own practice. Yet the Foucauldian approach itself only serves to pose anew questions about how and why people enter upon social life, the traditional questions of the disciplines in question. Ironically, the frequent narrowness of Foucauldian expla-nations of rationalities of rule can result in that tendency to "essentialize" modernity noted in my opening paragraph. This tendency has been particularly seen in Foucault's earlier work, with its invocation of the most traditional, conservative and functionalist explanations of "modernism," among them capitalism and the bourgeoisie.[60] How, then, can questions about the formation of the social and social life be pursued in ways that transcend the difficulties posed by older views of the social, views compromised by their roots in the project of modernity? At the level of social theory it is here that recent sociologies have important things to say about what I earlier termed the third of the "challenges" to established social history evident in postmodern thought, namely the understanding of social structure. Here I can only be brief and summary, by way of conclusion.

IV

If we wish to retain the concept of structure in a reconfigured social history then it needs to be viewed in the light of new conceptions of structure evident in contemporary sociologies, and elsewhere. And surely some concept akin to structure needs to be retained if we are to discern what Giddens has termed the "unconscious motivations" and "unintended consequences" of action. Giddens's account of "structur-ation" is one instance of a notion of "structure" which, as was said earlier, involves the agent in its creation and reproduction,[61] which is to say that the agent is built into the reproduction of society and the social themselves. What the newer sociologies involve is precisely this sense of "society" as constantly reproduced by its members, so that the emphasis, in Bauman for instance, is on "sociality" rather than "society," on "processual" understandings of the social rather than structural or static ones.[62] For instance, the conception of "structuration" Giddens draws on is derived from language, in the sense of an "absent totality" present only in its instantiation, rather than from static conception of "presences," as in visual analogies of structure evident in ideas of the body or the building.[63] As Giddens also puts it, arguing against the traditional dualism of action and structure and for what he calls a "duality of structure", "social structures are both constituted *by* human agency, and yet at the same time are the *medium* of this constitution."

This emphasis on the processual nature of understandings of the social, where the social is seen as continually reproduced by the agents who make it up, has of course many sources, and cannot simply be termed postmodern. The hermeneutic tradition, particularly in ethnome-thodology, has been very important.[64] There, emphatically anti-realist positions involve the argument that the action–structure dualism of the social sciences is something we simply impose on ourselves, unaware that it is a direct consequence of "being-in-the-world," part of the more fundamental activity of comprehending social life in the first place.[65] Post-Marxist traditions, evident for example in the relatively little dis-cussed work of Cornelius Castoriadis,[66] insist on the irreducible reality of fantasy and the unconscious, and the creative role of the "social imaginary" itself. The renaissance of interest in the work of Georg Simmel is also striking, and with it the emphasis on the self-constitution of the social world.[67] The sources are many, none the less they have been explored and developed most by self-consciously postmodernist sociologies, particularly the work of Bauman.[68] There the whole emphasis is against understandings of society as a system or a totality, and upon self-constitution, randomness and the reflexivity of subjects.

If the accent is now upon the continuous recreation of society, then the means and manner of this recreation become very important. Atten-tion shifts to this creative activity, which is always closely related to hermeneutic activity: to make the social is always to make meaning (in processes that may be conscious or not). Thus it is that the whole "linguistic turn" in history, with its emphasis on representation, has an affinity with these more recent, postmodernist sociologies and the con-cepts in which they deal.

The latter certainly serve as a critique of the dualism of action and structure which still continues to mark sociology and social history,[69] particularly in accounts of class. Yet the influence of not just new under-standings of structure, but of a whole set of concepts drawn from anti-system forms of theorizing about the social, still remains to be con-sidered within history, let alone worked out for historical practice.

Nevertheless, a start has been made in developing more hermeneutically driven accounts of change, including accounts of "structure" which build in access to and utilization of the recreative, representational activities of actors as they make the social world (one example would, again, be narrative itself, the concept of narrative, and who has access to what narratives, and to the means of communication themselves, serving to emphasize the centrality of hermeneutic activity for a reconfigured social history). The reproduction of the social world is seen to depend precisely on the processual activities which concepts like narrative give access to. And the same goes for all the categories employed by the "new cultural history" in its turn to language as the model of culture, especially its turn to the analogy of the text itself. This "aestheticization" of the social, what Hayden White calls "the content of the form,"[70] opens up many new questions. If the social world is at bottom a human construct, it is only by looking at the principles of its construction that headway will be made, and this applies to the history of the social, as well as to the theory of the social. The emerging history of the defining categories of Western modernity described here, that of the discursive practices of the "social," the "economic," the "cultural" and so on, itself invites new accounts of process and structure that will extend and criticize it.

NOTES

1. Raphael Samuel, "Reading the signs, part I," *History Workshop Journal*, xxxi, Autumn 1991, pp. 231–4; see also "Reading the signs, part II," *History Workshop Journal*, xxxiii, Spring 1992.
2. The meandering way of what may be termed the "discontents of social history" debate in *Social History* can be followed in David Mayfield and Susan Thorne, "Social history and its discontents: Gareth Stedman Jones and the politics of language," *Social History*, xvii, 2, May 1992; Jonathan Lawrence and Miles Taylor, "The poverty of protest: Gareth Stedman Jones and the politics of language – a reply," xviii, 1, January 1993; Patrick Joyce, "The imaginary discontents of social history: a note of response", ibid.; Mayfield and Thorne, "Reply," xviii, 2, May 1993; James Vernon, "Who's afraid of the 'linguistic turn'? The politics of social history and its discontents," xix, 1, January 1994; Neville Kirk, "History, language, ideas and postmodernism: a materialist view," xix, 2, May 1994. See also Anthony Easthope, "Romancing the Stone: history-writing and rhetoric," *Social History*, xviii, 2, May 1993.
3. For example, Lawrence Stone, "History and postmodernism," *Past and Present*, cxxxi, May 1991; "History and postmodernism iii," *Past and Present*, cxxxv, May 1992; Bryan Palmer, *Descent into Discourse: The Reification of Language and the Writing of Social History*, Philadelphia, 1990; "Critical theory, historical materialism, and the ostensible end of Marxism: the poverty of theory revisited," *International Review of Social History*, xxxviii, part 2, August 1993.

4. Geoff Eley and Keith Nield, "Classes as historical subjects: some reflections." An account of this paper is given in the report of the Portsmouth University conference by Kelly Boyd and Rohan McWilliam in this issue of *Social History*. The paper is to be published by Eley and Nield in 1995.

5. On the development of the "linguistic turn" in social history, and in history more widely, see G. Eley, "Is all the world a text? From social history to the history of society two decades later" in T. McDonald (ed.), *The Historical Turn in the Human Sciences*, 1993.

6. Patrick Joyce, *Work, Society and Politics: The Culture of the Factory in Later Victorian England*, Hassocks, 1980.

7. William H. Sewell, Jnr, "Towards a post-materialist rhetoric for labour history" in Leonard R. Berlanstein (ed.), *Rethinking Labor History: Essays on Discourse and Class Analysis*, Urbana, 1993. The majority of contributors to this volume wish to retain the essentials of the old labour history, but the level of the debate, particularly the seriousness of the engagement with ideas (especially those of Habermas), indicates that at least a part of US labour history is in singularly better shape than a now almost moribund British labour history.

8. Denise Riley, *"Am I That Name": Feminism and the Category of "Women" in History*, 1988; Joan W. Scott, *Gender and the Politics of History* (1988). See also J. Butler and J. W. Scott (eds), *Feminists Theorize the Political*, 1992.

9. Donna Haraway, *Simians, Cyborgs and Women: The Reinvention of Nature*, 1991.

10. W. H. Sewell, Jnr, "Towards a post-materialist rhetoric," op. cit., pp. 21–3.

11. Ibid. pp. 22–3.

12. Of course, conventional notions positing a separation of the material and the cultural, or the "discursive," are denied in Foucault's deployment of the idea of "discursive practice." Discursive practices are to be found not just in formal discourse (language) but in institutions, technical processes and so on, and they are also operative in, and on, the physicality of the body.

13. Michel Foucault, *The History of Sexuality*, esp. vol. 1, "An introduction", 1978.

14. For some observations on the relationship of "the self" and "the social" in nineteenth-century England, see P. Joyce, *Democratic Subjects: The Self and the Social in Nineteenth-Century England*, Cambridge, 1994, pp. 13–20.

15. Geoffrey Elton, *Return to Essentials: Some Reflections on the Present State of Historical Study*, Cambridge, 1991, Gertrude Himmelfarb, "Telling it as you like it: postmodernist history and the flight from fact," *Times Literary Supplement*, 16 November 1992.

16. Kirk, op. cit., Palmer, *Descent into Discourse*, op. cit., also "Critical theory, historical materialism," op. cit.

17. Palmer, "Critical theory", op. cit., p. 136. The misunderstandings of what is at issue are many. For instance, in a familiar ploy among historians engaging with postmodernist thought, it is claimed that historians know the essentials of this thought already, and have indeed been practising these for years. Palmer considers what he terms the "dialectic" between "agency" or "consciousness" and "the unrecognized material determinants" of life in this light, whereas postmodernist thought seeks to dissolve these traditional dualisms of thought, viewing their defence as part of modernity itself. See ibid., pp. 156–62. In a similar vein, Kirk equates "deconstruction" and the "decentring" at work in anti-foundationalist thought with the discovery of diversity and heterogeneity in the "working class" evident in the old social history. This is a rather spectacular misunderstanding, the effect of which is to allow Kirk to hold on to the centred collective subject of the working class despite any amount of evidence of difference and contradiction.

18. The evident cultural emphasis of this work notwithstanding, Thompson always thought of himself as an historical materialist, and this stance always brought him

back to some sense of social and economic "determination." See E. P. Thompson, *The Making of the English Working Class*, 1968, pp. 9–11, also "Eighteenth-century English society: class struggle without class?," *Social History*, III, 2, May 1978, pp. 146–51. For extended quotation from Thompson on these themes see P. Joyce, *Class: A Reader*, Oxford, 1995, pp. 130–42.

19. Joyce, *Democratic Subjects*, op. cit., pp. 5–9.

20. James Vernon, "Constructing the canon: the discourse of the real and the English historiographical tradition" in J. Vernon (ed.), *Re-reading the Constitution; New Narratives in the History of English Politics*, Cambridge, 1995. On the ideology of the real and history see also Roland Barthes, *The Rustle of Language*, New York, 1986.

21. On history's incarnation of the real see Mark Cousins, "The practice of historical investigation" in Derek Attridge *et al.* (eds), *Poststructuralism and the Question of History*, Cambridge, 1987; Lawrence Stone, "History and postmodernism," op. cit.; G. M. Spiegel, "History and postmodernism IV," *Past and Present*, CXXXV, May 1992, pp. 197–202, esp. 198, also "History, historicism, and the social logic of the text in the Middle Ages," *Speculum*, LXV, 1990 pp. 77, 84, 85. See also P. Joyce, "History and postmodernism," *Past and Present*, CXXXIII, November 1991 and Catriona Kelly, "History and postmodernism II" in the same issue.

22. Christine Stansell, "A response to Joan Scott," *International Labour and Working Class History*, XXXI, Spring 1987. See also Laura Lee Downs's invocation of "social life" and "social relations": "If 'Woman' is just an empty category, then why am I afraid to walk alone at night? Identity politics meets the postmodern subject," *Comparative Studies in Society and History*, XXXV, 2, April 1993, and the reply of Scott with the further response of Downs, "'The Tip of the Volcano'" and "Reply to Joan Scott," both in the 1993 number.

23. Joan W. Scott, "The evidence of experience," *Critical Inquiry*, XVII, Summer 1991.

24. Patrick Curry, "Towards a post-Marxist social history: Thompson, Clark and beyond" in Adrian Wilson (ed.), *Rethinking Social History: English Society 1570–1920 and its Interpretation*, Manchester, 1993.

25. Samuel, "Reading the signs, parts I and II," op. cit.

26. Anti-positivism, in the form of "Cambridge School" analysis of political language, has of course more than simply rightist manifestations among British historians. Originating in the work of J. G. A. Pocock and Quentin Skinner, this current is to the fore in the history emanating from Cambridge, and Cambridge is a major intellectual force in the make-up of contemporary historical writing in and on Britain. This particular "linguistic turn" owed next to nothing to the poststructuralist and postmodernist influences considered in this article. As Samuel indicates, its development was a more domestic affair, indebted as it was to Austin and Wittgenstein, rather than to Saussure. The secularism of this tradition, its narrow understanding of "language," and its conservative-liberal sympathies demarcate it from the "postmodernism" of Foucault, on the one hand, and right revisionism on the other. See R. Samuel, "Reading the signs, part II," op. cit., pp. 222–3.

27. J. C. D. Clark, "The past and the future of British history," unpublished paper, 1994.

28. Zygmunt Bauman, *Intimations of Postmodernity*, 1992, pp. 103–4.

29. Clark, "The past and the future of British history," op. cit.

30. Dipesh Chakrabarty, "The death of history? Historical consciousness and the culture of late capitalism," *Public Culture*, IV, 2, Spring 1992.

31. Nicholas B. Dirks, "History as a sign of the modern," *Public Culture*, II, 2, Spring 1990; Gyan Prakash, "Writing post-orientalist histories of the Third World: perspectives from Indian historiography," *Comparative Studies in Society and History*, XXXII, 2, April 1990, D. Chakrabarty, "Postcoloniality and the artifice of history: Who speaks for 'Indian' pasts?" *Representations*, XXXVII, Winter 1992.

32. Gyan Prakash, "Science as a sign of modernity in colonial India," paper presented at Warwick University, 1994.
33. As well as the feminist work cited in n. 8 above, Foucauldian perspectives on the history of identity have been important. See, for instance, Nikolas Rose, *Governing the Soul: The Shaping of the Private Self*, 1990.
34. See especially the essays in Graham Burchell, Colin Gordon and Peter Miller (eds), *The Foucault Effect: Studies in Governmentality*, 1991; Mike Gane and Terry Johnson (eds), *Foucault's New Domains* 1993.
35. Keith Tester, *Civil Society*, 1992.
36. Alain Touraine, "Is sociology still the study of society?", *Thesis Eleven*, xxiii, 1989; *Critique of Modernity*, 1994. Bauman, op. cit., esp. Introduction and chs 2, 4, 9; *Legislators and Interpreters: On Modernity, Postmodernity and the Intellectuals*, Cambridge, 1987; *Modernity and Ambivalence*, Cambridge, 1993; *Postmodern Ethics*, Oxford, 1994. See also Serge Moscovici, *The Invention of Society: Psychological Explanations for Social Phenomena*, Cambridge, 1993.
37. Bauman, *Intimations*, op. cit., pp. 190–1, 196, 204.
38. Touraine, "Is sociology still . . .," op. cit., pp. 177–9, 180–3: Bauman, *Intimations*, op. cit., pp. 104–10, 189–90.
39. Curry, op. cit., pp. 167–72.
40. William II. Sewell, *Work and Revolution in France: The Language of Labor from the Old Regime to 1848*, Cambridge, 1980; Gareth Stedman Jones, *Languages of Class: Studies in English Working Class History 1832–1982*, Cambridge, 1983; Scott, *Gender and the Politics of History*, op. cit., Jacques Rancière, *The Nights of Labor: The Workers' Dream in Nineteenth-Century France*, Philadelphia, 1980; Patrick Joyce, *Visions of the People: Industrial England and the Question of Class 1840–1914*, Cambridge, 1991.
41. Dror Wahrman, *Imagining the Middle Class: The Political Representation of Class in Britain c.1780–1840*, Cambridge, 1995.
42. For a possible development of this approach see Joyce, *Class: A Reader*, op. cit., section F.
43. Joyce, *Democratic Subjects*, op. cit., parts II and III; *Visions of the People*, op. cit., ch 2, p. 3.
44. E.g. Lynn Hunt, *The Family Romance of the French Revolution*, 1992; Joyce, *Democratic Subjects*, op. cit., pp. 153–61; Judith R. Walkowitz, *City of Dreadful Delights: Narratives of Sexual Danger in Victorian London*, 1993; Margaret R. Somers, "Narrativity, narrative identity and social action: rethinking English working class formation," *Social Science History*, Winter, 1992; Vernon (ed.), *Rereading the Constitution*, op. cit.
45. See the many citations in G. Eley, "Nations, publics and political cultures: placing Habermas in the nineteenth century" in Craig Calhoun (ed.), *Habermas and the Public Sphere*, 1993.
46. The journal *Economy and Society* has been important as a channel of this work. See, for instance, the "Special issue: liberalism, neoliberalism and governmentality," *Economy and Society*, xxii, 3, August 1993.
47. Eley, "Nations, publics and political cultures," op. cit., pp. 303–4.
48. Michel Foucault, "Governmentality," in Burchell *et al.* (eds), op. cit.
49. Colin Gordon, "Government rationality: an introduction" in *ibid.*; Graham Burchell "Peculiar interests: civil society and governing 'The System of National Liberty'" in *ibid.*
50. Jacques Donzelot "The mobilization of society" in *ibid.*; "The promotion of the social" in M. Gane and T. Johnson (eds), *Foucault's New Domains*; also *L'invention du Sociale*, Paris, 1984.
51. Nikolas Rose, "Towards a Critical Sociology of Freedom," inaugural lecture, Goldsmiths College, University of London, 1992, excerpted in Joyce, *Class: A Reader*, op. cit.

52. P. Rabinow, *French Modern: Norms and Forms of the Social Environment*, 1980; J. van Ginneken, *Crowds, Psychology and Politics 1871–1899*, Cambridge, 1988; T. Bennett, "The exhibitionary complex," *New Formations*, 4, 1988.
53. J. Donzelot, *The Policing of Families*, 1979; N. Rose, "Beyond the public/private division: law, power and the family," *Journal of Law and Society*, 14, 1987.
54. I. Hunter, *Culture and Government: The Emergence of Literary Education*, Basingstoke, 1988; I. Donald, *Sentimental Education: Schooling, Popular Culture and the Regulation of Liberty*, 1992; N. Rose, *The Psychological Complex: Psychology, Politics and Society 1918–1939*, 1985.
55. Joyce, *Democratic Subjects*, op. cit., pp. 15–17.
56. Rose, "Towards a critical sociology of freedom," *op. cit.*, pp. 10–13.
57. *Ibid.*, 14.
58. Jean Baudrillard, *In the Shadow of the Silent Majorities, or, The End of the Social*, New York, 1983.
59. Riley, *Am I That Name*, op. cit.
60. Samuel, "Reading the signs, I," op. cit., 106–7.
61. Anthony Giddens, *The Constitution of Society: Outline of the Theory of Structuration*, Cambridge, 1984, see also John B. Thompson, "The theory of structuration" in *Studies in the Theory of Ideology*, Cambridge, 1984, esp, pp. 52–5.
62. As well as the work of Bauman cited above see also Z. Bauman, *Freedom*, Milton Keynes, 1988.
63. Anthony Giddens, *Social Theory and Modern Sociology*, Cambridge, 1986, pp. 60–1, for a cogent explanation.
64. Wes Sharruck and Rod Watson, "Autonomy among social theories: the incarnation of social structure" in N. G. Fielding (ed.), *Action and Structure*, 1988.
65. *Ibid.*, pp. 58–9.
66. Cornelius Castoriadis, *The Imaginary Institution of Society*, Cambridge, 1987.
67. See, e.g., David Frisby, *Simmel and Since: Essays on George Simmel's Social Theory*, 1992.
68. For postmodern sociologies and sociologies of postmodernity see also Stephen Crook, Jan Pakulski and Malcolm Waters, *Postmodernisation: Change in Advanced Society*, 1992, Bryan S. Turner (ed.), *Theories of Modernity and Postmodernity*, 1990, Mike Featherstone (ed.), *Postmodernism*, 1988, Scott Lash, Paul Heelas and Paul Morris (eds), *Detraditionalization*, 1995.
69. For substantiation see Joyce, *Class: A Reader*, op. cit., section C, esp. pp. 127–49.
70. Hayden White, *The Content of the Form: Narrative Discourse and Historical Representation*, Baltimore, 1987.

30 Geoffrey Eley and Keith Nield

Starting over: the present, the post-modern and the moment of social history

These brief remarks have no claim to completeness. Their aim is to register a series of discomforts, our unease not that disagreements are occurring, but that an important debate is precisely not taking place, that questions are being raised in ways that ensure they are unlikely to be faced. We can agree with Patrick Joyce that historians are shying away from, or simply ignoring an important challenge of contemporary social and cultural theory, of politics, and of fundamental societal changes at the end of the twentieth century – all those phenomena collectively articulated *via* the discourse of postmodernity and postmodernism, which Joyce embraces, in fact.[1] To that extent, Joyce's complaints about the conservatism and timorousness of university history departments is well taken, and his recent role in being willing to voice questions of this kind is all to the good. On the other hand, his precise ways of raising these matters leave much to be desired. This response is a plea for more constructive discussion or, perhaps more accurately, for a discussion to be started in the first place, with an open-mindedness that neither the opponents of "postmodernism" nor this self-appointed historical advocate seem able to show!

First, there is an issue of tonality. One of the most striking features of Joyce's chosen mode of address is its sometimes peremptory, exhortatory timbre, its apocalyptic and apodictic tone. Historians *must* do this, they *cannot ignore* that, they had better get their general act together. Joyce's commentary presents itself as the new, self-evidently persuasive, overpowering logic of the age, of contemporary enquiry, a truth that cannot be opposed, that somehow supercedes everything else, everything that comes before. But we work in a more complicated intellectual environment than this. Patrick Joyce is not the only person to have been reading her or his way around the endlessly proliferating literatures of contemporary postmodernist celebration and critique. There are others, even among historians,[2] whose collective conservatism Joyce so laments, who have been giving these issues some thought. But these are also difficult and destabilizing questions, which go to the heart not only of the historian's practice, but also of our assumptions about the social and political world and its rules of intelligibility, questions for which there are no ready-made and ultimately convincing answers. The advocates of postmodernism above all, one might think, should not be surprised to encounter scepticism over the absolute acceptability of their claims. Reservations, that is, can be voiced from something other than mere recalcitrance.

In other words, there is a pre-existing pluralism of practices and discussion (a discourse of self-reflexive and theorized history before Joyce), which cannot be disposed of simply by pronouncing the truths of the new. To do the latter amounts to a closure; it creates no space; it forbids continuing intellectual exchange between a complex past and a complex present in theoretical terms; it denies creative conversations. It is a rhetoric of exhortation whose analytical purposes remain obscure. Why do we need this hortatory and apodictic instruction? What is it for?

Of course, the tonalities of Joyce's writing are generated partly by the closed-mindedness and arrogance of postmodernism's more extreme critics, among whom Lawrence Stone still has no peer. See, for instance, the latter's early warning cry, which called the profession to the defence of its integrity against the corrosive influences of relativism, poststructuralism, postmodernism, and other contemporary ideas.[3] There is an extremism of mutual hostility and miscomprehension that incites these tones of voice. They are not entirely the responsibility of Patrick Joyce, or any other single author, but the effect of a discursive field already shaped by multiple confrontations. All kinds of things are in play – anxieties, rage, disappointments, nostalgias, resistances, failures of intellectual generosity, refusals to take the risks of engagement. A theoretical *hauteur* instructs a redoubt of methodological conservatism, and the latter shouts defiantly back. Between the two lies a silence, a barrier that in these tones cannot be crossed.

Yet there are problems of closure not just at the level of tonality, but at the level of argument, too. To ease his argument Joyce undertakes an all-too-familiar simplification. An undifferentiated "Marxism" is assumed to be "past" in some irretrievable and unlamented way. This is a sign of our post-Communist times, in which not just the tired remnants of Stalinism and the state-socialist replications of Soviet-type economies have been brought to an end, but all forms of socialist thinking have been brought into question, tarred with the same brush, delegitimized as ways of thinking about society, its pasts and futures. We are being offered this closure by a neo-liberalism recklessly self-confident in its new-found ascendancy, through which not just the economy, but the possible forms of citizenship and social relations, and of meaningful communication among human agents, of cultural value, are being redefined – and limited – in particular ways. Unsurprisingly, Marxism as an intellectual tradition, as a set of theoretical perspectives, which only ever achieved a contingent and oppositional institutional place in the mainstream intellectual cultures of the West, varying from insecure and marginal footholds to relatively prestigious and ramified influence, has been a casualty of this situation. But in addressing this all-too-common dismissal of Marxism, its burial as Joyce and most of the critics see it, we need to remind ourselves of another truth of contemporary intellectual history, one which is not part of the post-Communist equation, and which has never been properly acknowledged by anti-Marxists, namely, that there are *many marxisms*. Marxism has long been a *plural* discourse.

The refusal to talk about Marxism as anything other than a single and undifferentiated *thing* is a big problem, a complacency for which our current post-Communist conjuncture has now delivered the permission. The vanished – or vanquished – utility or plausibility of Marxism is apparently connected in the minds of Joyce and others with the implosion of the Soviet Union, and the irreversible "failure" of the experiments begun in 1917. But for those of us educated in the New Left and the anti-Stalinist radicalisms after 1956, this reductive reading of Marxism makes absolutely no sense. It recalls Marxism to the orthodoxies of an older foundationalism. It reabsorbs the proliferating Marxisms of the last quarter-century into a single, oversynthesized and artificially conflated ideological construct, whose essential features (its structures of thought and logics of action) are supposed to have spawned the specific history of the Soviet Union and all the crimes and excesses of Stalinism, as well as the failures and inadequacies more generally of the state-centralized socialist tradition. But it is exactly a distancing from the Soviet Union that was the point. This mobilized the most creative modes of Marxist thought in the post-war world.

For one thing, the whole tradition of Western Marxism, as delineated by Perry Anderson,[4] gives the lie to this unitary view, in a double sense. On the one hand, there is the pluralizing of Marxism between the 1930s and the 1960s into a divergent and unmanageable theoretical repertoire, some of whose strands remained formally connected to official Communisms (various Marxisms in Italy and France), others of which situated themselves avowedly beyond the boundaries of the latter (most notable the Frankfurt School, but also the wide-ranging reception of both Gramsci and Althusser under way during the 1960s). On the other hand, first after 1956, and then increasingly after 1968, there are the many attempts to liberate Marxism from the need either to identify with the Soviet Union, or at least strategically to defend its existence. Such gains were always hard-won; they always had political consequences and implications; they always had political origins. Theory and politics were joined. It is a breathtaking negligence that can predicate an entire argument on the erasure of this history.

Since the 1960s, there have been many spaces for creative thought and politics within the copious boundaries of the Marxist tradition. There are many examples of fruitful discussion within the pluralities of Western Marxism, for which the influence and reworking of Gramsci's ideas have been one vital key. Foucault, too, was biographically grounded during the 1950s and 1960s in a culture of French Leftism – that is, a culture of taking Marx seriously, of admitting Marx and Marxist theory to the universe of legitimate thought, the kind of context of intellectual work that was replicated in a different form in Britain in the 1970s, not least in the project of the *New Left Review* and the systematic translation and diffusion of European theoretical Marxisms.

We don't wish to be misunderstood. We are not trying to subsume everything into an infinitely adaptable plurality of Marxist discourses, as though anything useful or innovative happening on the intellectual left could be credited and assimilated to an expansive and catholic "Marxism." But at the same time, Marxism does need to be acknowledged as an important – and continuing – element in the universe of living ideas. Nor is it our purpose to establish criteria for according or refusing the description of "Marxist" to a particular argument, tendency, insight or thinker. Our affirming of a plural Marxism is not a matter of establishing boundaries of procedure in that way – epistemological or whatever – or of analyses read off from a prior theoretical truth, but an upholding of the importance of the presence of Marxisms in the present intellectual discourse. Ill-considered and negligent rejections of the whole lead to a neglect of some valuable, maybe essential bodies of ideas. These include not just the value of Gramsci (which Joyce deals with explicitly, if briefly), but also of Althusser, and in a different way of Foucault, whose positions on "governmentality" and so on otherwise figure significantly in Joyce's argument. For even Foucault, a vital participant in Joyce's version of postmodernism, is taken only in bits. Again: we are not asking that some "whole package" be swallowed, of Gramsci or Foucault or whomsoever, but that some mind be paid to their reception and to the discussions thus initiated as a condition of possibility for important intellectual gains. Likewise, to recognize the value of Althusser's interventions, we don't need to be "Althusserians" in some essentialist or card-carrying sense, as opposed to seeing the ways in which Althusser's reception allowed certain departures and discussions to begin, or at any rate, helped them to occur.

Current treatments of class are subject to this same syndrome – an erasure of the many different ways of constructing class analytically, producing a conflation of complexities into a convenient and easily rejectable unity, the master narrative of a totalized and totalizing social analysis. The availability of class as a term useful in political analysis is wiped out. It is reduced by Joyce to a single, self-evidently wrong idea – namely, the reductive couplet of class interest and class consciousness, in which the logics of the second are structurally inscribed in the forms and formations of the first. But to pose the question in this way is to take the most reductive and discredited type of Marxist class analysis as the only possibility. (In passing, we might add, the corpus of contemporary social history is not exactly bursting with examples of the latter.) Again, the proponents of class analysis are being offered a zero-sum choice: any "serious" and internally consistent use of the class concept, they are told, requires both acceptance of "objective class interest" and belief in the narratives of class as the orthodoxies of Marxism–Leninism might have constructed them, and these positions (as every schoolgirl knows) have been exposed as wrong-headed once and for all. The débâcle of the political tradition that relied on "class" in this sense as the prime mover of history vitiates the very use of the term, it is argued, and measured by the destructive consequences of this failure, all the intricate efforts at theoretical interpretation and revision are so much hot air, merely academic, a scholastic irrelevance.

From this view, class analysis works neither as history nor as politics, and the concept should simply be given up. The usefulness of class analysis is being judged here by the bankruptcy of some of its orthodox Marxist versions, as if these exhaust the legitimate ways in which class can be understood. By implication, we are instructed, any usage of the concept of class automatically locks the user into a set of discourses and meanings properly belonging to discredited Stalinisms and bankrupted master-narratives. By this argument, only one kind of usage of the concept is recognized, and then promptly destroyed.

On the contrary, we want to argue, class can retain its analytical purchase on fundamental aspects of the present world. The licence for the blanket repudiation of class is insecure, itself resting on a perhaps surprising and casually imperious totalizing move, an underspecified assertion of the consequences of how the "world has changed."[5] Yet, we would argue, especially in the latest transnational and globalized forms, capitalism continues to entail necessary logics of inequality and exploitation, of who gets what, and through what mechanisms. In the world of these logics, class is more than the master category of a now allegedly discredited Marxist analytical "realism," and remains at the very least a useful descriptive term for the conjunctural outcomes of capitalism's distributive logics. And whatever the truth of the epistemo-logical arguments with and against Marx, whatever the substance of the allegations against Marxist practice of a now unusable and superseded "realism," capitalisms continue inexorably and inequitably to distribute the product. Capitalism continues to make many people poor. This, too, is a dimension – part of the "means and manner" – of "the continuous recreation of society."[6]

There remains a crucial and unacknowledged space between the spurious polarities of "understandings of society as a system or a totality" and "self-constitution, randomness and the reflexivity of sub-jects,"[7] in which more complex questions of power and its exercise need to be posed, and where the willingness to acknowledge the importance of society-wide analysis doesn't necessitate "totalizing" in the old way. We can agree with Joyce that some of the former languages of the "social" no longer work. We can even share some of his grounds of critique. Yet, at the same time, something else is being abandoned. Surely we can see real events occurring behind people's backs without reaffirming the entire conceptual lexicon of a problematic structuralism. In other words, contemporary arguments about postmodernism also entail understandings of the nature of power and raise issues of politics – political action and analysis – that need to be faced. Political dispo-sitions and limitations are inscribed in Joyce's discussion no less than in any other.

Restructurings of capitalism have, of course, occurred; classes have been reconfigured; identifying the relations of exploitation is harder than it used to be. We accept that class is being recomposed; it is not available in its previous manifest forms; it is no longer recognizable via former iconographies, typologies and embodiments. But this doesn't mean that either capitalism or its characteristic forms of exploitation have simply gone away. Current analyses of race, gender, space, sexuality, ethnicity are important not least for their purchase on changing modes of ensuring an inequitable distribution of the product. They provide access to the late capitalist modalities of exploitation and inequality – of class – in this sense. If this is so, if class can indeed be deployed analytically in the way we are suggesting, in a complex articulation with these other terms, perhaps there's something left after all of Marxism's core concept in a politically engaged tradition of social analysis. And, in that case, the question of the meanings of "post-Marxism" should now be called.

If elements of Marxism remain as useful knowledge, then what does *post-Marxism* entail? What is post-Marxism anyway? A world with no Marx, a world with no Marxism in it? Or a world which, no longer permitting many former "takes" on Marx, nevertheless acknowledges the reserves of analytical value for a territory of crucial and enduring importance: namely, the understanding of capitalism and all its effects? In other words: there has to be some care – more care than Joyce has evinced – and better clarity on the subject of the specific kinds of Marxism being invoked. The sloppiness of Joyce's notations of Marxism doesn't help a good discussion. They need to be more fully specified, if they're to be available for critique. A discourse has to be given its due. Marxism, no less than other bodies of thought, ought to be taken and criticized at its point of greatest strength.

But Joyce has a predilection for concentrating on weakness, for scoring easy polemical points, for focusing on the most extreme exponents of the anti-postmodernist stance in their most simplifying and most polemical moods. His attack on Palmer and Kirk is a good example of this effect, deriding their "fundamentalism" (again, the equation of the latter with "historical materialism" or "Marxism" *tout court*), and dismissing them as "sectarian" and "sanctimonious." He sees their arguments as "reproducing all the failings of the old social history at its worst",[8] the exemplification of which, he alleges, is the dismissal of poststructuralism by Kirk and Palmer as the ideological self-representation of postmodern society. There is certainly an element of this cheapness in Palmer's *Descent into Discourse*,[9] for instance, in which the latter comes perilously close to defining poststructuralist and postmodernist ideas as the self-rationalization, or careerist instrumentality, or at best the depoliticized intellectual plaything, of a late capitalist and privileged intelligentsia, the kind of theory we might expect from yuppies.

Yet there are ways of situating postmodernism historically (conjuncturally, socially, even materially) that don't require this reductive move, theorizing it instead as the "cultural logic" of our late capitalist present. Unfortunately, Joyce declines to take this more sophisticated version on, partly no doubt because the most influential exponent of *this* analysis is at the same time a key theorist of post-modernism itself. For he fails to engage the arguments about late capi-talism of a Fredric Jameson, who speaks in this sense from *inside* the discourse of postmodernity, while historicizing it in a manner at least recognizable, surely, from the perspective of a Palmer or a Kirk.

The critics of postmodernism, and especially those wanting to reaffirm historical materialism, according to Joyce, proceed from a "realist" epistemology that is no longer sustainable. In this manner, Joyce buries the "old" social history in a phrase, as well as some others, including varieties of feminist historical work. This is a truly polemical passage, in the time-honoured destructive sense. First, the object of polemical attack is nowhere adequately spelled out. Second, the argu-ment is supposedly proven before it is fully stated – "the least said of these positions the better."[10] The incantation of a magic hostility against conflation of the "real" and its "representation" is enough in itself to send to perdition those positions and "schools" which the author deplores. This is surely a sectarianism of theory of the purest kind, differentiated from past examples only by the absence of a sectarian political project, the kind meant to cleanse a political world of error (as in Thompson's *The Poverty of Theory*, a model Joyce presumably would be unwilling to embrace).

Joyce claims for himself a particular voice. He speaks on behalf of "contemporary anti-positivism."[11] This position is implicitly attributed to a variety of critics of diverse origins and interests – critics, that is, of the "liberal–left consensus of social history."[12] Speaking for our own part in this debate, we differ from Joyce in the following ways. First, we would argue for a greater generosity in appraising the given achieve-ments of the social history "tradition," which acknowledges the strengths of this body of work on its own terms. Second, we want to insist on the diversity and conflict within the alleged "consensus," a degree of contestation which in Joyce's exposition is wholly effaced. Third, we would point to the enduring elements of the social history project of the 1960s and 1970s, to the substance of what can still be sustained. We are saying in effect: this consensus must be given its due, allowed its coherence, in effect historicized. It is not an obsolete discourse to be entirely forgotten and suppressed, but a field of meanings and analysis, a coherent conjunctural project, which at the very least deserves serious conceptual recuperation. It should be considered at its strongest points by the best it has produced, as opposed to the self-evidently flawed or reductive, or derivative – that is, as complex, and creative, and sophisticated in its particular practice (the actual histories it has managed to produce).[13]

To admit that this corpus has been undertheorized, and insufficiently self-conscious about its own presuppositions and procedures (which may include an under-reflected "realism"), or in some other ways open to criticism, is not at the same time to dispose of it entirely as an "old" social history, which *ipso facto* no longer needs to be addressed. The corpus generated around the supposed consensus has been large, convincing, enriching and internally complex, as well as conceptually capable of change. Its internal divisions – conceptual, empirical – have been extensive, and sometimes ferociously contested (for instance, around issues of "experience," "consciousness," "agency," "base and superstructure", as well as around politics, party and present-day political action). This suggests at the very least that the liberal–left consensus is actually far less "consensual" than Joyce (largely for the ease of his argument, perhaps) invites us to assume.

But what, in fact, did that consensus comprise? We need, surely, some minimum explication of the terms in play. The key, perhaps, has been some strong notion of "social context," and of causalities proceeding outwards and upwards from this in a classical materialist manner. Some notion of social determination, conceptualized on the ground of material life, whether in demographic, political-economic, labour-process, class-sociological or class-cultural terms, generally provided social history with its common tissue of assumptions. This implied a willingness to understand *all* facets of human existence in terms of their social determinations – to "be as much concerned with questions of culture and consciousness as with those of social structure and the material conditions of life," as *Social History*'s first editorial put it.[14] Usually, some commitment to an idea of social totality also accompanied this underlying orientation, but this is perhaps a more contentious claim.

But to share that common explanatory disposition says little or nothing about the chosen objects of study, about empirical and other methods, or about the variety of available theoretical strategies, or the degree of interdisciplinarity, or especially the conceptual relationship with a complex Marxist canon. The amount of explicit or formal Marxism in this "old" social history has been at best modest. Joyce's glib talk about intellectual hegemony and institutional hegemony,[15] let alone the existence of an establishment,[16] shouldn't trick us into misremembering how embattled and maligned the presence of Marxism in academic history has actually been. Joyce gives us no grounds other than his assertion of the existence of this alleged hegemony. Any sociology of this kind of knowledge, or intellectual history of the present, demands a much fuller exposition than this. Joyce's account is so under-specified and under-resourced as to be difficult to engage with critically.

So we wish to formulate a different question, as an invitation to debate: what are the elements of this allegedly consensual project that can still be sustained, and how? The question now is not (*pace* Joyce) one of how to dispose magisterially of the historical materialist project by pronouncing upon it words drawn from a post-structuralist epistemology, whether "realist," or "positivist," or whatever. But nor is the question at issue one of trying to revive whole the social history project in one of its given forms. The question is to try to see, in our view, from a perspective sympathetic to the discourse of poststructuralism and postmodernism, what the continuities might be between this exceedingly complex, non-unitary consensus and the present practices of historical analysis.

What is still useful? What can properly be recuperated into the present practice of history, whether we retain the qualifier "social," or not? This is precisely the basis of our interest in class, precisely the focus of our own thinking: to resist the disavowal of key Marxist and "old" social historical concepts *without* seeking to restore commitment to some version of "realist" Marxist epistemology. We regret the repetition of this last point. But we are all too aware of the propensity of some critics to assume that our argument here is no more than a way "back to the future," a reluctance to face the bleakness of an intellectual world bereft of former realist certainties, a nostalgic, romantic attachment to histories which others claim are finished, a wilful attempt to sneak in by the back door what has been explicitly bade farewell to at the front.[17]

Postmodernism can be an all too satisfactory term for sectarian theoretical position-taking, a portmanteau of meanings inciting partial appropriations, standing service for a deeper and more ramified account of the contemporary discourse of postmodernity. So let's be perfectly clear: we're not disavowing the use of this term, we believe strongly that an adequate social history and a contemporary political analysis need to begin from the insights and recognitions the discourse of the postmodern has announced. On the contrary, what bothers us in Joyce's essentializing practice in respect of the latter, one which authorizes his award of central importance to oversynthesized elements of postmodernism's complex repertoire of meanings and practice. On the one hand the terms postmodernity and postmodernism encompass an incredibly heterogeneous range of contemporary movements and manifestations, phenomena extremely difficult to bring under a single head.[18] Joyce's practice brings a specious order to that turbulence. In Joyce's account, postmodernism is recreated as a group of complex but commensurable positions, flattened into a seductive and spurious singularity. Postmodernism encompasses something much more complex than this, and its distinction from poststructuralism requires to be acknowledged.

There are still other grounds on which Joyce's arguments need to be engaged – and here we mean not just the immediate text under discussion, but his larger *oeuvre* and what it represents. Here, as we have just said, Joyce's usage of the terms "modernity" and "postmodernity/ism" need to be unpacked. Mayfield and Thorne began this in their "Reply"[19] and there is more work still to be done. All we can do here is to signal our intention to contribute further to the explication of these terms in a future publication.[20] There's no question that Patrick Joyce has marked out a territory over the past decade which challenges the complacencies of historians, social and other, and provides an essential context of current debate. There were good grounds as we approached the 1980s, after all, for thinking that social history occupied a central conceptual space in the social sciences, as a result of achievements and histories during the previous two decades which by now we don't need to rehearse. This optimism is in shreds. Joyce deserves our acknowledgement for compelling this recognition. But quite aside from the tones and cadences of his writing, make no mistake, Joyce's arguments are intended to clear the decks, to start anew, to scorch the earth behind. He proclaims the "end of social history" by delegitimizing the conceptual basis on which he *believes* it was founded. At no point does he address the substantial and honourable and concrete historiographical achievements of the field. It is simply not enough to wipe out a scholarly discourse by first essentializing and then delegitimizing what are alleged to be its now superseded forms of knowledge.

We can do better than this. Twenty-five years ago, social history seemed a viable and exciting strategic ground from which to elaborate creative and valuable forms of analysis, and for some of us this was also linked to a politics. In the meantime, the strategic ground has shifted in all sorts of ways towards "culture," above all in two ways: first, in the transformation of the dominant discourses of social analysis; and second, in the necessary sites and purposes of politics, embracing all the familiar contemporary terms, of gender, race, sexuality, region, space, ethnicity, and the disordered micropolitical landscape of democratic citizenship and its characteristic forms of address.

Here we have been talking mainly about class, because Joyce evades the necessary difficulties of reconceptualizing the latter, we feel, at least in the terms that we have tried here to reaffirm. However, the question of class doesn't exhaust the range of difficulty. Axes of social difference formed outside and beyond the familiar habits of class analysis are fundamentally important too, have forced themselves, in fact, into the account. This simultaneity is at the nub of our argument: *none* of these things – the "social," capitalist reproductions and of course the constitutive forms of class itself – are graspable without the priorities which gender, race and the whole range of compelling questions of identity and subjectivity have pressed onto the agenda. The insufficiencies of class are fully a part of our own understanding. We *know* that the conditions and concepts of postmodernity are constitutive for the contemporary intellectual and political project.

But in Joyce's rendition of his own project, we really do resist the evacuation of the imperative to analyse capitalism and its necessary and characteristic inequities. To say that class as a concept has to be problematized differently now is not to give it up completely. To assert that former totalizing takes on "society" can no longer do the job is not to abandon the "social" altogether. To affirm the recognition of the creation, self and other, of subjectivity as a vital part of understanding social practice and relations is not entirely to vacate the analysis of powers and forces operating beyond them.

NOTES

1. See Patrick Joyce, "The end of social history?," *Social History*, xx, 1, January 1995. This substantial intervention in the continuing debate in *Social History* provides the starting-point for our discussion.

2. Consider the extensive and growing debate around these matters in this very journal, and the substantial archive of pertinent reference which it has generated.
3. Lawrence Stone, "History and post-modernism," *Past and Present*, cxxxi, May 1991.
4. Perry Anderson, *Considerations on Western Marxism*, London, 1976.
5. Joyce, op. cit.
6. *Ibid.*, p. 90.
7. *Ibid.*
8. Joyce, op. cit., p. 78. This passage continues in truly polemical style as follows: "The least said of these positions the better, perhaps, though it is unfortunately the case that this kind of apologia for a decaying social history is still given credence in some areas of labour and social history, particularly in the UK."
9. Bryan Palmer, *Descent into Discourse: The Reification of Language and the Writing of Social History*, Philadelphia, 1990.
10. Joyce, op. cit., p. 78.
11. *Ibid.*, pp. 79–80, and n. 26.
12. *Ibid.*, p. 80.
13. Here the archive of possible citation is enormous, requiring a bibliographical essay in itself. For the purpose here, and aside from the elaborated genres of writing on the labour aristocracy, on working-class formation, on artisanal trades and so on, simply consider the sophistication of various social historical approaches to class via community studies: M. Savage, *The Dynamics of Working-class Politics: The Labour Movement in Preston 1880–1940*, Cambridge, 1987; J. Seed, "Unitarianism, political economy and the antinomics of liberal culture in Manchester, 1830–1850," *Social History*, VII, 1, January 1982; R. J. Morris (ed.), *Class, Power and Social Structure in Nineteenth-century British Towns*, Leicester, 1986; J. Foster, *Class Struggle and the Industrial Revolution Early Industrial Capitalism in Three English Towns*, London, 1974; T. Roditschek, *Class Formation and Urban Industrial Society. Bradford 1750–1850*, Cambridge, 1990; P. Joyce, *Work, Society and Politics. The Culture of the Factory in Later Victorian England*, London, 1982.

For twenty years or more, some of the most usable and productive forms of exploring processes of class formation have been centred on community, on locally bounded studies such as these. Their practices are everywhere complex and conceptually sophisticated, never reductive in the senses alleged. The relative inability of this large, rich and complex social historiography to deal with questions composed around gender, or ethnicity or postmodern notations of subjectivity and identity, does not mean they are no longer usable. We have chosen here to focus on British work chiefly because the present debate has arisen on a base of largely British historiography. This is not to neglect the significance of other national historiographics and national voices, and their different saliences.
14. *Social History*, I, 1976.
15. Joyce, op. cit.
16. *Ibid.*, p. 80.
17. We want to stress here that our objective is to *engage* debate, not to polarize it, and what we are doing is not a sleight of hand simply to restore the centrality of class. But nor do we acquiesce in its utter banishment.
18. Postmodernism has produced a huge and burgeoning, variegated and extraordinarily unwieldly literature. Patrick Joyce seems to us to reduce the massive heterogeneity of discussion to one term, one description, using Zygmunt Bauman as his principal authority. Yet the literature continues to expand heterogeneously, and may not be reduced to some essentializing synthetic. If we go back to the release of this term into general currency we find a whole range of more complex takes. Fredric Jameson's important contributions have already been referred to in the text: especially, *Postmodernism, or the Cultural Logic of Late Capitalism*, London, 1990. The journal *Theory, Culture*

and Society, together with the work of its editor, M. Featherstone, has been a very important place of innovations as well as of insistence upon the heterogeneity of the postmodern project. In particular we should mention the "Special Issue on Postmodernism" published as *Theory, Culture and Society,* v. 2–3, June 1988. Of course this brief list could be easily and massively amplified.

19. David Mayfield and Susan Thorne, "Reply to 'The poverty of protest' and 'The imaginary discontents'," *Social History,* xviii, 2, May 1993. Mayfield and Thorne note Joyce's incomplete appropriation of linguistic and other theory: "We therefore find Joyce's effort to drape himself in the mantle of post-structuralism and deconstruction extremely misleading . . . *in this regard,* neither he nor Stedman Jones are quite postmodern or poststructuralist enough" (p. 224). It is surely worth suggesting that this line of criticism might be worth further amplification.

20. We feel somewhat disadvantaged here because Patrick Joyce refers extensively to a paper of ours which is not yet published and which was presented at a conference in Portsmouth in 1993 on "Historical Perspectives on Class and Culture." (See Kelly Boyd and Rohan McWilliam's brief report of this conference in *Social History,* xx, 1, January 1995. Our forthcoming book will be published by University of Michigan Press in 1996.

31 Patrick Joyce

The end of social history? A brief reply to Eley and Nield

It is good that Eley and Nield's response to my article on the future of social history opens up a space for debate between postmodernist and earlier positions,[1] especially the Marxist tradition in social history which these two authors espouse. However, the way in which they do this is not always helpful. Their (often justified) eagerness to defend Marxist traditions from the widespread, contemporary obloquy to which they have been subjected leads them into a complete misrepresentation of my position. They use me as a whipping boy for their own anxiety and anger, and the result, ironically, is to reproduce precisely what they claim to find in my original contribution, namely a tone which means that necessary questions are being raised in a way which makes it unlikely they will be faced. It is not my purpose to "dismiss" or "bury" Marxism, class and social history, as should be plain from the article, and my other published work.[2] Eley and Nield's acute sensitivity leads them at times into reckless and absurd statements, such as the equation of my questioning of social history with contemporary neo-liberalism. Theirs is too often that "denial of creative conversations" of which they accuse me.

Let me turn from the question of tone to substance (not that, in this highly politicized and moralized intellectual context, tone is so easily separable from substance). Eley and Nield make no attempt whatsoever to deal with the points of substance I raised, which I phrased in terms of identity, modernity and structure, as three areas where the challenge of postmodernist thought was especially evident. This being so, it is necessary to turn to their response, where the advocacy of Marxism as "a plural discourse" is central to their position. They call for clear statements of argumentative positions, but ought to heed this call themselves if debate is to go forward fruitfully.

What is the nature of the plurality of Marxism? What is plural about it, and what is singular? They talk, in the singular, of a "plural discourse," and "the whole tradition of Western Marxism." They also speak of "the copious boundaries of the Marxist tradition," and of "fruitful discussion within" Marxism's pluralities. The hard question they don't address is how a genuine plurality can subsist with a singular tradition or discourse which is for them clearly bounded. This is even more acutely raised when they talk of class as the "core concept" of Marxism: what happens to plurality when such a thing as a "core concept" is insisted upon? Eley and Nield ask for a "complex articulation" of class with other terms, and of Marxism with other currents, but one may be forgiven for thinking that the only complex articulation with other terms which they will allow is one that leaves core concepts unchanged and boundaries in place. Which is, of course, no articulation at all. This bears on the question of post-Marxism, which they seem to be appropriating for themselves. But a post-Marxism worthy of the name is a *post*-Marxism as well as a post-*Marxism*.[3] Theirs would seem to be the latter, a Marxism of "core concepts" and "boundaries," a Marxism after the event as it were, as opposed to a position in which the Marxist tradition is fundamentally reworked. "Seem to be" is appropriate, for Eley and Nield's position is not spelled out, and their own words about the sloppiness of notations of Marxism can with justice be returned to them. A debate about the nature of "post-Marxism" and its relationship to history would be greatly productive, and is overdue.

Eley and Nield spend much time talking about class, their "core concept." This, again, is a straw man when it comes to my work. I have not argued that the concept be abandoned, but that it be fundamentally reworked. My doubt, and my concern, is that this reworking cannot be generated out of the Marxist tradition, certainly as Eley and Nield seem to conceive it. This is especially apparent in their depiction of the "liberal left consensus" of social history, for which class was, and is, of central importance. This, of course, is *their* picture (one I tend to agree with, and indeed amply drew upon in my article in the form of their conference paper, which I cited). There, and in "Starting over", to my view rightly, they depict Marxism as providing the theoretical stiffening and even more the unstated theoretical "common sense" wisdom of social history. Of course, others will have a different account of social history. Given its heterogeneity, which I indicated in my article, this is not surprising. I was far from providing a history of social history. The provision of a detailed history would be of immense benefit to the thinking going into the reformulation of social history.

But this is not my present point, which is Eley and Nield's depiction of the social history consensus. Their attitude to this consensus is a ground for my concern about the capacity of at least some Marxist traditions to rework fundamental concepts. They depict this consensus as follows (whether rightly or wrongly not being my present point): the notion of "social context" is central, of "causalities proceeding outwards and upwards from this in a classical materialist manner." Equally important is the idea of "social determination," "conceptualized on the ground of material life." All facets of human existence are to be understood in terms of such "social determinations." Finally, a commitment to the idea of a "social totality" also accompanied this "underlying orientation" and "explanatory disposition." Conceptualized thus, they see this orientation as containing elements of enduring value. Their desire is to rescue what is of value in it (not that they tell us what is). To me, however, this outlook seems entirely reductive. It is decidedly essentialist in character, "the social" and "the material" taking reified forms. They profess to embrace postmodernism (in however a one-armed way), but neglect (or are unaware of?) the need to fundamentally rethink positions. Eley and Nield begin to look like old-fashioned base-superstructure men after all. My discussion of the concept of structure in "The end of social history?" opened some of the way here, concerned as it was with the relation of structure and action, so central to Marxism and social history. Eley and Nield make no reference to this, a crucial area for the whole debate.

As to the question of whether the "underlying orientation" and "explanatory disposition" of social history, as given by Eley and Nield, is correct or incorrect, I can only say here that we draw very different conclusions from our shared view that this is a passably accurate depiction (not that it is not in need of much development and qualification). Eley and Nield consider my view of social history to be reductive, even though it was taken from their own account. If social history, as they present it, is not reductive, then one would be hard pressed to find anything deserving the adjective.

Finally, some particular, and one more general point. It is disingenuous to try to recruit Foucault as a fellow-traveller of Marxism. He was (in)famous for ignoring it. And it is ingenuous to depict Fredric Jameson as a postmodernist critic of postmodernism. Ultimately, Jameson is firmly modernist and Marxist. Their reading of Jameson strongly indicates the need to bring different versions of postmodernism and postmodernity into open discussion (I am agreed with Eley and

Nield about this). They note my debt to Zygmunt Bauman's work, which is indeed considerable. His postmodernist critique of contemporary consumer capitalism is trenchant and profound. In being influenced by this (non-Marxist) critique of capitalism, I bridle at being lectured by Eley and Nield about the "evacuation of the imperative to analyse capitalism and its necessary and characteristic inequalities." Marxists should not be so quick to take the moral high ground in this way (particularly given the deficiencies of so much Marxist history of capitalism). So, contrary to what the two affirm, mine is not a "sectarianism of theory" differentiated from others by "the absence of a sectarian political project." We all have political projects, in which past and present ought to force us to disclose these projects, for it is new and troubling relationships with the changing conditions of our society which are at the root of the need to rethink social history. A dialogue between postmodernist thought and Marxism is possible and necessary, indeed imperative, but much ground still remains to be cleared. It is to be hoped that dialogue will go forward in a spirit of critical co-operation (one in which post-Marxism is not the exclusive possession of any one party). It is time to emphasize common purposes as well as differences. As for myself, I have never had the slightest desire to deny *tout court* the validity of social history, class and Marxism, only *particular* readings of all three, and the relationship between them, and I reject Eley and Nield's stereotyping of my position.

NOTES

1. Patrick Joyce, "The end of social history," *Social History*, xx, 1, January 1995; Geoff Eley and Keith Nield, "Starting over: the present, the postmodern and the moment of social history," *Social History*, xx, 3, October 1995, I should like to thank Patrick Curry for his comments on the latter.
2. The most recent of which Eley and Nield do not consider: Patrick Joyce, *Democratic Subjects: The Self and the Social in Nineteenth Century England*, Cambridge, 1994; *The Oxford Reader on Class*, Oxford, 1995.
3. Patrick Curry, "Towards a post-Marxist social history: Thompson, Clark, and beyond" in Adrian Wilson (ed.), *Rethinking Social History: English Society 1750–1920 and its Interpretation*, Manchester, 1993.

EDITOR'S INTRODUCTION

HISTORY AND THEORY, AND SAUL FRIEDLANDER (ED.) *PROBING THE LIMITS OF REPRESENTATION*: THE HOLOCAUST DEBATE

In 1992, *Probing the Limits of Representation* – a collection of articles much derived from a conference on representations of the Holocaust held at the University of California and edited by Saul Friedlander – was published. As Friedlander explained in his Introduction, the majority of the contributors to the volume were not necessarily scholars of the 1930s and 1940s but were historians and theorists interested in whether the Holocaust could be adequately represented and, if so, how. Friedlander's point is that the extermination of the Jews of Europe is, at one level, as accessible to representation as any other event of the past, but that in these poststructural, postmodern days wherein such events are indeed only known as representations – are indeed narrativized into existence as representations – in order to remember the Holocaust as it actually was then it seems that it should not be "distorted" or "banalized" by grossly inadequate representations . . . that "some claim to 'truth' appears particularly imperative." This suggests, as Friedlander adds, that there are limits to representation "which should not be but can easily be transgressed." Consequently, the essays of the volume variously rotate around the problem of whether such limits exist and, if so, if they could be enforced universally so that the resultant representations would be not so much "impositions" or "readings" or "positioned narratives" at all, but "the truth."

I give here a few pages from Friedlander's Introduction, pages especially dealing with his fear that Hayden White's postmodern position denies such a truth. As Friedlander puts it:

> White's by now familiar position aims at systematising a theory of historical interpretation based on a fundamental redefinition of traditional historical understanding. Language as such imposes on the historical narrative a limited choice of rhetorical forms, implying specific emplotments, explicative models, and ideological stances. These unavoidable choices determine the specificity of various interpretations of historical events. There is no "objective" outside criterion to establish that one particular interpretation is more true than another . . . White is [thus] close to what could be termed a postmodern approach to history.
>
> (p. 6)

I then give the beginning of White's own article in Friedlander's collection –

"Historical Emplotment and the Problem of Truth" – wherein his allegedly partial qualification of his relativism (a qualification alleged by Friedlander) is outlined. I then leave Friedlander's volume and move to four articles which appeared in 1994–5 in the pages of *History and Theory* and which pick up the issue of the representation of the Holocaust.

As indicated above, *History and Theory* is arguably the foremost philosophy of history journal in existence. In 1994, a large part of volume 33(2) was given over to a Forum entitled "Representing The Holocaust." In it Hans Kellner, Wulf Kansteiner and Robert Braun attacked historical realism and the possibility of finding "the facts" in order to get the Holocaust "story" straight. Either implicitly or explicitly they took a Hayden White line; parts of their articles are given here. In 1995, the philosopher Berel Lang replied to Kellner *et al.*, again in the pages of *History and Theory*, namely in his article, "Is it Possible to Misrepresent the Holocaust?" Lang's article is reproduced in full here.

It seems to me that this is a crucially important debate. For if – and this is in part Lang's argument – "facts" are to be significant, they can only gain that significance through being narrativized. This narrativization in its emplotment and troping confers on the facts a significance which a different emplotment and troping could take away. In effect the facts are narrative dependent and truth (facticity) is essentially an interpretive matter. Thus what happens if narratives produce different, even contradictory facts (significance)? How can these be then factually adjudicated except by what can only be another interpretation of the facts? And what if stories about the Holocaust cease to be told? This reminds me of Geras' statement, as noted in the Introduction to this volume; namely that if there is no Truth there is no injustice. For what could an injustice really be if there is no such thing as Injustice to act as the criterion? If there is no way of saying an account of what took place is factually true, then what is to stop any account, if it has the power to get away with it, to say its facts represent/constitute the truth? In other words – and this is what concerns Friedlander and many of the contributors to his volume (which incidentally included Berel Lang) – is might right? Well, it seems difficult to claim that this is not the case; that we live and have always lived within Foucault's "regimes of truth" and that philosophy, as Richard Rorty and Barbara Hernstein Smith have put it, may have to come to terms with this situation (for a limited discussion of Rorty on this point see, for example, my *On "What is History?": From Carr and Elton to Rorty and White* and, for a wider discussion – and advocacy of relativism – see B. H. Smith's *Contingencies of Value*, Cambridge, Mass., Harvard University Press, 1988, which bears very much on the concerns of Friedlander *et al.*). Be that as it may, however, the problematicization of the

Holocaust urgently raises the question of what might be the limits of historical representation in these postmodern (and indeed other) days.

32 Saul Friedlander

Probing the limits of representation

INTRODUCTION

> When I went into our little office this morning, it was a terrible
> mess; it had been requisitioned as a dressing room for the [musical]
> revue. The revue is taking over the whole camp. There are no overalls
> for people on outside duty, but the revue has an "overall ballet" –
> so day and night people sewed overalls with little puffed sleeves for
> the dancers. Wood from the synagogue in Assen has been sawed up
> to make a stage . . . Oh, Maria, Maria – Before the last transport, the
> people who were due to leave worked all day for the revue. Every-
> thing here has an indescribably clownish madness and sadness.

> Letter from Etty Hillesum to a friend, Westerbork camp (Holland),
> 2 September 1943. Hillesum died in Auschwitz on 30 November
> 1943.

Most of the contributors to this volume are not the usual interlocutors
in discussions of the Holocaust: although a few of them are scholars
who have dealt extensively with issues related to Nazism and the extermination of the Jews of Europe, the majority are not. The aim here is
not to deal with a specific historical aspect of these events or with their
particular expression in literature, in the arts, or in philosophy. The
underlying assumption is that we are dealing with an event of a kind
which demands a global approach and a general reflection on the difficulties that are raised by its representation.

This project evokes some doubts which are not easily dispelled. Can
the extermination of the Jews of Europe be the object of theoretical
discussions? Is it not unacceptable to debate formal and abstract issues
in relation to this catastrophe? It would be if these abstract issues were
not directly related to the way contemporary culture reshapes the image

of this past. Present memory of Nazism and its crimes is directly influenced by global intellectual shifts intrinsically linked to the questions raised in this volume. The necessity of such discussion is thus clear; it will be evident, moreover, that none of the contributors has forgotten the horror behind the words.

The basic problem we shall be dealing with has been on the minds of many since the very end of the war, and Theodor Adorno's (often misunderstood) utterance about writing poetry after Auschwitz has turned into its best-known point of reference. Nonetheless, the challenge has become more perceptible during the last two decades, as the result of an ongoing shaping and reshaping of the image of the Nazi epoch. During the seventies, film and literature opened the way to some sort of "new discourse." Historiography followed and the mid-eighties witnessed heated debates about new interpretations of the "Final Solution" in history (the best-known of these debates being the German "historians' controversy") and, in more general terms, about the proper historicization of National Socialism, that is, of "Auschwitz." In these various domains new narratives about Nazism came to the fore, new forms of representation appeared. In many cases they seemed to test implicit boundaries and to raise not only aesthetic and intellectual problems, but moral issues too. The question of the limits of representation of Nazism and its crimes has become a recurrent theme in relation to various concrete subjects. Here the overall aspect of this problem is our main concern.

The immediate incentive for the conference leading to this volume was a debate which took place in 1989 on "History, Event, and Discourse," during which Hayden White and Carlo Ginzburg presented opposing views on the nature of historical truth. The echoes of such a debate were reinforced by still-lingering controversies on the historicization of Nazism. The extermination of the Jews of Europe, as the most extreme case of mass criminality, must challenge theoreticians of historical relativism to face the corollaries of positions otherwise too easily dealt with on an abstract level. Of course the basic questions asked here refer also to forms of representation other than the historical.

The very nature of this project called for the expression of a great diversity of views, some of which I have reservations about. Therefore, this introduction is not merely a traditional presentation and pulling-together of the themes raised by the contributors from the point of view of a "neutral" editor; it is equally the expression of a personal stand.

The extermination of the Jews of Europe is as accessible to both representation and interpretation as any other historical event. But we are dealing
with an event which tests our traditional conceptual and representational categories, an "event at the limits."

* * *

The issue of historical knowledge, of historical "truth," which is at the
origin of this debate, must be referred to at the very outset. It is at this
initial point that the implications of Hayden White's positions can be
confronted. White does not call into question the possibility of assessing
the reality or even the exactness of historical *events*. But a mere enumeration of events leaves us at best with annals or a chronicle. In order to
provide a full-fledged historical narrative, a coherent emplotment
linking beginning, middle, and end within a specific *framework of interpretation* is unavoidable.

White's by now familiar position aims at systematizing a theory of
historical interpretation based on a fundamental redefinition of traditional historical understanding: language as such imposes on the
historical narrative a limited choice of rhetorical forms, implying specific
emplotments, explicative models, and ideological stances. These
unavoidable choices determine the specificity of various interpretations
of historical events. There is no "objective," outside criterion to establish
that one particular interpretation is more true than another. In that sense
White is close to what could be termed a postmodern approach to
history.

In his 1982 article, "The Politics of Historical Interpretation," White
suggested that traditional historiography has repressed the indeterminacy of the "sublime." The one exception in this regard is, according to
him, the fascist view of history. "The kind of perspective on history I
have been implicitly praising," he wrote, "is conventionally associated
with the ideologies of fascist regimes. Something like Schiller's notion
of the historical sublime or Nietzsche's version of it is certainly present
in the thought of such philosophers as Heidegger and Gentile and in
the intuitions of Hitler and Mussolini." However, he added, "We must
guard against a sentimentalism that would lead us to write off such a
conception of history simply because it has been associated with fascist
ideologies. *One must face the fact that when it comes to apprehending the
historical record, there are no grounds to be found in the historical record itself
for preferring one way of construing its meaning over another*" (my italics).
Although White has recognized the transparent horrors of fascism as
well as the dilemma stemming from his extreme relativism, he has not

offered any solution before attempting a compromise position in this volume.

For most historians a precise description of the unfolding of events is meant to carry its own interpretation, its own truth. This, for instance, is the impact of the empirical evidence presented in Christopher Browning's account of the murderous trail of *Ordnungspolizei* Unit 101 from Hamburg when transferred to the small Polish (Jewish) town of Jozefów on 13 July 1942. Browning's extremely detailed and precise description of the behavior of this unit and of individuals belonging to it, showing the passage from the "normality" of an ordinary police formation to its functioning as an instrument of mass murder, intuitively substantiates an interpretative framework which extends far beyond the history of this particular set of events. For Browning "there are no clearly distinct and separate categories of attestable fact on the one hand and pure interpretation on the other. Rather there is a spectrum or continuum": the very mass of ascertainable facts pertaining to the "Final Solution" determines the overall interpretation, not the other way around. There is still, however, the question of how one moves from the chronicle (Hayden White would probably consider Browning's harrowing account in the category of the chronicle) to levels of historiography where interpretive frameworks are determinant, notwithstanding the abundance of available material.

Whereas Christopher Browning's critique of White adopts in fact the "thick description" position, Amos Funkenstein attempts to demonstrate the paradox to which White's relativism may lead, by invoking the polemical-rhetorical genre of "counterhistory." He, too, however, has to substantiate the fact that some exercises in "worldmaking" are less arbitrary than others, by referring to an intuitive criterion not unlike Browning's. "If true," he writes, "reality, whatever its definition, must 'shine through it' [the narrative] like Heidegger's being – and, like the latter, without ever appearing directly."

Perry Anderson's critique confronts White's analytic categories directly. At the end of his analysis of one of the core texts of the "historians' debate," Andreas Hillgruber's *Zweierlei Untergang*, Anderson writes:

> First, certain absolute limits are set by the evidence. Denial of the existence of either – the regime or its crimes – is plainly ruled out. . . . Narrative strategies, to be credible, always operate within *exterior* limits of this kind. Second, however, such narrative strategies are in

turn subject to a double *interior* limitation. On the one hand, certain kinds of evidence preclude certain sorts of emplotment: the Final Solution cannot *historically* be written as romance or as comedy. On the other hand, any generic emplotment has only a weak determinative power over the selection of evidence. Hillgruber could legitimately depict the end of East Prussia as tragic; that choice, however, permitted by the evidence, did not in itself dictate the series of particular empirical judgments that make up his account of it.

Although the criticism of White's positions mentioned thus far opts for an epistemological approach, Carlo Ginzburg's passionate plea for historical objectivity and truth is as much informed by a deeply ethical position as by analytic categories. Ginzburg quotes a letter from the French historian Pierre Vidal-Naquet referring to the controversy, launched in France by "revisionists" such as Robert Faurisson, about the existence or nonexistence of gas chambers in the Nazi camps. "I was convinced that there was an ongoing discourse on gas chambers," writes Vidal-Naquet, "that everything should necessarily go through to a discourse; but beyond this, or before this, there was something irreducible which, for better or worse, I would still call reality. Without this reality, how could we make a difference between fiction and history?" Here we are indeed – as Hayden White himself perceived – at the "irreducible" core of our discussions; here we are confronted with the unavoidable link between the ethical and the epistemological dimensions of our debate.

33 Hayden White

Historical emplotment and the problem of truth

There is an inexpungeable relativity in every representation of historical phenomena. The relativity of the representation is a function of the language used to describe and thereby constitute past events as possible objects of explanation and understanding. This is obvious when, as in the social sciences, a technical language is so used. Scientific explanations openly purport to bear upon only those aspects of events – for example, quantitative and therefore measurable aspects – which can be denoted by the linguistic protocols used to describe them. It is less obvious in traditional narrative accounts of historical phenomena: first, narrative is regarded as a neutral "container" of historical fact, a mode of discourse "naturally" suited to representing historical events directly; second, narrative histories usually employ so-called natural or ordinary, rather than technical, languages, both to describe their subjects and to tell their story; and third, historical events are supposed to consist of or manifest a congeries of "real" or "lived" stories, which have only to be uncovered or extracted from the evidence and displayed before the reader to have their truth recognized immediately and intuitively.

Obviously I regard this view of the relation between historical storytelling and historical reality as mistaken or at best misconceived. Stories, like factual statements, are linguistic entities and belong to the order of discourse.

The question that arises with respect to "historical emplotments" in a study of Nazism and the Final Solution is this: Are there any limits on the *kind* of story that can responsibly be told about these phenomena? *Can* these events be responsibly emplotted in *any* of the modes, symbols, plot types, and genres our culture provides for "making sense" of such extreme events in our past? Or do Nazism and the Final Solution belong to a special class of events, such that, unlike even the French Revolution, the American Civil War, the Russian Revolution, or the Chinese Great

Leap Forward, they must be viewed as manifesting only one story, as being emplottable in one way only, and as signifying only one kind of meaning? In a word, do the natures of Nazism and the Final Solution set absolute limits on what can be truthfully said about them? Do they set limits on the uses that can be made of them by writers of fiction or poetry? Do they lend themselves to emplotment in a set number of ways, or is their specific meaning, like that of other historical events, infinitely interpretable and ultimately undecidable?

Saul Friedlander has elsewhere distinguished between two kinds of questions that might arise in the consideration of historical emplotments and the problem of "truth": epistemological questions raised by the fact of "*competing* narratives about the Nazi epoch and the 'Final Solution'" and ethical questions raised by the rise of "representations of Nazism . . . based on what used to be [regarded as] *unacceptable* modes of emplotment." Obviously, considered as accounts of events already established as facts, "competing narratives" can be assessed, criticized, and ranked on the basis of their fidelity to the factual record, their comprehensiveness, and the coherence of whatever arguments they may contain. But narrative accounts do not consist only of factual statements (singular existential propositions) and arguments; they consist as well of poetic and rhetorical elements by which what would otherwise be a list of facts is transformed into a story. Among these elements are those generic story patterns we recognize as providing the "plots." Thus, one narrative account may represent a set of events as having the form and meaning of an epic or tragic story, and another may represent the same set of events – with equal plausibility and without doing any violence to the factual record – as describing a farce. Here the conflict between "competing narratives" has less to do with the facts of the matter in question than with the different story-meanings with which the facts can be endowed by emplotment. This raises the question of the relation of the various generic plot types that can be used to endow events with different kinds of meaning – tragic, epic, comic, romance, pastoral, farcical, and the like – to the events themselves. Is this relationship between a given story told about a given set of events the same as that obtaining between a factual statement and its referent? Can it be said that sets of real events *are* intrinsically tragic, comic, or epic, such that the representation of those events as a tragic, comic, or epic story can be assessed as to its *factual* accuracy? Or does it all have to do with the perspective from which the events are viewed?

Of course, most theorists of narrative history take the view that emplotment produces not so much another, more comprehensive and synthetic factual statement as, rather, an *interpretation* of the facts. But the distinction between factual statements (considered as a product of object-language) and interpretations of them (considered as a product of one or more metalanguages) does not help us when it is a matter of interpretations produced by the modes of emplotment used to represent the facts as displaying the form and meaning of different kinds of stories. We are not helped by the suggestion that "competing narratives" are a result of "the facts" having been *interpreted* by one historian as a "tragedy" and *interpreted* by another as a "farce." This is especially the case in traditional historical discourse in which "the facts" are always given precedence over any "interpretation" of them.

Thus for traditional historical discourse there is presumed to be a crucial difference between an "interpretation" of "the facts" and a "story" told about them. This difference is indicated by the currency of the notions of a "real" (as against an "imaginary") story and a "true" (as against a "false") story. Whereas interpretations are typically thought of as commentaries on "the facts," the stories told in narrative histories are presumed to inhere either in the events themselves (whence the notion of a "real story") or in the facts derived from the critical study of evidence bearing upon those events (which yields the notion of the "true" story).

Considerations such as these provide some insight into the problems both of competing narratives and of unacceptable modes of emplotment in considering a period such as the Nazi epoch and events such as the Final Solution. We can confidently presume that the facts of the matter set limits on the *kinds* of stories that can be *properly* (in the sense of both veraciously and appropriately) told about them only if we believe that the events themselves possess a "story" kind of form and a "plot" kind of meaning. We may then dismiss a "comic" or "pastoral" story, with an upbeat "tone" and a humorous "point of view," from the ranks of competing narratives as manifestly false to the facts – or at least to the facts that *matter* – of the Nazi era. But we could dismiss such a story from the ranks of competing narratives only if (1) it were presented as a *literal* (rather than *figurative*) representation of the events and (2) the plot type used to transform the facts into a specific kind of story were presented as inherent in (rather than imposed upon) the facts. For unless a historical story is presented as a literal representation of real events, we cannot criticize it as being either true or untrue to the facts of the matter. If it were presented as a figurative representation of real events, then the question of its truthfulness would fall under the principles governing our assessment of the truth of fictions. And if it did not suggest that the plot type chosen to render the facts into a story of a specific kind had been found to inhere in the facts themselves, then we would have no basis for comparing this particular account to other kinds of narrative accounts, informed by other kinds of plot types, and for assessing their relative adequacy to the representation, not so much of the facts as of what the facts *mean*.

For the differences among competing *narratives* are differences among the "modes of emplotment" which predominate in them. It is because narratives are always emplotted that they are meaningfully comparable; it is because narratives are differently emplotted that discriminations among the kinds of plot types can be made. In the case of an emplotment of the events of the Third Reich in a "comic" or "pastoral" mode, we would be eminently justified in appealing to "the facts" in order to dismiss it from the lists of "competing narratives" of the Third Reich. But what if a story of this kind had been set forth in a pointedly ironic way and in the interest of making a metacritical comment, not so much on the facts as on versions of the facts emplotted in a comic or pastoral way? Surely it would be beside the point to dismiss *this* kind of narrative from the competition on the basis of its infidelity to the facts. For even if it were not positively faithful to the facts, it would at least be negatively so – in the fun it poked at narratives of the Third Reich emplotted in the mode of comedy or pastoral.

On the other hand, we might wish to regard such an ironic emplotment as "unacceptable" in the manner suggested by Friedlander in his indictment of histories, novels, and films which, under the guise of seeming to portray faithfully the most horrible facts of life in Hitler's Germany, actually aestheticize the whole scene and translate its contents into fetish objects and the stuff of sadomasochistic fantasies. As Friedlander has pointed out, such "glamorizing" representations of the phenomena of the Third Reich used to be "unacceptable," whatever the accuracy or veracity of their factual contents, because they offended against morality or taste. The fact that such representations have become increasingly common and therefore obviously more "acceptable" over the last twenty years or so indicates profound changes in socially sanctioned standards of morality and taste. But what does *this* circumstance suggest about the grounds on which we might wish to judge a narrative account of the Third Reich and the Final Solution to be "unacceptable" even though its factual content is both accurate and ample?

It seems to be a matter of distinguishing between a specific body of factual "contents" and a specific "form" of narrative and of applying the kind of rule which stipulates that a serious theme – such as mass murder or genocide – demands a noble genre – such as epic or tragedy – for its proper representation. This is the kind of issue posed by Art Spiegelman's *Maus: A Survivor's Tale*, which presents the events of the Holocaust in the medium of the (black-and-white) comic book and in a mode of bitter satire, with Germans portrayed as cats, Jews as mice, and Poles as pigs. The manifest content of Spiegelman's comic book is the story of the artist's effort to extract from his father the story of his parents' experience of the events of the Holocaust. Thus, the story of the Holocaust that is told in the book is framed by a story of how this story came to be told. But the manifest contents of both the frame story and the framed story are, as it were, compromised as fact by their allegorization as a game of cat-and-mouse-and-pig in which everyone – perpetrators, victims, and bystanders in the story of the Holocaust and both Spiegelman and his father in the story of *their* relationship – comes out looking more like a beast than like a human being. *Maus* presents a particularly ironic and bewildered view of the Holocaust, but it is at the same time one of the most moving narrative accounts of it that I know, and not least because it makes the difficulty of discovering and telling the whole truth about even a small part of it as much a part of the story as the events whose meaning it is seeking to discover.

To be sure, *Maus* is not a conventional history, but it is a representation of past real events or at least of events that are represented as having actually occurred. There is nothing of that aestheticization of which Friedlander complains in his assessments of many recent filmic and novelistic treatments of the Nazi epoch and the Final Solution. At the same time, this comic book is a masterpiece of stylization, figuration, and allegorization. It assimilates the events of the Holocaust to the conventions of comic book representation, and in this absurd mixture of a "low" genre with events of the most momentous significance, *Maus* manages to raise all of the crucial issues regarding the "limits of representation" in general.

34 Hans Kellner

"Never again" is now

The tacit presumption by writers and readers of history is that the magnitude of an event is dependent upon the magnitude of its cause. Great events have great causes, and chance is unacceptable on moral grounds. Battle history is held in low esteem because it so often seems to hinge upon the courage or ineptness of small groups of soldiers, or of one. "All for the want of a horseshoe nail," goes the old rhyme, and few are willing to believe that kingdoms may be lost so trivially.[1] To believe that would remove one from the realm of linear understanding, the linear equations that describe its operation, and the linear narrative force of its explanations. Yet, as Donald McCloskey has recently suggested in this journal, the mathematics of nonlinearity reinforces the possibility of an absurd disproportion, an unpredictability of cause and effect: "As students of chaos theory since Poincaré have pointed out, simple models can generate astonishingly complicated patterns. The slightest perturbation can yield an entirely different history. (And in catastrophe theories, quickly.)"[2] McCloskey may jibe that "one does not avoid nonlinearities by not knowing what they are called," but I think that this is precisely what is avoided.[3] It is the diction, the speech register, the decorum of mathematics that rules it out of historical consideration for matters outside the griminess of economics. Humans are presumed to live stories, not equations.

This problem is called to mind by the exchange of letters between Hannah Arendt and Karl Jaspers shortly after World War II. Arendt: "The Nazi crimes, it seems to me, explode the limits of the law, and that is precisely what constitutes their monstrousness. For these crimes, no punishment is severe enough. It may be essential to hang Goering, but it is totally inadequate. That is, the guilt, in contrast to all criminal guilt, oversteps and shatters any and all legal systems. That is the reason why the Nazis in Nuremberg are so smug."[4] What is the law that Arendt believed was exploded, overstepped, and shattered by the actions of the defendants at Nuremberg? Why did she feel that hanging Goering was inadequate? Surely she did not have a more theatrical treatment, like public torture, in mind. Her expressed frustration, I think, was that no available conclusion to the drama was adequate to the events. The stage of representation offered by the Nuremberg courtroom and its noose was absurdly disproportionate to the acts represented. In wishing to emplot the events of the Holocaust as beyond emplotment, she dreamed of an imaginary mode of representation that would place the characters and their deeds in a proper relation to reality.

But no such mode of representation existed, as Jaspers knew, and prudent wisdom must see things within the bounds and psychological necessities of audience expectations. So Jaspers replied, "a guilt that goes beyond all criminal guilt inevitably takes on a streak of 'greatness' – of satanic greatness – which is, for me, as inappropriate for the Nazis as all the talk about the 'demonic' element in Hitler and so forth." Jaspers saw immediately that the situation was literary. The cast of characters at Nuremberg would be seen in a context of culturally available models; above all, he wanted to deny them the grandeur of the Miltonic Satan or of Goethe's "demon." The great revenge he proposed would be that of the critic, to deny any stature at all to the actors. "It seems to me that we have to see these things in their total banality, in their prosaic triviality, because that's what truly characterizes them. Bacteria can cause epidemics that wipe out nations, but they remain merely bacteria. I regard any hint of myth and legend with horror, and everything unspecific is just such a hint." And, to be sure, Arendt took his point. Evil in her Eichmann book would be banal. The furor over the "banality of evil" that dominated Holocaust discussions in the 1960s derived from the point McCloskey makes, that we take as a historical given that great events have great causes. But horseshoe nails or brave junior officers at key places on a battlefield at crucial moments may decisively change the course of things, assuming that things have a course.

Hilberg stresses that the most important fact about the Holocaust was its unexpectedness. This is an essential part of history, which I have described elsewhere as its "terror."[5] What is particular about the Holocaust, as opposed to the Terror of the French Revolution, is not that it was unforeseen (almost everything is), but that it cannot be made to seem inevitable through narrativization. It is hard to make any story that accounts for this event; perhaps it is misleading to try.[6] Challenging the rhetoric of "large causes – large effects," even the logic of cause and effect itself, the Holocaust is a scandal for rational representation. A writer about the Holocaust will either be seen as adding what does not belong, or omitting something that does. The unprocessed oral reports of witnesses will tell us many things, but not about the Holocaust, because no one witnessed the Holocaust.

So the question arises whether a special kind of representation may be found, suitable for coping with the special nature of this event. Berel Lang and Hayden White have separately posed this question. Implicitly acknowledging the "rules" cited by Hilberg, they see the key to preserving the "responsible," "proper" representations of the Holocaust in maintaining a restricted discourse before it. This is what Lang and White call for in their advocacies of a literalism and a writerly intransitivity, respectively.[7] Something must be silenced, and each of them conceives of that something as a form of language use.

White finds in the ancient Greek grammatical form of the "middle voice" a possible way of avoiding the unwanted intrusion of the subject into the action it wants to represent. In this form, "the subject is presumed to be interior to the action."[8] As he works it out, the rhetorical stance of the middle voice asserts the disappearance of the writer, dissolution of any point of view outside the work, the questioning of epistemological assumptions, and the use of chance characteristic of modernist writing. In short, it seems to be the sort of modernist historiography that he has called for since *History and Theory* published "The Burden of History" in 1966.

White's suggestion that a certain sort of language found under the heading of modernism is available which might prove suitable for putatively *special sorts of events* is challenging. The essence of intransitive writing seems to be that it erases the separation of subject and object that dominates the terminology of linguistic "voice" in normal usage. Active voice ("I kick you") and passive voice ("I am being kicked" [by you]) both separate the world from the position of the speaker as he or she speaks. There are, however, ways of seeing the world that efface the distinction and create a more fluid sense of things. To use an analogy, Barry Manilow sings "I write the songs" actively; a passive phrasing (and reversal of perspective) of this would be "I am written by the songs" or perhaps "The songs write (me?)"; a middle-voiced phrasing would be "I am the song and it (I) is (am) writing me (it)." This last example, which is not so absurd as it seems when seen in a Heideggerian context in which "language speaks," throws attention on the being of the agents (subject, object) and their mutual involvement in the historical moment of writing.

The middle voice of ancient Greek is far older than the passive, a latecomer in Indo-European languages. It corresponds somewhat to modern reflexive sentences ("I am washing myself") or it may be transitive in a certain way (as in the Greek *loúomai khitôna*, "I am washing [my] shirt," or the French *Je me lave une chemise*, "I am washing [myself] a shirt"). Thus, there are two forms of middle voice.

> From the glosses that have been attached to some of the examples it will be clear that the subject of the "middle" can be interpreted as "non-agentive" or "agentive" according to the context or the meaning of the verb; and, if the subject is taken as "non-agentive," it can also be identified in certain instances with the object of a corresponding transitive sentence in the active voice. Under these conditions, the distinction between the middle and the passive is neutralized.[9]

White seems to want a poststructuralist version of the middle voice, which will not give way to the passive under the pressure of context. (The linguist Lyons's example of this is the middling "I am getting [myself] shaved" becoming the passive "I am being shaved.") White's version suggests rather that the intransitivity of the middle voice is the answer to Yeats's question "How can we tell the dancer from the dance?" by denoting that the ambiguity derives from a poor fit between reality and language. There is an undecidability here which can be glossed only by changing the terms. (This middle voice would almost be the voice of the Zen Buddhist who told the hot dog vendor, "Make me one with everything.")

When Roland Barthes put the concept of the middle voice into circulation among literary theorists at the fabled Johns Hopkins structuralism conference in 1966, he was immediately interrogated by members of his audience. Jean-Pierre Vernant posed (and answered) the question why the middle voice had in effect died out in most Western languages. Vernant's answer had to do with responsibility and the developing Greek sense of self (or subjecthood, as one says today):

> The psychological conclusion that Benveniste doesn't draw, because he is not a psychologist, is that in thought as expressed in Greek or ancient Indo-European there is no idea of the agent being the *source* of his action. Or, if I may translate that, as a historian of Greek

civilization, there is no category of the *will* in Greece. But what we see in the Western world, through language, the evolution of law, the creation of a vocabulary of the will, is precisely the idea of the human subject as agent, the source of actions, creating them, assuming them, carrying responsibility for them.[10]

So I conclude that the middle voice, once a relic from before the birth of the subject, is what may be spoken again after the death of the subject, the death of the author, and so forth, these "deaths" being understood as the figural signs of an awareness of the historicity of discourse and the situated nature of any speech act.[11] In fact, if one acknowledges the social construction of the self and reality, or at least their effective linguistic construction as we can know them, all utterances may be understood as middle-voiced, even when they are not explicitly so. For example, Caesar's "all Gaul is divided into three parts" might be read as "Gaul is having its tripartite being hailed here, now." (Is this the same Hayden White who wrote, "But the moral implications of the human sciences will never be perceived until the faculty of the will is reinstated in theory"?[12]) The will finds its expression in rhetoric, which is entailed in any use of language which involves free choice among socially sanctioned alternatives. The will and the restricted middle voice find themselves in tension.

White cites Art Spiegelman's *Maus: A Survivor's Tale*, a comic strip account of a man's confrontation with his father and his father's experience of the Holocaust and Auschwitz. Although White does not associate *Maus* with the middle voice he is promoting, I suggest that it is an instructive example of the middle-voiced *stance* White advocates. Spiegelman is both the author of his work and a character in it. The subject is both the Holocaust and the process of writing about it; within the text, there is no distinguishing between the two because each intrudes upon the other constantly. Spiegelman, one might say, is neither active nor passive. He does not create his tale (and yet he does), but it does not happen to him (and yet it does). He is part of the event of its creation, which changes him. His evidence, his father, is difficult; their relationship is not at all objective or stable. Memory and its vagaries plays a role at every turn. The story is Spiegelman's and it is not. It is his father's, and it is not. The willful authority of these figures is present in the narrative, but it is always questioned and undermined. Finally, as I read it, the story of *Maus* and its sequel becomes no one's story, but without asserting a falsifiable claim to objective realism.

Writing the kind of self-reflexive history that places the historian in the moment – or better, process – of creating the historical text, enacting the work of research, has its current exemplars and theoreticians. Robert Rosentone's *Mirror in the Shrine: American Encounters with Meiji Japan* (Cambridge, Mass., 1988), begins with his encounter with Japan, and contrasts his feelings and experiences confronting the foreignness of Japan with those of his chosen texts. Linda Orr describes her emotional and sensual responses to the mildewed, crumbling books she discusses in *Headless History: Nineteenth-Century French Historiography of the Revolution*. This work is a full-length account of the reflexivity of romantic French historiography, and a thoughtful presentation of the paradoxes and ironies of authority.

> Seen from the "mimetic" perspective by which the representation of the real gets its legitimacy from a possible coincidence (word with object, word with signification), the author assumes a position of authority second only to reality, which occupies the sovereign position. In the beginning a simple mediator of the real, the author eventually seizes all power, since the real in question appears only by his or her doing. But let us invert this mimetic view of representation. Without looking any different on the outside, the once established hierarchy of power is turned inside out. (Roland Barthes's short essay "Historical Discourse" is a good example of this exercise.) If the hypothetical center is now the text, no matter how unstable, upon which the characters, both narrator and narratee, depend, then author and reader also assume an identity by the effect of the text. They occupy a position whose insignificance is exceeded only by the real itself, a projection both phantasmatic and material, that derives its legitimacy from rhetoric and language. The figure of the author, after the exercise of inversion, refers then to a space opened up by the narrative. It is a metaphorical space that this narrative, however, cannot grasp – but that gives the author ostensible authority, parental authenticity.[13]

Although few historians since Michelet have participated in the hypothetical extremes of textual inversion that Orr describes, there has been a noticeable change in authorial practice. Philippe Carrard notes in his recent *Poetics of the New History* that there has been a general relaxation of the classic positivist rules restricting the presence of the scholar in the historical enunciation. "They [the changes] point to a questioning of the possibility of objective knowledge, and, since this questioning started in the early twentieth century, to the lag between rhetoric and epistemology: the now commonplace argument that all knowledge is grounded in a subject keeps being made in the human sciences (and in this very sentence) through a rhetoric which signals the researcher's reluctance to leave marks of his involvement, or even his hope of dispensing with them altogether."[14] What we have here is a willed choice on the part of those who are calling the will into question, a rhetorical stance assumed in order to annul the privilege of the rhetorical subject. The moment represented must be the moment of representation. The distance between the knower and what is known dissolves somewhat through refocusing. Representing the Holocaust becomes representing "coming to know the Holocaust." At least, this is the illusion offered by the new rhetoric that enacts the grammatical function of the old middle voice.

White, I suspect, understands the voracious dynamism of professional history, its need to recreate the past as a set of ever-varied commodities, and its absolute inadequacy as a memorializing force of any kind. It would be then his genuine wish to protect a certain image of the Holocaust that impels him to suggest the enormous self-restraints of middle-voiced writing as suitable to that event. This is not, however, his stated reason – namely, that some social and institutional changes in modernity have made this mode of writing appropriate to certain kinds of subjects. To pursue this notion, borrowed from Erich Auerbach, would harken back to sixty-year-old visions of correspondences between social structures, events, and aesthetic forms. Lukács *redivivus*! It would imply that there is a language of translation (in every era?) by which events may be made into discourse responsibly. *Metahistory*, however, effectively denies this possibility, noting "elective affinities" only among discursive options, but not between those options and something outside discourse, not even "events, such as the Holocaust, which are themselves 'modernist' in nature."[15] Furthermore, while one might call an event "modernist," following the postmodern trend of aestheticizing history, it is surely wrong to call an event "'modernist' in nature."[16]

The philosopher Berel Lang also proposes a special status for the Holocaust, as an event that virtually speaks for itself, at least in the sense that its *literal* presentation will constitute an adequate account of the event, an account that does not lessen its moral weight by the intrusion of rhetorical decisions.

Whatever else it does, figurative discourse and the elaboration of figurative space obtrudes the author's voice and a range of imaginative turns and decisions on the literary subject, irrespective of that subject's character and irrespective of – indeed defying – the "facts" of that subject which might otherwise have spoken for themselves and which at the very least, do not depend on the author's voice for their existence. The claim is entailed in imaginative representation that the facts *do not* speak for themselves, that figurative condensation and displacement and the authorial presence these articulate will turn or supplement the historical subject (whatever it is) in a way that represents the subject more compellingly or effectively – in the end, more truly – than would be the case without them.[17]

Lang claims that the "Final Solution" is one instance (he suggests no others) of an event that challenges the premise that all representation is a figural work of the imagination. He justifies this conclusion by asserting that figural language and emplotment contradict the "denial of individuality and personhood" and the "abstract bureaucracy" of evil that characterize the event. A literal "chronicle" lessens the risks entailed in any historical representation.

Lang's suggestion – that in some cases the facts speak for themselves – runs so drastically against the stream of current opinion on historical representation that one hesitates to restate the case against it, a case with which he is certainly familiar. Lang understands chronicle to be "foundational" for historiography, and believes that an emphasis on chronicle rather than the fully-figured narrative emplotment, which he takes to be logically subsequent to chronicle, will provide the sort of representation that will avoid the risks and disruptions inherent in discourse. But this is mistaken. A chronicle is the result of a pre-existing narrative; it is not the origin of such a narrative. For example, Andreas Hillgruber's notorious *Zweierlei Untergang*, which parallels somewhat the respective plights of the Jews and the displaced Eastern Germans, contains a very different chronicle of facts from Hilberg's *Destruction of the European Jews*.[18] Hilberg wanted to tell a different story. To object that one might sort out a proper chronicle from even Hilberg's work is simply to reiterate that chronicles depend on pre-existing narratives that tell us which facts are proper and which are not.

The troubles even of naming the events point to the issue at hand: Holocaust, Greek for a sacrificial burnt offering with Homeric overtones; "Final Solution," a bitterly ironic assumption of the Nazi's language;

Shoah, with the defamiliarization of a word from a language that was the vernacular of virtually none of the participants in the event, and generalized by a work of cinematic art. All of these terms are figural, imaginative, literary. "The destruction of the European Jews," Raul Hilberg's title, is the simplest, most literal of all, and perhaps the most effective in its minimal descriptiveness. That effectiveness, however, is aesthetic. It indeed possesses the sparse, modernist decorum now deemed suited to the event, reminding us that decorum is a fluid social convention. Even literality is the handmaiden of rhetoric. When Hayden White notes, "In point of fact I do not think that the Holocaust, Final Solution, Shoah, Churban, or German genocide of the Jews is any more unrepresentable than any other event in human history," his list of names tells us the problem.[19] There are too many possible and competing representations of these events. This new literalism seems today not so much a return to "the positivist paradigm" Carrard describes at the beginning of *The Poetics of the New History*.[20] It seems instead a sort of postmodern literalism, a self-critical (or self-deconstructing, if you will) literalism that points querulously to its own impossibility.

Ironically, in one example the literality that Lang has in mind is of a special, mimetic sort. He writes of the Holocaust literature that does not exist, the works from Vilna, Prague, Warsaw, or Vienna that might have existed had the Holocaust not taken place. "Their absence," he comments, "remains in fact the most closely literal representation of the Holocaust."[21] Since representation requires a presence, we would ordinarily say that the presence of an absence represents the absence of a presence. We do not know the titles of the works we do not have, but we know that those works would have existed. It was Isaac Babel who described this as a "genre of silence," but historians know it as the *argumentum ex silentio*. John Lange, in his essay "The Argument from Silence," emphasized the risks of this traditional strategy of historical logic, concluding that historians must still rely on their hunches, skill, and good sense, but surely his reasoning would be misapplied to Lang's statement.[22] There is an intuitive certainty that the "genre of silence" exists that overrides any of the probabilities suggested by analysis.

Of course, it is possible that there is a certain form of discourse that is appropriate for a certain kind of event, and one should not rule this out. Freud suggested that, at times, the subject of writing takes command of the writing subject, but his description of this does not bode well for any hope to control the process: "But one cannot always carry out one's reasonable intentions. There is often something in the material itself which takes charge of one and diverts one from one's first intentions. Even such a trivial achievement as the arrangement of a familiar piece of material is not entirely subject to an author's own choice; it takes what line it likes and all one can do is to ask oneself after the event why it has happened in this way and no other."[23] It is hard to imagine a topic more likely than the Holocaust to tap some unconscious source, with unpredictable results. Things do not turn out as planned.

If the Holocaust requires a certain form of discourse, however, there is no way of proving it, one way or the other. Such an idea also runs counter to White's project of the last twenty years, as I understand it. For this reason, I attribute his advocacy of a subject-effacing middle voice and Lang's call for an unfigured chronicle to an act of will, and a revealing one. These attempts to silence a certain aspect of the full narrative voice bespeak a fear, but I think a different one from the fears expressed by Lang and White. The threat to a "responsible" representation of the Holocaust, this ostensibly modern event, is modern, responsible historical scholarship.

Martin Jay correctly identifies the missing ingredient in most of the discussions of historical representations, namely, the reader. By reader here I mean, although Jay does not, anyone who has experienced a representation of some part of the past, whether a scholar who has studied, say, the Holocaust, or a student being taught about it in school or the mass media, or even someone who has the vaguest sense (what "everybody knows") that "Hitler" did something "bad" to the Jews. Any intended representation of the Holocaust will have an intended audience. That audience, which is always an imaginary and often unconscious construction of the author, will be expected to make sense and grasp the intended force of the representation that is aimed at it.[24]

Creating a reader for the Holocaust has been the work of writers, artists, filmmakers, poets, and historians since the end of the war. As Jay notes, there was no Holocaust for anyone to experience or witness; it was an imaginative creation, like all historical events.[25] The witness to a massacre is a witness to a massacre, a participant in a meeting may tell what he saw and heard. The events we have named Babi Yar or Wannsee, however, are not the Holocaust, nor even part of it until it has been imaginatively constituted. Creating the event means creating the reader who will recognize the event as an event when it is presented, and who can then follow its course according to the prevailing conventions of readability.[26] No writer can be sure of his audience, however.

Genre, *topoi*, emplotment are the traditional formal devices of rhetoric that are supposed to secure the adherence of a reader to a vision of the subject. We expect a different protocol from what announces itself as a novel than from a film, or an academic history. We expect to see perpetrators and victims differentiated, atrocities linked together, concepts defined and exemplified. We expect that certain events will not be made comic or absurd; we object when certain events are made tragic. Use of the old, the expected, secures the creation of the new by making its novelty nevertheless recognizable as meaning.

This rhetorical constitution of events depends for its existence on the social codes that prevail in a group, a time, a place. The signs of gravity, clarity, and sense that are appropriate to a subject are given in advance, and the creation of meaning in discourse is indeed, as Jay puts it, a negotiation among a number of forces. Among these, I suggest, are the factual material itself (which has already been constituted by a negotiation with other forces); the intention of the author (never to be ignored, but far from dominant); the resources of discourse that govern authorial choices; and the reading expectations of the audience (which is constituted ideally in the text long before the unpredictable appearance of any actual reader). Formal possibilities and the social institutions that guide them create the verisimilitude of real events, especially of such real events that seem as untrue to real – that is, imaginable – life as the Holocaust. Jay, however, follows Carlo Ginzburg in expressing an unwillingness to accept that the meaningfulness of our truth is a product of an enormously complex and diffuse cultural process. Or, to put it another way, Jay admits that this is indeed the case, but places his faith in *one of the social institutions* that creates the standard of verisimilitude. He asserts that the historical profession, with all its faults and limitations, raises knowledge above the merely conventional, at least in terms of the verification of facts, by relentless institutional criticism.

Let us suppose that the profession of history in a non-totalitarian world functions more or less as it represents itself. It certifies the skills and standards of its members through granting degrees; it informally designates the hierarchy of prestige and reputations that determines professional credibility; it culls published material for errors of documentation or false inferences. It is able to maintain its control of justified belief; what the consensus of professional historians believe to be the best information and judgment is taken to be the best information and judgment. Most importantly, this process is dynamic; the work of criticism is ongoing. This is how the system is supposed to work, and I believe that it does, for the most part. The critical dynamism of the profession is driven by professionalism itself, the need to make careers. Proximate truth results from constant historical revision. Rewards exist to keep the structure moving.

It is the dynamism of the structure, however, that should undermine any confidence one might place in it of maintaining the memory of any event whatever. In practice, the profession eats up historical events through normal professional behavior. Professional historical accounts do not appear to serve a great or continuous image of what truly, responsibly, properly happened in the past. They are rather sent into a marketplace or exchange of texts where, once they have been admitted by meeting certain standards, they will be valued precisely to the extent that they differ from or challenge existing accounts. Every ambitious historian, even in the bureaucratized and team-oriented feudalism of old world historical institutions, knows that a name and career are advanced by novelty. At the most basic level, the doctoral degree is attained by producing something new, and thus different.

Now the most elementary fact about the modern historical profession is that it produces an enormous amount of discourse. This avalanche of solid historical work relates less to the past than to other historical accounts; it must be so because of the vast quantity of material that has to be taken note of to gain entry to the marketplace. The historical work that does not change our view of a given topic by adding information that alters our picture, or by reframing the conventional questions in such a way as to produce a different topic entirely, will not get more than a grudging 750-word notice in the *American Historical Review*. With each successful work things must *change*, if the profession is working as it should. It may be argued that this process must bring us more comprehensive, better documented, and more finely argued represen-tations of past events. There is no question but that this is often the short-term result, especially in regard to events with no immediate impact. For events, however, that have a special pressure within them (and the Holocaust is surely such an event, as was in the 1960s and 1970s the question of the black family in slavery and reconstruction), the research will yield too much, will inevitably stray from any centrality of the event into areas that relate to other aspects of life, will produce nuances and exceptions to any pertinent generalizations, will bring forth schools of interpretation that cannot be reconciled by any possible appeal to evidence because at the heart of the dispute is the question of what shall *be* the appropriate evidence. At a certain point, the question will no longer bear professional reward. The things that are interesting to say will have been said, the possible encodings exhausted for the moment, at least until newer forms of representation are offered (as the large-scale, novelistic narrative offered Gibbon opportunities for considering Roman history that Montesquieu did not use). The centrality of the political will give way to intellectual history which will give way to social history which will give way to group histories, histories of the everyday, or the intimate, of the body, of death. On this process, F. R. Ankersmit has written:

> The logic in this development is that in each phase, with each new set of historical topics, meaning is given to what seemed historically irrelevant, meaningless, static, or belonging to an a-historical domain during a previous phase in the development of historiography. One might say that history always moves *backwards* instead of *forwards*: it does not penetrate deeper into what at a certain phase is seen as the essence of historical reality, but tends to turn away from that essence. Historiography is, to use another metaphor, centrifugal instead of centripetal. What were mere details under a previous dispensation becomes the center or the essence under a later one.[27]

The narrative plots of the Western tradition may pass, along with a focused interest in the history of Europe, of which the Holocaust is unmistakably a part. Certainly, the account given by Peter Novick in *That Noble Dream* (Cambridge, 1988) of the decentering of American historical practice should warn anyone who places his or her faith in professionalism to safeguard any historical subject. It is not that the system of modern research and institutional verification does not work. It works all too well, producing an endless supply of competing verifiable accounts, the significance of which is always in question. The institution in which Martin Jay believes will do its task; it will swallow the event. Raul Hilberg, however, senses the danger of successful historical practice to the desire to memorialize. Echoing Adorno's judgment that it is barbaric to write poetry after Auschwitz, Hilberg suggests that it may be equally barbaric to write footnotes, for historians "usurp history" precisely when they succeed.

If the modern historical profession cannot well serve any memorializing function, nor sustain a stable referent, and if there is no particular form of writing that naturally suits the sort of event exemplified by the

Holocaust, then what conclusion must be drawn by someone who sees the ethical truth of the matter in the vow "Never Again?," and who believes that no responsible historical imagination may disregard it? However strong our belief in the transcendent truth of the evil, uniqueness, and centrality of the Holocaust in history, we must confront the fact that this is *our* belief; any efforts to maintain this for the future will be an essentially conservative task to preserve a certain sort of moral community, as Lang calls it, or interpretive community, as a literary critic might.

NOTES

1. Donald N. McCloskey, "History, Differential Equations, and the Problem of Narration," *History and Theory* 30, 1991, p. 25–36.
2. *Ibid.* p. 28.
3. *Ibid.* p. 36.
4. *Arendt-Jaspers Correspondence*, cited in Gordon A. Craig, "Letters on Dark Times," *New York Review of Books*, May 13, 1993, p. 12.
5. Hans Kellner, "Beautifying the Nightmare: The Aesthetics of Postmodern History," *Strategies: A Journal of Theory, Culture, and Politics* 4–5, 1991, pp. 289–313.
6. Klüger: "Already at that time, a thought struck me and is unfortunately still deeply impressed upon me more than the indignation about the great atrocity, namely the consciousness of the absurdity of the whole thing, the nonsensical about it, the complete senselessness of those murders and deportations, which we call the Final Solution, Holocaust, Jewish catastrophe, and recently Shoah – always new names because the words for it very quickly rot in our mouths. The absurdity, unreasonableness of it, how easily it could have been avoided, how nobody profited from my carrying tracks [and] railroad ties instead of sitting at a school bench, and the role that coincidence had in it. I don't mean that I don't understand how it came about. At least I know as much as others about the backgrounds. But this knowledge doesn't explain anything. We recount on our fingers what went on before and rely upon the fact that the radical Other occurred out of those events. Everyone before our time who drew attention to himself in Germany must be accountable. Then it was Bismarck and Nietzsche and the Romantics and even Luther, who supposedly created the preliminary conditions for the great genocide of our century. But why? Because every child has a great grandmother, so every thing must have its cause. And the poor grandmother suddenly holds the responsibility for the wrongs that her progeny perpetrate. If this were so, one would have to be able to state: if Calvin rather than Luther or realistic novels rather than Hoffmann's tales, then no horrors in the 1940s. That doesn't compute. One could not predict because everything was possible, because no idea is so absurd that it can't be carried out in highly civilized societies." (Klüger, *Weiter leben*, pp. 147–8).
7. Berel Lang, "The Representation of Limits," and Hayden White, "Historical Emplotment and the Problem of Truth," in *Probing the Limits of Representation: Nazism and the "Final Solution,"* (ed.) Saul Friedlander, Cambridge, Mass., 1992, pp. 300–17 and 37–53 respectively.
8. White, "Historical Emplotment," p. 48.

9. John Lyons, *Introduction to Theoretical Linguistics*, Cambridge, Eng., 1968, p. 374.
10. Vernant, "Discussion: Barthes-Todorov," in (ed.) Richard Macksey and Eugenio Donato *The Structuralist Controversy: The Languages of Criticism and the Sciences of Man*, Baltimore, 1972, p. 152.
11. Langer, in *Holocaust Testimonies*, tells of the narration of Edith P., who yearns for someone who knows her *really*, having found a "permanent estrangement" (Langer's words) in her life after Auschwitz. Langer draws a connection with White's discussion in *The Content of the Form* of the annalistic genre of reflection on the past. In medieval annals, White tells us, things happen to people, rather than people doing things. Disorder and fear characterize that world, and the form that represents it. "Up to a point, this is the experience of which the surviving victim speaks" (Langer, 108).

    The disrupted narrative selfhood that Edith P. experiences corresponds to the absence of any central authority, an absence which White associates with the drift of annalistic presentation, and which is perhaps not terribly far from his decentered middle-voiced writing. Langer, however, takes the traditional humanistic view: "The key factor is a responsive and transforming consciousness. At this point, annals become narrative, and narrative makes possible the birth of history for succeeding generations." It is interesting to note that Langer's study of the "raw" data of survivor videotapes leads him to yearn for the processing voice of narrative that White and Lang distrust.
12. Hayden White, *Tropics of Discourse: Essays in Cultural Criticism*, Baltimore, 1978, p. 23.
13. Linda Orr, *Headless History: Nineteenth-Century French Historiography of the Revolution*, Ithaca, NY, 1990, pp. 74–9.
14. Philippe Carrard, *The Poetics of the New History: French Historical Discourse from Braudel to Chartier*, Baltimore, 1992, p. 104.
15. White, "Historical Emplotment and the Problem of Truth," p. 50. From *Metahistory*: "In my view, a historiographical style represents a particular *combination* of modes of emplotment, argument, and ideological implication. But the various modes of modes of emplotment, argument, and ideological implication cannot be indiscriminately combined in a given work. For example, a Comic emplotment is not compatible with a Mechanistic argument, just as a Radical ideology is not compatible with a Satirical emplotment. There are, as it were, elective affinities among the various modes that might be used to gain an explanatory effect on the different levels of composition. And these elective affinities are based on the structural homologies which can be discerned among the possible modes of modes of emplotment, argument, and ideological implication. . . . These affinities are not to be taken as *necessary* combinations of the modes in a given historian. On the contrary, the dialectical tension which characterizes the work of every master historian usually arises from an effort to wed a mode of emplotment with a mode of argument or of ideological implication which is inconsonant with it." (White, *Metahistory: The Historical Imagination in Nineteenth-Century Europe*, Baltimore, 1973, p. 29).

    F. R. Ankersmit puts the matter somewhat differently in *Narrative Logic: A Semantic Analysis of the Historian's Language*, The Hague, 1983: "The idea that the historian should offer a narrative 'translation' of what the past really is like is the misunderstanding that this and similar proposals have in common. For there are no translation-rules which, when carefully applied, can guarantee the objectivity of a narratio" p. 236).
16. Allan Megill discusses the postmodern aestheticization of "the whole of reality" in *Prophets of Extremity: Nietzsche, Heidegger, Foucault, Derrida*, Berkeley, 1985, *passim*. Stephen Kern has described how modernism changed the experience of time and space, creating a parallel between the arts and historical events; see *The Culture of*

Time and Space: 1880–1918, Cambridge, Mass, 1983, esp. ch. 11: "The Cubist War." He does not, however, suggest that World War I was cubist "in nature."

17. Lang. "The Representation of Limits," p. 316.

18. Martin Jay points this out in "Of Plots, Witnesses, and Judgments," *Probing the Limits of Representation*. p. 103.

19. White, "Historical Emplotment," p. 52.

20. "Finally, the *Introduction* [by Langlois and Seignobos] proposes a stylistics: a set of rules about selecting the proper word, phrase, and sentence pattern. This stylistics advocates what Anglo-Saxon composition teachers call the 'plain style': a language that would be 'unadorned by figures, unmoved by emotions, unclouded by images, and universalistic in its conceptual or mathematical scope,' as LaCapra (1985, p. 12) defines it with obvious irony. Langlois and Seignobos again proscribe 'literary effects,' in this instance the 'rhetoric' whose ornaments are incompatible with the sobriety that must characterize historical writing (pp. 67, 273). The main culprit is of course metaphor, since this trope combines the drive to 'do literature' with a wrong view of what the world is 'really like.'" Carrard, *Poetics*, p. 8.

21. Lang. "Introduction," in *Writing and the Holocaust*. p. 15.

22. John Lange, "The Argument from Silence," *History and Theory* 5, 1966, pp. 300–1.

23. *The Standard Edition of the Complete Psychological Works of Sigmund Freud*, trans. James Strachey, London, 1953, XVI, p. 379.

24. "If the writer succeeds in writing, it is generally because he can fictionalize in his imagination an audience he has learned to know not from daily life but from earlier writers who were fictionalizing in their imaginations, audiences they had learned to know in still earlier writers, and so on back to the dawn of written narrative." Walter J. Ong. "The Writer's Audience Is a Fiction," in *Interfaces of the Word*, Ithaca, NY, 1977, p. 60.

25. The notion that events are narratively constructed from an undifferentiated "advent" is put forth in Hans Kellner, "Naive and Sentimental Realism: From Advent to Event," *Storia della storiografia* 22, 1992, pp. 117–23.

26. It may be objected that some events are named at once, and thus experienced in their historical identity. World War II, for example, was experienced as such, at least after the entry of the United States. Yet World War II was seen and named immediately as the counterpart of World War I, although World War I had not existed before World War II caused it to be so named. It was transformed from the vaguely named Great War by the happenings that were its completion and repetition, and which changed its nature entirely, from a unique and self-consuming tale (the war to end war) into an example of a modern form of activity, world war. It is also instructive to note that the subsequent conflict in Korea became the Korean War despite the efforts of American leaders to represent it as a police action. The Vietnam War became that without the formal congressional speech act declaring legal hostilities. One may say that "readers" constituted these events against the official actions and intentions of the principal participants. They knew the plot that constructed a certain kind of event when they saw it, and refused to believe that anything else could occur under that description.

27. F. R. Ankersmit, "On Historiographical Progress," *Storia della storiografia* 22, 1992, p. 107.

35 Wulf Kansteiner

From exception to exemplum: the new approaches to Nazism and the "Final Solution"

Two intellectuals who contributed to the theoretical foundations of the new discourse on Nazism, Hayden White and Jean-François Lyotard, have themselves considered the consequences of their theories for the representation of Nazism and the "Final Solution." In the process White has met with similar difficulties as Young. White has proposed a structuralist system for the analysis of historical discourse in which he differentiates between two levels in the historiographical texts. The primary referent of historical discourse is the different events which are dealt with in the respective historical texts. The secondary referent, on the other hand, is the narrative structures which historians employ to insert these different events within general interpretations of the respective historical processes. White asserts that these two levels are independent of each other. While the truthfulness of primary referents can be checked according to accepted rules of evidence, the truthfulness of the meanings conveyed by specific narrative structures depends on the interpretive, tropological tastes which prevail in the scientific and social community.[1]

Applied to the study of Nazism this means that those practitioners of history who do not deal in historical facts, as for instance the radical revisionists who deny the facticity of the Holocaust, have no chance of being admitted into the community of scholars.[2] All others who respect the factual record of the National Socialist period are considered to have produced truthful accounts if their interpretation of the history or segments thereof are compatible with the range of narrative modes and interpretations which are currently accepted among scholars. White gives two examples to show that even the facts of the Nazi past do not speak for themselves, that they can be successfully incorporated into redemptive narrative structures if the social context allows for that. In Israel, the Shoah has been sublated within the traditional plot type of catastrophe and redemption. In addition, the extermination of the Jews could be framed as a success story under certain historical conditions, for example, a revival of Nazism.[3] The theory of the singularity of the Holocaust might itself serve as another example. As defined above, the concept of singularity is a specific form of emplotment that excludes all kinds of figurative equivalences between Nazism and its historical context, such as historical continuity and qualitative similarity. As long as this interpretive truth was acknowledged by historians, in Germany roughly until the *Historikerstreit*, all historical interpretations which posited a substantial equivalence, for instance between Nazism and the Federal Republic, were excluded from the range of accurate, professional representations of the past.[4] As the examples above indicate, this "plot barrier" has been substantially undermined by current scholarship.

Apparently, White has recently reconsidered his position and conceded that in the case of the Holocaust some interpretations of the Nazi period are to be excluded because of their incompatibility with the historical facts.[5] He has also come closer to the theory of the incomprehensibility of Nazism. White denies that Nazism and the Holocaust are in principle unrepresentable but contends that our current historiographical representational repertoire stemming from the nineteenth century might very well be insufficient for the representation of modernist events like the "Final Solution" and should be replaced by more adequate means.[6] Thus White approaches the traditional consensus in the field of Holocaust studies which takes the reality of the Holocaust to surpass our linguistic abilities and conventional interpretive strategies. The reasons for this transformation are not apparent in White's texts. It seems that White, when confronted with the allegedly disturbing implications of his structuralist poetics for the representation of Nazism, decided to contain the more radical implications of his theory and to reconsider the standards for representing the Holocaust that most scholars of his generation endorse.[7]

As already indicated by Sande Cohen's critique of Habermas, the concept of singularity has been most thoroughly displaced by Lyotard's rethinking of Auschwitz's exceptionality. Like White, Lyotard seeks to expose the referential illusion manifest in most linguistic constructs, but he also criticizes the illusion of stability provided by systems of secondary signification, as for instance structuralist poetics. For him, Auschwitz represents the most powerful example to date which testifies to the singularity of all events and our inability to represent them conclusively and adequately in language. Auschwitz has brought to the forefront a radical incommensurability between eventhood and meaning. It has made us understand that an event always carries an excess of significance which surpasses any given interpretation, or to put it differently, that events disrupt the preexisting frameworks of reference so that we lack certainty about the relevant interpretive contexts for any given event. Events mark the site of dispute, "differends" between the incommensurable genre of phrases which seek to explain them; they also partake in incommensurable temporalities, "an unthinkable future history and a past become uncannily present."[8]

With regard to Auschwitz, Lyotard demonstrates his arguments in two steps. The radical heterogeneity between the law of the perpetrators and the silence of the victims has disrupted our mode of historical understanding and displayed the inadequacy of our cognitive forms of representation. The revisionists have inadvertently exposed this double-bind inherent in the process of representation. The survivors of the Holocaust cannot attest to the crime committed because they did not experience the gas chambers themselves, while the victims cannot testify because they have been killed. From the vantage point of our cognitive rules of representation the events remain indescribable since the victims were robbed of any "legitimate" way to voice their resistance to the process of extermination. Their silence, which is linked to the name of Auschwitz, shows that "something which must be able to be put into phrases cannot yet be."[9]

Lyotard directs his criticism against any positive definition of the singularity of the "Final Solution" which is based on the idea of historical truth as directly linked to past reality or as guarded by the scholarly community. He does so because he claims these cognitive genres were themselves implicated in the "Final Solution" and displaced by the events. At the same time he uses the example of Auschwitz to point out the shortcomings of a structuralist, and especially a narratological, analysis of its history. In emphasizing the conventional grounds of historical writing, critics such as White turn the event into an absolutely inaccessible past which is open to all kinds of subjective interpretations. For Lyotard they thus evade the necessary although futile challenge to find an expression for the wrong committed to the victims.

Against both approaches Lyotard insists that philosophy has to attest to the incommensurability of our modes of understanding and representation which forces us to make indeterminate judgments, to judge without recourse to any stable epistemological, ethical, or aesthetic framework which would bridge the gap between the just and the true.

Auschwitz is here "merely" a case in point; the same dilemma character-izes all our efforts to judge in language.

Lyotard has compared Auschwitz to an earthquake which destroys all seismographic devices and therefore cannot be measured and repre-sented within the applicable sign systems. Like such an earthquake Auschwitz has left only a vague but powerful feeling of its enormity and unrepresentability. Lyotard's metaphor is on the way to becoming as popular and misunderstood a phrase as Adorno's dictum about poetry after Auschwitz. At first glance, Lyotard attests here to the incom-prehensibility of the Holocaust in a way similar to Adorno's or Friedlander's position. Like them, he asserts that the meaning of Ausch-witz can never be known or even felt satisfactorily. For Lyotard, however, the event has destroyed the possibility of knowledge and representation in principle, or, to stay within the metaphor, the earth-quake has destroyed the measuring devices and the trust in their accuracy beyond repair so that all future earthquakes of whatever mag-nitude cannot be represented any longer. Also, unlike Adorno and Friedlander, Lyotard is not concerned with the consequences of the process. To him, the disintegration of the discourse of identity and of such concepts as "subject" and "history" represents the only chance to escape the forces that have set the "Final Solution" in motion.

NOTES

1. Hayden White, *The Content of the Form: Narrative Discourse and Historical Representation*, Baltimore, 1987, especially pp. 43–7; see also Hayden White, *Metahistory: The Historical Imagination in Nineteenth-Century Europe*, Baltimore, 1973; and Hayden White, *Tropics of Discourse: Essays in Cultural Criticism*, Baltimore, 1978.
2. The problem remains, however, that these revisionists might be successful in other than scholarly contexts where they might be politically much more dangerous. On the activities of the radical revisionists see most recently Deborah Lipstadt, *Denying the Holocaust: The Growing Assault on Truth and Memory*, New York, 1993.
3. White, *The Content of the Form*, pp. 76, 80. For a critique of White's provocative form of contextualism that links truthfulness with effectiveness see for instance Carlo Ginz-burg, "Just One Witness," in *Probing the Limits*, pp. 82–96 and Martin Jay, "Of Plots, Witnesses, and Judgements," in *Probing the Limits* pp. 97–107.
4. Obviously, historians treat existential truth claims about single events and abstract truth claims like that of the singularity of Nazism differently. But as long as paradigms such as that stipulating the singularity of the Holocaust are in place they help define the border between professional and amateur historiography. The relativity of interpretive truth is often only revealed with hindsight. Compare Christopher R. Browning, "German Memory, Judicial Interrogation, and Historical Reconstruction: Writing Per-petrator History from Postwar Testimony," in *Probing the Limits*, pp. 22–36, 33.

5. Hayden White, "Historical Emplotment and the Problem of Truth," in *Probing the Limits*, pp. 37–53, especially 40. See also Hayden White, "'Figuring the Nature of the Times Deceased': Literary Theory and Historical Writing," in Ralph Cohen (ed), *The Future of Literary Theory*, New York, 1989, pp. 19–43.
6. White, "Historical Emplotment and the Problem of Truth," 51–53.
7. See on this point also Wulf Kansteiner, "Hayden White's Critique of the Writing of History," *History and Theory* 32 (1993), 273–95.
8. Jean-François Lyotard, *The Differend: Phrases in Dispute* Minneapolis, 1988, 128; quote from Bill Reading's *Introducing Lyotard: Art and Politics*, London, 1991, 60.
9. Lyotard, *The Differend*, 3–4, 40, 56–8, 97–100, quote from 13; see also Cohen, "Between Image and Phrase."

36 Robert Braun

The Holocaust and problems of representation

INTRODUCTION

Historiography is bound up with notions of "objectivity," "reality," and "truth." Representations of the past should offer, so historians say, a direct and close link to past "reality" on the basis of "facts." The realism of historical representation may be contextualized, extratextualized, detextualized but, in the end, the factual reality of the past is not questioned. Evidence and proof is used to establish the "truth" of historical representation.[1] Thus, historiography displays an inexpungible realism.

On the other hand, in conveying "historical reality" historical representation employs narrative form as a mode of emplotment, thereby weakening the direct connection between factual statements and the means of representation.[2] The "transferentiality" of categories such as "experience" in historical representation, which point to the ambivalence of the relationship between historians' frameworks of analysis and the objects of their study, make the direct relationship between representation and "reality" even more problematic.[3] Moreover, theories about the "narrative construction of reality," as an instrument of mind in the creation of present as well as past reality, show that the psychological bases of the connection between perception and reality are less unequivocal than more traditional interpretations would suggest.[4] All this seems to question the traditional understanding of the relationship between "facts," "representation," and "reality." "Facts" may be constructions of "reality" rather than mirrors of it; "representation" a mode of meaning production rather than a re-enactment of the past; and historical "reality" a web of constructions of distant minds and representations themselves. In this way, historical representation displays an ineradicable element of relativism.

In a 1966 publication Hayden White wrote about historiography's internal contradictions and emphasized the need to leave behind the nineteenth-century "burden of history."[5] He analyzes the conflict between the nineteenth-century conception of historiography-as-science and modernity. According to White, the former is based on two points of reference: positivist science and realist art. The core of the problem is that while both art and science found new ideals, time passed over historiography unnoticed and the discipline continued to view itself in the original framework. White marks the broader context signified by modern reservedness towards history as follows:

> when historians claim that history is a combination of science and art, they generally mean that it is a combination of *late nineteenth-century* social science and *mid-nineteenth century* art. That is to say, they seem to be aspiring to little more than a synthesis of modes of analysis and expression that have their antiquity alone to commend them. . . . Many historians continue to treat their "facts" as though they were "given" and refuse to recognize, unlike most scientists, that they are not so much "found" as "constructed" by the kind of questions which the investigator asks of the phenomena before him. It is the same notion of objectivity that binds historians to an uncritical use of the chronological framework for their narratives.[6]

White calls on historiography to employ the achievements of modern scientific theory and artistic representation in order to find appropriate forms of representation for different aspects of the historical past. White concludes that acceptance of this formula is the only way historiography can avoid radical relativism and propagandistic application.[7]

Ever since the end of World War II, numerous scholars have sought appropriate forms of representation for that singular, spectacular operation known as the Holocaust. Primo Levi wrote several books in which he attempted to depict the experience of the Holocaust with documentary–literary–biographical methods. In addition, there is Paul Celan's famous poem which, according to legend, provoked T. W. Adorno's famous dictum about the barbarity of post-Holocaust poetry.[8] In 1990, almost half a century after the events took place, the Hungarian writer and Holocaust survivor Imre Kertész wrote that "we may form a realistic view of the Holocaust, this incomprehensible and confusing reality, only with the help of our aesthetic imagination."[9] The faith of Levi and

Celan however, both of whom attempt to represent the "reality" of the Holocaust with the help of aesthetic imagination, bears witness to the conflict between the various possibilities of representation and reality. Those living reality often find its representation inadequate; nor do they see an escape from this situation. It seems to me that there is an unresolvable conflict, often apparent to the narrator/witness him or herself, between the experience of an event and his or her narration of it. Sometimes historians writing on the Holocaust claim that research did not facilitate their understanding of the event.[10] This should be taken as a sign that similar conflicts may exist between the acquired knowledge of the researcher – whose methods are based on modern rationality – and the form chosen for the task. The question is further complicated by the interplay between the researcher's "experience" as present condition and "experience" as evidence employed in the representation of the past. This is marked by the different levels of and claims for referentiality with "reality" contained in the "experience" of both those in the present and those in the past.[11]

Turning to historical problems posed by the Holocaust might be fruitful for a number of reasons. Forty-five years after the event, we are at the moment in which past "reality" turns into "history"; the "experience" of the former is to be preserved as those who nurtured its memory give way to a new generation. There are few events in history better documented than the Holocaust; historians and archivists have collected an incomparable quantity of documents and relics. At the same time, the event in which a "nation with the authority of its leader decided and announced that it would kill off as completely as possible a particular group of humans, including old people, women, children and infants, and actually put this decision in practice, using all the means of governmental power at its disposal" confronts anyone thinking about it with a moral challenge unparalleled in history. Notwithstanding that questions posed by and answers gained from the Holocaust might be extended to the whole of history, special care must be taken that moral outrage not be intermingled with rational judgements.

Historiographical debates centering on the Holocaust bring us to a core problem of the theory of history: the conflict between the "meaning" of past "reality" as knowledge (*epistemé*), the formation of representations of the past as opinion (*doxa*), and the relationship between past "reality" as construction of mind in the present *and* in the past. In the final analysis, it seems futile to speak about the "reality" of the past as an object of study. Not only do interpretations in the form of historical narratives serve as legitimation of present political, moral, or aesthetic judgements about the past, but the referentiality between "facts," "representation," and "truth" in the past seems to be less unequivocal than some historians would like to believe. Thus, past "reality" does not exist; in its place are an endless number of realities tantamount to the various judgments and viewpoints one can find in the present. There is a continuous interplay between a web of reality-constructions *both* in the present and the past. Since present judgments are constantly changing, they are in need of continuous legitimization – as is the "reality" of the past.

CONCLUSION

This essay has not attempted to deal with historical literature on the Holocaust. As far as debates on problems of historical consciousness, historical judgment, and interpretation of the National Socialist past in Germany are concerned, the essay has attempted to show that the representation of past "reality" is closely connected to problems that lie outside the sphere of purely scholarly activity. Problems of historical representation are politically and socially significant in the individual and communal search for legitimation – the past, it seems, is granted its own legitimation by the authority of the present.

When employing narrative strategies to make sense of a historical past as morally, politically, and intellectually disturbing as the Holocaust, fundamental problems of historical representation can be seen. Theories that view historical representations as "narrative substances," and therefore speak about an exclusive self-referentiality of such texts, face an extreme challenge.[13] Discussions about meaning, truth, and reference in connection with such narrative substances, both as names ("the Holocaust") and as a set of statements, are influenced by questions posed by twentieth-century philosophical discourse from Wittgenstein to Rorty. This understanding of historical representation works in the context of representation being a "language game," an entity that is not a medium for determining relations to unities such as the self or reality, but stands on its own.

In connection with historical representations of the Holocaust the self-referentiality of the historical text and its propositional nature seem to conflict with fundamentally held notions about the "reality" of the events and thus the correspondence of their representation to this "reality"[14] It is not surprising that critics of the realist project in historical writing, such as Hayden White, have to face accusations by historians that their ideas come close to ideologies commonly connected to fascist regimes.[15] It is then not so peculiar that White revised his thesis about the inexpungible relativism in historical representation in a way that gives him ground to counter such accusations (though his new position weakens his overall relativist arguments).[16] What passed unnoticed is that his approach to the limits of representation in connection to the Holocaust comes close to opinions held by theorists who subscribe to the absolute evil nature, and thus argue for the implicit moral contents, of the events.[17]

Droysen's insight in his *Historik* reveals how the realism of historical representation is not based on the criterion of truth, but, with reference to the social reality of the historian's own time, on a criterion of *plausibility* which is different from the *possible* (aimed at by science) and the *imaginary* (represented by art). The criterion of plausibility may be considered as the social *modus vivendi* of the present, as the consensus between different interests, morals, and "objective" perceptions of the world by individuals and groups.[18]

This is of great significance with respect to problems of representation of the Holocaust. In the case of those who have experienced the Holocaust as a "boundary event," this lived reality is mediated through a moral, political, and intellectual perception of the world in which the differentiation between the possible, imaginary, and plausible cannot take place. In the social reality of the Holocaust, brought to us by the documents and testimonies of survivors, the "facts" are equal to the politically possible and the morally imaginary. History, seen as an "objective" representation of past "reality," must be based on the criterion of the "possible" only; as the mediation of past "reality" through legitimation of the moral or political authority of the present on the criterion of "plausible" only; and as scholarship, on the criterion of the "factual" only. "Objectivity" of representation is questioned by theorists of science as well as philosophers of language. "Plausibility" as moral and political authority becomes problematic when the politics of interpretation is discussed. "Factuality" as an unproblematic use of evidence and proof is less unequivocal once questions related to the construction of evidence are raised. Seen in this way, historical representation of the Holocaust that is true to the traditional understanding of the criteria of objectivity, legitimacy, and factuality is not possible. The problem is evident in Gershom Scholem's critique of Hannah Arendt on the Eichmann trial. Scholem mentions the lack of balanced judgment in Arendt's narrative, and implicitly questions the possibility of any historical judgment on the Holocaust, claiming that the judge "was not there."[19]

Considering these insights into the broader perspective of history, we may conclude that in our perception of past social reality *vis-à-vis* documents and other "facts," there is no difference between the politically possible, the socially plausible, and the morally imaginary – nor do we know with which we are dealing. The narrator of past "reality" orders "facts" into the form of a story emplotted as desired, and at times names the politically possible as "reality" in order to establish mythic continuity with the past. At other times, the morally imaginary is called "reality" in order to establish continuity with the past through a moral imperative. Occasionally, the socially plausible is referred to as "reality," but in order to separate it from the possible and imaginary, identification with the past is sought. It seems to me that historiography which looks at past reality as a substance to be epistemologically revealed has to be given up.

To paraphrase Adorno's maxim, it seems that after Auschwitz poetry can be written, but history, as the "realistic" interpretation of the past, cannot. It seems to me, remembering Walter Benjamin's Angel of History, that in order to save some value from the debris of history a more pragmatist view of our past has to be taken.[20] It has to be accepted that scholars are concerned with the "public use of history," that is with substituting the absent past with a historical text. In the realm of politics, this means attending to questions of identity, communal and individual searches for legitimation, and culture understood as power. In the realm of aesthetics this means questions related to the form of representation, the propositional nature and self-referentiality of texts. A more pragmatist view of our past would then be that of accepting historical representation as a tool, as are language games in general, that work better for certain purposes than other tools. They serve our understanding of identity, community, and culture better than other means. They do not take us closer to hidden truths behind these notions, nor do they offer a picture of how things really were or really happened. The purpose of using these tools is to establish a human solidarity that is not dependent on universal validity appealing to reason to reveal "reality," but is understood as a temporary consensus arrived at in the course of free and open encounters. This may be the case even with phenomena as morally, politically, and intellectually challenging as the Holocaust. In the final analysis, traditional criteria of truth and falsity do not apply to historical representations of the past. I believe that in order to satisfy Hayden White's call for a new historiography, a new theory of history is needed, one that is free of the burden of the past seen as "reality."

NOTES

1. Carlo Ginzburg, "Checking the Evidence," *Critical Inquiry* 18, Autumn, 1991, pp. 79–92; Wulf Kansteiner, "Hayden White's Critique of the Writing of History," *History and Theory* 32, 1993, p. 287.
2. Hayden White, "Historical Emplotment and the Problem of Truth," in Saul Friedlander (ed.), *Probing the Limits of Representation*, Berkeley, 1992, pp. 37–53.
3. Joan W. Scott, "Experience as Evidence," *Critical Inquiry* 17, Summer, 1991, pp. 773–97; cf. Dominick LaCapra, *History & Criticism*, Ithaca, NY, 1985, pp. 71–94.
4. Jerome Bruner, "The Narrative Construction of Reality," *Critical Inquiry* 18, Autumn, 1991, pp. 1–21.
5. Hayden White, "The Burden of History," *History and Theory* 5, 1966, pp. 111–34.
6. *Ibid.*, p. 127.
7. Hayden White modified his view about relativism and found – to my mind, correctly – epistemological skepticism and relativism as important intellectual forces of social inquiry; cf. White, *Metahistory*, Baltimore, 1973 and *The Content of the Form*, Baltimore, 1987, esp. p. 227, n. 12. In a manner which could be understood as a retreat, his recent articles qualify his relativism in connection with the representation of the Holocaust. Cf. White, "Historical Emplotment and the Problem of Truth." For the development White's work from *Metahistory* to the present see Kansteiner, "Hayden White's Critique of the Writing of History."
8. Sidra DeKoven Ezrahl, "The Grave in the Air," in Friedlander (ed.), *Probing the Limits*, pp. 259–60.
9. I. Kertész, *A holocaust mint kultura*, [Holocaust as Culture], Budapest, 1993, p. 22.
10. Cf. Arno Mayer, *Why Did the Heavens Not Darken?*, New York, 1989.
11. Scott, "Experience as Evidence," pp. 776–7.
13. F. R. Ankersmit, "Reply to Professor Zagorin," *History and Theory* 29, 1990, pp. 278–84.
14. It is at this point that a note on the so-called "Holocaust Revisionists" must be included. It seems to me theoretically unsatisfactory to state, as Hayden White did, that their claims are "as morally offensive as [they are] intellectually bewildering," and settle the problem with claiming that "an interpretation falls into the category of a lie when it denies the reality of the events of which it treats, and into the category of an untruth when it draws false conclusions from reflection on events whose rationality remains attestable on the level of 'positive' historical inquiry." Not only do "revisionists" hold a more detailed view which enables them to counter such statements by questioning the number of victims and the purpose of gas chambers thus leaving the "reality" of events intact, but White's approach leaves problems related to the "reality" of historical representation unnoticed. In my opinion, it is exactly this problematic relation to the referentiality of historical representation that makes such views, their bewildering moral and intellectual claim notwithstanding, difficult to deal with. For White's position see *The Content of the Form*, pp. 76–8
15. Carlo Ginzburg, "Just One Witness," in Friedlander (ed.) *Probing the Limits*, pp. 82–96; cf. White, *The Content of the Form*, pp. 74–5.

16. Kansteiner, "Hayden White's Critique," p. 293.
17. Cf. Lang, *Act and Idea*, pp. 117–61.
18. J. G. Droysen, *Historik: Vorlesungen über Enzyklopedie und Methodologie der Geschichte*, Munich, 1937. Cf. White, *The Content of the Form*, pp. 93–4.
19. "Letter of Gershom Scholem to Hannah Arendt," in Arendt, *The Jew as Pariah*, p. 243.
20. Cf. Richard Rorty, *Consequences of Pragmatism*, Minneapolis, 1982, pp. 160–75; Rorty, "Science as Solidarity," in H. Lawson and L. Appignanesi (eds), *Dismantling Truth: Reality in the Postmodern World*, New York, 1989, pp. 6–22.

37 Berel Lang

Is it possible to misrepresent the Holocaust?

ABSTRACT

The essays by Hans Kellner, Wulf Kansteiner, and Robert Braun in the Forum, "Representing the Holocaust" (*History and Theory*, May 1994) attack historical realism as a legitimate form of such representation. Like any other part of narrative, "facts" do not speak for themselves in respect to the Holocaust or any other historical "event"; they are context-dependent and thus speak only in the voice of their interpreters. The symposiasts adopt this view on the assumption that an alternative to historical realism will yet reaffirm the primary data of the Holocaust: the number of deaths, identities, places, dates. But I argue to the contrary: that ontologically there is but one alternative to historical realism, and that this alternative offers no ground even in principle for acknowledging a contradiction between an assertion and a denial that, for example, "On January 20th, 1942, Nazi officials at Wannsee formulated a protocol for the 'Final Solution of the Jewish Question.'" Thus, at least in respect to items of chronicle, historical realism (and the principle of contradiction) must be granted – unless one is ready to affirm, as the symposiasts apparently are not, a radical epistemic and moral (and of course historical) skepticism.

Metaphysics may be a mug's game, but those who think they can avoid it by burying their heads in the sand are likely to wind up playing the game anyway but from the other end (reviving the "Posterior Analytics"?). This is, it seems to me, a lesson taught by the three essays in the *History and Theory* Forum on "Representing the Holocaust" (May, 1994) by Hans Kellner, Wulf Kansteiner, and Robert Braun respectively.

Those essays differ tactically and rhetorically, but a common enemy – realism in all its guises – motivates them and then serves as the alien "other" against which their conclusions stand in solidarity. This oppositional stance may explain why the essays do not bother to consider – let alone to defend – the implications of their own views of historical representation, but obviously it does not justify that avoidance which has the effect of undercutting their initial criticism. As it is unlikely, for any two conceptual alternatives, that the choice of either will come without certain costs, the reluctance of the three authors to weigh the price of their own proposal is proportionate to the strength of the one they reject.

The topic of the Forum has, of course, been much discussed; indeed the history of this discussion is what concerns the three contributors. The principal question at issue in that history can be simply formulated: what special limitations or demands (if any) does, or should, the character of the Holocaust impose on its historical representation? This question evidently assumes a "normal" – that is, "*non*-special" – form of historical representation as a background against which specific representations (including those of the Holocaust) will be assessed. The question cited thus asks whether changes in the normal form are required by the (allegedly) unusual character of the Holocaust – either on a "one-off" basis or in the normal form as such. Although the three authors differ on certain aspects of the normal form of historical representation, there is no disagreement among them either on what they consider the most essential element of that form (that is, its contextualist and anti-realistic drive) or on their negative answer to the historiographical question concerning the Holocaust's special representational status. There are, in their common view, *no* special limitations or requirements in the historical representation of the Holocaust – certainly none that would alter the normal and thus generally applicable form of historical representation.

The last part of this response is controversial only in its rejection of accounts of the Holocaust which assert its historical uniqueness and/or its historical "unrepresentability." *Those* two claims are by no means equivalent or mutually entailed (as Kansteiner assumes), but this objection is a small matter in the larger context. At least it would be a small matter if the rejection of the two claims were itself based on historical grounds. Admittedly, some advocates of the Holocaust's uniqueness or unrepresentability have argued from theological or other transhistorical premises, and such claims can hardly be contested in historical terms.

But there is *also* a historical claim about the failure of precedents for the Holocaust (and/or the phenomenon of genocide), as is demonstrated in Steven Katz's broadly-based thesis that the convergence of causal factors in the Holocaust is historically unprecedented.[1] Whatever one infers from Katz's thesis – and indeed even if one rejects it – he surely demonstrates that the historical question of Holocaust-precedents is not intrinsically mystifying or ideologically tendentious – which is how Kellner, Kansteiner, and Braun finally "represent" it.[2] This non-historical dismissal of claims of the Holocaust's historical distinctiveness is symptomatic of their more basic and also a priori premise concerning the normal form of historical representation: on the one hand, a rejection of any such representation as even possibly referential or factual; on the other hand – in its positive version – the assertion that historical representation (with all history *as* representational) is uniformly contextual and interpretive. They assume that historical accounts are frozen between brackets all the way down.

Their other differences aside, the agreement among the three authors on these two contentions is firm and unquestioned. From these premises they then conclude that no exceptions need be made for representing the Holocaust. At this poststructuralist stage on the mind's way, we are to understand, only the naif would credit historical discourse with a "stable referent" (Kellner) or the possibility of "factual singularity" (Kansteiner) or the "'reality' of the past as an object of study" (Braun). Their common oppositional stance is epitomized by Braun's use of quotation marks wherever he finds himself compelled even to mention the terms "fact" or "truth" (or "reality"). Like the skeptic's raised eyebrows, those marks surround and presumably defeat any use of language hinting at an extra-linguistic or extra-interpretive historical referent. Since there is no extra-interpretive fulcrum, any historical claim of uniqueness must also allow for another representation in which the object at issue is not exceptional but commonplace – a possibility that by itself defeats the original claim.

The point at issue here, again, is not the substantive question of the Holocaust's uniqueness, but the normal form prescribed by the symposiasts for historical analysis. In both their practice as well as in principle they assert that historical representations are not permitted the reactionary invocation of nineteenth-century realism or positivism, such as Ranke's tropological and thus self-refuting view of history as the search for the "eigentlich." Insofar as this proscription applies to the normal form of historical discourse in general, it holds also for historical representations of the Holocaust: harder justice in that case, perhaps, but justice nonetheless. (Even if Kellner allows that some forms of discourse may be more "appropriate" than others for "some" events, this does not entail a point-zero at which the structure of discourse is not itself part of the subject of discourse.) The Hayden White of *Metahistory* is thus recalled nostalgically by all three authors. (Their erstwhile forebear, groundbreaker in the discovery of history as narrative form, has recently regressed, honorably but mistakenly troubled by the phenomenon of the Holocaust in relation to his own earlier historiographical tour de force. Now he looks to the middle-voice or, in any event, to *some* voice that will speak for non-interpreted facts.)

What arguments are made for this dismissal of historical realism? One might dispute this question itself on the grounds that where the status of facts or truth is at issue, it begs the question to require arguments in their traditional form. To be sure, the latter consideration doesn't prevent certain voluntary inconsistencies (so, Kellner: "The most elementary fact about the modern historical profession is that it produces an enormous amount of discourse": What silent miracle keeps the subject of this sentence afloat?). In general, however, the oppositional point of departure in the three essays carries over into their positive moment, shaping their respective versions of an adequate (or at least *more* adequate) view of historical representation, although still without adducing proof or evidence. (Kansteiner claims only to be identifying the "limits and blind spots" in each of the two major paradigms; but he leaves no doubt about which, in his view, is the blinder of the two which he associates, perhaps more than metaphorically, with their respective ages). Again, like the negative critique in the three essays' origins, the refrain here is constant:

> *Kellner*: The rhetorical constitution of events depends for its existence on the social codes that prevail in a group, a time, a place.
> *Kansteiner*: Only *Alltagsgeschichte* ... offers the kind of consistent, intuitively [!] convincing image of Nazism which furthers historicization proper, that is the routinization of the representation of Nazism compatible with the parameters of historiography and of more popular forms of historical culture.
> *Braun*: In our perception of past social reality *vis-à-vis* documents and other "facts," there is no difference between the politically possible, the socially plausible, and the morally imaginary – nor do we know with which we are dealing.

To be sure, some room remains at the edges of these assertions. Kellner's reference to "the rhetorical constitution of events" may leave open the possibility of another means of constituting them; Kansteiner elsewhere cites a "problem inherent in structuralist poetics" (as in James Young's *Writing and Rewriting the Holocaust*),[3] in that it provides no grounds for dismissing "certain appropriations of the Holocaust" as compared to others; Braun, in claiming the legitimization of the past "by the authority of the present" acknowledges the latter as at least a provisional terminus. But what is thus given offhandedly is invariably taken back directly. The locus of history is always and only a point at the convergence of vectors of social custom or political power or linguistic figuration or moral tendency. Not only do facts never speak for themselves, but post-Kantians all, have we not suffered enough from political and literary and historical mystification to recognize in the ontology of facts a second world of "things-in-themselves" still more inaccessible than anything we might hope for (also in vain) from "facts-in-themselves"? We should rather be confident and glad of the "irredeemably earthly and immanent status of interpretation"; that "after Auschwitz poetry can be written, but history, as the 'realistic' interpretation of the past, cannot".

Here occurs the metaphysical failure of nerve that disables at once the symposiasts' criticism of one normal form of historical representation and the form by which they mean to replace it. This failure is evident from a critique of ordinary usage: if representation or interpretation is representation or interpretation *of* some "thing," what is the ontological status of whatever the representation or interpretation is of? Or more bluntly, in reconceiving the Forum's title: "Representing the *What*?" No one would deny that the term "Holocaust" is a matter of (disputed) convention; but are we to suppose that the ontology of conventions (itself neither simple nor conventional) applies also and directly to whatever the convention incorporates or cites? If "factual material itself . . . [is] constituted by a negotiation with other forms", does not this imply that some *non*-negotiated material is part of the negotiation with the "other forces"? But what then would be the status of this material?

Kellner objects to the proposal in one of my own essays that at least chronicles are non-interpretive: "But this," he announces, "is mistaken. A chronicle is the result of a pre-existing narrative; it is not the origin of such a narrative". There are two alternative positions that Kellner might be disputing with this objection. The first would construe a chronicle as a corporate structure of selected, albeit elementary, data. To call such a chronicle mimetic or directly referential would, *of course*, be "mistaken": the act of selection precludes such claims. Who, one might ask, would deny that chronicle in this sense is narrative-dependent (although why one of them should "precede" the other or even why they should be distinguished at all are questions Kellner – who makes both these claims – ignores)?

There *is* an issue, however, in the question of whether the items constituting a chronicle (that is, its atomic elements or, more prosaically, the facts: who did what to whom, when or where) are individually dependent – ontologically and epistemically – on a "pre-existing" narrative. This indeed is the issue I reiterate here against the three contextualist views of historical representation in the Forum as they would place the Holocaust or any other historical event (that is, "event") always and entirely within the circle of interpretation. If the narrative-dependence of facts holds in general, then for any particular narrative (and its derivative "facts") an alternate "pre-existing" narrative might produce other, even contradictory, "facts." In other words, narrative and interpretation first, facts, second. The implication here is – or should be – clear: not only is history accessible only in variant, sometimes conflicting narratives, but nothing that the narratives tell or talk *about* is exempt. We must distrust the tale as well as the teller – with no place else to turn.

That the Holocaust has at times been proposed as a test case for historical representation is due, of course, to its moral enormity. So far as concerns the normal form of historical representation *in general*, the judgment about this test case by the authors of "Representing the Holocaust" – to the effect that the Holocaust changes nothing in this normal form – may well hold. But one could accept *this* claim and still maintain that the Holocaust is a test case of the normal form itself. So indeed I would argue – not for its uniqueness as a test but because the consequences that hinge on the status of alternate Holocaust-narratives (consequences which the contributors to the Forum consistently ignore) demonstrate graphically what is at stake in the issue of historical representation more generally.

Consider this item of chronicle: "On January 20, 1942, Nazi officials at Wannsee formulated a protocol for the 'Final Solution of the Jewish Question'." There are, to be sure, matters that might require specification in this statement – for example, the status of the officials or whether the formulation of the "Final Solution" originated then or before. But with or without such additional clauses, the crucial question remains whether what the statement asserts (and so its truth or falsity) is *essentially* a matter of interpretation. Is the statement's truth or falsity a function only of a larger narrative – and thus open to contradiction in each or even every point when transposed to another narrative?

A large and obvious difference exists between answering "Yes" or "No" to these two questions. In everything they affirm and nothing they deny, Kellner, Kansteiner, and Braun seem committed to answering "Yes" to both questions – and then to accepting the consequence that an alternate narrative to the one they presumably accept (which affirms the occurrence of the Wannsee Conference) could equally legitimately find the Conference *not* to have occured. Moreover, these two claims are not even contradictory since there is no metanarrative by which to judge the two. Is this what the authors and the several versions of contextualism they propose, mean to affirm? If not, on what grounds do they deny it?

The issue here is perilously Either/Or. *Either* there is, at the ground of historical writing (whatever subsequent appropriations make of it), an element of reference: facts.

Or history is as you like it, not only in the stratosphere where historians and readers might on any account enjoy free flight, but in the trenches, with the masses of names, dates, and numbers elbowing each other for place. Can any possible narrative appear as superstructure for any sub- or infra-structure of fact, undoing or redoing any or all of the latter's elements? The Holocaust can be described as one event or many, and as soon as narrative connectives are imposed on individual items of chronicle, alternate paths open up for alternate narratives. But to say that historical narratives when they thus move beyond the items of chronicle are unfettered by anything more than the historian's imagination or will is to imply that the items of chronicle also are functions of imagination or will – thus (for example) that it is the *historian's* responsibility whether or not Nazi officialdom met at Wannsee. Most people (including, I would guess, the symposiasts themselves) would be reluctant to concede that whether or not they existed five minutes ago depends entirely on what historians (singly or collectively) say about them. The basis for this reluctance is not a matter of psychology or physics or linguistic tropology. But this is how, in various combinations reflecting *their* imaginations and will, Kellner, Kansteiner, and Braun represent history. And the Holocaust.

NOTES

1. Steven Katz, *The Holocaust in Historical Context*, New York, 1994.
2. I would instance here – symptomatically – their misreading of my own work as maintaining the "uniqueness" *and* the "unrepresentable" or incomprehensible nature of the Holocaust – all of which views I have opposed in *Act and Idea in the Nazi Genocide*, Chicago, 1990, and elsewhere (cf., e.g., "The History of Evil and the Future of the Holocaust," in Peter Hayes (ed.) *Lessons and Legacies*, Evanston, Ill., 1991, pp. 90–105; "The Interpretation of Limits," in Saul Friedlander (ed.) *Probing the Limits of Representation*, Cambridge, Mass., 1992, pp. 300–17; "Genocide," in Lawrence Becker (ed.) *Encyclopedia of Ethics*, New York, 1992, pp. 60–1.
3. James E. Young, *Writing and Rewriting the Holocaust: Narrative and the Consequences of Interpretation*, Bloomington, Ind., 1988.

Bibliography

The literature on postmodernism in general, and the relationship between postmodernism and historiography, is growing at an ever increasing rate. This Bibliography is therefore merely indicative of this developing discourse. For convenience I have divided it into three sections: (1) further texts written by those historians/theorists featured in this Reader which are of particular relevance; (2) books by other writers on postmodernism as such and/or postmodernism and historiography (generally not already cited), and (3) articles by writers especially on postmodernism and historiography who are again not generally cited in the above text.

FURTHER TEXTS BY WRITERS FEATURED IN THIS READER

Ankersmit, F. R., *Narrative Logic*, The Hague, Martinus Nijhoff, 1993.

——, *History and Tropology*, Berkeley, University of California Press, 1994.

Appleby, J. *et al.* (eds), *Knowledge and Postmodernism in Historical Perspective*, New York, Routledge, 1996.

Barthes, R., *Empire of the Signs*, New York, Hill and Wang, 1982.

——, *A Barthes Reader*, (ed.) S. Sontag, London, Cape, 1982.

Bennett, T., *Formalism and Marxism*, London, Methuen, 1979.

——, *The Birth of the Museum*, London, Routledge, 1995.

Baudrillard, J., *Jean Baudrillard: Selected Writings*, (ed.) M. Poster, Cambridge, Polity, 1988.

——, *Simulacra and Simulation*, Michigan, University of Michigan Press, 1994.

——, *Seduction*, New York, St Martin's Press, 1990.

——, *The Perfect Crime*, London, Verso, 1996.

Berkhofer, R., *Beyond the Great Story*, Princeton, Princeton University Press, 1995.

Chambers, I., *Border Dialogues*, London, Routledge, 1990.

Chambers, I. and Curti, L. (eds), *The Post Colonial Question*, London, Routledge, 1996.

Elam, D. and Wyegam, R. (eds), *Reflections on Feminism, Narrative and Desire*, London, Routledge, 1995.

Eley, G., "Edward Thompson, Social History and Political Culture," in, H. Kaye and K. McClelland, (eds) *E. P. Thompson: Critical Perspectives*, Cambridge, Polity, 1990, pp. 12–49.

Elton, G., *The Practice of History*, London, Fontana, 1969.

Ermarth, E. D., *Realism and Consensus in the English Novel*, Princeton, Princeton University Press, 1983.

Foucault, M., *The Order of Things*, London, Tavistock, 1970.

——, *Power/Knowledge*, New York, Pantheon, 1980.

——, *The Foucault Reader*, (ed.) P. Rabinow, London, Penguin, 1986.

Fox-Genovese, E., *Within the Plantation Household*, Chapel Hill, North Carolina University Press, 1988.

Friedlander, S., *When Memory Comes*, New York, Farrar, Strauss and Giroux, 1987.

Friedman, S. S., *Penelope's Webb*, Cambridge, Cambridge University Press, 1990.

Himmelfarb, G., *New History and the Old*, Harvard, Harvard University Press, 1987.

——, *On Looking into the Abyss?*, Vintage, 1995.

Hunt, L. (ed.), *The New Cultural History*, Berkeley, University of California Press, 1992.

Jacob, M., *The Cultural Meaning of the Scientific Revolution*, London, McGraw-Hill, 1988.

Joyce, P., *Democratic Subjects*, Cambridge, Cambridge University Press, 1994.

——, *The Oxford Reader on Class*, Oxford, Oxford University Press, 1995.

Kansteiner, W., "Hayden White's Critique of the Writing of History," *History and Theory*, 32, 3, 1993, pp. 273–95.

Kellner, H. and Ankersmit, F. R. (eds), *A New Philosophy of History*, London, Reaktion, 1995.

——, "Narrativity in History . . .", *History and Theory*, Beiheft, 26, 1987, pp. 1–29.

Lang, B., *Act and Idea in the Nazi Genocide*, Chicago, Chicago University Press, 1990.

Lyotard, J. F., *Just Gaming*, Manchester, Manchester University Press, 1985.

——, *The Differend*, Manchester, Manchester University Press, 1988.

——, *The Lyotard Reader*, (ed.) A. Benjamin, Oxford, Blackwell, 1989.

——, *The Postmodern Explained to Children*, London, Turnaround, 1992.

Nield, K. and Eley, G., "Why Does Social History Ignore Politics," *Social History*, 5, 1980, pp. 249–71.

Norris, C., *What's Wrong with Postmodernism*, Hemel Hempstead, Harvester Wheatsheaf, 1990.

——, *The Truth About Postmodernism*, Oxford, Blackwell, 1993.

——, *Truth and the Ethics of Criticism*, Manchester, Manchester University Press, 1994.

Palmer, B., *Descent Into Discourse*, Philadelphia, Temple University Press, 1990.
——, *Edward Thompson: Objections and Oppositions . . .*, London, Verso, 1994.
Spiegel, G., *Romancing the Past*, Berkeley, University of California Press, 1993.
Stone, L., *The Past and the Present*, London, Routledge, 1981.
White, H., *Metahistory*, Baltimore, Johns Hopkins University Press, 1973.
——, *Tropics of Discourse*, Baltimore, Johns Hopkins University Press, 1978.
——, *The Content of the Form*, Baltimore, Johns Hopkins University Press, 1987.
Young, R. (ed.), *Untying the Text*, London, Routledge, 1981.
——, *Colonial Desire*, London, Routledge, 1991.
——, *Torn Halves . . .* Manchester, Manchester University Press, 1996.
Zagorin, P., *Rebels and Rulers 1500–1660* (2 vols) Cambridge, Cambridge University Press, 1982.

TEXTS ON POSTMODERNISM/POSTMODERNISM IN HISTORY/ HISTORIOGRAPHY

Alcoff, L. and Potter, E. (eds), *Feminist Epistemologies*, London, Routledge, 1993.
Bauman, Z., *Intimations of Postmodernity*, London, Routledge, 1992.
Bennington, G., *Legislations*, London, Verso, 1994.
Berman, M., *All That Is Solid Melts Into Air*, London, Verso, 1982.
Bertens, H., *The Idea of the Postmodern*, London, Routledge, 1995.
Best, S. and Kellner, D., *Postmodern Theory*, London, Macmillan, 1992.
Bhaba, H., *The Location of Culture*, London, Routledge, 1994.
Bhaskar, R., *Philosophy and the Idea of Freedom*, Oxford, Blackwell, 1991.
Callinicos, A., *Against Postmodernism*, London, Macmillan, 1990.
Canary, R. H. and Kozicki, H. (eds), *The Writing of History*, Michigan, University of Wisconsin Press, 1978.
Carrard, P., *The Poetics of the New History*, Baltimore, Johns Hopkins University Press, 1992.
Connor, S., *Theory and Cultural Value*, Oxford, Blackwell, 1992.
D'Amico, R., *Historicism and Knowledge*, London, Routledge, 1989.
d'Certeau, M., *The Writing of History*, New York, Columbia University Press, 1988.
Derrida, J., *Of Grammatology*, Baltimore, Johns Hopkins University Press, 1976.
—— *Specters of Marx*, New York, Routledge, 1994.
Dews, P., *The Limits of Deconstruction*, London, Verso, 1995.
Docherty, T. (ed.), *Postmodernism: A Reader*, Hemel Hempstead, Harvester Wheatsheaf, 1993.
Fish, S., *Doing What Comes Naturally*, Oxford, Clarendon Press, 1989.
Füredi, F., *Mythical Past, Elusive Future*, London, Pluto, 1992.
Geras, N., *Solidarity in the Conversation of Humankind*, London, Verso, 1995.

Ginzburg, C., *Clues, Myths and the Historical Method*, Baltimore, Johns Hopkins University Press, 1989.

Munslow, A. *Deconstructing History*, London, Routledge (forthcoming).

Rorty, R., *Contingency, Irony, and Solidarity*, Cambridge, Cambridge University Press, 1989.

Royle, N., *After Derrida*, Manchester, Manchester University Press, 1995.

Ryan, M., *Marxism and Deconstruction*, Baltimóre, Johns Hopkins University Press, 1982.

Said, E., *Culture and Imperialism*, New York, Knopf, 1993.

Scott, J. W., *Gender and the Politics of History*, New York, Columbia University Press, 1988.

Southgate, B., *History: What and Why?* London, Routledge, 1996.

Tallack, D. (ed.), *Critical Theory: A Reader*, Hemel Hempstead, Harvester Wheatsheaf, 1995.

Veeser, H. A., *The New Historicism*, New York, Routledge, 1989.

Wilson, A. (ed.), *Re-Thinking Social History*, Manchester, Manchester University Press, 1993.

ARTICLES

Ankersmit, F. R. "Reply to Professor Zagorin," *History and Theory*, 29, 3, 1990, pp. 275–96.

——, "Historical Representation," *History and Theory*, 27, 3, 1988, pp. 205–28.

——, "Historicism: An Attempt at Synthesis," *History and Theory*, 34, 3, 1995, pp. 143–61.

Ahmad, A., "Reconciling Derrida . . .," *New Left Review*, 208, 1994, pp. 88–106.

Bann, S., "Towards A Criticial Historiography," *Philosophy*, 56, 1981, pp. 365–85.

Bevir, M., "Objectivity in History," *History and Theory*, 33, 3, 1994, pp. 328–44.

Caplan, J., "Postmodernism, Poststructuralism and Deconstruction: Notes for Historians," *Central European History*, 22, 3/4, 1989, pp. 260–78.

Cronon, W., "A Place for Stories . . .," *The Journal of American History*, March, 1992, pp. 1347–76.

de Bolla, P., "Disfiguring History," *Diacritics*, 16, 4, 1986, pp. 49–58.

Eagleton, T., "The Crisis of Contemporary Culture," *New Left Review*, 196, 1993, pp. 29–41.

Harlan, D., "Intellectual History and the Return of Literature," *American Historical Review*, 94, 3, 1989, pp. 581–609.

Himmelfarb, G., "Some Reflections on the New History," *American Historical Review*, 94, 3, 1989, pp. 661–70.

Hollinger, D., "The Return of the Prodigal . . .," *American Historical Review*, 94, 3, 1989, pp. 610–21.

Jameson, F., "Marx's Purloined Letter," *New Left Review*, 209, 1995, pp. 75–109.

Klein, K. W., "In Search of Narrative Mastery: Postmodernism and the People Without History," *History and Theory*, 34, 4, 1995, pp. 275–98.

Norman, A. P., "Telling It Like It Was: Historical Narratives on their Own Terms," *History and Theory*, 30, 2, 1991, pp. 119–35.

Norris, C., "Truth, Science and the Growth of Knowledge," *New Left Review*, 210, 1995, pp. 105–23.

Levine, L. W., "The Unpredictable Past," *American Historical Review*, 94, 3, 1989, pp. 671–9.

Lorenz, C., "Historical Knowledge and Historical Reality . . .," *History and Theory*, 33, 3, 1994, pp. 297–327.

Lovibond, S., "Feminism and Pragmatism . . .," *New Left Review*, 193, 1992, pp. 56–74.

McCullagh, C. B., "The Truth of Historical Narrative," *History and Theory*, pp. 30–46.

Magill, A., "Recounting the Past . . .," *American Historical Review*, 94, 3, 1989, pp. 627–53.

Partner, N., "Making Up Lost Time: Writing on the Writing of History," *Speculum*, 61, 1, 1986, pp. 90–117.

Scott, J. W., "History in Crisis?," *American Historical Review*, 94, 3, 1989, pp. 680–92.

White, H., "The Rhetoric of Interpretation," *Poetics Today*, 9, 2, 1988, pp. 253–74.

——, "Historical Pluralism," *Critical Enquiry*, 12, 1986, pp. 480–93.

Zammito, J., "Are We Being Theoretical Yet . . .," *The Journal of Modern History*, 65, 4, 1993, pp. 783–814.

Index of Names

Vincent, J. 327

Wahrman, D. 354
Walkowitz, J. 269
Walsh, W.H. 142, 143, 145
White, H. 14, 17, 18, 22, 23, 28, 91, 96, 101, 117, 131, 135, 141, 142, 152, 156, 157, 162, 164, 165, 167, 170, 173, 234, 274, 284, 298, 299, 313, 361, 384, 388, 389, 390, 391, 392–6, 399, 400, 401, 403, 405, 406, 413, 414, 419, 422, 424, 429

Williams, R. 182, 192, 263, 323, 336
Wolff, J. 251
Wright, G. 163

Young, J. 413, 430
Young, R. 22, 35, 75–6, 110, 111, 117, 119, 220

Zagorin, P. 23, 257, 274, 275, 276, 298–312
Zammito, J. 20
Zeldin, T. 161